APPROPRIATE BUILDING MATERIALS

For our children
Matthias Juan, Elena Anina, Natalia and Nikil

APPROPRIATE BUILDING MATERIALS

A Catalogue of Potential Solutions

Revised, Enlarged Edition

Roland Stulz
Kiran Mukerji

SKAT

it

gate

Original edition	1981, 750 copies, SKAT
Second impression	1983, 3000 copies, co-publication SKAT & IT Publications Ltd.
Second revised edition	1988, 2800 copies, co-publication SKAT Publications, Swiss Centre for Development Cooperation in Technology and Management, St.Gallen / Switzerland Intermediate Technology Publications Ltd., London / UK GATE, German Appropriate Technology Exchange, Eschbom / FRG
Third revised edition	1993, 1500 copies SKAT Publications & IT Publications
Second impression	1998, 1000 copies SKAT Publications & IT Publications
Authors:	Roland Stulz, Zürich / Switzerland Kiran Mukerji, Stamberg / FRG
Illustrations	Kiran Mukerji and Roland Stulz (if no other source is mentioned)
Copyright	SKAT Publications, Switzerland, 1988
Comments	Please send any comments to SKAT Publications Vadianstrasse 42 CH-9000 St. Gallen, Switzerland
Distribution by:	SKAT-Bookshop Vadianstrasse 42 CH-9000 St. Gallen, Switzerland Fax: +41 71 23 75 45 and Intermediate Technology Publications Plymbridge House, Estover Road Plymouth PL6 7PZ, United Kingdom
ISBN	SKAT: 3 908001 44 7 ITP: 1 85339 225 1

Printed and bound in the United Kingdom

PREFACE

"Appropriate Building Materials" was first published in 1981 and quickly established itself as one of the most important source books in the field of building materials for the Third World. Up to this date, this book is in very high demand and used from various groups such as: engineers, architects, planners, practitioners, government officials as well as do-it-yourself makers etc. SKAT receives still many letters, comments and also enquiries. Relevant journals reviewed the book and since then, almost any publication about appropriate building materials refers to it and/or includes it in the bibliography.

Since 1981 the development of the appropriate building materials sector has undergone a swift development and soon up-dating was necessary. Therefore, in 1988 a revision was made and the second edition published. The book also became available in Spanish under the title "Construyendo co Materiales de Bajo Costo" as a co-publication SKAT-CETAL (Chile). Now a new translation of the previous Spanish version is on the way.

In 1993 a new print became necessary. This opportunity has been made use of by a mini revision (third revised edition) to add certain information such as Micro Concrete Roofing (MCR), new equipment and machine designs as well as new addresses.

Only a mini revision was made, because the content of the second edition is still very much up to date with the prevailing situation in the field of appropriate building materials .

In order to maximize the dissemination of the information contained, this book is being published jointly by SKAT, IT Publications (Great Britain) and GATE (Federal Republic of Germany)

SKAT
Swiss Centre for Development Cooperation in Technology and Management

St.Gallen, August 1993

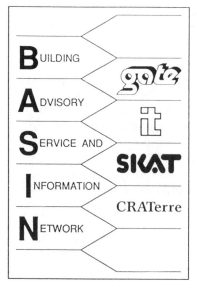

BUILDING

ADVISORY

SERVICE AND

INFORMATION

NETWORK

BASIN

Building materials and construction technologies that are appropriate for developing countries, particularly in the low-income sector, are being developed, applied and documented in many parts of the world. This is an important prerequisite for providing safe, decent and affordable buildings for an ever-growing population.

But such new developments can do little to improve the building situation, as long as the information does not reach potential builders. The types and sources of information on standard and innovative building technologies are numerous and very diverse, making access to them difficult.

Thus, in order to remedy this drawback, GATE, ITDG, SKAT and CRATerre are cooperating in the Building Advisory Service and Information Network, which covers four principal subject areas and coordinates the documentation, evaluation and dissemination of information.

All four groups have a coordinated database from which information is available on Documents, Technologies, Equipment, Institutions, Consultants as well as on Projects and Programs. In addition, printed material or individual advice on certain special subjects is provided on request. Research projects, training programs and other field work can be implemented in cooperation with local organizations, if a distinct need can be identified and the circumstances permit.

BASIN is a service available to all institutions and individuals concerned with housing, building and planning in developing countries, but can only function efficiently if there is a regular feedback. Therefore, any publications, information, personal experiences, etc. that can be made available to BASIN are always welcome and will help BASIN to help others.

Advisory Service provided by

WAS/BASIN
GATE-GTZ
P.O.Box 5180
D-65 726 Eschborn
Federal Republic of Germany
Tel. + 49 - 6196 - 79 4810
Telefax + 49 - 6196 - 79 4820
Telex 407501-0 gtz d
Cables GERMATEC Eschborn

Wall Building

GATE (German Appropriate Technology Exchange) a programme of the Deutsche Gesellschaft für Technische Zusammenarbeit (GTZ) GmbH, acts as a centre for the dissemination and promotion of appropriate technologies for developing countries.

The Information and Advisory Service on Appropriate Technologies (ISAT), a project of GATE, has accumulated specific know-how in the wall building sector through its own research and development programmes, studies and publications. Own capacities and a team of experts are available for advice on wall construction and wall building materials.

Advisory Service provided by

ITDG
Myson House
Railway Terrace
Rugby CV21 3HT
United Kingdom
Tel. + 44 - 788 - 560631
Telefax + 44 - 788 - 540270
Telex 317466 itdg g
Cables ITDG Rugby

Cements and Binders

The Intermediate Technology Development Group (ITDG) is an independent British charity, founded by Dr. E.F. Schumacher, author of Small is Beautiful, to help increase the income-generating and employment opportunities of small-scale industrial activities in developing countries.
ITDG offers expertise in a wide range of technical areas (eg Mineral Industries, Shelter, Agro Processing, Textiles), provides advice and assistance in the selection and application of appropriate technologies aimed at improving the productivity of communities and small enterprises, and provides several other services through the Group's subsidiaries.

Advisory Service provided by

SKAT
Vadianstrasse 42
CH-9000 St. Gallen
Switzerland

Tel. + 41 - 71 - 237475
Telefax + 41 - 71 - 237545
Telex 881226 skat ch
Cables LATAMI St. Gall

Roofing

SKAT

SKAT (Swiss Center for Development Cooperation in Technology and Management) is a documentation centre and consultancy group which is engaged in promoting appropriate technologies in the Third World.
The services of SKAT are: 1. Technical Enquiry Service; 2. Consultancies, Projects, Studies; Documentation Centre; 4. Bookshop; 5. Publishing Department; 6. International Cooperation; 7. Public Relations for Appropriate Technologies.
SKAT's main fields of activity are Building Materials, Energy (with emphasis on hydro-power), Small-Scale Industrial Development (with emphasis on the metal-working industry), as well as Water, Sanitation and Wastewater.

Advisory Service provided by

CRATerre – EAG
Centre Simone Signoret
BP 53
F - 38090 Villefontaine
France

Tel. + 33 - 74 96 60 56
Telefax + 33 - 74 96 04 63
Telex 308658 F CRATERE

Earth Building

CRATerre

CRATerre, the International Centre for Earth Construction, is a non-governmental, non-profit organization of the School of Architecture of Grenoble, dedicated to the promotion of earth as a building material.
CRATerre has an integrated working method in which research, application, consultancy, training and communication are permanently linked.
The three main programs of development are: i. Industrialization; ii. Economic Housing; iii. Preservation.
The competence of CRATerre covers every aspect of the different earth construction technologies at all levels.

Introductory section
(white pages)

How to use this catalogue	!
Contents	C
Introduction	I

Annex
(grey triangle on top)

Machines and equipment	
Conversion factors	in/cm
Useful addresses	
Bibliography	
Abbreviations	
Index	?

Building elements
(Fundamental information : grey triangle on top)
(Examples: white pages)

Foundations	
Floors and ceilings	
Walls	
Roofs	
Building systems	
Protective measures	

Building materials
(Fundamental information : grey triangle on top)
(Examples: white pages)

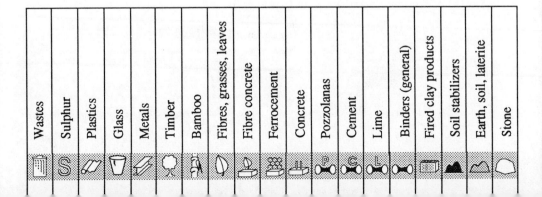

Wastes | Sulphur | Plastics | Glass | Metals | Timber | Bamboo | Fibres, grasses, leaves | Fibre concrete | Ferrocement | Concrete | Pozzolanas | Cement | Lime | Binders (general) | Fired clay products | Soil stabilizers | Earth, soil, laterite | Stone

II

HOW TO USE THIS CATALOGUE

This catalogue has *three* main parts:

Part one
FUNDAMENTAL INFORMATION
This part contains general
information about the raw materials,
processing and use of
BUILDING MATERIALS,
design guidelines for
BUILDING ELEMENTS
and practical hints on
PROTECTIVE MEASURES

Part two
EXAMPLES
This part is a
CATALOGUE
of
traditional and experimental
applications of
BUILDING MATERIALS
for each category of
BUILDING ELEMENTS

Part three
ANNEXES
This part is designed to facilitate the practical
implementation of the technologies in this catalogue

Information can be found in various different ways, as shown by the questions overleaf:

IV

Question	Section(s) with this (these) sign(s)		Answer under this heading
Is the locally available soil suitable for building?			Field and laboratory tests
What happens when cement hardens?			Hydration of cement
What are the problems of using bamboo, and how are they overcome?			Problems, remedies
What kind of roof is appropriate for hot-dry climates?			Roofs for hot-dry climates
How are masonry walls made earthquake resistant?			Earthquake: Protective measures
What type of roof can be constructed with ferrocement?			Ferrocement roofs
How can houses be built entirely with mud bricks?			Mud brick vaults and domes
Where can information on building materials be obtained in Guatemala?			Guatemala
Which publications are recommended for further reading on pozzolana?			08. Pozzolanas
What does "pfa" stand for and on which page is it found?			Abbreviations under "P"

Readers are advised to read the INTRODUCTION before using this catalogue.

CONTENTS

VI

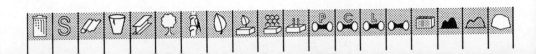

VIII

Aim of this Catalogue

The International Year of Shelter for the Homeless (IYSH 1987) was initiated by the United Nations to draw the world's attention to the disastrous housing situation in developing countries. While there are numerous political, social and economic aspects of the problem, there is also a great need for appropriate technical solutions, and these are what the book is about.

More than sufficient information on building materials and construction technologies for developing countries is available in the world today, but only very few people – and least of all the local house builders – have access to it. Therefore, this catalogue has been prepared for architects and engineers, educational and scientific institutions, producers and suppliers of building materials, and above all, for the building practitioner in the field of low-cost constructions in all parts of the world.

The aim of the catalogue is:

• to summarize technical data and practical information from a large number of publications, enabling the reader to identify appropriate solutions for almost any given construction problem in low-cost housing in developing countries, without having to study volumes of literature, which is rapidly increasing every year;

• to list traditional materials and methods, as well as methods which are still in the experimental stage, but seem promising for the future;

• to provide theoretical background information, coupled with numerous practical examples of building material usage, which together will hopefully generate ideas for a series of new construction methods, with a view to further reduction of cost, construction time, energy input, wastage and pollution;

• to contribute to a worldwide exchange of information and experiences between all those who are involved in the research, development and implementation of more appropriate building construction in developing countries.

X

Choice of Appropriate Building Materials

The "appropriateness" of a building material or construction technology can never be generalized. The following questions show some of the main factors which determine appropriateness:

• Is the material produced locally, or is it partially or entirely imported?

• Is it cheap, abundantly available, and/or easily renewable?

• Has it been produced in a factory far away (transportation costs!); does it require special machines and equipment, or can it be produced at lower cost on the building site? (Good quality and durability are often more important than low procurement costs).

• Does its production and use require a high energy input, and cause wastage and pollution? Is there an acceptable alternative material which eliminates these problems?

• Is the material and construction technique climatically acceptable?

• Does the material and construction technique provide sufficient safety against common natural hazards (eg fire, biological agents, heavy rain, hurricanes, earthquakes)?

• Can the material and technology be used and understood by the local workers, or are special skills and experience required?

• Are repairs and replacements possible with local means?

• Is the material socially acceptable? Is it considered low standard, or does it offend religious belief? Does it match with the materials and constructions of nearby buildings?

Important Note

Readers are requested to keep in mind the following points:

• While it was an important aim to make this sourcebook as comprehensive as possible, it cannot be considered complete and does not represent a scientific analysis of construction technology.

• All technical data in this manual are taken from publications or producers' data sheets. Therefore, neither the authors nor the publishers can be held responsible for any inaccuracies.

• The building materials, elements and general information presented in this manual have principally been dealt with in the context of one- and two-storey low-cost buildings. The construction of multi-storey buildings requires careful consideration of the structural requirements and expert advice should be sought.

• A house cannot be built without fundamental knowledge of building materials and construction. Unfortunately, appropriate building materials and technologies are generally considered to be simple enough to be handled by people without special skills or training. The poor results – and even failures – have led to a great deal of criticism and to the general belief that appropriate technologies are "inferior technologies". It is, therefore, important to stress that a material that has failed or performed poorly, was evidently not appropriate for that particular application, or it had been produced and used incorrectly.

Building materials which are produced with appropriate technologies, therefore, have to be prepared and used with the same skill and care as a high technology product.

XII

Acknowledgements

Many of the readers of the previous edition of this book sent a number of useful comments and suggestions, which have greatly influenced the work on the new edition. The authors are extremely grateful for all the trouble taken to communicate so much valuable information, and hope that this new edition will generate a similar response.

The authors sincerely thank SKAT, ITDG and GATE for their support and cooperation, and particularly for their understanding and patience, when the preparation of this book took longer than originally expected. Special thanks are due to Hannah Schreckenbach of GATE for her detailed comments and suggestions, and for providing so many useful illustrations.

A number of international experts generously provided information and illustrative material, as well as comments, suggestions and technical advice, for which the authors are deeply grateful. It is not possible to include all the names, but mention should be made of Victor Beck (SKAT, St. Gall), Lilia Casanova (RENAS-BMTCS, Manila), Professor Lutz Christians (TU Berlin), Thomas Gieth (CTA, Asunción), Nicolas Hall (London), Urs Heierli (SDC, Dhaka), Neville Hill (TERRE, Portsmouth), Hugo Houben (CRATerre, Ville-fontaine), Carlos Lola (ATI, Washington, D.C.), Kosta Mathéy (TRIALOG, Munich), G.C. Mathur (NBO, New Delhi), Professor Gernot Minke (Gh Kassel), John Norton (DW, Fumel), Alvaro Ortega (Montreal), John Parry (ITW, Cradley Heath), Helmut Stiehler (GATE, Eschborn), Klaus Vorhauer (Karlsruhe), Wolfgang Willkomm (Hanover), Werner Wilkens (DESWOS, Cologne), Ad Wouters (CICAT, Delft).

The sources of information and illustrations have been mentioned wherever relevant. Illustrations without statement of a source are by the authors.

The authors owe special thanks to the Human Settlements Unit of The ESCAP/UNIDO Division of Industry, Human Settlements and Technology, on whose behalf Kiran Mukerji undertook a survey of building materials and technologies in ten Asian countries (January to April 1987), for their permission to use some of the material collected during the mission.

And finally, a very special acknowledgement is due to Annette Grevé (Starnberg) for so excellently accomplishing the task of preparing the entire text and layout on the computer and for her patience in making so many changes and corrections, before the book was ready for printing.

1

FUNDAMENTAL INFORMATION
ON
BUILDING MATERIALS

2

STONE

General

Natural stone is perhaps the oldest, most abundant and most durable "readymade" building material, found predominantly in hilly areas. Various types and forms of natural stone can also be processed to produce other building materials.

The main stones used in building are divided into three geological categories:

1. *Igneous rocks*, generally crystalline, formed by the cooling of molten magma forced up through cracks in the earth's crust. It, therefore, cannot contain fossils or shells. Most common examples: granites and volcanic stones.

2. *Sedimentary rocks*, commonly found in layers, formed by the disintegration and decomposition of igneous rocks due to weathering (water, wind, ice), or by accumulations of organic origin. Most common examples: Sandstones and limestones.

3. *Metamorphic rocks*, which are structurally changed igneous or sedimentary rocks, caused by immense heat and pressure. Most common examples: Slates (derived from clay), quartzites (from sandstone) and marble (from limestone).

Extraction of rocks is possible with simple tools such as drills, wedges and hammers, but skill and experience is essential to ensure accurate cuts. Harder rocks, such as granite, require more sophisticated mechanized equipment. Natural stone can be used as quarried, ie irregularly shaped, or can be shaped with simple tools or machines, depending on the ultimate construction. The material can be used completely, without wastage.

Applications

- Rubble (undressed stone) for foundations, floors, walls, or even corbelled roof structures, in all cases with or without mortar.
- Ashlar (squared or shaped stone) for regular course masonry, window sills, lintels, steps and paving.
- Impermeable stone (eg granite) as damp proof courses; also as external cladding of walls, though less suited for low-cost constructions.
- Slate for roofing.
- Gravel and stone chippings as aggregate for concrete and terrazzo.
- Granules for surfacing bituminous felts.
- Powders for extending paint.
- Limestone for lime and cement production.

4

BUILDING STONE MATERIALS AND APPLICATIONS
(from United Nations: Stone in Nepal, 1977)

Type	Limestone	Sandstone	Granites
Use	Walling and Cladding		Walling, Cladding plinths, surrounds and steps
Composition	Largely calcium carbonate	Quartz in all mica and felspar grains in some. Bonded largely with silica or calcium carbonate	Mainly felspar, quartz and mica
Method of production	Quarried, cut to size (masoning and sawing), finish as required, eg patterned, rock faced, fair picked, fine axed, rubbed, eggshell or polished		
Specific weight kg/m³	1900 - 2700	1950 - 2550	2400 - 2900
Compressive strength MN/m²	9 - 59	21 - 105	90 - 146
Water absorption %	2.5 - 11	2 - 8.5	0.1 - 0.5
Effect of fire	All non-combustible		
Moisture expansion %	about 0.01	0.07	none
Effect of chemicals	Attacked by acids	Resistant to most acids except calcareous types which are attacked	Resistant to most chemicals
Resistance to effect of soluble salts	Poor to very good	Poor to good	Poor to good
Thermal expansion co-efficient (per °C approximations)	4×10^{-6}	12×10^{-6}	11×10^{-6}
Thermal conductivity (W/m.°C approximations)	1.5	1.5	3.0
Resistance to frost	Poor to very good	Poor to excellent	Good to excellent
Durability	Dependent on thermal performance, resistance to chemicals and application in construction		
Ease of working	Easy to hard	Hard	Hard
Liability to become dirty	Become soiled in urban atmosphere		Resistant to soiling
Ease of cleaning	Fairly easy to clean	Difficult to clean	Difficult to clean

Marbles	Slates	Quartzites
Window surround, floors and stairs	Cladding sills, coping steps and paving	Cladding plinths, floors, paving and stairs
Mainly calcium carbonate	Mainly silica, alumina and iron oxides	Mainly quartz
Same as limestone, sandstone, granites		Finish natural, riven
2725 - 2900	2400 - 2900	about 2600
about 60	75 - 200	about 100
0.1 - 0.5	0.1	0.1 - 0.5
	Negligible	
Attacked by acids	Mainly resistant to acids	Resistant to most acids
Good	Good	Good
4×10^{-6}	11×10^{-6}	11×10^{-6}
2.5	1.9	3.0
Good to excellent	Good to excellent	Good to excellent
Dependent on thermal performance, resistance to chemicals and application in construction		
Fairly hard	Hard	Hard
Fairly resistant to soiling	Resistant to soiling	
	Difficult to clean	

Advantages

• Usually abundantly available and easily accessible in hilly regions; extraction generally requiring low investment cost and energy input.
• Immense strength and durability of most varieties of stone; negligible maintenance requirements.
• Impermeability of most stone varieties, providing good rain protection.
• Climatically appropriate in highland and arid zones, due to high thermal capacity of stone.

Problems

• Deterioration may result from atmospheric pollution, eg when sulphur compounds dissolved in rainwater produce sulphuric acid, which reacts with carbonates in limestones, causing skin formation and blisters.
• Efflorescence and spalling caused by certain salts and sea spray.
• Damage due to thermal movement of some stones, especially when fixed rigidly to materials with differing thermal movement, eg concrete.
• Surface damage due to water, which slowly dissolves limestones; or by prolonged wetting and drying of certain sandstones; or by freezing of water trapped in cracks.
• Low resistance to earthquake forces, thus likelihood of destruction and endangering lives.

Remedies

• Avoidance of using limestones and calcareous sandstones close to sources of atmospheric pollution eg where sulphur dioxide is emitted (from burning coal and oil).
• Avoidance of surface treatments that seal in salts; occasional sponging of affected stones helps to remove salts, especially in coastal areas.
• Construction of movement joints to accomodate differences between the thermal movements of adjoining materials.
• Construction details that will allow water to be removed by evaporation or drainage, to avoid frost damage or washing out of limestones.
• Careful building design, especially with corner reinforcements, ring beam, etc., in earthquake prone areas; especially avoidance of stone vaults or corbelled roofs.

EARTH, SOIL, LATERITE

General

When referring to *earth* or *soil* in building construction, both terms mean the same material. *Mud* is a wet, plastic soil mixture, with or without additives, which is used to make mud bricks (adobe) or monolithic mud walls.

Soil

Soil is the loose material that results from the transformation of the underlying parent rock by the more or less simultaneous interaction of climatic factors (sun, wind, rain, frost) and chemical changes, brought about by biological agents (flora and fauna) and migration of chemical substances through rain, evaporation, surface and underground water.

Laterite

Of the various soil types that occur in the tropics and sub-tropics, laterites are of special interest in conjunction with building construction. These are highly weathered soils, which contain large, though extremely variable, proportions of iron and aluminium oxides, as well as quartz and other minerals. They are found abundantly in the tropics and sub-tropics, where they generally occur just below the surface of wide grasslands or forest clearings in regions with high rainfall. The colours can vary from ochre through red, brown, violet to black, depending largely on the concentration of iron oxides.

The special characteristics of laterites, by which they differ from other soils, are:
•   Soft occurances tend to harden on exposure to air, which is why blocks have traditionally (eg in India) been cut in situ, allowed to harden and then used for masonry wall construction (hence the name was derived from "later", the Latin word for "brick").
•   The darker the laterite, the harder, heavier and more resistant to moisture it is.
•   Some laterites are found to have a pozzolanic reaction when mixed with lime (which can be explained by the high clay content), producing hard and durable building materials (eg stabilized blocks).

However, irrespective of the type of soil, it is always composed of particles of different size and nature, as summarized in the following chart.

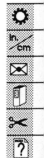
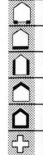

8

Material	Character	Particle Size	Short Description
Gravel		60 to 2 mm	Coarse pieces of rocks like granite, lime, marble, etc., of any shape (round, flat, angular). Gravel forms the skeleton of the soil and limits its capillarity and shrinkage.
Sand		2 to 0.06 mm (ie the smallest grain size that can be discerned by the naked eye).	Particles mainly comprising silica or quartz; beach sands contain calcium carbonate (shell fragments). Sand grains lack cohesion in the presence of water, and limit swelling and shrinkage.
Silt		0.06 to 0.002 mm	Physically and chemically the same as sand, only much finer. Silt gives soil stability by increasing its internal friction, and holds together when wet and compressed.
Clay		Smaller than 0.002 mm (2 μ)	Clay results from chemical weathering of rocks, mainly silicates. The hydrated aluminosilicate particles are thin plates of extremely great specific surface area, causing strong cohesion in the presence of water, also excessive swelling and shrinkage.
Colloids		Smaller than 0.002 mm (2 μ)	Fine particles resulting from decomposition of minerals and organic matter (clay is the chief mineral colloid), forming a gluey substance.
Organic matter		Several mm to several cm	Micrograins and fibres resulting from decomposition of plants and soil fauna. It has a spongy or stringy structure and smells like wet decaying wood.

In addition to the solid particles, soil also comprises:
• Air, which is a weakening factor and undesirable in building construction, as it also entraps micro-organisms and water vapour, both of which can cause deterioration of the building component.
• Water, without which the soil cannot be used for building, but which can carry dissolved substances (salts) that may create problems.

Most soils are suitable for use as building materials, though in various cases, the addition or removal of certain constituents is required to improve their quality. Several tests need to be carried out in order to identify the characteristics of the soil and its appropriateness for building construction. The procedures are described under *Soil Testing*.

It must be stressed that, contrary to common belief, building with earth is **not a simple technology**. The mere fact that natives of many countries have been building their houses with earth since thousands of years does not mean that the technology is sufficiently developed or known to everyone. It is indeed the lack of expertise that brings about poor constructions, which in turn gives the material its ill reputation. However, with some guidance, virtually anyone can learn to build satisfactorily with earth, and thus renew confidence in one of the oldest and most versatile building materials.

Applications

Soil constructions are found in all parts of the world, though to a lesser extent in areas of extreme rainfall.

Buildings can consist entirely or partially of soil, depending on the location, climate, available skills, cost and use of the buildings. The construction can be monolithic or made of various components (bricks, renders, infills).

In areas where there is a large diurnal temperature variation (arid zones or highlands) the walls and roofs are preferably thicker than in more uniform climates (humid zones), where the need for materials of high thermal capacity is less.

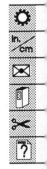

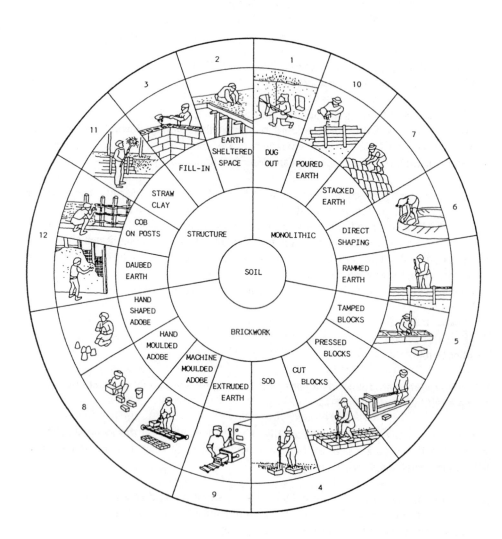

The various earth construction methods (Bibl. 02.19)

Soil can be used for all major parts of the building:

Foundations

- Hard varieties of laterite, with good particle size distribution (sand to gravel), lightly compacted, for small buildings in dry regions.
- Similar laterite as aggregate in concrete.
- Stabilized air-dried soil blocks, with 10 % cement content, laid in laterite-cement mortar, only in dry regions.

Walls

- Base course same as for foundations.
- Direct moulding, without shuttering, just by pressing moist earth by hand.
- Rammed earth construction by tamping lightly moistened soil in shuttering (similar to concrete) for monolithic walls. Stabilization with straw, cement, lime, bitumen, cow dung, etc. as required.
- Straw clay construction, similar to rammed earth, but with straw (any kind) as the major ingredient and clay as the binder. (Good thermal insulation, eg for highland regions).
- Daubed earth applied on a supporting substructure, eg wooden or bamboo frame with wickerwork or plaited straw (wattle and daub).
- Masonry constructions, using air-dried mud blocks (adobe) laid in a mud mortar (with addition of some sand). Rain protective rendering required.
- Masonry constructions, using compressed, air-dried stabilized soil blocks laid in soil-cement or soil-lime mortar. In areas of moderate rainfall, no rendering required.
- Renders, using soil with or without additives, such as binders (cement, lime, gypsum), waterproofing agents (bitumen, plant extracts, chemicals), fibrous material (plant or animal fibres, cow dung), or using plain cow dung.
- Paints based on soil mixes.

Floors

- In reasonably dry areas, with good drainage and low water tables: subbase of well compacted, clay-rich soil, covered by large sized gravel (to break capillary action), topped by small sized gravel and a layer of sand, the surface layer made of a silty soil, mixed with 5 % linseed oil and compacted with tamper or vibrator.

• Same as before, but surface layer of stabilized soil bricks or tiles, laid on the sand bed and jointed with soil cement mortar.
• Traditional rural house floors (Asia, Africa) made of compacted stone or earth and smoothened with a mixture of soil and cow dung, or only cow dung (for resistance to abraison, cracks and insects).
• Other surface hardeners: animal (horse) urine mixed with lime, ox blood mixed with cinders and crushed clinker, animal glues, vegetable oils, powdered termite hills, crushed shells, certain silicates and other synthetic products.

Roofs

• Traditional flat roof with timber sub-structure covered with soil (same as for rammed earth walls) and compacted well, only suitable for dry regions.
• Fibre-soil reels laid moist between timber purlins, on flat or sloped roofs, evened out with a fibre-soil layer and covered with roofing felt or bitumen coat; not recommended in termite prone areas.
• Grass roofs, requiring a water and rootproof membrane, gravel to drain water and ventilate roots and a soil layer on which grass grows, providing favourable indoor climate and sound-proofing, as well as air-purification; suitable for all climates.
• Soil brick vaults and domes, constructed with or without formwork, such that each brick rests on the layer below, passing on the compressive forces in a curved line within the thickness of the structure; a traditional construction found in most arid and semi-arid regions.

Soil brick vault construction (Bibl. 00.56)

Advantages

- Availability in large quantities in most regions,
- hence low cost (mainly for excavation and transportation) or no cost, if found on the building site.
- Easy workability, usually without special equipment.
- Suitability as construction material for most parts of the building.
- Fire resistance.
- Favourable climatic performance in most regions, due to high thermal capacity, low thermal conductivity and porosity, thus subdueing extreme outdoor temperatures and maintaining a satisfactory moisture balance.
- Low energy input in processing and handling unstabilized soil, requiring only 1 % of the energy needed to manufacture and process the same quantity of cement concrete.
- Unlimited reuseability of unstabilized soil (ie recycling of demolished buildings).
- Environmental appropriateness (use of an unlimited resource in its natural state, no pollution, negligible energy consumption, no wastage).

Problems

- Excessive water absorption of unstabilized soil, causing cracks and deterioration by frequent wetting and drying (swelling and shrinkage) as well as weakening and disintegration by rain and floods.
- Low resistance to abraison and impact, if not sufficiently stabilized or reinforced, thus rapid deterioration through constant use and possibility of penetration by rodents and insects.
- Low tensile strength, making earth structures especially susceptible to destruction during earthquakes.
- Low acceptability amongst most social groups, due to numerous examples of poorly constructed and maintained earth structures, usually houses of the underprivileged population, thus qualifying earth as being the "poor man's material".
- On account of these disadvantages, lack of institutional acceptability in most countries, which is why building and performance standards often do not exist.

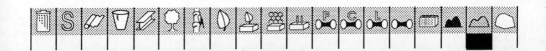

14

Remedies

• Avoidance of excessive water absorption can be achieved by selection of the most appropriate type of soil and/or correcting the particle size distribution; also by adding a suitable stabilizer and/or waterproofing agent; good compaction; and more important, by good design and protective measures.
• Resistance to abraison and impact is generally improved by the same measures as above; waterproofing agents, however, do not necessarily impart higher strength and hardness; hence special additives may be needed and special surface treatment.
• Soil constructions in earthquake zones require careful designing to minimize the effect of destructive forces, but also the use of additional materials, which possess high tensile strength (especially for reinforcements).
• Building important public buildings and high standard housing with earth can be convincing demonstrations of the advantages of the technology and thus improve its acceptability.
• By eliminating the major disadvantages, the lack of institutional acceptability can be overcome. Because of the importance of the material, methods of testing and improving soils for building construction are dealt with in more detail.

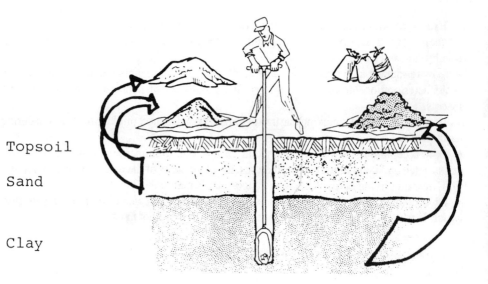

Topsoil

Sand

Clay

Extracting soil samples with an auger (Bibl 02.10).

Soil Testing

Whether the aim is to build a single house or to start a production unit for stabilized soil blocks, it is essential to test the soil used, not only in the beginning, but at regular intervals or each time the place of excavation is changed, as the soil type can vary considerably even over a small area.

Basically there are two types of tests:
- indicator or field tests, which are relatively simple and quickly done,
- laboratory tests, which are more sophisticated and time consuming.

In certain cases, soil identification on the basis of experience can be sufficient for small operations, but normally some indicator tests are indispensable. They provide valuable information about the need for laboratory tests, especially if the field tests give contradicting results. Not all the tests need to be carried out, as this can be tiresome, but just those that give a clear enough picture of the samples, to exclude those that show deficiencies. This is not only necessary to achieve optimum material quality, but also to economize on costs, material, stabilizers, manpower and energy input.

It should further be remembered that soil identification alone does not provide assurance of its correct use in construction. Tests are also necessary to evaluate the mechanical performance of the construction material.

Collecting Samples

- The soil is best excavated directly at the building site and several holes are dug in an area that is big enough to supply all the required soil.
- First, the topsoil containing vegetable matter and living organisms is removed (unsuitable for construction).
- The soil samples are then taken from a depth of up to about 1.5 m for manual excavation, or up to 3 m if a machine will be doing the work.
- A special device, an auger, is used to extract samples from various depths. Each different type of soil is put on a different pile.
- The thickness of each layer of soil, its colour and the type of soil, as well as an accurate description of the location of the hole should be recorded on labels attached to each bag of soil taken for testing.

Indicator or Field Tests

The implementation of these simple tests should preferably *follow the order presented here.*

Odour test

Equipment: none
Duration: few minutes

Immediately after removal, the soil should be smelt, in order to detect organic matter (musty smell, which becomes stronger on moistening or heating). Soils containing organic matter should not be used or tested further.

Touch test

Equipment: none
Duration: few minutes

After removing the largest particles (gravel), a sample of soil is rubbed between the fingers and palm of the hand. A sandy soil feels rough and has no cohesion when moist. A silty soil still feels slightly rough, but has moderate cohesion when moist. Hard lumps that resist crushing when dry, but become plastic and sticky when moistened indicate a high percentage of clay.

Similar tests can be done by crushing a pinch of soil lightly between the teeth (soils are usually quite clean!).

Lustre test

Equipment: knife
Duration: few minutes

A slightly moist ball of soil, freshly cut with the knife will reveal either a dull surface (indicating the predominance of silt) or a shiny surface (showing a higher proportion of clay).

Adhesion test

Equipment: knife
Duration: few minutes

When the knife easily penetrates a similar ball of soil, the proportion of clay is usually low. Clayey soils tend to resist penetration and to stick to the knife when pulled out.

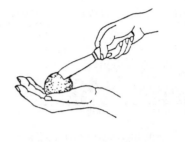

Washing test

Equipment: bowl of water or water tap
Duration: few minutes

When washing hands after these tests, the way the soil washes off gives further indication of its composition: sand and silt are easy to remove, while clay needs to be rubbed off.

Visual test

Equipment: two screens with wire mesh of 1 mm and 2 mm

Duration: half an hour

With the help of the screen the dry gravel and sand particles should be separated on a clean surface to form two heaps. Crushing of clay lumps may be necessary beforehand. By comparing the sizes of the heaps a rough classification of the soil is possible.

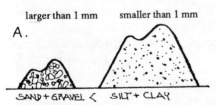

A. The soil is either silty or clayey if the "silt + clay" pile is larger; a more precise classification requires further tests.

B. Similarly the soil is sandy or gravelly, if the "sand + gravel" pile is larger.

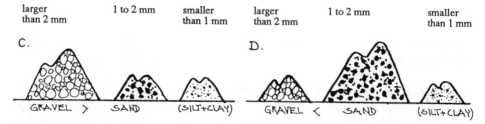

| larger than 2 mm | 1 to 2 mm | smaller than 1 mm | larger than 2 mm | 1 to 2 mm | smaller than 1 mm |

C. and D. Further sieving with a 2 mm mesh screen will reveal whether the soil is gravelly or sandy.

In the case of sandy or gravelly soil, a handful of the original material (before sieving) should be moistened, made into a ball and left to dry in the sun. If it falls apart as it dries, it is called "clean", and thus unsuitable for earth constructions, unless it is mixed with other materials.

If the soil is not "clean", the silt and clay pile should be used for the next tests.

Water retention test

Equipment: none
Duration: 2 minutes

A sample of the fine material is formed into an egg-sized ball, by adding just enough water to hold it together but not stick to the hands. The ball is gently pressed into the curved palm, which is vigorously tapped by the other hand, shaking the ball horizontally.

• When it takes 5 - 10 taps to bring the water to the surface (smooth, "livery" appearance), it is called *rapid* reaction. When pressed, the water disappears and the ball crumbles, indicating a *very fine sand* or *course silt*.
• When the same result is achieved with 20 - 30 taps (*slow* reaction), and the ball does not crumble, but flattens on pressing, the sample is a *slightly plastic silt* or *silty clay*.
• *Very slow* or no reaction, and no change of appearance on pressing indicate a *high clay content*.

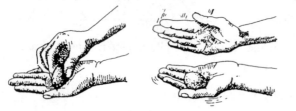

5 to 10 taps = rapid
20 to 30 taps = slow
over 30 taps = very slow

CRATERRE

Dry strength test

Equipment: oven, if no sun available
Duration: four hours for drying

2 to 3 moist samples from the previous test are slightly flattened to 1 cm thickness and 5 cm Ø and allowed to dry completely in the sun or in an oven. By attempting to pulverize a dry piece between thumb and index finger, the relative hardness helps to classify the soil:

- If it is broken with great difficulty and does not pulverize, it is *almost pure clay*.
- If it can be crushed to a powder with a little effort, it is a *silty* or *sandy clay*.
- If it pulverizes without any effort, it is a *silt* or *fine sand* with *low clay content*.

Thread test

Equipment: flat board, approx. 30 x 30 cm
Duration: 10 minutes

Another moist ball of olive size is rolled on the flat clean surface, forming a thread. If it breaks before the diameter of the thread is 3 mm, it is too dry and the process is repeated after re-moulding it into a ball with more water. This should be repeated until the thread breaks just when it is 3 mm thick, indicating the correct moisture content. The thread is re-moulded into a ball and squeezed between thumb and forefinger.

- If the ball is hard to crush, does not crack nor crumble, it has a *high clay content*.
- Cracking and crumbling shows *low clay content*.
- If it breaks before forming a ball, it has a *high silt or sand content*.
- A soft spongy feel means *organic soil*.

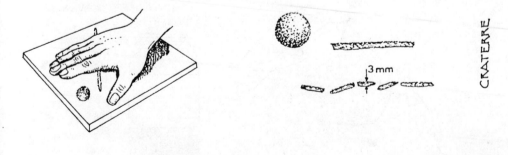

Ribbon test

Equipment: none
Duration: 10 minutes

With the same moisture content as the thread test, a soil sample is formed into a cigar shape of 12 to 15 mm thickness. This is then progres-
sively flattened between the thumb and forefinger to form a ribbon of
3 to 6 mm thickness, taking care to allow it to grow as long as possible.

- A long ribbon of 25 to 30 cm has a *high clay content.*
- A short ribbon of 5 to 10 cm shows *low clay content.*
- No ribbon means a *negligible clay content.*

Sedimentation test

Equipment: cylindrical glass jar of at least 1 litre capacity, with a flat bottom and an opening
that can be just covered with the palm; centimetre scale
Duration: 3 hours

The glass jar is filled quarter full with soil and almost to the top with clean water. The soil
is allowed to soak well for an hour, then with the opening firmly covered, the jar is shaken
vigorously and then placed on a horizontal surface. This is repeated again an hour later and
the jar then left standing undisturbed for at least 45 minutes.

After this time, the solid particles will have settled at the bottom and the relative proportions
of sand (lowest layer), silt and clay can be measured fairly accurately. However, the values
will be slightly distorted, since the silt and clay will have expanded in the presence of water.

ORGANIC
MATERIAL

CLAY
SILT
SAND
GRAVEL

CRATERRE

Laboratory Tests

Linear shrinkage test

Equipment: long metal or wooden box with internal dimensions 60 x 4 x 4 cm (l x b x h), open on top; oil or grease; spatula
Duration: 3 to 7 days

The inside surfaces of the box are greased to prevent the soil from sticking to them. A sample of soil with optimum moisture content is prepared (ie when squeezing a lump in the hand, it retains the shape without soiling the palm, and when dropped from about 1 metre height, breaks into several smaller lumps). This soil mix is pressed into all corners of the box and neatly smoothened off with the spatula, so that the soil exactly fills the mould. The filled box is exposed to the sun for 3 days or left in the shade for 7 days.

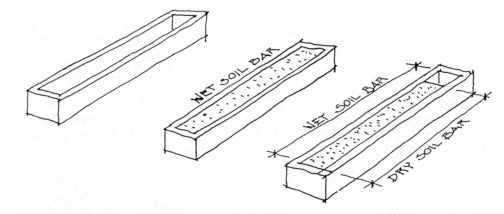

After this period, the soil will have dried and shrunk, either as a single piece or forming several pieces, in which case they are pushed to one end to close the gaps. The length of the dried soil bar is measured and the linear shrinkage is calculated as follows:

$$\frac{\text{(Length of wet bar) - (Length of dried bar)}}{\text{(Length of wet bar)}} \times 100$$

To obtain good results in construction, the soil should shrink or swell as little as possible. The more the soil shrinks, the larger is the clay content, which can be remedied by adding sand and/or a stabilizer, preferably lime.

Wet sieving test

Equipment: a set of standardized sieves with different meshes (eg 6.3 mm, 2.0 mm, 0.425 mm and 0.063 mm); flat water container below the sieves; 2 small buckets, one filled with water; stove or oven for drying samples; 2 to 5 kg balance with an accuracy of at least 0.1 g
Duration: 1 to 2 hours

A 2 kg soil sample is weighed dry, placed in the empty bucket and mixed with clean water. The water-soil mix, well stirred, is poured into the sieves, which are placed in descending order one on top of the other, with the finest mesh at the bottom, below which is the flat container. The bucket is rinsed clean with the remaining water, which is also poured into the sieves.

Each sieve will have collected a certain amount of material, which is dried by heating on the stove or in the oven, then weighed accurately and recorded. The fine particles in the bottommost container is a mixture of silt and clay, which cannot be separated by sieving. This is carried out by the next test.

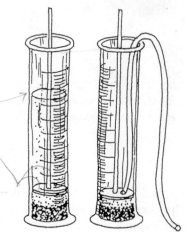

Siphoning test

Equipment: a 1-litre graduated glass measuring cylinder, with an inside diameter of about 65 mm; a circular metal disk on a stem, which can be lowered down inside the cylinder; a rubber tube and heat resistant drying dishes for siphoning; a watch; a pinch of salt; stove or oven and balance, as in previous test
Duration: 1 to 2 hours

A dry sample of 100 g of the fine material from the previous test is carefully weighed and put into the cylinder. A pinch of salt is added, to improve dispersion of the clay particles, and water is filled up to the 200 mm mark. With the cylinder kept firmly closed with the palm of the hand, the contents are shaken vigorously until a uniform suspension of the grains is achieved. The cylinder is placed on a firm level surface and the time taken.

After 20 minutes, the metal disk is carefully lowered down to cover the material that has settled at the bottom of the cylinder, without disturbing it. The clay, which is still in suspension, is removed by siphoning off the liquid, which is subsequently dried out and the residue weighed. The weight in grams is also the percentage of clay in the sample.

Grain size distribution analysis

With the results of the wet sieving and siphoning tests of one sample showing the relative proportions of the various constituents, as defined by their particle sizes, several points can be plotted on a chart. A curve is then drawn so that it passes through each point successively, giving the grain size distribution of that particular soil sample. This can be repeated for other samples on the same chart, showing the range of soil types analyzed.

The chart below shows an example of a gravelly soil (G) and a clay soil type (C). The horizontally shaded area indicates the types of soils that are suitable for rammed earth construction, while the vertically shaded area shows appropriate soils for compressed block production. The overlapping area is thus good for most soil constructions, so that a curve (I) running through the middle symbolizes a soil of ideal granulation.

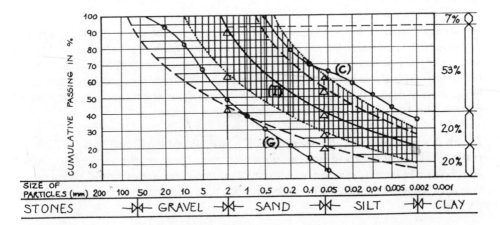

The purpose of this exercise is to determine whether the available soil is suitable for building. If the soil is too gravelly, the gaps between the particles are not properly filled, the soil lacks cohesion and is consequently very sensitive to erosion. If the soil is too clayey, it lacks the large grains that give it stability, and is thus sensitive to swelling and shrinkage. An optimum grain size distribution is one in which the proportion of large and small grains is well balanced, leaving practically no gaps, and sufficient clay particles are present to facilitate proper cohesion.

If the tests reveal a poor grain size distribution, it can be corrected to some extent by:
• sieving the gravelly fraction, if the soil contains too much coarse material;
• partly washing out the clayey fraction, if finer particles are in excess;
• mixing soil types of different granular structure.

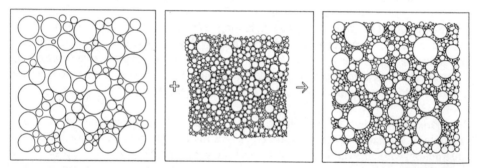

(Bibl. 02.34)

Atterberg limit tests

These tests, developed by the Swedish scientist Atterberg, are needed to find the respective moisture contents at which the soil changes from a liquid (viscous) to a plastic (mouldable) state, from a plastic consistency to a soft solid (which breaks apart before changing shape, but unites if pressed), and from this state to a hard solid. While the previous tests determined the quantity of each soil constituent, the Atterberg tests show which type of clay mineral is present. This has an influence on the kind of stabilizer required.

For all practical purposes, the determination of the "liquid limit" and "plastic limit" is sufficient, the other Atterberg limits are not so important. However, the determination of the Atterberg limits is usually carried out with the "fine mortar" fraction of the soil, which passes through a 0.4 mm sieve. This is because water has little effect on the consistency of larger particles.

Liquid limit test

Equipment: a curved dish, about 10 cm in diameter and 3 cm deep, with a smooth or glazed inner surface; a grooving tool (as illustrated); a metal container with tightly fitting cover (eg large pill box); a drying oven which maintains a temperature of 110° C; a balance, accurate to at least 0.1 g, preferably to 0.01 g.
Duration: about 10 hours

A sample of fine soil (about 80 g) is mixed with drinkable water to a consistency of a thick paste and evenly filled into the dish such that the centre is about 8 mm deep, gradually diminishing towards the edge of the dish.

This is divided into two equal parts by drawing the grooving tool straight through the middle, making a V-shaped groove (of 60° angle) and a 2 mm wide gap at the bottom. Alternatively, a knife can be used.

The dish is held firmly in one hand and tapped against the heel of the other hand, which is held 30 to 40 mm away. The motion must be a right angles to the groove. If it takes exactly 10 taps to make the soil flow together, closing the gap over a distance of 13 mm, the soil is at its liquid limit.

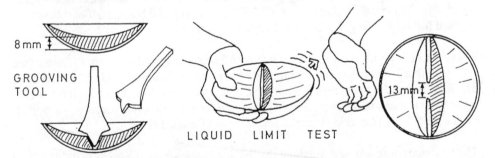

8 mm

GROOVING
TOOL

13 mm

LIQUID LIMIT TEST

If it takes less than 10 taps, the soil is too moist; more than 10 taps means that it is too dry. The moisture content must then be corrected, whereby moist soils can be dried by prolonged mixing or adding dry soil. The process is repeated until the liquid is found.

With an accurate balance, it is sufficient to take just a small sample of soil, scraped off from a point close to where the groove closed. The sample is put into the container, which is tightly covered and weighed before the moisture can evaporate. The soil container is then put into the 110° C oven until the soil is completely dry. This may take 8 - 10 hours and can be checked by weighing several times, until the weight remains constant.

Knowing the wet (W_1) and dry weight (W_2) of the soil and container, and the weight of the clean dry container (W_c), the liquid limit, expressed as the percentage of water in the soil, is calculated as follows:

$$\text{Liquid Limit} = \frac{\text{Weight of Water}}{\text{Weight of oven dried soil}} \times 100 \qquad\qquad L = \frac{W_1 - W_2}{W_2 - W_c} \times 100 \ \%$$

Some examples of liquid limits are:
Sand: $L = 0$ to 30
Silt: $L = 20$ to 50
Clay: $L =$ over 40

Plastic limit test

Equipment: a smooth flat surface, eg glass plate 20 x 20 cm; a metal container, drying oven and balance, as for the liquid limit test.
Duration: about 10 hours

About 5 g of fine soil is mixed with water to make a malleable but not sticky ball. This is rolled between the palms of the hands until it begins to dry and crack. Half of this sample is rolled further to a length of 5 cm and thickness of 6 mm.

Placed on the smooth surface, the sample is rolled into a thread of 3 mm diameter (see illustration for *Thread test*). If the sample breaks before the diameter reaches 3 mm, it is too dry. If the thread does not break at 3 mm or less, it is too moist. The plastic limit is reached, if the thread breaks into two pieces of 10 - 15 mm length. When this happens, the broken pieces are quickly placed in the metal container and weighed (W_1).

The next steps of drying and weighing the soil and container are the same as for the liquid limit test, determining the values W_2 and W_c. The whole procedure is repeated for the second half of the original sample. If the results differ by more than 5 %, the tests must be repeated one again.

The plastic limit is calculated in the same way as the liquid limit:

$$\text{Plastic Limit} = \frac{\text{Weight of Water}}{\text{Weight of oven dried soil}} \times 100 \qquad\qquad P = \frac{W_1 - W_2}{W_2 - W_c} \times 100 \ \%$$

Plasticity index

The plasticity index (PI) is the difference between the liquid limit (L) and plastic limit (P):

$$PI = L - P$$

The simple mathematical relationship makes it possible to plot the values on a chart. The advantage is that the areas can be defined in which certain stabilizers are most effective.

It should, however, be noted that laterite soils do not necessarily conform to this chart. There is in fact no substitute for practical experimentation, using the recommended stabilizers to begin with, and starting with small dosages.
The choice of soil stabilizers is dealt with in detail in the next chapter.

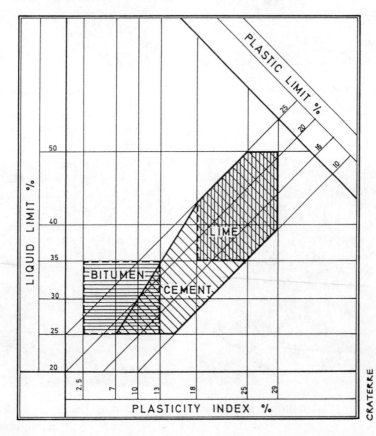

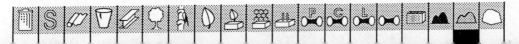

Traditional Mud Brick Production in Egypt (Photos: K. Mathéy)

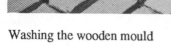

Washing the wooden mould

Filling the mould with mud

After smoothing the top surface, removal of
the mould

Sun-dried mud bricks, ready for use in
building construction

SOIL STABILIZERS

General

Soils that do not possess the desired characteristics for a particular construction can be improved by adding one or more stabilizers.

Each stabilizer can fulfil one (or at the most two) of the following functions:

• Increase the compressive strength and impact resistance of the soil construction, and also reduce its tendency to swell and shrink, by *binding* the particles of soil together.

• Reduce or completely exclude water absorption (causing swelling, shrinking and abrasion) by *sealing* all voids and pores, and covering the clay particles with a waterproofing film.

• Reduce cracking by *imparting flexibility* which allows the soil to expand and contract to some extent.

• Reduce excessive expansion and contraction by *reinforcing* the soil with fibrous material.

The effect of stabilization is usually increased when the soil is compacted. Sometimes compaction alone is sufficient to stabilize the soil, however, without an appropriate stabilizer, the effect may not be permanent, particularly in the case of increased exposure to water.

But, *before considering the use of a stabilizer* the following points must be investigated:

• Does the available soil satisfy the main requirements even without stabilization? This is largely dependent on the local climate, natural hazards and type of construction.

• Does the building design take into account the characteristics and limitations of the material? Building on a high level and incorporating damp-proof courses (to minimize damage by rising water) and providing wide roof overhangs (for protection against rain and solar radiation) are examples of appropriate design.

• Is the stabilization of the entire construction really necessary, or can a good surface protection (eg stabilized render) be sufficient?

By reducing the need for stabilization, considerable costs, time and effort can be saved.

Kinds of Stabilizers

A great number of substances may be used for soil stabilization, and much research is going on to find the most suitable stabilizer for each soil type. But, despite these research efforts, there is no "miracle" stabilizer that can be used in all cases. Stabilization is not an exact science, so that it is up to the builder to make trial blocks with various kinds and amounts of stabilizers which can be tested.

The most common *naturally available stabilizers* used in traditional constructions are:
- sand and clay
- straw, plant fibres
- plant juices (sap, latexes, oils)
- wood ashes (cinders)
- animal excreta (mainly cow dung, horse urine)
- other animal products (blood, hair, glues, termite hills).

The most common *manufactured stabilizers*, (ie products or by-products of local village industries or large industrial processes) are:
- lime and pozzolanas
- portland cement
- gypsum
- bitumen
- commercial soil stabilizers
- sodium silicate ("water glass")
- resins
- whey (casein)
- molasses

The listed stabilizers are briefly described below. The choice of the most suitable stabilizer will mainly depend on local availability and costs, but also to some extent on social acceptance.

Sand and clay
- These are used to correct the quality of soil mix, that is, addition of sand to clayey soils or addition of clay to sandy soils.
- Mixing should be done in the dry state, otherwise it cannot be uniform.
- Dry clay is usually found in the form of hard lumps, which have to be well crushed before mixing.

Straw, plant fibres
- These act as reinforcements, especially to check cracking in soils with a high clay content.
- They also make the soil lighter, increase its insulating properties (good in arid and highland regions) and accelerate the drying process (by providing drainage channels).
- Straw is universally the most common soil reinforcement; almost any type is acceptable (wheat, rye, barley, etc.), also the chaff of most cereal crops.
- Other fibrous plant materials are sisal, hemp, elephant grass, coir (coconut fibre), bagasse (sugar cane waste), etc.

- To achieve satisfactory results, the minimum proportion of plant reinforcements is 4 % by volume; 20 to 30 kg per m³ of soil are common.
- Since plant reinforcements tend to weaken the end product and increase water absorption, excessive use should be avoided.
- The straw and fibres should be chopped to lengths of not more than 6 cm, and mixed thoroughly with the soil to avoid nests.

Plant juices
- The juice of banana leaves precipitated with lime improves erosion resistance and slows water absorption.
- Reduced permeability is also achieved by adding the latex of certain trees (eg euphorbia, hevea) or concentrated sisal juice in the form of organic glue.
- Vegetable oils and fats must dry quickly to be effective and provide water resistance. Coconut, cotton and linseed oils are examples; castor oil is very effective, but expensive.
- Kapok oil can also be effective. It is made by roasting kapok seeds, grinding them to a fine powder and mixing it with water (10 kg powder : 20 to 25 l water).

A freshly decorated soil house in Ghana. The walls are treated with the decoction of the Locust bean pods and polished with a flat stone (Photo: H. Schreckenbach, Bibl. 00.49)

Wood ashes
• Ash from hardwood is usually rich in calcium carbonate and has stabilizing properties, but is not always suitable for clayey soils. Some ashes can even be harmful to the soil.
• The addition of 5 to 10 % (by volume) of fine, white ashes from fully burnt hardwood appears to be most effective, that is, improvement of the dry compressive strength.
• Ashes do not improve water resistance.

Animal excreta
• These are mainly used to stabilize renderings.
• Cow dung is the most common stabilizer, which is valued mainly for its reinforcing effect (on account of the fibrous particles) and ability to repel insects. Water resistance is not significantly improved, while compressive strengths are reduced.
• Horse or camel dung are less common alternatives.
• Horse urine as a substitute for mixing water effectively eliminates cracking and improves resistance to erosion. Even better results are obtained by adding lime.
• Despite their advantages, these materials face low social acceptance in most regions, while in others (mainly rural areas in Asia and Africa) they are well accepted traditional materials.

Other animal products
• Fresh bull's blood combined with lime can greatly reduce cracking, however, here again low social acceptance.
• Animal hair or fur is often used to reinforce renders.
• Animal glues, made from horn, bone, hooves and hides, improve moisture resistance.
• Termite hills, which are known to resist rain, can be pulverized and used as a stabilizer for sandy soils.

Lime and pozzolanas
(see also chapters on *Lime* and *Pozzolanas*)
• Clayey soil (with liquid limits in the region of 40 % or more) can be stabilized only with lime, as it reacts with the clay particles in the soil to form a binder.
• For soils with a lower clay content, a suitable pozzolana (eg fly ash, rice hush ash) can be added to the lime, to produce a cementitious binder.
• Quicklime (CaO), produced by burning limestone, can be used for stabilizing, but has several drawbacks: it has to be well crushed before use; it becomes very hot (up to 150° C) and can burn the skin; the heat of hydration tends to dry the soil quickly, with the risk of delayed hydration after several months.
• Hydrated or slaked lime ($Ca[OH]_2$), made by adding water to quicklime, has less drawbacks. It can be used as a dry powder (available in bags), as milk of lime (slaked lime with excess water) or as lime putty (a viscous mass).

- The correct proportion of lime (with or without a pozzolana) cannot be generalized and needs to be found by a series of tests. The required amount can range between 3 and 14 % by dry weight, depending largely on the clay content (more clay requires more lime).
- Dry soil must be crushed (as clayey soils usually contain hard lumps) and thoroughly mixed with the lime. Most soils can be dried and broken with quicklime.
- The wet soil-lime mix is best kept in that state under cover for a day or two, after which the lime will have broken the remaining clay lumps. The soil is mixed again (if necessary, with addition of a pozzolana) producing a homogenious mass, which can immediately be used in construction. (Proportion of lime : pozzolana can range between 1 : 1 and 1 : 3).
- The curing of lime-stabilized soil takes about six times that of cement-stabilized soil. High temperatures and humidity help to improve the ultimate compressive strength. This can be achieved by curing under a plastic sheet, or in an enclosed space built with corrugated iron sheets, for at least two weeks. Final strength is gained after two to six months.
- Curing can be accelerated by adding cement just before use in construction.
- Limestone with a high clay content produces a special type of lime, called hydraulic lime, which sets and hardens like cement. Soil stabilization with hydraulic limes reduces the period of curing, but may not achieve sufficient strengths.

Portland cement
(see also chapter on *Cement*)
- Soils with low clay contents are best stabilized with portland cement, which binds the sand particles and gravel in the same way as in concrete, that is, it reacts with the water in the soil mixture to produce a substance which fills the voids, forming a continuous film around each particle, binding them all together.
- The reaction of cement and water (known as *hydration*) liberates calcium hydroxide (slaked lime) which reacts with the clay particles to form a kind of pozzolanic binder. If the clay content is too low the lime remains free. This can be remedied by replacing a proportion (15 to 40 % by weight) of the cement with a pozzolana, which is usually cheaper than cement.
- Just as in cement-sand mortars, soil-cement mixes become more workable by adding lime. If the clay content is high, the additional lime reacts with it to further stabilize the soil.
- The appropriate cement content will vary according to the aspects mentioned above. A minimum of 5 % is recommended, while cement contents exceeding 10 % are considered unsuitable, because of the high cost of cement.
- Soil and cement must be mixed dry, and the water added and thoroughly mixed just before use, as the cement begins to react with water immediately.
- Once the cement has begun to harden, it becomes useless. Soil cement cannot be recycled.
- The more thoroughly the soil is mixed, the higher the ultimate strength, which is obtained by compaction (eg with a ramming device or block press).
- Portland cement is the stabilizer that provides the greatest strength as well as resistance to water penetration, swelling and shrinkage.

Gypsum
- Soil stabilization with gypsum is not common practice and information on its performance is very limited.
- Gypsum is abundantly available in many countries, either as natural gypsum or as an industrial by-product, and is cheaper than lime or cement (produced with less energy and equipment).
- Since gypsum mixed with water hardens rapidly, adobe blocks stabilized with gypsum require no lengthy curing period, but can be used for wall constructions soon after production. Gypsum contents around 10 % are best.
- The advantages of stabilization with gypsum are low shrinkage, smooth appearance and high mechanical strength. In addition, gypsum binds well with fibres (particularly sisal), is highly fire resistant and is not attacked by insects and rodents.
- The main disadvantage of gypsum is its solubility in water, which requires careful protective measures: protection from rain on outer walls by plastering, cladding or wide overhanging roofs; protection from indoor moisture development by avoiding steam (in kitchens) and condensation; protection against rising water by means of waterproof membranes.

Bitumen
(see also chapter on *Binders*)
- For soil stabilization, bitumen can either be used as a cutback (ie mixed with a solvent such as gasoline, kerosene or naphtha), or as an emulsion (ie dispersed in water).
- After mixing a soil with bitumen cutback, it should be spread out to allow the solvent to evaporate before the material is used for blockmaking. It is best to mix the cutback with a small quantity of soil, which is then mixed with the remaining soil.
- Bitumen emulsions are usually very fluid and mix easily with moist soil. Excessive mixing must be avoided to prevent a premature break-down of the emulsion, leading to increased water absorption after drying. Emulsions should be diluted in the mixing water.
- Soil mixes required for compaction should not be too moist, hence a less quantity of stabilizer should be added.
- The bitumen content should be between 2 and 4 %. Higher proportions result in dangerously low compressive strengths.
- Bitumen stabilized soils should be cured in dry air at temperatures around 40° C.
- While bitumen stabilization does not improve the strength of the soil, it significantly reduces water absorption. In other words, while the dry strength of the soil is not very high, the strength is not reduced when wet.
- Bitumen stabilization is most effective with sandy or silty soils with a liquid limit between 25 and 35 % and plasticity index between 2.5 and 13 %.
- The presence of acid organic matter, sulphates and mineral salts can be very harmful. The addition of 1 % cement is a possible remedy.

Commercial soil stabilizers
• These are mainly industrially produced chemical products, which were developed primarily to stabilize the soil used in road construction.
• These chemical stabilizers work mainly as a waterproofer. In general, they do not improve the compressive strength of the soil.
• The required quantities of these stabilizers range between 0.01 and 1 % by weight, hence very thorough mixing is required to achieve a uniform distribution.
• A long list of commercial stabilizers is given in Bibl. 02.19.

Sodium silicate
• Sodium silicate, known as "water-glass", is cheaply available in many parts of the world.
• It works best with sandy soils, like clayey sands and silty sands, but is not suitable for clay soils.
• Sodium silicate works as a waterproofer, and also prevents fungal growth.
• If it is mixed with the soil, the usual quantity is 5 %.
• However, it is best to use it as a surface coating, made of 1 : 3 parts of commercial sodium silicate : clean water.
• Soil blocks are dipped into the solution for about a minute, after which the solution is applied with a stiff brush. The procedure is repeated a second time and the blocks are left to dry in a protected place for at least 7 days.
• Deeper penetration of the solution is achieved by adding a very small amount of a surfactant (surface active agent).

Resins
• Resins are either processed plant extracts, such as sap from trees, or by-products of various industrial processes.
• Much research work is being undertaken on these materials and extraordinary results have been obtained with resin stabilization.
• The main advantages are water resistance (though not in all cases), rapid setting and solidification of very moist soils.
• The main drawbacks, however, are high cost, sophisticated production technology and the need for larger quantities than conventional stabilizers. Resins are often toxic and degradable by biological agents.

Whey
• Whey (casein) is the protein-rich liquid formed by making curd. Its use for building will be very limited in most developing countries, on account of its nourishing value. However, in regions where a surplus of whey is produced, its use as a surface stabilizer for soil constructions is well worth considering.

- By adding whey to a soil-lime plaster or to a limewash, a weather-proof surface protection is achieved, without forfeiting the capability of the soil to breathe.
- In order to achieve good adhesion and avoid cracks, the limewash should be applied in two or three thin coats. The use of whey as a primer can also give good results.

Molasses
- Molasses are a by-product of the sugar industry.
- Adding molasses to the soil improves its compressive strength and reduces the capillarity of the soil.
- They work well with silty and sandy soils. In the case of clayey soils, small quantities of lime should be added to the molasses.
- The quantity of molasses normally added to the soil is about 5 % by weight of soil.

How to Use Stabilizers

Although the use of each stabilizer is mentioned above, some general rules are summarized here:
- The full benefit of using a stabilizer is achieved only if it makes contact with each particle of soil, hence, thorough mixing is necessary.
- Much preparation and testing is required to find the best combination and proportions of stabilizers for a given soil. It is certainly worth the time and effort, even if it takes one or two months of preparation.
- The only way to determine the correct proportion of stabilizer is to make 5 to 7 trial blocks from each mix and subject them to a series of tests, such as compression strength tests after different periods of drying, prolonged wetting and drying tests, and immersion in water.
- Portland cement and lime stabilized blocks need to be moist cured for at least 7 days to gain strength.
- Testing programs should take into account the local climatic conditions, the possible occurance of frost, and the like. The choice of stabilizer will also differ between arid and humid regions.
- It should be remembered that trial blocks need only a small amount of soil, which is easy to mix. During the actual construction or mass block production, the mixing of large quantities of the soil is more difficult, so that a slightly higher proportion of stabilizer should be added (except in the case of cement).
- The aim of the tests should always be to find the lowest amount of stabilizer to satisfy the requirements. Very often the specified requirements are unjustifiably high, leading to unnecessarily high costs.

FIRED CLAY PRODUCTS

General

The technique of firing clay to produce bricks and tiles for building construction is more than 4000 years old. It is based on the principle that clayey soils (containing 20 to 50 % clay) undergo irreversible reactions, when fired at 850 - 1000° C, in which the particles are bonded together by a glassy ceramic material.

A large variety of soils are suitable for this process, the essential property being plasticity to facilitate moulding. While this depends on the clay content, excessive proportions of clay can cause high shrinkage and cracking, which is unsuitable for brickmaking. The qualities of fired clay products vary not only according to the type and quantity of other ingredients of the soil, but also to the type of clay mineral. For the production of good quality bricks and tiles, careful testing of soils is necessary.

Burnt brick production has reached a high level of mechanization and automation in many countries, but traditional small-scale production methods are still very widespread in most developing countries. Thus there is a great variety of non-mechanized and mechanized methods for clay winning, preparation, moulding, drying and burning, which can only be dealt with briefly in this manual.

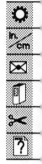

Clay winning

• Clay deposits are found at the foot of hills or on agricultural land close to rivers (which naturally generates conflicting interests between the use of land for brickmaking and for agriculture).
• The criteria for choosing a suitable location are the quality of clay, availability of level ground and closeness of a motorable road for transports.
• Hand-digging in small and medium-sized production plants is usually done to a depth of less than 2 m. (After excavation of large areas, they can be returned to agricultural use.)
• Mechanical methods, using drag-line and multi-bucket excavators, are required for large-scale brickmaking plants. These methods require proportionately less excavating area, but make deep cuts in the landscape.

Clay preparation

• This includes sorting, crushing, sieving and proportioning, before the material is mixed, wetted and tempered.

• Sorting is done by picking out roots, stones, limestone nodules, etc., or in some cases by washing the soil.
• Crushing is required because dry clay usually forms hard lumps. Manual pounding is common, but laborious. However, simple labour-intensive crushing machines have been developed (see *ANNEX*).
• Sieving is needed to remove all particles larger than 5 mm for bricks, or 0.6 mm for roof tiles.
• Proportioning is required if the clay content or grain size distribution is unsatisfactory. In some cases, rice husks, which serve as a fuel, are added to the clay, in order to obtain lighter and more uniformly burnt bricks.
• Thorough mixing is needed and a correct amount of water. Since manual mixing (traditionally by treading with bare feet) is laborious and often unsatisfactory, motor-powered mixers are preferred. The effort of mixing can be greatly reduced by allowing the water to percolate through the clay structure for some days or even months. This process, known as "tempering", allows chemical and physical changes to take place, inproving its moulding characteristics. The clay must be kept covered to prevent premature drying.

Moulding

• Moulding is done by hand or by mechanized methods.
• Hand-moulding methods make use of simple wooden moulds: the clay is formed into a clot, thrown into the mould, and the excess cut off.
• There are two traditional techniques for releasing the brick from the mould: a. the slop-moulding method, by which the mould is kept wet and the clay is mixed with more water, and b. the sand-moulding method, by which the clot is rolled in sand to prevent the clay from sticking to the mould.
• Bricks made by slop-moulding are vulnerable to slumping and distortion, while sand-moulding produces firmer, well-shaped bricks. Where sand is not available, finely ground clay can also be used, according to a technique developed at the ITW (Intermediate Technology Workshop in the United Kingdom).
• With table moulds (as developed by ITW, United Kingdom, and Central Building Research Institute, India), less effort, more accurately shaped bricks and higher outputs are achieved. While the moulding is done in the same way as with simple wooden moulds, the bricks are ejected by means of a foot-operated lever.
• Roofing tiles are made with specially shaped moulds, but principally in the same way as bricks. The main difference is that other material characteristics, with regard to uniformity, particle size and clay content, are needed.

• Mechanized brickworks use machines which extrude the clay through a dye to form a clay column, which is wirecut into brick-sized pieces. This method produces denser and stronger bricks, which can also be perforated.

• An intermediate solution is brick and tile moulding with mechanical compression. Two machines produced in Belgium (CERAMAN and TERSTARAM) were specially designed for this purpose, but are also used to make air-dried, stabilized soil bricks. Mechanical compression allows for considerably lower moisture contents, thus shortening the drying period.

Brickmaking in Ghana: Preparing the clots, cutting off surplus clay, removing the bricks from the mould, for placing in drying racks; ready fired bricks. (Photos: H. Schreckenbach, Bibl. 00.49)

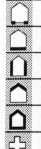

Drying

• Green bricks are likely to be crushed in the kiln, under the weight of those piled on top; they can shrink and crack during firing; the water driven off can condense on cold bricks away from the heat source; or steam is developed, building up excessive pressures within the bricks; and, finally, too much fuel is required to drive out the remaining water. Hence, thorough drying is vital.

• Drying should be relatively slow, that is, the rate at which moisture evaporates from the surface should not be faster than the rate at which it can diffuse through the fine pores of the green brick. Air should have access to all sides of the bricks, so that they must be stacked with sufficient gaps between them.

• Natural drying is done in the open under the sun, but a protective covering (eg leaves, grass or plastic sheeting) is advisable to avoid rapid drying out. If it is likely to rain, drying should be done under a roof. But traditionally, bricks are only made in the dry season.

• Artificial drying (as in large mechanized plants) is done in special drying chambers, which make use of heat recovered from the kilns or cooling zones.

• Drying shrinkage is inevitable, and causes no special problems if below 7 % linear shrinkage. 10 % linear shrinkage should not be exceeded, thus, if necessary, the clay proportion must be reduced by adding sand or grog (pulverized brick rejects).

Typical clamp in India: The crushed coal, being screened in the foreground, is the fuel used. On the right are green bricks stacked for drying (Photo: K. Mukerji)

Burning

- There are two types of kilns for burning bricks: intermittent and continuous kilns.
- Intermittent kilns include clamps and scove kilns (traditional field kilns), updraught and downdraught kilns. Their fuel efficiency is very low, but they are adaptable to changing market demands. They vary in size from 10 000 to 100 000 bricks.
- Continuous kilns include various versions of the Hoffmann kiln (particularly the Bull's trench kiln) and the high-draught kiln. These are very fuel efficient. Tunnel kilns, in which the bricks are passed through a stationary fire, are too sophisticated and capital-intensive to be considered here.
- *Clamps* are basically a pile of green bricks interspersed with combustible material (eg crushed coal, rice husks, cow dung). Some holes are left at the base of the clamp, where the fire is lit. The holes are closed and the fire allowed to burn out, which can take a few days or several weeks. The bricks near the centre of the clamp will be the hardest. Sorting out is necessary, as about 20 to 30 % are not saleable. These are refired or used in the clamp base, sides or top.
- *Scove kilns*, plastered on all sides with mud, are principally the same as clamps, except that tunnels are built across the base of the pile, in order to feed additional fuel. This is the best method for burning wood.
- *Updraught kilns* (also known as Scotch kilns) function in the same way as scoves, except that the tunnels and walls are permanent.
- *Downdraught* kilns have a permanent arched roof. The hot gases from the fuel burnt ant the sides of the kiln, rise to the arched roof and are drawn down between the bricks by the chimney suction, through the perforated floor and out through the chimney.
- The *Hoffmann kiln*, which was originally circular but now more commonly oval, is a multi-chamber kiln in which the combustion air is preheated by cooling bricks in some chambers, and passes through the firing zone, from which the exhaust gases preheat the green bricks. While the cooled bricks are removed from one side of the empty chamber, green bricks are stacked on the other side. The fuel is fed from the top, through holes in the permanent arched roof. The daily output is about 10 000 bricks.
- The *Bull's trench kiln* operates on the principle of the Hoffmann kiln, except that the expensive arched roof is omitted and the exhaust gases are drawn off through 16 m high moveable metal chimneys with a wide base, which fit over the openable vent holes set in the brick and ash top of the kiln. The fuel, generally crushed coal, is fed in through the holes on the top. Depending on the size of the kiln, daily outputs can be between 10 000 and 28 000 bricks, 70 % of which being of high quality.

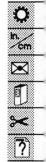

- The *high-draught kiln* is a further development of the Bull's trench kiln, whereby temporary cross-walls of green bricks leave openings on alternate sides, thus making the hot air travel a longer distance in a zig-zag fashion, achieving a larger transfer of heat from a given quantity of fuel (wood and coal). Fans are installed to provide the necessary draught. Daily outputs of 30 000 bricks are possible.
- Wood, coal and oil are the main types of fuel used. Coal is suitable for all purposes, while wood is less suited for clamps and oil is not used for clamps, downdraught, Bull's trench and high-draught kilns.

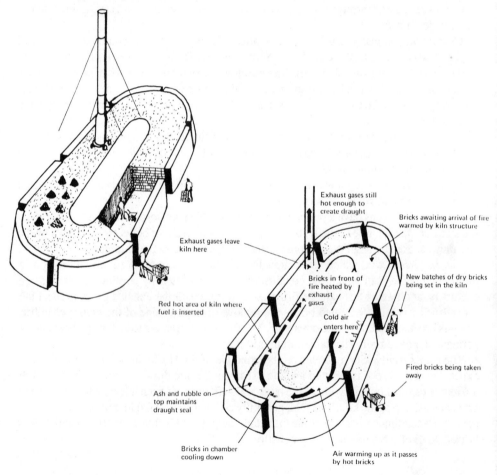

Working principle of the Bull's trench continuous kilns used in Pakistan and India (Bibl. 04.11)

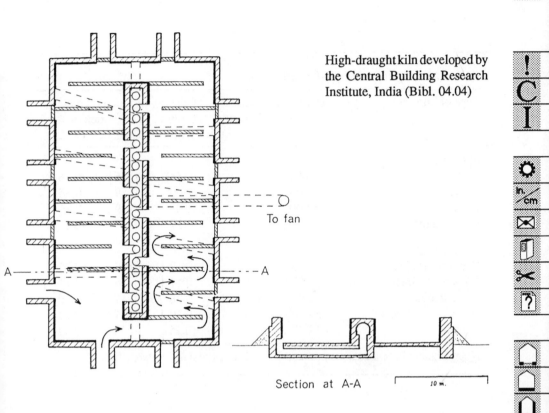

High-draught kiln developed by the Central Building Research Institute, India (Bibl. 04.04)

To fan

Section at A-A   10 m.

Scales of production in brick manufacturing (Bibl. 04.04)

Scale of production	Number of bricks per day (average)	Example of process used	Appropriate for market area
Small	1 000	Hand made, clamp-burnt	Rural village
Medium	10 000	Mechanized press, Bull's trench kiln	Near towns
Large	100 000	Fully automated, Extruded wire cut, Tunnel kiln	Industrialized areas of high demand and well-developed infrastructure

Typical fuel requirements of kilns (Bibl. 04.04)

Type of kiln	Heat requirement (MJ / 1 000 bricks)	Quantity of fuel required (Tonnes / 1 000 bricks)		
		Wood	Coal	Oil
Intermittent				
Clamp	7 000	(0.44)	0.26	(0.16)
Scove	16 000	1.00	0.59	0.36
Scotch	16 000	1.00	0.59	0.36
Downdraught	15 500	0.97	0.57	(0.35)
Continuous				
Original Hoffmann	2 000	0.13	0.07	0.05
Modern Hoffmann	5 000	0.31	0.19	0.11
Bull's trench	4 500	0.28	0.17	(0.10)
Habla (high-draught)	3 000	0.19	0.11	(0.07)
Tunnel	4 000	(0.25)	(0.15)	0.09

Note: Figures in brackets mean that the fuel is not suitable for that kiln.

Applications

• Solid or perforated bricks of all shapes and sizes for standard masonry constructions, including foundations, floors, and load-bearing walls, arches, vaults and domes.
• Roof tiles of various shapes and sizes for roof slopes ranging between 1 : 3 (18°30') and 1 : 1 (45°).
• Floor tiles and facing bricks for waterproof and durable surface finishes, and for improving appearance.
• Special products, such as engineering bricks which have high densities and compressive strengths; refractory bricks, with high heat resistance, used for lining kilns and furnaces; acid resisting bricks and tiles to withstand chemical attack; pipes and channel elements for various purposes.
• Specially shaped, hollow clay blocks for composite reinforced concrete beam slabs (for ceilings and roofs).
• Brick rejects can be used to construct kiln walls, as a filler in wall or floor cavities, as an aggregate in concrete, or, when finely ground, underfired rejects produce a pozzolana (surkhi) and others produce grogs for brickmaking.

Advantages

• Fired clay products can have high compressive strengths, even when wet, and are thus resistant to impact and abrasion.
• The porosity of fired clay permits moisture movement, without significant dimensional changes. Brick and tile constructions can "breathe".
• Solid bricks have a high thermal capacity, required for most climates, except for the predominantly humid zones; perforated bricks can be used (with perforations running vertically) for cavity walls, which provide thermal insulation, or (with perforations perpendicular to the wall face) for ventilation or screen walls.
• Fired clay products provide excellent fire-resistance.
• Bricks and tiles are weather resistant and can remain without any surface protection, thus saving costs. However, exposed brickwork is often considered unfinished and hence not always accepted.
• Poor quality and broken bricks are useable for other purposes, hence no wastage.
• The production process can be extremely labour-intensive and thus create many jobs, even for unskilled workers.

Problems

• Relatively high fuel consumption of the firing process. In many countries, where firewood is used, large forest areas have disappeared causing serious ecological damage. Where firewood is still available, it is usually extremely expensive, but this is also true for other fuels. Therefore, good quality fired clay products tend to be expensive.
• Simple field kilns do not always produce good quality and uniform bricks, and generally operate with very low fuel efficiency. Capital investments for fuel efficient kilns that produce good bricks are often too high for small-scale producers. They are also not justified, if continuous or large supplies of bricks are not required.
• A common defect of bricks is "lime blowing" (or "lime bursting"), a weakening or breaking of bricks, which is caused by the hydration of quicklime particles, derived from limestone in brickmaking clays.
• Another defect is "efflorescence", which appears temporarily on the surface of the brick, and is caused by soluble salts inherent in the clay or process water.

Remedies

- Fuel efficiency is primarily dependent on the design of the kiln: continuous kilns retain the heat longest and utilize the heat from the cooling bricks, while the green bricks are preheated by the exhaust gases. Intermittent kilns have to heat up the entire heap anew, each time a batch is fired.
- Firewood should not be used up faster than it can be regrown. Hence plantations of fast-growing trees are vital. Considering their lower calorific value, larger numbers of fast-growing trees are needed than slow-growing trees. However, such plantations can be difficult to maintain in dry regions or when the rains fail.
- Agricultural wastes and other biomass, such as rice husks, coffee husks, papyrus, are useful and cheap (partial) substitute fuels. Mixing them with the clay helps to burn the bricks uniformly, avoiding unburnt cores.
- The Bull's trench and highdraught kilns have a fuel efficiency comparable to sophisticated, mechanized kilns. They are also cheaper to build than the Hoffmann kiln. It is, therefore, worth considering using the first batch of bricks from a clamp to build a more fuel efficient kiln, whereby the size is tailored to suit the local market demands. A certain minimum size is nevertheless needed to provide the requisite draught.
- Lime blowing can be minimized by reducing the particle size of the raw mix and firing at $1000°$ C. The addition of 0.5 to 0.75 % of common salt (sodium chloride) before firing has also proved effective. After firing, the bricks can be soaked in water for 10 minutes, during which the lime is slaked. The process, called "docking", is not always successful.
- Improvements are possible and greatly needed in all phases of brick manufacture, so that a good deal of research is still required to find simple, inexpensive methods for proper clay preparation, fast and uniform moulding, and - most important of all - maximum fuel efficiency.

General

Binders are substances which are used to bind inorganic and organic particles and fibres to form strong, hard and/or flexible components. This is generally due to chemical reactions which take place when the binder is heated, mixed with water and/or other materials, or just exposed to air.

There are four main groups of binders:
- Mineral binders
- Bituminous binders
- Natural binders
- Synthetic binders.

Mineral Binders

These can be divided into three categories:
- Hydraulic binders, which require water to harden and develop strength.
- Non-hydraulic binders, which can only harden in the presence of air.
- Thermoplastic binders, which harden on cooling and become soft when heated again.

Hydraulic binders

- The most common hydraulic binder is cement (see chapter on *Cement*).
- Hydraulic and semi-hydraulic limes (see chapter on *Lime*) are obtained from burning limestone, which contains a large or moderate amount of clay. This can be easily understood, since limestone and clay are the main raw materials for cement production.
- Pozzolanas (see chapter on *Pozzolanas*), when mixed with non-hydraulic lime, form a hydraulic cement.
- Hydraulic binders are usually available in the form of a fine powder: the finer they are ground (usually in a ball mill), the larger is the specific surface area (of the sum of the particles) per unit weight. And the larger the surface area, the more effective and complete is the chemical reaction with the water that it comes into contact with.
- On account of their affinity to water, hydraulic binders must be stored in absolutely dry conditions, to avoid premature setting and hardening. Even humid air can cause hydration.

Non-hydraulic binders

• The most common non-hydraulic binder is clay, which is present in most soils, causing them to harden on drying and soften when wet. Its main uses are in earth constructions and in the manufacture of burnt clay products.

• Another common non-hydraulic binder is high calcium or magnesium lime (see chapter on *Lime*). Hardening depends on its combination with carbon dioxide from the air (carbonation), by which it again becomes calcium carbonate (limestone). But limes are rarely used as the only cementitious binder, and more usually react with clay or a pozzolana to form a hydraulic cement.

• Gypsum is a non-hydraulic binder which occurs naturally as a soft crystalline rock or sand. The chemical name is calcium sulphate di-hydrate ($CaSO_4 \cdot 2H_2O$). By gentle heating up to about 160° C, calcium sulphate hemi-hydrate ($CaSO_4 \cdot 1/2H_2O$) is produced, more commonly known as "Plaster of Paris", which when mixed with water sets in 8 to 10 minutes. Gypsum plaster has successfully been produced by means of solar energy. Further heating of gypsum, slightly beyond 200° C (not achieved by solar energy) produces anhydrite gypsum ($CaSO_4$), which when mixed with water, sets very slowly.

Calcination of gypsum
with solar energy
(Photo: N. Nolhier)

• Gypsum is also abundantly available as an industrial by-product from the evaporation of seawater to produce common salt, or from the manufacture of fertilizer from phosphate rock. The latter is called phosphogypsum, which contains more water than natural gypsum, is more acidic and has more impurities, so that costly processing is required. It is also to some extent radioactive and therefore not recommended for use in building.

• Gypsum is used as a building material, mainly as a retarder to regulate the setting of various types of hydraulic cements, and in conjunction with a variety of other materials (eg lime, sand, sawdust, jute, sisal, linseed oil, paper) to produce renders, boards and masonry blocks.
• The main advantages of gypsum are the low energy input during burning to produce gypsum plaster; rapid drying and hardening, with negligible shrinkage (needing no form-work); good adhesion to fibrous and other materials; good fire resistance; good sound reflection (if made dense and hard); superior surface finish; resistance to insects and rodents.
• The principle drawback of gypsum plaster is its solubility in water (2 g gypsum per litre of water). Humid air can also soften gypsum plaster. Frost and sudden temperature changes can also cause damage.
• On account of this drawback, gypsum should not be used on external surfaces in humid climatic zones, unless it is well protected by wide overhanging roofs and a water resisting coating (eg hot linseed oil).

Thermoplastic binders

• Thermoplastic materials require heat in order to be processed, and harden on cooling. Their properties remain unchanged on reheating and cooling, so that they can be reclaimed and reprocessed numerous times.
• Probably the only thermoplastic mineral binder used for building is sulphur. For details, see chapter on *Sulphur*.

Bituminous Binders

• *Bitumens* are mechanical mixtures of different hydrocarbons (compounds of carbon and hydrogen) and a few other substances, and is obtained as a residue in the distillation of crude oil, either in petroleum refineries or in nature (in pores of rocks or in the form of lakes, close to petroleum deposits). Bitumens are generally dark black, oily, fluorescent thermoplastic, substances, which are highly viscous to almost solid at normal temperatures. Compounds consisting of at least 40 % of heavy hydrocarbons are called bitumens.
• *Asphalts* are defined as mixtures containing bitumen and a substantial proportion of inert mineral matter (sand, gravel, etc.). In the USA, bitumen is called asphalt, thus causing some confusion.
• *Tar* is the thick black substance produced by the destructive distillation (or carbonisation) of organic matter, such as wood or coal.
• *Pitch* is the residue after distilling tar from coal.
• Bitumen is not affected by either light, air or water individually, but in combination they can make it brittle, porous and susceptible to oxidation, forming blisters and cracks. It

becomes soft at temperatures between 30° and 100° C (no sharp melting point), and therefore must be protected from exposure to heat. It is insoluble in water and fairly resistant to most acids. Although bitumen is combustible, composite products, such as mastic asphalt, are not readily ignited. Bitumen and coal tar products may be poisonous, hence contact with drinking water should be avoided.

• Bituminous products can be used as waterproofing materials (in soil stabilization, as paints, damp-proof membranes, roofing felt, joint fillers, etc.), as paving materials (roads and floors) and as adhesives (for wood block flooring, insulating linings and felts).

• When bitumen is used, it must be either heated; or mixed with solvents (eg gasoline, kerosene or naphta), which is called "bitumen cutback"; or dispersed in water, which is called "bitumen emulsion".

Natural Binders

• A variety of binders are obtained from plants and animals, and can be used in their natural form or after processing.

• Examples of natural binders are plant juices (eg juice of banana leaves; latex of certain trees; sisal juice; coconut, cotton and linseed oils), animal excreta (eg cow dung; horse urine) and other animal products (eg bull's blood; animal glues from horn, bone, hooves and hide; casein or whey, made from milk).

• Natural binders have played an important role in traditional constructions since prehistoric times, but nowadays face low social acceptance. However, research today is giving such materials increasing importance, especially with a view to cost effectiveness and environmental acceptability.

Synthetic Binders

• These binders are generally produced by industrial processes and, therefore, often expensive. Some synthetic binders are toxic.

• They can either be used as admixtures, as adhesives or as surface coatings and are either applied hot, or as an emulsion, or with a solvent.

• Synthetic admixtures which bond loose particles together are mainly resins derived from plant materials or mineral oil. The variety of commercial products is very large and their use depends on the required performance (strength development, waterproofing, elasticity etc.).

• Adhesives are used to stick larger particles, components, membranes, sheets, boards, tiles, etc. on another surface. Some adhesives are designed specifically for one job, whilst others can be used for a number of applications. Adhesives can have one or two components. Some adhesives are thermoplastic and retain their properties when reheated and cooled.

• Surface coatings can be used as a protective film, as a decoration or even to achieve a surface bonding. Here again the variety of products is too large to be dealt with here.

General

The production of lime in kilns is a more than 2000 year old technology, believed to have been developed by the Romans around 300 B.C. The process of burning limestone at temperatures above 900° C to produce quicklime, which is subsequently slaked with water to produce hydrated lime, has since become traditional practice in most countries, as lime is one of the most versatile materials known, being used for numerous industrial and agricultural processes, environmental protection and building construction.

Lime is also obtained as a by-product in the form of lime sludge (which contains calcium carbonate and various impurities) from sugar manufacture, and from acetylene and paper industries.

The chemical reactions in lime burning are:

Reaction 1: (900° C, depending on type of limestone)

$$CaCO_3 \quad + \quad heat \quad \rightarrow \quad CaO \quad + \quad CO_2$$

| Calcium | Calcium | Carbon |
| carbonate | oxide | dioxide |

Limestone   Quicklime
Chalk   Lump lime
Coral/Shells

or

Reaction 2: (at around 750° C):

$$CaMg(CO_3)_2 + \quad heat \quad \rightarrow \quad CaCO_3 \quad + \quad MgO \quad + \quad CO_2$$

Dolomitic   Calcium   Magnesium
limestone   carbonate   oxide

then Reaction 1 (at around 1100° C)

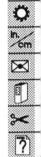

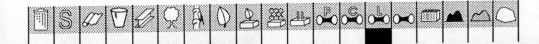

Raw materials

• The chemical process of lime burning shows that the main constituent in the raw material (limestone) is necessarily calcium carbonate ($CaCO_3$). Limestone can have $CaCO_3$ contents exceeding 98 % (as in chalk and various types of shells and coral) or as low as 54 % (in pure mineral dolomite).

• Each type of limestone yields a different quality of lime, depending on the type and quantity of impurities. The purest forms of lime are needed for chemical and industrial use, while impurities can be desirable in limes used for building and road construction. Limestones, called "kankar" in India, that contain 5 to 25 % of clay can produce a *hydraulic lime*, which hardens in the presence of water, like a cement.

• By-product lime sludge is moulded into bricks or briquettes before firing in kilns.

• The presence of impurities in the limestones influences its behaviour during burning, so that the kiln design and choice of fuel are largely dependent on the raw material and the kind of end product required. Expert advice is therefore essential at a very early stage, in order to achieve satisfactory results, both for the lime producer and user.

• Preparing the raw material is extremely important as only one size of stone (about the size of a man's fist) should be used, in order to facilitate an even gas flow and uniform burning of the lumps. Small-scale firing trials are important to study the behaviour of the raw material and the quality of quicklime it yields, and also to make sure that the lumps do not break apart until they leave the kiln.

Kiln for small scale firing trials (Bibl. 06.08)

Fuels

• Wood and coal are the most common, traditional fuels. Wood firing produces some of the best quality limes, as it burns with long, even flames generating steam (from the moisture content of the wood), which helps to lower the temperature needed for dissociation (separation of CO_2 from the carbonates), thus reducing the danger of overburning.

• The wood must be seasoned (dried) and cut into relatively small pieces. The wood supply should be close to the kiln in order to avoid heavy transport costs. About 2 m³ bulk of wood is needed for each tonne of hydrated lime produced. This is a problem, in view of the rapid depletion of timber resources, but a possible solution is to establish fuelwood plantations for continuous replacement of the harvested wood.

• Charcoal gives a higher fuel efficiency, but the lime produced is not as good as that burnt with wood.

• Coal with a high carbon content produces a good lime and can show good fuel economy even in small kilns. Coke is preferable because of its low volatile content (hydrocarbons which can be driven off as vapour), but is hard to ignite, and is, therefore, often mixed with coal.

• Liquid and gaseous fuels, though more expensive, are easier to handle than solid fuels, and burn without producing ash which contaminates the lime.

• The main types are heavy fuel oils, often mixed with used motor oil. The fuel is vaporized, mixed with air and ignited in chambers located around the kiln, producing a fully developed flame before it comes into contact with the limestone.

• Liquified petroleum gases, mainly propane (C_3H_8) and butane (C_4H_{10}), are other useful liquid fuels. Natural gas, such as methane (CH_4), and producer gas, which is made from wood, plant material or coal, are used in the same way.

• Whether oil or gases are used, the kilns will necessarily be more sophisticated than those needed for solid fuels.

• Possible alternative fuels are peats and oil shales, and biomass energy, derived from plant material including agricultural and forestry wastes. There are several ways in which they can be used.

• Solar and wind energy are unlikely to be used in the near future.

Kiln design and operation

• A lime kiln is a built structure, in which limestone is heated to a temperature at which CO_2 is released, converting the stone into quicklime. The heat is provided by burning suitable fuels, which are either placed in layers between the limestone or mixed with it. Liquid or gaseous fuels are either injected from the sides of the kiln or burnt in adjacent chambers, from which hot gases are passed through the kiln.
• Careful control is needed to maintain the correct temperature long enough to burn the stone completely. Underburnt limestone will not hydrate, while overburnt material is too hard and dense for slaking, or hydrates very slowly.
• As the variety of kiln types is extremely wide, they can only be described here in general terms. The more sophisticated types (eg rotary and fluidized bed kilns) are not dealt with, although in certain situations their use may indeed be worth consideration.

• *Batch or intermittent kilns* are generally used in remote places, where continuous supplies are not needed (eg small building projects or road construction). They are loaded with limestone and fired until all the stone has been burnt. After cooling, the quicklime is extracted, the limestone reloaded and the kiln fired again. The fuel efficiency is naturally very low, as the kiln walls have to be reheated each time a new batch is fired. On the other hand, it requires little attention during firing. The fuel is burnt below the limestone (in updraught or flare kilns) or within the entire batch (in mixed feed batch kilns).

• *Vertical shaft kilns* are designed mainly for continuous production: the stone, fed in from the top, gradually drops into the burning zone, then into the cooling zone, and is finally extracted from below, making room for the next load, and so on. The top layer is preheated by the exhaust gases and the air intake below is preheated by the cooling quicklime, thus achieving maximum use of the available heat.

The main design features and operational considerations with regard to vertical shaft mixed feed kilns are:

• *Foundations and kiln base:* built on a firm ground and dimensioned to carry the shaft and kiln contents; an engineer's advice is needed.
• *Shaft dimensions and shape:* the cross-sectioned area is related to the desired output (rule of thumb: 1 m^2 produces about 2.5 tonnes per day); a circular plan provides better heat distribution; the ratio of height to diameter should be at least 6 : 1 for optimum gas flow; the height must be related to the type of limestone, as soft stones tend to get crushed under the pressure, thus restricting the gas flow (kilns for soft chalk should not exceed 5 m height); shafts that taper towards the top (angle about 3°) minimize "hanging" (stone sticking to the sides and forming arches).

- *Structural walls:* must support the lateral pressure of the limestone (by provision of greater wall thickness at the base, or buttresses, or by means of steel tension bands at intervals of 80 cm, as developed by the Khadi and Village Industries Commission, Bombay); must resist cracking due to heat expansion (by using small bricks rather than big blocks, and lime-sand mortar in narrow joints); wall thicknesses of at least 50 cm for good thermal performance; weather resistant material (natural stone or well-burnt bricks) at least for the top wall courses.

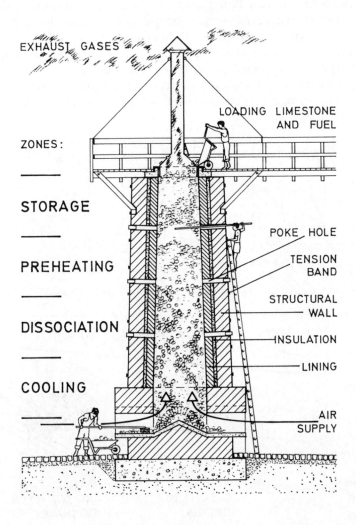

EXHAUST GASES

LOADING LIMESTONE AND FUEL

ZONES:

STORAGE

PREHEATING

DISSOCIATION

COOLING

POKE HOLE

TENSION BAND

STRUCTURAL WALL

INSULATION

LINING

AIR SUPPLY

• *Linings:* at least 22 cm thick, in the upper part of the kiln, resistant to abrasion (eg hard stone or blue engineering bricks); in the firing zone and below, resistant to heat and chemical action (hard, fine-textured refractory bricks laid with very fine joints of fireclay mortar).

• *Insulation:* usually 5 to 10 cm thick, between wall and lining to retain the heat in the kiln, especially around the calcining zone; different insulations are possible (eg air-gap, rice husk ash or other pozzolana, light-weight aggregate, rockwool).

• *Openings:* at the top for charging, preferably with lid, if a chimney extends beyond the opening; at the bottom for air to flow in and to remove the cooled quicklime, whereby with a single opening in the centre (inflow type) draught control is easier than with two or more openings (outflow type); around the kiln at different levels as pokeholes and inspection holes, usually the size of a brick (which is used for closing), to regularly loosen stuck limestone lumps and to monitor the temperature within the kiln.

• *Chimney:* between 2.5 and 6 m high, to improve the draught and thus provide sufficient oxygen for combustion, to cool the quicklime, and to draw the exhaust gases away from operators loading the kiln.

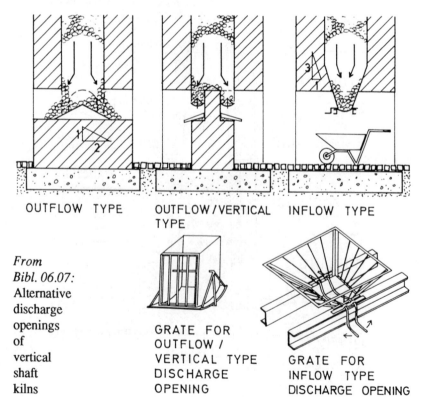

OUTFLOW TYPE   OUTFLOW/VERTICAL   INFLOW TYPE
TYPE

From Bibl. 06.07: Alternative discharge openings of vertical shaft kilns

GRATE FOR OUTFLOW / VERTICAL TYPE DISCHARGE OPENING

GRATE FOR INFLOW TYPE DISCHARGE OPENING

Hydration

• The type of lime that is used for building and numerous other processes is *hydrated or slaked lime*. This is obtained by adding hot water or steam to quicklime. Pure quicklimes react vigorously evolving considerable heat, while impure limes hydrate slowly, or only after the lumps are ground.

Reaction 3:

$$CaO \quad + \quad H_2O \quad \rightarrow \quad Ca(OH)_2 \quad + \quad heat$$

Calcium oxide   Water   Calcium hydroxide

Three forms of hydrated lime are commonly produced:

a. *dry hydrate,* a dry, fine powder, formed by adding just enough water to slake the lime, which is dried by the heat evolved;

b. *milk of lime,* made by slaking quicklime with a large excess of water and agitating well, forming a milky suspension;

c. *lime putty,* a viscous mass, formed by the settling of the solids in the milk of lime.

• The most common form is dry hydrate, which is very suitable for storage in silos or air-tight bags, and easy to transport. Lime putty, which is an excellent building material, can be stored indefinitely under moist conditions. Milk of lime is generally produced in conjunction with other process industries.

• In small limeworks, slaking is usually done by hand, either on platforms to produce a dry hydrate or in shallow tanks to make lime putty.

• Although the hydration of quicklime is a simple process, it must be carried out with special care, for instance, to see that all the quicklime is completely slaked. Pieces that hydrate too slowly and as a result are overlooked, can cause serious problems later on.

• If water is added too slowly, the temperature of the lime may rise too fast, forming an inactive white gritty compound ("water burnt" lime). If water is added too quickly, a skin of hydroxide may develop, preventing further hydration ("drowned" lime).

The Central Building Research Institute in India has developed a small hydration plant, which requires very little space and eliminates most of the problems of hydration, producing uniform qualities of dry hydrate in a relatively short time.

Site organization

The location and layout of a lime-works are vital factors that influence the economy and quality of lime production. The illustration (from Bibl. 06.08) shows an appropriate site organization in which distances between successive operations are relatively short.

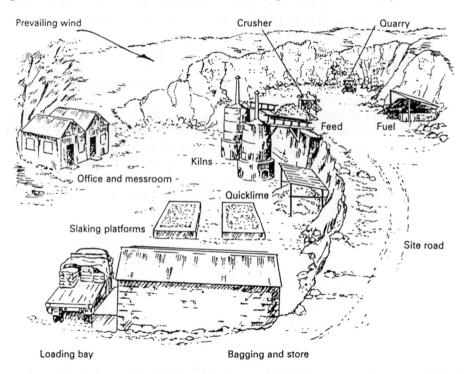

Applications

• Lime is used as a stabilizer in soil constructions with clayey soils, because the lime reacts with clay to form a binder.
• Lime is mixed with a pozzolana (rice husk ash, fly ash, blast furnace slag, etc.) to produce a hydraulic binder, which can partially or completely substitute cement, depending on the required performance.
• Hydraulic lime (made from clay-rich limestone) can be used without a pozzolana.
• Non-hydraulic lime (pure calcium hydroxide) is also used as a binder in renders. It hardens on reaction with the carbon dioxide in the air to change back to limestone (calcium carbonate). This process can take up to 3 years, depending on the climatic conditions.
• Lime is used in cement mortars and plasters to make it more workable.
• Limewash (diluted milk of lime) is used as an external and internal wall coating.

Advantages

• Lime is produced with less energy input than cement, making it cheaper and environmentally more acceptable.
• In mortars and plasterwork, lime is far superior to portland cement, providing gentle surfaces which can deform rather than crack and help to control moisture movement and condensation.
• Since the strengths produced by portland cement are not always required (and sometimes can even be harmful), lime-pozzolanas provide cheaper and structurally more suitable substitutes, thus conserving the cement for more important uses.
• Limewashes are not only cheap paints, but also act as a mild germicide.

Problems

• Soil stabilization with lime requires more than twice the curing time needed for soils stabilized with cement.
• If quicklime is stored in moist conditions (even humid air), it will hydrate.
• Hydrated lime, stored for long periods, gradually reacts with the carbon dioxide in the air and becomes useless.
• Lime bursting (hydration of remaining quicklime nodules) can take place long after the component has dried, causing blisters, cracks and unsightly surfaces.
• Plain limewashes take a long time to harden, and are easily rubbed off.
• Traditional lime burning in intermittent kilns waste a great deal of fuel (usually firewood) and often produce non-uniform, low quality limes (overburnt or underburnt).
• The value of lime is greatly underestimated, especially since portland cement has become a kind of "miracle" binder almost everywhere.

Remedies

• The curing time of lime stabilized soils can be shortened by using hydraulic limes or adding a pozzolana to non-hydraulic limes.
• Quicklime has to be hydrated before use in construction work, therefore this should be done soon after it is unloaded from the kiln, as hydrated lime is much easier to store and transport.
• To prevent rapid deterioration of dry hydrated lime, it should be stored in air-tight bags.
• It is advantageous to store the lime in the form of lime putty. This can be done indefinitely, as the quality of the lime putty improves the longer it is stored. By this method, even the slowest hydrating quicklime particles are slaked, thus avoiding lime bursting at a later stage.
• A great deal has to be done to disseminate information and assist local lime producers in constructing more efficient lime kilns (in terms of fuel consumption and lime output).
• Similar efforts are needed to rehabilitate lime as one of the most important building materials.

CEMENT

General

Of the large variety of cements available today, ordinary portland cement (OPC) is the most common, and usually the type referred to when speaking of cement. It is the fine, grey powder that can be mixed with sand, gravel and water to produce a strong and long lasting mortar or concrete.

Portland cement was developed in the 19th century and was so named because it resembled a popular building stone quarried in Portland, England. It has since been associated with high strength and durability, and has consequently become one of the most prestigious building materials.

Cement is usually produced in large centralized plants, which incur high capital costs and long transportation distances to most building sites. In most developing countries, production capacities are far below the demand and also on account of losses and deterioration in transports and storage, cement is generally associated with high costs and short supplies.

In order to improve the situation, efforts have been concentrated on the development of small-scale cement plants (also called "mini-cement" plants), particularly in China and India.

Large-scale cement production

- About 95 % of the world's cement is being produced in rotary kilns with daily outputs ranging between 300 and more than 5000 tonnes.
- Limestone (calcium carbonate) and clay (silica, alumina and iron oxide) are ground and mixed with water to form a slurry, which is fed into the upper end of the slightly inclined, refractory lined rotating furnace, which can be more than 100 m long. Hot air of temperatures between 1300° and 1400° C is blown in at the lower end, drying the slurry, which is then sintered and fused into hard balls known as clinker. These drop out of the kiln, are cooled and interground in a ball-mill with about 3 % gypsum to retard the setting of the cement. The finer it is ground, the higher is the rate of the setting and strength development reactions.
- The wet process, described here, has largely been superceded by the dry process, which needs less energy to dry the raw material feed.
- OPC is sold in 50 kg bags, preferably heavy quality multi-ply paper bags. However, in some countries (eg India) reusable jute bags are used, leading to great wastage and difficulties in maintaining quality control.

Small-scale cement production

• This production method utilizes small vertical shaft kilns, a technology that accounts for more than half of China's annual cement production.
• The kiln feed is made of crushed limestone, clay and coal, which are proportioned and finely interground in a ball mill and then made into nodules in a disc nodulizer.
• The nodules are fed into the top conical portion of the kiln, in which the rising preheated air causes the fuel in the nodules to ignite, forming clinker.
• The clinker nodules gradually drop into the cylindrical portion, where it is cooled by the air introduced from below.
• A rotary grate discharges the clinker, which is then interground with gypsum in a ball-mill. Since the nodules are porous, less energy is required for grinding.
• Daily outputs of a vertical shaft kiln can range between 2 and 30 tonnes of ordinary portland cement.

Cement varieties

• Numerous varieties of cement are produced by altering the types and proportions of the raw materials to be calcined, or by blending or intergrinding portland cement with other materials. A few common types are:
• *Rapid hardening portland cement* (more finely ground than OPC; ultimate strength same as OPC).
• *Sulphate resisting portland cement* (made by adjusting the chemical composition of the raw mix).
• *Portland-pozzolana cements* (made by blending or intergrinding a pozzolana, eg rice husk ash or fly ash, in proportions of 15 to 40 % by weight, thus saving on cement and improving some of its properties).
• *Portland blastfurnace cements* (made by blending ground granulated blast furnace slag, thus achieving slower hardening and sulphate resistance).
• *Magnesium oxychloride or sorel cement* (obtained by calcining magnesium carbonate, achieving much higher strengths than OPC, but is attacked by water).
• *High alumina cement* (obtained by calcining limestone and bauxite, achieving high early strengths, optimum sulphate resistance, good acid resistance, and heat resistance up to 1300°C; but 3 times the cost of OPC and not suitable for structural concrete).

Hydration of cement

• Water reacts on the surface of the cement grains and diffuses inwards to reach unreacted cement. Therefore, the finer the grains the quicker the reaction.
• The water in the capillary space between the grains is filled with products of the hydration process. The more water used, the larger is the space that needs to be filled, and if there are insufficient hydration products, capillary pores remain, which weaken the cement. Hence, the correct *water-cement ratio* is important for strength development.
• During hydration, lime is set free. This hardens (by combining with CO_2) very slowly and expands in doing so, causing cracking and failure of concrete. By adding a pozzolana, it forms a hydraulic binder, which sets and hardens like cement.
• Setting (which means stiffening) takes place within 45 minutes, but hardening (which means useful strength development) takes several weeks. Specifications are, therefore, based on strengths achieved after 28 days.
• Because they set quickly, cement mixes have to be used as soon as possible.
• In hot climates, cements dry out too quickly and must be kept wet for at least two weeks.

Applications

• Cement is used as a binder for several inorganic and organic materials, eg soil-cement, sand-cement blocks, cement-bonded fibre boards.
• It is primarily used together with sand and gravel (and reinforcements) to produce (reinforced) concrete.
• It is used with sand and chicken-wire mesh (or fibres) to produce ferrocement (or fibre concrete).
• Mortars and plaster are made from cement and sand, often mixed with lime for better workability. With a very fine sand it is used for screeding.
• A paint can be made from cement mixed with excess water.

Advantages

• Cements can achieve extremely high strengths, generally remain unaffected by water, and do not significantly swell and shrink.
• Cements are resistant to fire and biological hazards, if kept clean.
• Cement constructions have a high prestige value.
• With regard to decentralized, small-scale cement production, the advantages are: low capital investment; use of cheaper quality coke or coal; lower transportation costs, due to shorter distances to consumer; lower technical sophistication, thus providing job opportunities even for unskilled labour; adaptability to market demands; capability of using different raw materials and producing a variety of cementitious products; increase of supporting industries around the plant.

Problems

• In most developing countries, cement is still too expensive for the majority of the population, and usually in short supply.
• Storage requires great care to avoid premature setting.
• Cracks occur in hot dry conditions due to rapid setting or due to temperature fluctuations.
• Sulphates and salts can cause rapid deterioration.
• Due to the high reputation of cement, it is often used to make over-strong mortars which cause brittleness, or porous mortars which lack durability.

Remedies

• Increase of supplies and reduction of costs are possible by introducing decentralized, small-scale cement plants.
• Improved bagging and storage methods in dry conditions, but also quick turnover can avoid wastage through premature setting.
• Proper wet curing avoids cracking, and special cements are used to avoid damage by sulphates and salts.
• Unnecessary and wrong usage of cement can be reduced by increased dissemination of information and increased use of lime, eg to improve the quality of cement mixes.

POZZOLANAS

General

Pozzolanas are natural or artificial materials which contain silica and/or alumina. They are not cementitious themselves, but when finely ground and mixed with lime, the mixture will set and harden at ordinary temperatures in the presence of water, like cement.

Pozzolanas can replace 15 to 40 % of portland cement without significantly reducing the long term strength of the concrete.

Most of the pozzolanic materials described here are by-products of agricultural or industrial processes, which are produced in large quantities, constituting a waste problem, if they remain unused. Even if there were no other benefits, this aspect alone would justify an increased use of these materials. But compared with the production and use of portland cement, these materials contribute to cost and energy savings, help to reduce environmental pollution and, in most cases, improve the quality of the end product.

Types of pozzolanas

* There are basically two types of pozzolanas, namely natural and artificial pozzolanas.
* Natural pozzolanas are essentially *volcanic ashes* from geologically recent volcanic activity.
* Artificial pozzolanas result from various industrial and agricultural processes, usually as by-products. The most important artificial pozzolanas are *burnt clay, pulverized-fuel ash (pfa), ground granulated blast furnace slag (ggbfs)* and *rice husk ash (RHA).*

Volcanic Ashes

* The first natural pozzolana to be used in building construction was the volcanic ash from Mt. Vesuvius (Italy), found closeby in the town Pozzuoli, which gave it the name.
* Although the chemical compositions are similar, the glassy material formed by the *violent projection* of molten magma into the atmosphere is *more reactive with lime*, than the volcanic ash formed by less violent eruptions.
* The occurrance of suitable natural pozzolanas is therefore limited to only a few regions of the world.
* Good pozzolanas are often found as fine grained ashes, but also in the form of large particles or tuffs (solidified volcanic ash), which have to be ground for use as a pozzolana. However, the qualities of such pozzolanas can vary greatly, even within a single deposit.
* Natural pozzolanas are used in the same way as artificial pozzolanas.

Burnt Clay

• When clay soils are burnt, the water molecules are driven off, forming a quasi-amorphous material which is reactive with lime. This is also true for shales and bauxitic and lateritic soils. This was discovered in ancient times and the first artificial pozzolanas were made from crushed pottery fragments, a traditional technology that is still being widely practiced on the Indian subcontinent, Indonesia and Egypt, using underfired or reject bricks. (In India it is called "surkhi", in Indonesia "semen merah", and in Egypt "homra").

• Alternatively, as reported from a project in India, soils which contain too little clay and too much sand for brickmaking, are cut and removed in blocks, forming circular pits. The blocks are then replaced in the pits, together with alternate layers of firewood. The residue obtained from firing is very friable and needs no pulverization. This is used as masonry mortar by just adding it to lime putty and mixing it, without sand or cement (Bibl. 05.10).

• A similar technique is reported from Java, Indonesia, where clay blocks are burnt in a clamp, disintegrated, sieved and used with lime and sand, sometimes also cement (Bibl. 05.11).

• The qualities of these traditional methods are very variable, but improved methods of calcination have been developed to produce pozzolanas of higher quality and uniformity.

• The illustration shows a vertical shaft kiln (after Thatte and Patel) developed in India. The feed consists of a mixture of clay lumps 50 to 100 mm in size and coal slack (comprising 48 % ash, 31 % fixed carbon and 20 % volatiles). Calcination takes place at 700° C for 3 hours, with the temperature monitored by thermocouples and controlled by an air blower and feed input. The capacity is 10 tonnes per day. A fluidized bed process has been developed by the National Buildings Organization, New Delhi, by which the clay feed is calcined within a few minutes, thus achieving high output rates in a continuous process (Bibl. 08.07).

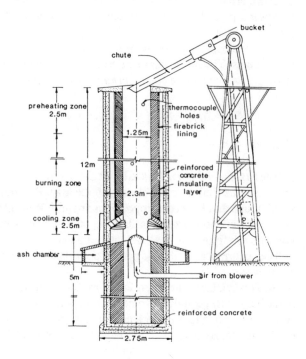

Pulverized-Fuel Ash (Fly Ash)

- By comparing the production processes of pulverized-fuel ash (pfa), commonly known as fly ash, and ordinary portland cement (OPC), it becomes clear, why pfa can be used as partial replacement of the latter.
- Finely ground coal is injected at high speed with a stream of hot air (about 1500° C) into the furnace at electricity generating stations. The carbonaceous content is burnt instantaneously, and the remaining matter (comprising silica, alumina and iron oxide) melts in suspension, forming fine spherical particles on rapid cooling while being carried out by the flue gases.
- In the production of OPC, limestone and clay, finely ground and mixed, are fed into an inclined rotary kiln, in which a clinker is formed at 1400° C. The cooled clinker is finely ground and mixed with gypsum to produce OPC.
- Depending on the type of coal, pfa contains varying proportions of lime, low-lime pfa being pozzolanic and high-lime pfa having cementitious properties itself. As with other pozzolanas, the lime liberated by the hydration of OPC combines with the pfa to act as a cementitious material.
- The glassy, hollow, spherical particles of pfa have the same fineness as OPC, hence no further grinding is needed. The addition of pfa makes fresh concrete more workable (probably due to the ball-bearing effect of the spherical particles) and homogeneous (by dispersing the cement flocs and evenly distributing the water).

Other advantages of using pfa are:
- With increasing age, higher strengths than concrete without pfa are developed.
- Pfa does not adversely influence the structural performance of concrete members.
- Compared to OPC concrete, pfa concrete is lighter, less permeable (due to denser compaction) and with a better surface finish.
- Pfa concrete is also more resistant to sulphate attack and alkali-silica reaction.
- Concretes in which 35 - 50 % by weight of OPC is replaced by pfa have shown satisfactory performances.
- Aggregates derived from fly ash show excellent bonding in pfa concretes, contributing favourably to their performance and durability.

Freshly mixed ordinary portland cement concrete

10 μm

Dispersion of the cement grains by adding pfa

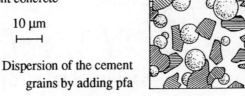

Ground Granulated Blast Furnace Slag

• Blast furnace slag is a molten material which settles above the pig iron at the bottom of the furnace. It is produced from the various input constituents in the furnace when it reaches 1400° to 1600° C.

• Slow cooling of the slag produces a crystalline material, which is used as aggregate. Rapid cooling with air or water under pressure forms glassy pellets (expanded slag > 4mm, suitable as lightweight aggregate) and granules smaller than 4 mm, which possess hydraulic properties when finely ground.

• The ground slag is blended with OPC to produce portland blast furnace cement (PBFC), whereby the slag content can reach 80 %. However, since PBFC is slower to react than OPC, the reactivity is reduced the higher the percentage of slag.

• Although the early strength of PBFC concretes is generally lower than OPC concretes, the final strength is likely to be higher. The slower reactivity of PBFC develops less heat and can be advantageous in situations where thermal cracking is a problem.

• Apart from improving the workability of fresh concrete, PBFC has high resistance to chemical attack, and its capability of protecting steel reinforcement makes it suitable for use in reinforced and prestressed concrete.

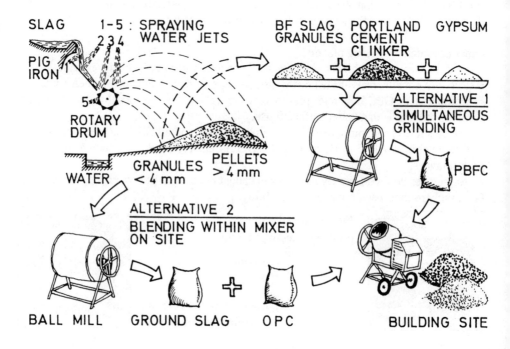

Rice Husk Ash

• The combustion of agricultural residues removes the organic matter and produces, in most cases, a silica-rich ash. Of all the common agricultural wastes, rice husks (also called paddy husks) yield the largest quantity of ash - around 20 % by weight - which also has the highest silica content - around 93 % by weight. It is this high silica content that gives the ash its pozzolanic properties.

• However, only amorphous (non-crystalline) silica possesses these properties, which is why the temperature and duration of combustion are of importance in producing rice husk ash (RHA). Amorphous silica is obtained by burning the ash at temperatures below 700° C. Uncontrolled combustion of rice husks, eg when used as a fuel or in heap burning, usually at temperatures above 800° C leads to crystallization of the silica, which is less reactive.

• The illustrated incinerator, first developed by the Pakistan Council of Scientific and Industrial Research (PCSIR) and later improved by the Cement Research Institute of India (CRI), is made of bricks with many openings to allow good air flow through the rice husk mass. The inner surface is covered with a 16 gauge fine-wire mesh. The husks are filled in from the top and the ash removed from the bottom discharge door. A pyrometer monitors the temperature, which can be controlled by shutting or opening the holes, maintaining a temperature around 650° C for 2 - 3 hours.

• The reactive ash is dark grey to white, depending on the residual carbon in it, which has no negative effects if below 10 %. To improve its reactivity, the ash is ground in a ball mill for about one hour, or longer if it contains crystalline silica. The ash can replace up to 30 % of cement in mortar or concrete. Alternatively, it can be mixed with 30 to 50 % of hydrated lime to be used like cement in mortars, renderings and unreinforced concrete.

• In another process, the ash obtained from heap burning or the production of parboiled rice, is mixed with about 20 to 50 % (by weight) of hydrated lime. This is ground for 6 or more hours in a ball mill to produce ASHMOH, a hydraulic binder suitable for masonry, foundations and general concreting work other than reinforced concrete. A variation of this is ASHMENT, in which the lime is substituted by portland cement (Bibl. 08.04).

• A method has also been developed, using waste lime sludge obtained from sugar refining. This is dried and mixed with an equal amount (by weight) of crushed rice husks and some water. Tennis ball sized cakes are made by hand and sun-dried. These are fired on a grating in an open clamp, to produce a soft powder, which is ground in a ball mill. The hydraulic binder is used in the same way as ASHMOH.

• A variation of this method utilizes soils with at least 20 % clay content instead of lime sludge. The resulting binder can be used as a 30 % mixture with portland cement to make portland pozzolana cement. Tests have shown that the pozzolana is best if the clay is bauxitic.

• At the National Building Research Institute, Karachi, Pakistan:
The first low-cost house to be built predominantly with rice husk ash and lime, substituting cement completely in the production of hollow load-bearing block, mortar and plaster. 30 % of the portland cement in the precast concrete lintels and roof beams were substituted by RHA.

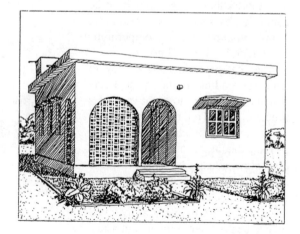

CONCRETE

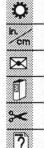

General

The essential ingredients of concrete are cement, aggregate (sand, gravel) and water. When mixed in carefully prescribed proportions, they produce a workable mass, which can take the shape of any formwork into which it is placed and allowed to harden in.

Concrete technology is one that requires a great deal of know-how and experience. Therefore, only very general aspects can be dealt with here. *If detailed information is required, specialized literature should be consulted, or professional advice sought.*

Typical method of preparing concrete mix in India The fresh mix is filled in metal pans and carried to the formwork, or passed from one worker to another, forming a chain between the mixer and formwork.
(Photo: K. Mukerji)

Preparation of concrete mix

• Depending on the use and desired performance of the concrete, careful selection of the type and proportion of cement, aggregates and water is necessary, which is best done by a series of tests (if the qualities of the materials are not standardized or well-known from experience).
• In most cases, a good grain size distribution of fine and coarse aggregate (sand and gravel) is necessary, in order to leave no voids, which weaken the concrete. The more voids, the more cement and water are needed.

• Aggregate particles with rough surfaces and angular shapes create more friction than smooth, rounded particles, which are easier to compact. Silt, clay and dust should be removed, as they interfere with the bond between cement and aggregate, and require more water.

• The water should be as clean as possible, as salts and other impurities can adversely affect the setting, hardening and durability of the concrete. Seawater should be avoided as far as possible, especially in reinforced concrete, in which the steel easily corrodes.

• In special cases, a variety of admixtures can be used, depending on whether the setting should be accelerated or retarded, waterproofing and chemical resistance should be improved, and so on. Correct dosage and quality control are vital to achieve satisfactory results and save costs.

• The aggregate and cement should be well mixed in the dry state. Just before the concrete is used, water is added gradually while the mixing continues. As the water : cement ratio determines the strength and durability of the concrete (excess water produces air voids!), the addition of water requires special care.

• In ready-mixed concrete, supplied from a central batching/mixing plant, by truck mixers (which are still rare in developing countries) principally the same criteria apply. However, a study by the Cement Research Institute, India, recommends the transportation of "semi-dry" mixes in small non-agitating vehicles (cheaper!) and completion of mixing prior to final placing.

• The uniformity of fresh concrete is usually measured by the slump test: filling a conical mould in four layers of equal volume and rodding each layer 25 times, smoothing the top, lifting off the mould and measuring the difference in heights of the mould and the fresh concrete specimen. Slumps between 25 and 100 mm are most suitable.

• Mixes are specified primarily by grade designations, eg C7, C10, C25, etc., which refer to their compressive (C) strengths in N/mm² (MPa).

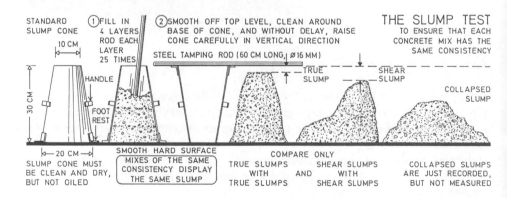

STANDARD SLUMP CONE   ①FILL IN 4 LAYERS ROD EACH LAYER 25 TIMES   10 CM   ②SMOOTH OFF TOP LEVEL, CLEAN AROUND BASE OF CONE, AND WITHOUT DELAY, RAISE CONE CAREFULLY IN VERTICAL DIRECTION   STEEL TAMPING ROD (60 CM LONG, ⌀ 16 MM)   THE SLUMP TEST TO ENSURE THAT EACH CONCRETE MIX HAS THE SAME CONSISTENCY

HANDLE   30 CM   FOOT REST   TRUE SLUMP   SHEAR SLUMP   COLLAPSED SLUMP

20 CM   SLUMP CONE MUST BE CLEAN AND DRY, BUT NOT OILED   SMOOTH HARD SURFACE   MIXES OF THE SAME CONSISTENCY DISPLAY THE SAME SLUMP   COMPARE ONLY TRUE SLUMPS WITH TRUE SLUMPS   AND   SHEAR SLUMPS WITH SHEAR SLUMPS   COLLAPSED SLUMPS ARE JUST RECORDED, BUT NOT MEASURED

Formwork

• Formwork, which can be reused many times, is usually made of timber boards or steel panels, with joints sufficiently tight to withstand the pressure of compacted concrete, and without having any gaps through which the cement paste can leak.
• The texture of the hardened concrete surface can be predetermined by the type of formwork. If smooth surfaces are needed, concrete remnants from previous castings should be scraped off the forms.
• In order to facilitate removal, the inner surfaces of the formwork should be oiled with a brush or spray.
• If reinforcement is required, it is placed in the formwork after oiling, and spacers (pieces of stone or broken concrete) are placed between the steel and the oiled surface, such that the formwork and steel do not come into contact with each other. This is needed to prevent the steel from remaining exposed on the concrete surface, where it can easily rust.
• The choice of formwork must take into account ease of assembly and removal. In some cases, the formwork can be designed to remain in place (permanent shuttering); for example, where an insulating layer or special facing is needed, these can constitute the formwork (or part of it).

Placing and curing

• The concrete is transported from the mixer to the formwork by cranes, dumpers, barrows, buckets, pipes, or other means, depending on the available facilities. In many developing countries, long chains of workers pass the concrete in small metal pans from one to another. If the concrete is not produced on the site, ready-mixed concrete is brought in a special truck.
• The concrete must be placed without interruption to fill complete sections each time, since joints between concrete placed at different times are weak points.
• After a certain amount of concrete is in the formwork it needs to be compacted to fill up all voids. This is most effectively done by means of a vibrator (either attached to the formwork, or immersed in the concrete) which releases the trapped air. However, for most low cost constructions, which do not need high strengths, hand compaction with a suitable rod can be quite sufficient.
• It is important to immediately wash all the equipment that has been in contact with the concrete, as it will be difficult to remove after hardening.
• The formwork is removed after a few days when the concrete it hard enough. But strength development (curing) takes place over several weeks and a vital prerequisite is that the concrete is kept wet for *at least 14 days*, eg by covering it with wet jute bags which are regularly watered.
• All the above points, from preparation of concrete mix to curing, apply likewise to in situ construction (at the building site) and to prefabrication.

Applications

• *Plain mass concrete*, with graded or predominantly small sized aggregate, for foundations, floors, paving, monolithic walls (in some cases), bricks, tiles, hollow blocks, pipes.
• *No-fines concrete*, a lightweight concrete with only single size coarse aggregate (dense or lightweight) leaving voids between them, suitable for loadbearing and non-loadbearing walls, in-fill walls in framed structures or base coarse for floor slabs. No-fines concrete provides an excellent key for rendering, good thermal insulation (due to air gaps), and low drying shrinkage. The large voids also prevent capillary action.
• *Lightweight aggregate concrete*, using expanded clay, foamed blast furnace slag, sintered fly ash, pumice, or other light aggregate, for thermal insulating walls and components, and for lightweight building blocks.
• *Aerated concrete*, made by introducing air or gas into a cement-sand mix (without coarse aggregate), for thermal insulating, non-structural uses and lightweight building blocks. Disadvantages are low resistance to abrasion, excessive shrinkage and permeability. However, it is easy to handle and can be cut with a saw and nailed like timber.
• *Reinforced concrete*, also known as RCC (reinforced cement concrete), which incorporates steel bars in sections of the concrete which are in tension (to supplement the low tensile strength of mass concrete and control thermal and shrinkage cracking), for floor slabs, beams, lintels, columns, stairways, frame structures, long-span elements, angular or curved shell structures, etc., all these cast in situ or precast. The high strength to weight ratio of steel, coupled with the fortunate coincidence of its coefficient of thermal expansion being about the same as concrete, make it the ideal material for reinforcement. Where deformed bars (which have ribs to inhibit longitudinal movement after casting) are available, they should be given preference, as they are far more effective than plain bars, so that up to 30 % of steel can be saved.
• *Prestressed concrete*, which is reinforced concrete with the steel reinforcement held under tension during production, to achieve stiffness, crack resistance and lighter constructions of components, such as beams, slabs, trusses, stairways and other large-span units. By prestressing, less steel is needed and the concrete is held under compression, enabling it to carry much higher loads before this compression is overcome. Prestressing is achieved either by *pre-tensioning* (in which the steel is stressed before the concrete is cast) or by *post-tensioning* (after the concrete has reached an adequate strength, allowing the steel to be passed through straight or curved ducts, which are filled with grout after the reinforcement has been tensioned and anchored). This is essentially a factory operation, requiring expensive, special equipment (jacks, anchorages, prestressing beds, etc.), not suitable for low-cost housing.
• However, the *cold-drawn low-carbon steel wire prestressed concrete* (CWPC) technology, developed in China, where about 3000 CWPC factories produce 20 million m³ of precast components annually, is a promising alternative. The tensile strengths of low-carbon

steel wires (normal steel wires) of Ø 6.5 to 8 mm are doubled by drawing them through a die at normal temperatures, producing 3, 4 or 5 mm Ø wires, and saving 30 to 50 % of the steel. Concrete grades of C30 are used. The technology is easily understood and implemented, the equipment is simple (Bibl. 09.09).

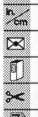

Prestressed concrete production plant in Bangladesh (Photo: K. Mukerji)

Advantages

• Concrete can take any shape and achieve compressive strengths exceeding 60 N/mm².
• Reinforced concretes combine high compressive strengths with high tensile strengths, making them adaptable to any building design and all structural requirements. They are ideally suited for prefabrication of components and for constructions in dangerous conditions (earthquake zones, expansive soils, etc.).
• The energy requirement to produce 1 kg of plain concrete is the lowest of the manufactured building materials (1 MJ/kg, equalling timber; Bibl. 00.50), while reinforced concrete (with 1 % by volume of steel) requires about 8 MJ/kg.
• The high thermal capacity and high reflectivity (due to light colour) are especially favourable for building in hot dry or tropical highland climates.

- Properly executed concrete is extremely durable, maintenance-free, resistant to moisture penetration, chemical action, fire, insects, and fungal attack.
- Concrete has an extremely high prestige value.
- A variety of processed agricultural and industrial wastes can be profitably used to substitute cement and/or improve the quality of concrete.

Problems

- High cost of cement, steel and formwork.
- Difficult quality control on building sites, with the risk of cracking and gradual deterioration, if wrongly mixed, placed and insufficiently cured with water.
- In moist climates or coastal regions, corrosion of reinforcement (if insufficiently protected), leading to expansion cracks.
- Fire resistance only up to about 500° C, steel reinforcement begins to fail (if not well covered) and after fires, RCC structures usually have to be demolished.
- Demolishing concrete is difficult and debris cannot be recycled, other than in the form of aggregate for new concrete.
- Negative electromagnetic effects of reinforced concrete create unhealthy living conditions.

Remedies

- Cement proportions can be reduced by careful mix design, grading of aggregates, testing, quality control and by substitution with cheaper pozzolanas; also, increased decentralized cement production with sufficient supplies and low wastage (by better bagging) can reduce costs.
- Saving in steel reinforcement can be achieved by good structural design and use of deformed bars or prestressing with cold-drawn low-carbon steel wire.
- Quality control is only possible with a well-trained team and continuous supervision.
- The improvement fire resistance of non-structural components is possible by using high-alumina cements with crushed fired brick, which resist temperatures up to 1300° C (refractory concrete).
- Crushed fired brick (brick rejects) can be used to substitute gravel aggregate, where these are scarce (eg Bangladesh), resulting in a relatively lightweight concrete of slightly less strength but higher abrasion resistance. Since the brick aggregate absorbs water, more water is required in preparing the concrete mix.
- Expansion joints should be designed, if excessive thermal movement is expected.

FERROCEMENT

General

Ferrocement is principally the same as reinforced concrete (RCC), but has the following differences:

- Its thickness rarely exceeds 25 mm, while RCC components are seldom less than 100 mm.
- A rich portland cement mortar is used, without any coarse aggregate as in RCC.
- Compared with RCC, ferrocement has a greater percentage of reinforcement, comprising closely spaced small diameter wires and wire mesh, distributed uniformly throughout the cross-section.
- Its tensile-strength-to-weight ratio is higher than RCC, and its cracking behaviour superior.
- Ferrocement can be constructed without formwork for almost any shape.

Ferrocement is a relatively new material, which was first used in France, in the middle of the 19th century, for the construction of a rowing boat. Its use in building construction began in the middle of the 20th century in Italy. Although its application in a large number of fields has rapidly increased all over the world, the state-of-the-art of ferrocement is still in its infancy, as its long-term performance is still not known.

In 1976, the International Ferrocement Information Centre (IFIC) was founded at the Asian Institute of Technology, Bangkok, Thailand. It serves as a clearing house for information on ferrocement and publishes the *Journal of Ferrocement* and a number of other publications. The picture below shows the Ferrocement Park in Bangkok with some typical items made of ferrocement. (Photo: K. Mukerji)

Mortar composition

• The essential ingredients of the mortar which represents about 95 % of ferrocement are portland cement, sand, water, and in some cases an admixture.
• Most locally available, standard *cement* types are suitable, but should be fresh, of uniform consistency and without lumps or foreign matter. Special cement types are needed for special uses, eg sulphate-resistant cement in structures exposed to sulphates (as in seawater).
• Only clean, inert *sand* should be used, which is free from organic matter and deleterious substances, and relatively free from silt and clay. Particle sizes should not exceed 2 mm and uniform grading is desirable to obtain a high-density workable mix. Lightweight sands (eg volcanic ash, pumice, inert alkali-resistant plastics) can also be used, if high strengths are not required.
• Fresh drinking *water* is the most suitable. It should be free from organic matter, oil, chlorides, acids and other impurities. Seawater should not be used.
• *Admixtures* can be used for water reduction, thus increasing strength and reducing permeability (by adding so-called "superplasticizers"); for waterproofing; for increased durability (eg by adding up to 30 % fly ash); or for reduced reaction between mortar and galvanized reinforcements (by adding chromium trioxide in quantities of about 300 parts per million by weight of mortar).
• The recommended *mix proportions* are: sand/cement ratio of 1.5 to 2.5, and water/cement ratio of 0.35 to 0.5, all quantities determined by weight. For watertightness (as in water- or liquid-retaining structures) the water/cement ratio should not exceed 0.4. *Great care should be exercised in choosing and proportioning the constituent materials*, especially with a view to reducing the water requirement, as excessive water weakens the ferrocement.

Reinforcement

• The reinforcing mesh (with mesh openings of 6 to 25 mm) may be of different kinds, the main requirement being flexibility. It should be clean and free from dust, grease, paint, loose rust and other substances.
• Galvanizing, like welding, reduces the tensile strength, and the zinc coating may react with the alkaline environment to produce hydrogen bubbles on the mesh. This can be prevented by adding chromium trioxide to the mortar.
• The volume of reinforcement is between 4 and 8 % in both directions, ie between 300 and 600 kg/m^3; the corresponding specific surface of reinforcement ranges between 2 and 4 cm^2/cm^3 in both directions.
• *Hexagonal wire mesh*, commonly called chicken wire mesh, is the cheapest and easiest to use, and available almost everywhere. It is very flexible and can be used in very thin sections, but is not structurally as efficient as meshes with square openings, because the

wires are not oriented in the principal (maximum) stress directions.

• *Square welded wire mesh* is much stiffer than chicken wire mesh and provides increased resistance to cracking. However, inadequate welding produces weak spots.

• *Square woven wire mesh* has similar characteristics as welded mesh, but is a little more flexible and easy to work with than welded mesh. Most designers recommend square woven mesh of 1 mm (19 gauge) or 1.6 mm (16 gauge) diameter wires spaced 13 mm (0.5 in) apart.

• *Expanded metal lath*, which is formed by slitting thin gauge sheets and expanding them in the direction perpendicular to the slits, has about the same strength as welded mesh, but is stiffer and hence provides better impact resistance and better crack control. It cannot be used to make components with sharp curves.

• *Skeletal steel*, which generally supports the wire mesh and determines the shape of the ferrocement structure, can be smooth or deformed wires of diameters as small as possible (generally not more than 5 mm) in order to maintain a homogenous reinforcement structure (without differential stresses). Alternatively, skeletal frameworks with timber or bamboo have been used, but with limited success.

• *Fibres*, in the form of short steel wires or other fibrous materials, can be added to the mortar mix to control cracking and increase the impact resistance.

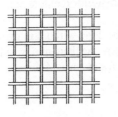

Hexagonal wire mesh
Square welded wire mesh

Square woven wire mesh
Woven mesh (undulated wires)

Expanded metal lath
Plaited mesh

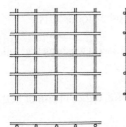
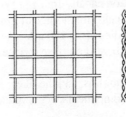

Construction method

- The first step is to prepare the skeletal framework onto which the wire mesh is fixed with a thin tie wire (or in some cases, by welding). A minimum of two layers of wire mesh is required, and depending on the design, up to 12 layers have been used (with a maximum of 5 layers per cm of thickness).
- The sand, cement and additives are carefully proportioned by weighing, mixed dry and then with water. Hand mixing is usually satisfactory, but mechanical mixing produces more uniform mixes, reduces manual effort and saves time. The mix must be workable, but as dry as possible, for greater final strength and to ensure that it retains its form and position between application and hardening.
- After checking the stability of the framework and wire mesh reinforcement, the mortar is applied either by hand or with a trowel, and thoroughly worked into the mesh to close all voids. This can be done in a single application, that is, finishing both sides before initial set takes place. For this two people are needed to work simultaneously on both sides.
- Thicker structures can be done in two stages, that is, plastering to half thickness from one side, allowing it to cure for two weeks, after which the other surface is completed.
- Compaction is achieved by beating the mortar with a trowel or flat piece of wood.
- Care must be taken not to leave any reinforcement exposed on the surface, the minimum mortar cover is 1.5 mm.
- Each stage of plastering should be done without interruption, preferably in dry weather or under cover, and protected from the sun and wind. As in concrete construction, ferrocement should be moist cured for at least 14 days.

Applications

- Boat construction (one of the most successful uses, especially in China).
- Embankment protection, irrigation canals, drainage systems.
- Silos (above ground or underground) for storage of grain and other foodstuffs.
- Water storage tanks, with capacities up to 150 m^3.
- Septic tanks and aqua privies, and even complete service modules with washing and toilet facilities.
- Pipes, gutters, toilet bowls, washbasins, and the like.
- Walls, roofs and other building components, or complete building, either in situ or in the form of precast elements.
- Furniture, such as cupboards, tables and beds, etc. and various items for children's playgrounds.

Some Applications of Ferrocement

Furniture, sanitary units, roofing elements at the Structural Engineering Research Centre, Madras, India.

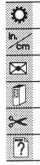

Latrine squatting slab, washing basin, toilet flush cistern and water tank (made of 5 square elements, assembled on site) at the Housing & Building Research Institute, Dhaka, Bangladesh.

(Photos: K. Mukerji)

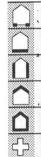

Advantages

- The materials required to produce ferrocement are readily available in most countries.
- It can take almost any shape and is adaptable to almost any traditional design.
- Where timber is scarce and expensive, ferrocement is a useful substitute.
- As a roofing material, ferrocement is a climatically and environmentally more appropriate and cheaper alternative to galvanized iron and asbestos cement sheeting.
- The manufacture of ferrocement components requires no special equipment, is labour intensive and easily learnt by unskilled workers.
- Compared with reinforced concrete, ferrocement is cheaper, requires no formwork, is lighter, and has a ten times greater specific surface of reinforcement, achieving much higher crack resistance.
- Ferrocement is not attacked by biological agents, such as insects, vermin and fungus.

Problems

- Ferrocement is still a relatively new material, therefore its long-term performance is not sufficiently known.
- Although the manual work in producing ferrocement components requires no special skills, the structural design, calculation of required reinforcements and determination of the type and correct proportions of constituent materials requires considerable know-how and experience.
- Galvanized meshes can cause gas formation on the wires and thus reduce bond strength.
- The excessive use of ferrocement for buildings can create unhealthy living conditions, as the high percentage of reinforcement has deleterious electromagnetic effects.

Remedies

- Research on the condition of older ferrocement structures.
- Development of simple construction guidelines and rules of thumb which can be applied without special technical knowledge.
- Galvanized mesh can be immersed in water for 24 hours and then dried for 12 hours, in order to allow the salts used during galvanizing to come to the surface. The residue can then be brushed off.
- Problems with galvanized mesh can be reduced by adding chromium trioxide to the mixing water.
- Complete enclosure of dwelling units with ferrocement components (ie for floor, walls and roof) should be avoided.

FIBRE AND MICRO CONCRETE

General

Fibre concrete (FC) is basically made of sand, cement, fibres and water. In the case of micro concrete (MC) fine aggregate is used instead of fibre. It is one of the newest building materials used in low-cost building. However, through intensive research and wide practical experience in many parts of the world, it has become a mature technology.

The types and characteristics of fibre concrete are extremely diverse, depending on the type and quantity of fibre used, the type and quantity of cement, sand and water, the methods of mixing, placing and curing, and - not least - on the skill of production, supervision and quality control.

The most well-known and, until recently, most successful fibre reinforced concrete was asbestos cement (ac), which was invented in 1899. The serious health risks (lung cancer) associated with mining and processing asbestos have led to the successive replacement of asbestos by a mixture of other fibres (fibre cocktail) in most places.

In the 1960s fibre reinforced concretes, using steel fibre, glass fibre, polypropylene and some other synthetic fibres, were developed and research on them is still underway. However, these can generally be considered inappropriate for applications in developing countries, due to the high costs and limited supplies of such fibres. This section, therefore, mainly deals with *natural fibre concrete*.

Depending on the available resources in different places, a wide range of natural fibres has been tested. These are essentially organic fibres, since the only practical example of a natural inorganic fibre is asbestos. The organic fibres are either of vegetable (cellulose base) or animal origin (protein base).

Vegetable fibres can be divided into four groups:
- Bast or stem fibres (eg jute, flax, hemp, kenaf)
- Leaf fibres (eg sisal, henequen, abaca)
- Fruit hair fibres (coir)
- Wood fibres (eg bamboo, reeds, bagasse).

Animal fibres include hair, wool, silk, etc., but are less recommended if not perfectly clean, as contaminants, such as grease, weaken the bond between fibre and matrix.

A variety of building elements can be made out of natural fibre concrete or micro concrete, but its most widespread application is in the production of Roman tiles and pantiles for roofing. After a few years of experimental work, large-scale applications in low-cost housing projects with FC sheets began in the late 1970s in several countries. However, the results of these field experiences with FC sheets were extremely diverse, ranging from "very satisfactory" to "complete failure" (leaking roofs, breakage of sheets, etc.), creating controversies and uncertainty about the viability of the new technology.

This situation led SKAT (Swiss Centre for Appropriate Technology) to undertake, together with a number of international experts, a systematic evaluation of production experiences in 19 developing countries, resulting in a state-of-the-art report on "FCR - Fibre Concrete Roofing" in 1986 (Bibl. 11.08). The main conclusions of the study were:

• Most failures in FCR production and application were due to the lack of know-how transfer, inadequate professional training, and consequently insufficient quality control.
• The present level of know-how is sufficiently advanced to ensure the provision of good quality and durable roofing, with a minimum life-span of 10 years or more.
• A square metre of FC sheets or tiles can be produced at a cost of 2 to 4 US$ (that is, 4 to 8 US$ for the FC roof including the supporting structure), which is cheaper than any comparable roofing material, but this cost benefit can be completely reversed, if certain minimum standards of production and installation are not observed.
• The fibre content of FCR is required primarily to hold together the wet mix during manufacture, to inhibit drying shrinkage cracking and to provide early strengths until the roof is installed. In normal portland cement matrices, the fibres decay within months or a few years on account of alkali attack. Hence, FCR must be installed and treated with the same care and precautions as for burnt clay materials or unreinforced concrete.
• The main advantage of the technology is that a cheaper, and thermally, acoustically and aesthetically more satisfactory substitute for galvanized corrugated iron (gci) sheeting can be manufactured locally on any desired scale (usually small or medium scale), with a relatively small capital investment and large job creating effect. Compared to asbestos cement (ac) one advantage is the absence of any health risk.

The FCR study also identified the need for a follow-up program to assist and advise potential and existing producers and users of FCR. So, in collaboration with ITDG, GATE and other AT organizations, a Roofing Advisory Service (RAS) was established in 1987, at SKAT, St. Gall. RAS issues manuals and periodicals and generally serves as a clearing house for information and technical assistance on all aspects of fibre and micro concrete roofing.

For a general understanding of the role played by the respective constituent materials, some of the main points are discussed here:

Fibres

- The main purpose of reinforcing concrete with fibres is to improve its tensile strength and inhibit cracking. While steel and asbestos reinforcements fulfil this function over many years, natural fibres maintain their strength only for a relatively short period (quite often less than a year), on account of their tendency to decay in the alkaline matrix, especially in warm humid environments.
- For many applications (eg roofing), this loss of strength is not necessarily a drawback. The fibres hold together the wet mix, inhibit cracking while it is being shaped and during drying, and give the product sufficient strength to survive transports, handling and installation.
- When the fibres lose their strength, the product is equivalent to an unreinforced concrete. However, by then the concrete will have attained its full strength, and since cracking had been inhibited in the early stages, it might be stronger than a similar product made without reinforcement.
- The same end-strength of the product can be achieved without fibre (MC). However, during manufactur and transport greater care is required.
- The fibre content is generally about 1 to 2 % by weight, never by volume, as fibre densities can vary greatly.
- Fibre concrete products have been produced with long fibres as well as with short (chopped) fibres, both methods having advantages and disadvantages.

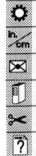

• With properly aligned long fibres higher impact resistance and bending strengths are achieved. The method of working several layers of fibre into the concrete, such that each fibre is fully encased in the matrix, is, however, relatively difficult, and thus rarely done.
• In the short fibre method, the chopped fibres are mixed with the mortar, which is easy to handle as a homogeneous mass. Since the fibres are randomly distributed, they impart crack resistance in all directions. The length and quantity of the fibres is of importance, since too long and too many fibres tend to form clumps and balls, and insufficient fibres lead to excessive cracking.
• Extremely smooth and uniform fibres (eg some varieties of polypropylene) that can easily be pulled out, are ineffective. On the other hand, too good a bond of mortar to fibre will result in a sudden, brittle mode of failure, when the fibres fail in tension.
• If methods can be found to overcome the weakening and decay of natural fibres, a wide range of semi-structural applications of natural fibre concrete will be possible, eg hollow beams, stair treads, etc. Therefore, intensive research is being conducted on fibre durability (see *BIBLIOGRAPHY*).
• Since natural fibre decay is caused by the alkaline pore water in the concrete, it is necessary to reduce the alkalinity. This is achieved by using high alumina cement or replacing up to 50 % of the portland cement with a highly active pozzolana (eg rice husk ash or granulated blast furnace slag). Best results were obtained by adding ultra-fine silica fume (a by-product of the ferro-silicon and silicon metals industries), but this pozzolana is unlikely to be available in most developing countries.
• In order to seal the pore system of the concrete matrix several methods were tested (eg use of higher proportion of fines, lower water-cement ratio, etc.), and interesting results were achieved by adding small beads of wax to the fresh mortar. When the set concrete is heated (eg by the sun), the wax melts and fills the pore system, thus reducing absorption of water which causes fibre decay.
• A vital requirement is that the fibres are free from all impurities, such as grease which interferes with the fibre-mortar bond, and sugar (as on bagasse fibres) which retards the setting of cement.

Cement

• The cementitious matrix of the earlier specimens of the composite contained a large proportion of cement (2 parts cement : 1 part sand), which was why it was named "fibre cement". The new generation of mechanically compacted fibre reinforced composites contains only 1 part cement : 1 to 2 parts sand (depending on the quality of cement, therefore the name "fibre concrete" became more appropriate.
• For MC a proportion of 1 part cement, 2 parts sand and 1 part aggregate is usually suitable.
• The proportion of cement needs to be higher if the sand is not well graded and if compaction cannot be done by a vibrating machine. For manual compaction by tamping the cement : sand ratio should be 1 : 1.

• Ordinary portland cement of the standard quality available in most places is usually suitable. For the production of roofing components, slow setting qualities should be avoided, as they delay demoulding and thus require far more moulds and working space.

• For applications in which the improvement of fibre durability is essential (and slow setting causes no problems), the cement should be partially replaced by a pozzolana (eg rice husk ash). Since the qualities of cement, pozzolana and fibres differ greatly, the proportion of cement replacement should be determined by laboratory tests.

Sand and aggregate

• In order to obtain as small a proportion of voids, angular sand particles of good grain size distribution should be used. The small particles fill the gaps between the large ones, requiring less cement and resulting in a less permeable matrix.

• For FC products only sand between 0.06 and 2.0mm is used.

• For MC products between 25 and 50% aggregate is used. The maximum grain size should not exceede two thirds of the product's thickness.

• The sand and aggregate should be of silicious origin or have similar characteristics. They should not contain minerals which may react chemically with the cement.

• Fine particles of silt and clay should be reduced as far as possible, as clay interferes with the bond between sand and cement.

• The correct proportion of sand must be determined by sample tests. Too much sand will result in a brittle, porous product. Too little sand means a wastage of the far more expensive cement and a greater tendency to develop cracks on setting.

Water

• In order to safeguard against corrosion of the steel reinforcements, clean drinkable water is used to prepare concrete mixes. In fibre concrete, impurities, such as salts, do not necessarily affect the fibres, and satisfactory results have already been achieved with brackish water. But it is always recommended to use the cleanest available water.

• A correct water to cement ratio is vital for the quality of the product. The tendency is to use too much water because it makes working with the mix easier. Excessive water gradually evaporates, leaving pores which weaken the product and increase its permeability. The correct water to cement ratio is 0.5-0.65 by weight.

Additives

• Admixtures may be useful to accelerate or retard setting, or to improve the workability of the fresh mix, but are likely to be expensive and difficult to get. Generally, no additives are needed for FC/MC products, except in cases where fibre durability requires

improvement and waterproofing is vital.

• As discussed above (see *Fibres*), fibre decay can be retarded by reducing the alkalinity of the cement matrix. This is achieved by adding a suitable pozzolana, such as rice husk ash, fly ash or granulated blast furnace slag.

• Reducing the permeability of the product also retards fibre decay. An interesting method (also discussed above) is to add small beads of wax to the fresh mix. In the hardened concrete, the wax melts on heating, forming an impervious film in and around the voids (Bibl. 11.07).

• A variety of other waterproofing agents is also available, and their selection should be governed by availability, cost and effectiveness.

• The colour of FC/MC products can be changed as desired by adding a pigment (in powder form) to the fresh mix, approximately 10 % by volume of the cement for red pigments, but considerably more for other colours. However, pigments are usually more expensive than cement and constitute a significant cost increase in the end product (Bibl. 11.15).

Hydraulic press and drag mould, for the production of corrugated fibre-cement roofing sheets, reinforced with coir fibre or wood wool. In this method, developed at the Central Building Research Institute, Roorkee, India, the cast sheets are kept pressed in the form during the setting period (4 hours), after which they are demoulded and cured in vertical stacks (Photo: K. Mukerji).

Applications

• Corrugated roofing sheets and tiles.
• Flat tiles for floors and paving.
• Light wall panels and cladding elements.
• Render for masonry or concrete walls.
• Door and window jambs, window sills, sunshades, pipes.
• Most other non-structural uses.

Advantages

• A large variety of cheap, locally available natural fibres (even agricultural by-products) can be used.
• If correctly manufactured and applied, FC/MC products can be the cheapest, locally produced durable material.
• The technology is adaptable to any scale of production, right down to one-man production units, as in the case of small-scale pantile production.
• The thermal and acoustical performance of FC/MC roofing is superior to that of gci sheets.
• The alkalinity of the concrete matrix prevents the fibres from being attacked by fungi and bacteria.

Problems

• In many developing countries, the limited availability and high price of cement can make FC/MC an inappropriate alternative to other locally produced materials.
• Good quality FC/MC products can only be made by well-trained workers, with great care in all stages of production and with regular and thorough quality control. Without these, failure is almost certain.
• The introduction of this relatively new material faces great reluctance and mistrust, on account of past negative experiences or lack of information.
• Incorrect handling, transportation and installation of FC/MC products can easily develop cracks or break, becoming weak or useless before beginning its service life.

Remedies

• In areas of limited supplies, the local production and distribution of cement should receive special attention and support, as without the availability of sufficient, standard priced, good quality cement, the FC/MC technology is not viable.
• Know-how transfer in the form of training courses and technical assistance by experienced practitioners is an essential requirement at the outset of every FCR/MCR project (Information available through RAS at SKAT, St. Gall).
• Problems of damage during handling, transports and installation can be reduced by making smaller products. Roofing sheets should not be longer than 1 m, and they should be transported (eg in trucks) standing vertically and tied securely, rather than lying, to avoid

breakage.
- FC/MC roofs must be treated like clay tile roofs, and moving on them should not be done without crawling boards.
- The more successful FC/MC applications there are in a country, the greater will be the acceptance of the new technology.

NATURAL FIBRES, GRASSES, LEAVES

General

Considering that various living creatures build shelters out of leaves, grasses and natural fibres, these materials were perhaps the earliest building materials of mankind, where caves or other natural dwellings were not available.

These materials are available in continuous supply in all but the most arid regions. In some places, they constitute the only useful construction material available, in others they are used together with a variety of additional materials.

The common features of these vegetable (cellulose based) materials are their renewability and their low compressive strengths, impact resistance and durability. Single fibres, grasses or leaves are usually too weak to support their own weight, but in larger quantities, when twisted, interwoven, bundled or compressed, can be used for various structural and non-structural applications in building construction.

Reed houses of the Uru-Indians, Lake Titicaca, Peru

Mudhif (guest house) of the Ma'dan (Marsh Arabs), Iraq: bundled giant reeds as frame structure and scaffold, reed mats as cladding

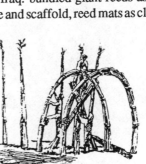

Sidamo dwelling, Ethiopia: basket-like structure

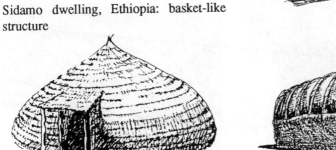

Examples of traditional dwellings made of grasses and leaves (Bibl. 23.17)

Applications

- Natural fibres (such as sisal, hemp, elephant grass, coir) as reinforcements in soil constructions or fibre concrete and other composite elements (eg fibre boards).
- Natural fibres, twisted to ropes, to tie building elements together or to produce tensile structural members, especially in roof construction.
- Straw for thatch roofs or for making particle boards. In an industrial process, compressed straw slabs (Stramit) are produced by heat and pressure, without any binders, but with paper on both sides.
- Reeds, bundled or tied together as boards, or split and woven as mats, for various uses as columns, beams, wall cladding, sun screens, or roofing material, or as substructure for wattle and daub constructions.
- Leaves, mainly palm leaves, for thatch roofs or for making mats and woven panels for floors, walls and roofs.

Production and installation of Raphia palm leaf tiles, Ghana
(Photos: H. Schreckenbach, Bibl. 00.49)

Advantages

- Usually locally available abundant, cheap (or even no-cost), quickly renewable materials (which can also be grown in the backyard).
- Traditional techniques (in most cases), easily comprehended and implemented by local people.
- Thatch roofing, if properly implemented, can be perfectly waterproof and possesses good thermal and acoustical properties.
- Reed constructions have high tensile strengths, good strength-weight ratio, hence usually good earthquake performance. In case of collapse, their light weight causes less damage and injuries than most other materials.
- Compressed straw slabs have high dimensional stability, and resistance to impact and splitting, are not easily ignitable, and (if kept dry) are not attacked by biological agents. The slabs are used like timber boards.

Fixing of palm leaf thatch (view from below), Brazil, (Photo: K. Mathéy)

Typical coconut palm thatch on bamboo framed house with bamboo mat walls, Trivandrum, India (Photo: K. Mukerji)

Problems

• In most cases, low life expectancy, about 2 to 5 years, though with good constructions and maintenance useful service lives of 50 or more years are achievable (in the case of reed thatching).
• Vulnerability to biological agents (attraction and nesting of insects, rodents, birds, and development of fungi and rot).
• Risk of fire, either originating within the building or spread through flaming or glowing fragments carried by wind.
• Tendency to absorb moisture, thus becoming heavy, accelerating deterioration and creating unsanitary conditions.
• Low resistance to destruction by hurricanes.
• Deformation and gradual destruction due to impact, structural stresses and fluctuations in temperature and humidity.
• Low acceptance due to general view that these materials are inferior, used only for "poor people's houses.

Remedies

• Impregnation of materials against biological hazards and fire, either by pretreatment or surface application, similar to bamboo and timber preservation. (Caution: these are costly, and easily washed out by rain, contaminating surroundings and drinking water collected from roofs. Moreover, fire resistant treatments may promote mould growth, leading to rapid decay.)
• Wide roof overhangs and roof pitches of at least 45° help to protect exposed surfaces and drain off rainwater quickly.
• Reduction of fire risk on thatch roofs by application of a coat of stabilized soil on the exterior surface to prevent ignition by wind-borne fragments, and restrict air-flow through the thatch in the event of fire.
• Maintenance of dry conditions and good ventilation to avoid attack by biological agents. In many traditional dwellings, smoke is developed inside the houses to prevent rot and nesting of insects.

BAMBOO

General

The use of bamboo as a building material probably dates back to the invention of the earliest tools for construction. Thus, being such an old and well established, traditional technology, it has produced a great wealth of forms and construction techniques, which resulted from all kinds of requirements and constraints governed by climate, environment, religion, security, social status and so on. But despite this immense variety of applications of a single material, it evidently possesses an almost unlimited potential for the development of new forms and methods of construction, making use of its characteristic properties.

Growth characteristics

• Bamboo is a perennial grass found in most tropical and subtropical regions, and also some temperate zones. Well over 1000 species of some 50 genera are known, the largest number occuring in Southern Asia and the islands between Japan and Java.
• Bamboos differ from grasses in the long life-span of the culms (hollow stalk), their branching and lignification (development of woody tissues). Like leaf-bearing trees, they shed their leaves annually and grow new branches, increasing their crown every year.
• Bamboo is the fastest growing plant, and has been reported to grow more than one metre in a single day. Bamboo culms can reach their full height (giant species grow 35 metres or more) within the first six months of growth, but it takes about 3 years to develop the strengths required for construction, and full maturity is generally achieved after 5 or 6 years of growth.
• Bamboos flower only once in their lifetime. Depending on the species this happens every 10 to 120 years, and every bamboo of the same species, even if planted in different countries, will flower simultaneously. The leaves that are shed before flowering are not replaced by new ones and the culms die. Regeneration takes place after 10 or more years. In places where a bamboo species constitutes a valuable natural resource, its death can have serious economic consequences for the people. But also animals, like the rare giant panda in Chinas's Sichuan Province, are threatened with extinction now that their food source, the arrow bamboo, is flowering and dying en masse.
• There are two main types of bamboo:
a) sympodial, or clump forming bamboo, found in the warmer regions, and
b) monopodial, or running bamboo, found in the cooler zones.
• The roots of bamboo are called rhizomes, which grow sideways below the ground. The rhizomes of sympodial bamboo multiply with short links symmetrically outward in a circle from which the bamboo shoots grow, forming clumps. Monopodial bamboo sends its rhizomes in all directions covering a large area with widely spaced culms.

• The hollow, cylindrical bamboo culms comprise a fibrous, woody outer wall, divided at intervals by nodes, which are thin, hard transverse walls that give the plant its strength. Branches and leaves develop from these nodes.

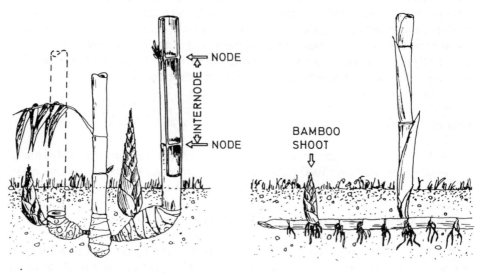

Sympodial bamboo   Monopodial bamboo

Harvesting and preservation

• Untreated bamboo deteriorates within 2 or 3 years, but with correct harvesting and preservative treatment, its life expectancy can increase about 4 times.
• Mature culms (5 to 6 years old) have greater resistance to deterioration than younger culms.
• Since fungal and insect attack increases with the moisture content, bamboo should be harvested when the moisture content is lowest, that is in the dry season in the tropics, and autumn or winter in cooler zones.
• The culms should be cut 15 to 30 cm above the soil level immediately above a node, so that no water can accumulate in the remaining stub, as this could destroy the rhizomes.
• The freshly cut culms, complete with branches and leaves, should be left standing for a few days (avoiding contact between the cut surface and the soil), allowing the leaves to transpire and reduce the starch content of the culm. This method, called "clump curing", reduces attack by borer beetles, but has no effect on termites or fungi.

- When considering preservative treatments of bamboo, non-chemical methods should be given priority.
- Stacks of bamboo are smoked above fire places or in special chambers, destroying the starch and making the outer wall layer unpalatable to insects. However, cracks can occur, which eventually facilitate insect attack.
- Immersion of bamboo in (preferably flowing) water for 4 to 12 weeks removes starch and sugar which attract borer beetles. Large stones are needed to keep the poles submerged.
- Application of lime slurry or coat of cow dung, creosote (a product of coal tar distillation) and borax, though not indoors, because of strong odours.
- Effective resistance to termites, most types of fungus and fire is achieved mainly by chemical treatment. However, great care must be exercised in the choice of preservative, application method and security measures. *In most industrialized countries, a number of highly poisonous preservatives are banned, but suppliers and government institutions in developing countries and even recent publications still recommend their use. No chemical preservative should be used without full knowledge of its composition, and those containing DDT (dichlor-diphenyl-trichlorethane), PCP (pentachlorphenol), Lindane (gamma-hexachloro-cyclohexane) and arsenic SHOULD BE AVOIDED.*
- Research on non-poisonous preservatives is still underway and full clarity on the toxicity of the recommended and currently available chemicals has not yet been attained. However, it seems safe to use preservatives based on borax, soda, potash, wood tar, beeswax and linseed oil. Their resistance to biological agents is less than that of the poisonous chemicals mentioned above, but can be equally effective in conjunction with good building design (exclusion of moisture, good ventilation, accessibility for regular checks and maintenance, avoidance of contact with soil, etc.). Several methods of chemical treatment are possible:
- Brushing and spraying of culms, which has only a temporary effect, because of the low penetration of the preservatives.
- Immersing the lower portion of freshly cut culms (which still have leaves), in a preservative solution, which is drawn up the capillary vessels by the transpiration of the leaves. This method (called "steeping") only works with fairly short culms, as the liquid may not rise to the top of long culms.
- Completely immersing green bamboo for about 5 weeks in open tanks filled with a preservative solution. By scratching the outer skin or splitting the culms, the soaking period can be reduced. With alternate hot and cold baths, the process can be still quicker and more effective.

Steeping

• Replacing the sap with a preservative solution, by allowing it to slowly flow from one end of the culm to the other, where the sap is forced out. When the sap is removed, the preservative solution can be collected and reused. The process (called the "Boucherie" method) takes 5 days, but can be reduced to a few hours by pressure treatment.

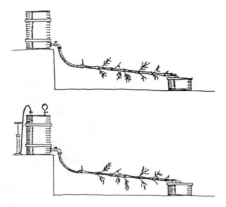

Bamboo houses on stilts,
Dhaka, Bangladesh

Bamboo scaffolding,
Dhaka, Bangladesh

(Photos: K. Mathéy)

Applications

• Whole culms for pile foundations (but of low durability), building frame structures, beams, trusses, grid shell structures, stairs, ladders, scaffolding, bridge constructions, pipes, fencing, furniture, musical instruments.
• Half culms as purlins, roof tiles, gutters, and for floors, walls, concrete reinforcement ("Bamboocrete"), grid shell structures.
• Split bamboo strips for matting and woven panels, ornamental screens, concrete reinforcement, grid shell structures, fencing, furniture.
• Bamboo boards (split and flattened whole culms) for floor, wall and ceiling panels, doors and windows.
• Bamboo fibres and chips for fibreboards, particle boards and fibre concrete.

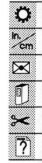

Advantages

• Bamboo is abundantly available, cheap and is quickly replaced after harvesting, without the serious consequences known from excessive use of timber (environmental acceptability!). The annual yield by weight per unit area can reach 25 times the yield of forests in which building timber is grown. Bamboo can be grown in the backyard.
• Handling during felling, treatment, transporation, storage and construction work is possible with simple manual methods and traditional tools.
• No waste is produced: all parts of the culm can be used; the leaves can be used for thatching or as animal feed.
• The pleasant smooth, round surface requires no surface treatment.
• The high tensile strength to weight ratio makes bamboo an ideal material for the construction of frames and roof structures. With proper design and workmanship, entire buildings can be made of bamboo.
• Bamboo houses provide comfortable living conditions in hot climates.
• On account of their flexibility and light weight, bamboo structures can withstand even strong earthquakes, and in case of collapse, cause less damage than most other materials. Reconstruction is possible within a short time and at low cost.

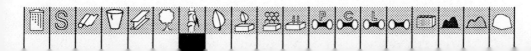

Problems

• Bamboo has relatively low durability, especially in moist conditions, as it is easily attacked by biological agents, such as insects and fungus.
• Bamboo catches fire easily.
• The low compressive strength and impact resistance limit its application in construction. Wrong handling, bad workmanship and incorrect design of bamboo structures can lead to cracking and splitting which weaken the material and make it more vulnerable to attack by insects and fungus. Nails cause splitting.
• The irregular distances between nodes, the round shape and the slight tapering of the culms towards the top end makes tight-fitting constructions impossible, and therefore, cannot replace timber in many applications.
• Bamboo causes greater tool wear than timber.
• Bamboo preservative treatments are not sufficiently well-known, especially the high toxicity of some chemical preservatives recommended by suppliers and official bodies.

Remedies

• Certain bamboo species have a natural resistance to biological attack, hence their cultivation and use should be encouraged.
• Only mature culms should be used, properly treated (see *Harvesting and preservation*), not stored for too long (if at all, then without contact with the ground), carefully handled (avoiding cracks or damage of the hard outer surface), and installed in carefully designed structures (ensuring dry conditions, good ventilation of all components, accessibility for inspection, maintenance and replacement of attacked members).
• Fire protection is achieved by treatment with boric acid (also effective fungicide and insecticide) and ammonium phosphate.
• Predrilling is essential to avoid splitting, if nails, screws or pegs are used. Fastening of joints by means of lashing materials is more appropriate for bamboo constructions.
• Bamboo should not be used where tight-fitting components are required. Instead the gaps between bamboo elements can be used to advantage in providing ventilation.
• *Recommendations for preservative treatments with chemicals should not be followed blindly. Different opinions of experts should be sought. And irrespective of the type of preservative used, care should be taken to protect the skin and eyes from coming into contact with it. The need for thorough safety precautions cannot be overstressed.*

TIMBER

General

Timber is not only one of the oldest building materials, along with stone, earth and various vegetable materials, but has remained until today the most versatile and, in terms of indoor comfort and health aspects, most acceptable material.

However, timber is an extremely complex material, available in a great variety of species and forms, suitable for all kinds of applications. This diversity of timber products and applications requires a good knowledge of the respective properties and limitations as well as skill and experience in order to derive maximum benefits from timber usage.

Although only a small proportion of the timber harvested is used for building, the universal concern about the rapid depletion of forests, especially the excessive felling of large old trees (which take hundreds of years to replace) and the great environmental, climatic and economic disasters that follow deforestation, has led to a great deal of research into alternative materials and rationalized timber utilization. Since timber cannot be completely replaced by other materials, it shall long remain one of the most important building materials, and hence great efforts are required to maintain and renew timber resources with continuous, large scale re-afforestation programs.

Growth characteristics

• The cross-section of a tree trunk or branch reveals a number of concentric rings, with the innermost ring being the oldest. The trunk thickness increases by the addition of new rings, usually one ring each year, but because of the exceptions to this rule, they are called *growth rings* (instead of annual rings).

• The rings comprise minute tubular or fibrous cells (tracheids) which transport moisture and nutrients to all parts of the tree. The *early wood* (springwood) formed during the growth period has large cells, while in the dry season the *late wood* (summerwood) grows more slowly, has thicker cell walls and smaller apertures, forming a narrower, denser and darker ring, which gives the tree structural strength.

• As each new ring forms a new band of "active" *sapwood*, starch is extracted from an inner sapwood ring (sometimes substituted by natural toxins) adding a further ring to the "inactive" *heartwood* core. Mechanically there is hardly any difference between sapwood and heartwood, but sapwood is usually lighter in colour and contains substances (eg starch, sugar, water) which attract fungi and some insects.

• The slower the tree grows, the narrower are the growth rings, and the denser and stronger is the timber. Its resistance to biological hazards is also usually greater.

STRUCTURE OF A TREE TRUNK
(HARDWOOD AND SOFTWOOD)

USABLE PARTS OF A COCONUT PALM

- Timbers are generally classified as hardwoods or softwoods. *Hardwoods* are from broad-leaved trees, in the tropics usually evergreen, in temperate zones usually deciduous (shedding their leaves annually). *Softwoods* are generally from coniferous (cone-bearing) trees, found mainly in temperate zones. The differentiation is only in botanical terms, not in mechanical properties, as some hardwoods (eg balsa) are much softer than most softwoods.
- In recent years, coconut timber has been found to be a good substitute for the common timber varieties. While *cocowood* is related to hardwood, there are some basic differences in growth characteristics: cocowood has no heartwood and sapwood, no annual rings and hence no increase in diameter; the age is determined by circumferential demarcations along the length of the bark; it has no branches and knots; the density decreases from the outer part to the centre, and from the lower part to the upper portion of the trunk. Coconut timber is commercially useful only after 50 years of age, when the copra yield begins to decrease rapidly.

Types and properties of timbers

• Timber for building construction is divided into two categories: primary and secondary timber species.
• *Primary timbers* are generally slow-grown, aesthetically appealing hardwoods which have considerable natural resistance to biological attack, moisture movement and distortion. As a result, they are expensive and in short supply.
• *Secondary timbers* are mainly fast-grown species with low natural durability, however, with appropriate seasoning and preservative treatment, their physical properties and durability can be greatly improved. With the rising costs and diminishing supplies of primary timbers, the importance of using secondary species is rapidly increasing.
• Research activities in several Asia-Pacific countries have shown *cocowood* to be a viable secondary timber, which is abundantly available in most tropical costal areas. However, special knowledge and equipment is required in processing cocowood, as each portion of the coconut trunk has a different density and strength, and its high silica content and hard outer portion causes rapid dulling of sawteeth (requiring special tungsten-carbide blades).
• Without considering the many exceptions, the main properties of timber are: relative low density compared with other standard building materials; high strength : weight ratio with the highest tensile and compressive strengths displayed parallel to the grain; elasticity; low thermal conductivity; growth irregularities; tendency to absorb and release moisture (hygroscopicity); combustibility; renewability.
• The shrinkage of wood is a common feature and varies according to the direction of shrinkage: radial shrinkage is about 8 % from the green to the dry state; the corresponding tangential shrinkage is about 14 to 16 %; in the longitudinal direction shrinkage is negligible (0.1 to 0.2 %).

Seasoning and preservative treatment

• Seasoning is the process by which the moisture content of timber is reduced to its equilibrium moisture content (between 8 and 20 % by weight, depending on the timber species and climatic conditions). This process, which takes a few weeks to several months (depending on timber species and age, time of harvesting, climate, method of seasoning, etc.), makes the wood more resistant to biological decay, increases its strength, stiffness and dimensional stability, and reduces its weight (and consequently transportation costs).
• *Air seasoning* is done by stacking timber such that air can pass around every piece. Protection from rain and avoidance of contact with the ground are essential.
• *Forced air drying* is principally the same as air seasoning, but controls the rate of drying by stacking in an enclosed shed and using fans.

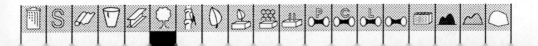

Solar timber seasoning kilns

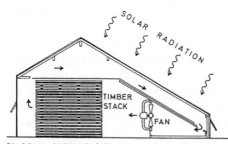

DIAGRAM SHOWING THE AIR FLOW AROUND THE KILN

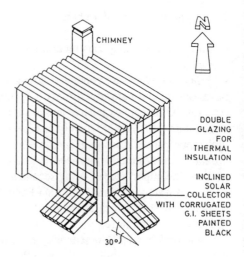

designed by the Commonwealth Forestry Institute (CFI) and ITDG, UK: Solar heat is collected by a series of black-painted panels; hot air is circulated through the stacks by two large fans; the humidity is released through a series of vents.

designed by CBRI, Roorkee, India: two solar collectors transport heated fresh air into the seasoning chamber and the humid air escapes through the chimney; the kiln works without fans on the principle of thermal air circulation.

• *Kiln drying* achieves accelerated seasoning in closed chambers by heating and controlling air circulation and humidity, thus reducing the time by 50 to 75 %, but incurring higher costs. An economic alternative is to use solar heated kilns.

• *Seasoning time* is greatly reduced if the timber is harvested in the dry or winter season, when the moisture content of the tree is low.

• Seasoning alone is not always sufficient to protect timbers (particularly secondary species) from fungal decay and insect attack. Protection from these biological hazards and fire is effectively achieved by preservative treatments with certain chemicals.

• The *chemicals* and methods of application are generally the same for timbers, as are described in the previous section on *Bamboo*. Hence the comments about the *avoidance of highly poisonous preservatives* are equally valid in the case of timber.

• When considering preservative treatment of timber, it should be remembered that *timber is the healthiest of all building materials and it is paradoxical to "poison" it*, especially when other methods can be implemented to protect it, for instance, with non-toxic preservatives and good building design (exclusion of moisture, good ventilation, accessibility for periodical checks and maintenance, avoidance of contact with soil, etc.).

Timber products

• *Pole timbers*, generally from young trees (5 - 7 years) with the barks peeled off, seasoned and treated as required. The cost and wastage incurred by sawing is eliminated and 100 % of the timber's strength is used. A timber pole is stronger than sawn timber of equal cross-sectional area, because the fibres flow smoothly around natural defects and are not terminated as sloping grain at cut surfaces. Poles also have large tension growth stresses around their perimeters and this assists in increasing the strength of the compression face of a pole in bending.

• *Sawn timber*, mainly from older trees with large diameter trunks, cut in rectangular sections as beams or boards. The part of the trunk from which they are cut and the slope of grain have a great effect on the quality of the product (as shown in the diagrams). The cutting of logs before seasoning is called conversion; re-sawing and shaping after seasoning is called manufacture.

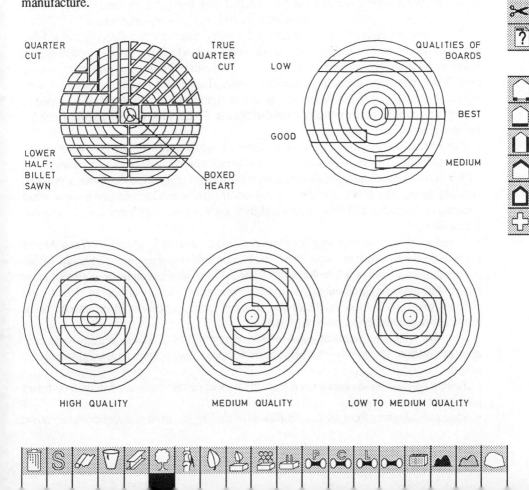

- *Plywood*, made of several plies ("peeled" off a pre-boiled log by rotating it against a knife) glued together such that the direction of grain of each ply runs at right angles to the ply on either side, producing extremely large panels of greater strength and lower moisture movement than sawn timber boards. As the outer sides must have uniform strength and moisture movement properties, there must always be an odd number of plies. Thicknesses range from 3 to 25 mm. A major problem is the use of formaldehyde-based glues, which are highly toxic.
- *Blockboard*, comprising a solid core of (usually secondary timber) blocks up to 25 mm wide, faced each side with veneers (of primary timbers), with their grain at right angles to that of the blocks.
- *Glue-laminated wood*, composed of layers of wood with the orientation of the grain of each layer usually in the same direction, or varied according to the intended use of the product. By this method, straight or curved structural members of very large (even varying) cross-sections and great lengths can be produced with low grade timbers of small sizes, achieving high strengths, dimensional stability and very pleasing appearance.
- *Particle board* (also called chipboard), principally made of wood chips (but also from other fibrous or small-sized ligno-cellulose materials), which are dried, blended with a synthetic resin and hot-pressed (requiring about 8 % binder) or extrusion-pressed (requiring only 5 % binder) to almost any desirable shape. Hot-pressed boards are stronger than extruded boards; and moisture movement acts at right angles to the plane of hot-pressed boards, and parallel to the plane of extruded boards. To improve their strengths, extruded boards are invariably veneered.
- *Fibre board* (ranging from "softboards" having good thermal insulation, to "hardboards" having properties similar to plywood) principally made of wood (or other vegetable) fibres, which interlock mechanically, requiring no adhesive as the lignin in the fibres acts as the bonding agent. The sheets are either hot-pressed (hardboards) or simply dried without pressing (softboards), and may contain additives such as water repellents, insecticides and fungicides.
- *Wood-wool slabs*, comprising long wood shavings saturated with an inorganic binder (such as portland cement or magnesium oxychloride) and compressed (for 24 hours, before demoulding and curing for 2 to 4 weeks). Various wood species can be used, except those that contain appreciable amounts of sugar, which retards the setting of cement. Wood-wool slabs are relatively light in weight, elastic, resistant to fire, fungal and insect attack, can be easily sawn like timber boards and plastered.
- *Saw dust*, and other finely chipped forestry or sawmill by-products, as additive in clay brick production. The wood particles are burnt out, producing porous, lightweight fired clay bricks.
- *Tannin based adhesives*, extracted from the bark of certain trees, used in particle board production.
- *Wood tar*, obtained from the dry distillation of timber, and used as a timber preservative.

Applications

• Complete or partial building and roof frame structures, using pole timber, sawn timber beams, or glue laminated elements.
• Structural or non-structural floors, walls and ceilings or roofs, made of pole timber (block construction), sawn timber boards, or large panels from plywood, particle board, fibre board or wood-wool slabs; in most cases, suitable for prefabricated building systems.
• Insulating layers or panels made of wood-wool slabs or softboard.
• Facing of inferior quality timber elements with timber ply or veneer, to obtain smooth and appealing surfaces, or facing of other materials (brickwork, concrete, etc.) with boards and shingles.
• Door and window frames, door leaves, shutters, blinds, sun-screens, window sills, stairs and similar building elements, mainly from sawn timber and all kinds of boards and slabs.
• Roof constructions, including trusses, rafters, purlins, lathing and wood shingles, mainly from pole or sawn timber.
• Shuttering for concrete or rammed earth constructions and scaffolding for general construction work, from low grade pole and sawn timber.
• Furniture, using any or combinations of the timber products described above.

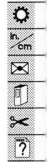

Advantages

• Timber is suitable for construction in all climatic zones, and is unmatched by any other natural or manufactured building material in terms of versatility, thermal performance and provision of comfortable and healthy living conditions.
• Timber is renewable and at least secondary species are available in all but the most arid regions, provided that re-afforestation is well planned and implemented.
• Most species have very high strength : weight ratios, making them ideal for most constructional purposes, particularly with a view to earthquake and hurricane resistance.
• Timber is compatible with traditional skills and rarely requires sophisticated equipment.
• The production and processing of timber requires less energy than most other building materials.
• Timber provides good thermal insulation and sound absorption, and thicker members perform far better than steel in fire: the charred surface protects the unburnt timber, which retains its strength.
• The use of fast growing species helps to conserve the slow growing primary species, thus reducing the serious environmental problems caused by excessive timber harvesting.
• Using pole timber saves the cost and wastage of sawing and retains its full strength, which is greater than sawn timber of the same cross-sectional area.

• Since cocowood was previously considered a waste material with immense disposal problems, its utilization as a building material not only solves a waste problem but provides more people with a cheap, good quality material and conserves a great deal of other expensive and scarce timber resources.

• All the timber-based sheets, boards and slabs provide thin components of sizes that can never be achieved by sawn timber. Apart from requiring less material by volume (which generally consists of lower grade timber or even wastes), larger, lighter and sufficiently strong constructions are possible.

• Demolished timber structures can often be recycled as building material, or burnt as fuelwood, the ash being a useful fertilizer, or processed to produce potash (a timber preservative).

Problems

• High costs and diminishing supplies of naturally resistant timber species, due to uncontrolled cutting and exports, coupled with serious environmental problems.

• Extreme hardness of some dried timbers (eg cocowood) making sawing difficult and requiring special saws.

• Thermal and moisture movement (perpendicular to the grain) causing distortions, shrinkage and splitting.

• Susceptibility of cheaper, more abundantly available timber species to fungal decay (by moulds and rot) and insect attack (by beetles, termites, etc.).

• Fire risk of timber members and timber products with smaller dimensions.

• High toxicity of the most effective and widely recommended chemical preservatives, which represent serious health hazards over long periods.

• Failure of joints between timber members due to shrinkage or corrosion of metal connectors.

• Discoloration and embrittlement or erosion of surface due to exposure to sunlight, wind-borne abrasives or chemicals.

< Logs at a sawmill in Kumasi, Ghana
  (Photo: H. Schreckenbach, Bibl. 00.49)

Remedies

• Conservation of forest resources by comprehensive long-term re-afforestation programs, and use of fast growing timber varieties and forestry by-products, thus also reducing costs.
• Harvesting timber in the dry or winter season, when the moisture and starch content, which attracts wood-destroying insects, is lowest.
• Sawing of hard timber species (eg cocowood) when still green, since the moisture in the fresh logs lubricates the saw.
• Reduction of moisture content to less than 20 % by seasoning, in order to prevent fungal growth. Care should be taken to control and slow the rate of drying to avoid cracking, splitting or other defects.
• Temperatures below 0° C and above 40° C also prevent fungal growth, as well as complete submersion in water.
• *Chemical treatment of timber against fungi, insects and fire should only be done with full knowledge of the constituent substances, their toxicity (especially the long-term environmental and health hazards associated with their production and use), the correct method of application and the requisite precautionary measures.* Opinions from different experts should be sought, in order to determine the least hazardous option. Proposals, such as facing of particle board with wood veneer or plastic laminate, are not always acceptable, as the emission of formaldehyde fumes is not reduced but takes place over a longer period.
• Indoor and outdoor uses of timber should be differentiated according to durability and degree of toxicity: under ideal (dry, well-ventilated, clean) conditions, even low-durability timbers can be used indoors; treated timbers that could represent a health hazard should only be used externally, but well protected from rain, if leaching out of toxic chemicals is expected.
• Good building design using well seasoned wood, good workmanship and regular maintenance can considerably reduce the need for chemically treated timbers.
• Good design of timber constructions includes: avoidance of ground contact; protection against dampness by means of moisture barriers, flashing and ventilation; avoidance of cavities, which can act as flues spreading fire rapidly; accessibility to all critical parts for regular maintenance; provision of joints designed to accomodate thermal and moisture movement; avoidance of metal connectors in places exposed to moisture; protection of exterior components from rain, sunlight, and wind by means of wide roofs and vegetation.

General

Metals are not generally considered appropriate materials for low-cost constructions in developing countries as they are usually expensive, in most cases imported, and very often require special tools and equipment. However, only a very small percentage of buildings are constructed without the use of metals, either as nails, hinges, roofing sheets or reinforcement in concrete components.

Metals used in construction are divided into two main groups:
- *Ferrous metals*: irons and steels
- *Non-ferrous metals*: aluminium (Al), cadmium (Cd), chromium (Cr), copper (Cu), lead (Pb), nickel (Ni), tin (Sn), zinc (Zn).

Ferrous metals

- All ferrous metals are made from pig iron, which is produced by heating iron ore, coke, limestone and some other materials, in a blast furnace.
- *Cast irons* are alloys of iron, carbon (in excess of 1.7 %), silicon, manganese and phosphorus. They have relatively low melting points, good fluidity and dimensional stability.
- *Wrought iron* is pure iron with only 0.02 to 0.03 % carbon content, is tough, ductile and more resistant to corrosion than steel, but is expensive and unsuitable for welding, so that it has almost completely been replaced by mild steel.
- *Steels* are all alloys of iron with carbon contents between 0.05 and 1.5 %, and with additions of manganese, silicon, chromium, nickel and other ingredients, depending on the required quality and use.
- *Low carbon steels*, with less than 0.15 % carbon, are soft and used for wire and thin sheet for tin plate.
- *Mild steels*, with 0.15 to 0.25 % carbon, are the most widely used and versatile of all metals. They are strong, ductile and suitable for rolling and welding, but not for casting.
- *Medium carbon steels*, with up to 0.5 % carbon, are specialist steels used in engineering.
- *High carbon steels*, with up to 1.5 % carbon, have high wear resistance, are suitable for casting, but difficult to weld. They can be hardened for use as files and cutting tools.

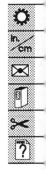

Non-ferrous metals

• *Aluminium*, the third most common element, but difficult to recover as a metal (produced with very high energy input and high costs), is the lightest metal, has good strength, high corrosion resistance, high thermal and electrical conductivity, and good heat and light reflectivity. Aluminium and its alloys have numerous applications in building construction, but their high costs and limited availability in most developing countries makes them less appropriate building materials.

• *Copper* is an important non-ferrous metal, available in its pure form, or as alloys, such as brass, bronze, etc., and suitable for a large number of special uses, but with few applications in low-cost constructions.

• *Lead*, mainly used in its pure form, is the densest metal, but also the softest, and thus weakest metal. Its good corrosion resistance makes it useful for external applications, eg in roofing (flashings, gutters, etc.), but rarely in low-cost constructions. Its high toxicity makes it a less recommended material, especially where alternatives are available, as for pipes and paint pigments.

• *Cadmium, chromium, nickel, tin, zinc* and a few other metals are mainly used as constituents of alloys to suit a variety of requirements, or as coatings on less resistant metals to improve their durability, a common example being galvanization (zinc coating) of corrugated iron sheets (gci).

Applications

• Structural steel components (columns, beams, joists, hollow sections, etc.) for complete framed structures, or individual elements, such as lintels, trusses, space frames and the like.

• Sheets, usually corrugated for stability, for roofs (mainly galvanized corrugated iron, less commonly corrugated aluminium sheets), walls (infill panels or cladding), sun-shades, fencing, etc.

• Plates, strips or foil for flashings (eg steel, copper, lead), fastenings (as in timber trusses) and facing (for protection against physical damage or for heat reflection).

• Steel rods, mats, wire mesh for reinforcement in concrete and ferrocement. The use of deformed bars (twisted or ribbed) gives higher mechanical bond between steel and concrete, reducing construction costs by up to 10 %. Mild steel wires of Ø 6.5 to 8 mm, drawn through a die at normal temperatures, producing 3, 4 or 5 mm Ø wires, have twice their original tensile strength and low plasticity, and are used (predominantly in China) in making prestressed concrete components, saving 30 to 50 % of the steel.

• Wire of various types and thicknesses, eg steel wire for tying steel reinforcements or other building components together, copper wire for electrical installations and thick galvanized

steel, aluminium or copper wire for lightning conductors.
• Galvanized steel wire mesh or expanded metal (made by slotting a metal sheet and widening the slots to a diamond shape) as a base for plaster or for protection of openings.
• Nails, screws, bolts, nuts, etc., usually galvanized steel, for connections of all kinds of construction components, formwork, scaffolding and building equipment.
• Rolled steel sections or extruded aluminium sections of various profiles for door and window frames, shading devices, fixed or collapsible grilles.
• Ironmongery of all kinds, eg hinges, handles, locks, hooks, various security devices, handrails, etc.
• Pipes, channels, troughs for sanitary, electrical, gas installation.
• Construction tools and equipment.
• Miscellaneous metal components for tanks, furniture, outdoor facilities.

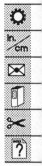

Advantages

• Most metals have high strength and flexibility, can take any shape, are impermeable and durable.
• Prefabricated framed construction systems of steel or aluminium are assembled extremely quickly. With strong connections, such systems can be very resistant to earthquake and hurricane destruction.
• Roofing sheets are easy to transport without damage, easy to install, require minimum supporting structure, permit large spans, are relatively light, are wind- and waterproof, and resistant to all biological hazards. In most developing countries they have a high prestige value.
• Many concrete constructions are only possible with steel reinforcements.
• Similarly, there are often no alternatives to certain uses of metals, eg electrical installations; screws, bolts, etc.; tools; security devices.

Problems

• High costs and limited availability of good quality metal products in most developing countries. As a result, inferior quality products are supplied, eg extremely thin roofing sheets, insufficiently galvanized components.
• With regard to roofing sheets: lack of thermal insulation (causing intolerable indoor temperatures, especially with extreme diurnal temperature fluctuations); condensation problems on the underside of roofs (causing discomfort, unhealthy conditions and moisture

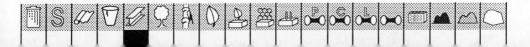

related problems, such as corrosion and fungal growth); extreme noise during rainfall; tendency of thin sheets to be torn off at nailed or bolted points (particularly those without or with only small washers) under strong wind forces; havoc caused by whirling sheets that have been ripped off in hurricanes.

• Poor fire resistance of most metals: although they are non-combustible and do not contribute fuel to a fire or assist in the spread of flames, they lose strength at high temperatures and may finally collapse.

• Corrosion of most metals: corrosion of ferrous metals in the presence of moisture and some sulphates and chlorides; corrosion of aluminium in alkaline environments; corrosion of copper by mineral acids and ammonia; corrosion of various metals by washings from copper; corrosion by electrolytic action due to contact of dissimilar metals.

• Toxicity of some metals: lead poisoning through lead water pipes or paints containing lead; toxicity caused by fumes emitted when welding metals coated with or based on copper, zinc, lead or cadmium.

Remedies

• Cost reduction by limited use of metals and design modifications which permit the use of cheaper alternative materials.

• To counteract heat and condensation: avoidance of sheet metal roofs in areas of intense solar radiation and large temperature fluctuations; double layer roofs with ventilated air space and absorptive lower layer; reflective outer surface.

• To prevent corrosion: avoidance of use in moist conditions; periodic renewal of protective coating; in case of dissimilar metals, prevention of contact with non-metallic washers; avoidance of contacts between aluminium and cement products (mortar or concrete).

• For noise reduction: shorter spans and coating of bitumen on underside of roofing sheet; also careful detailing of suspension points, and application of insulating layers or suspended ceiling.

• For resistance to uplift: thicker gauged sheets and stronger connections.

• To reduce toxicity: avoidance of lead or lead compounds where they may come into contact with food or drinking water; good ventilation of rooms in which toxic fumes are produced.

GLASS

General

Like metals, glass is a solidified liquid. It is produced by melting sand, soda ash, limestone, dolomite, alumina, feldspar, potash, borax, cullet (broken glass) and/or other ingredients, at about 1500° C, shaping it, and allowing it to cool slowly (annealing) to prevent cracking. Although the earliest forms of glass were produced a few thousand years ago, its large-scale production and use in buildings is less than two centuries old.

Glass is not an essential material for low-cost constructions in developing countries, but certain glass products or even waste glass can be quite useful in improving the quality of other materials, or indoor comfort in buildings.

Applications

• Flat glass, either as clear float glass (with undistorted vision and reflection), cast glass (usually translucent) or special variety (for solar control, thermal insulation, decoration, etc.) mainly for glazing of windows, sometimes doors, also for solar collectors, greenhouses, Trombe walls (thermal storage walls).
• Hollow glass blocks (made by fusing two trays of glass together) for non-loadbearing walls or screens to provide light and solar heat transmission.
• Glass fibre, in conjunction with other materials such as cement, polyester and epoxide resins, for lightweight roofing materials or infill wall panels, sun shades, cisterns and other items of any desirable shape.
• Glass wool, made of glass fibres sprayed with a binder and formed into boards or rolls, as thermal insulating material.
• Old bottles used as a substitute for hollow glass blocks.
• Waste glass, crushed to a fine powder and mixed with clay (7 parts powder : 3 parts clay), acts as a flux and reduces the temperature needed to fire the bricks by more than 50° C (saving nearly 50 % of the fuel). The bricks are tough and resistant to wind and rain. Very strong and resistant bricks are also made from 31 % crushed glass, 6 % clay, 7 % water and 56 % crushed old bricks.

Advantages

- Durability, usually high in normal conditions, and good resistance to chemicals (with a few exceptions) and biological hazards.
- Sufficient strength and elasticity, so that an ordinary glazed pane will safely deflect up to 1/125th of its span.
- In regions with cold seasons, utilization of solar energy by trapping the heat within the building ("greenhouse effect"), providing indoor comfort and saving fuel for heating.
- Glass can be recycled.

Problems

- Glass is brittle and thus difficult to transport; incorrect installation, thermal stresses, sudden impact, etc. can lead to breakage.
- Broken glass can cause serious injuries.
- Most modern varieties of glass absorb most of the sun's ultra-violet rays, which is vitally important (especially for children) for the synthesis of vitamin D and to destroy harmful bacteria.
- Hydrofluoric and phosphoric acids, and strong alkalis (eg caustic soda, alkaline paint removers, cement products) attack glass; deterioration is also caused by prolonged action of water.
- Although glass is non-combustible, it breaks and later melts in fires.

Remedies

- Small glass components are easier to transport and less likely to break. A good alternative to standard glazed windows are adjustable glass-louvred windows, especially in the humid tropics, where cross-ventilation is desirable.
- Cheaper, low quality glass, made primarily from quartz sand, does not permit undistorted vision, but allows the healthy ultra-violet rays to pass through.
- Water running off from fresh concrete or mortar must be properly removed from glass to prevent deterioration. In dry conditions, with regular cleaning, glass can be extremely durable.

General

Plastics are synthetic materials based on carbon compounds derived from petroleum and to a small extent from coal. All plastics materials are polymers (long chains of molecules loosely tangled together), the lengths and characters of which can easily be adjusted in manufacture, which explains the immense variety of plastics.

All plastics materials can be classified as either thermoplastic or thermosetting:
• *Thermoplastics* soften on heating without undergoing chemical change (if not over-heated) and harden again on cooling.
• *Thermosets* undergo an irreversible chemical change during moulding, so that they do not soften on heating and thus cannot be recycled.

While some developing countries have their own plastics industries, many others have to import the raw materials or finished products, which consequently are expensive. This is not always a disadvantage in building construction, as plastics are not essential materials, but if available, they have numerous applications in building, either to substitute or protect other materials, or to improve comfort conditions.

Applications

• Rigid plastics for various uses in water supply and sanitation; transparent, translucent or opaque sheets for non-loadbearing wall and roofing elements, glazing, facing, etc.; extruded profiles for window frames, furniture elements, etc.; fibre reinforced plastics (eg with glass, jute or sisal fibres) for (double curved or folded) self-supporting wall and roof elements (complete building systems).
• Plastic films and membranes for damp-proof courses; covering for concrete curing; temporary rain and wind protection of openings; tent structures. Thicker varieties and tubes for electrical insulation.
• Synthetic fibres for high strength ropes and fabrics, and as alkali resistant reinforcements (eg in fibre concrete roofing elements).
• Foamed plastics mainly as thermal insulation materials, lightweight ceiling panels, or as aggregate in lightweight concrete components.
• Synthetic resins and adhesives for production of various composite materials, such as particle board, plywood, all kinds of laminated and sandwich panels.
• Emulsion paints, distempers, enamel paints, varnishes.
• Sealants for movement joints, weather and waterproof joints.

Advantages

- Impermeability and resistance to most chemicals, hence no corrosion.
- Good strength : weight ratios of most plastics materials; lightness in weight makes handling and transportation easier and cheaper; no heavy supporting structure is required.
- Capability to take on a wide variety of forms, colours and other physical properties; imitation and substitution of scarce and expensive materials.
- Generally good resistance to biological hazards.
- Excellent electrical insulation.

Problems

- High costs and limited availability in many developing countries.
- Flammability of most plastics, with development of noxious fumes and dense smoke.
- High thermal expansion, up to ten times that of steel, and rapid decline of mechanical properties at elevated temperatures.
- Deterioration of most plastics due to prolonged exposure to the sun's ultra-violet rays.

Remedies

- Use of plastics only for special purposes, eg for waterproofing, thermal and electrical insulation, easier and cheaper transports or for use in earthquake prone areas.
- Avoidance of combustible materials installed close to plastics, and provision of sufficient ventilation openings to remove smoke and fumes in case of fire.
- Provision of sufficient movement joints for plastics components.
- Avoidance of uses of plastics exposed to sunlight.

SULPHUR

General

Although there are several very useful applications of sulphur as a building material, the technology is not yet widely known. This is probably because research and development has taken place almost exclusively in Canada and the United States and only few prototype buildings have been constructed in developing countries. However, the increasing supplies of sulphur, mainly from the desulphurization of petroleum and natural gas, are causing disposal problems in some countries, problems that can be solved if sulphur is used extensively as a building material.

Sulphur also occurs naturally in volcanic regions and has since long served as a basic material for the chemical industry, particularly for producing sulphuric acid, a primary material for large-scale industrialization. Sulphur is also used in the production of fertilizers and insecticides.

At normal temperatures, pure sulphur is a yellow crystalline material, which melts at about 119° C and hardens rapidly on cooling. In the molten state it adheres firmly to a wide range of materials rendering them waterproof and resistant to salts and acids. Sulphur can be stored indefinitely and recycled any number of times by heating and recasting.

The use of sulphur also has several limitations which must be recognized. Further research is needed, preferably in sulphur producing developing countries, especially with a view to the use of low-cost additives, development of practical, inexpensive equipment and simple construction methods.

Sulphur products

• *Sulphur concrete*, comprising elemental sulphur (about 30 % by weight) and coarse and fine inorganic aggregate (about 70 %), forming a concrete-like material that can be moulded and which is impervious to water. It contains neither water nor cement. The powder sulphur and aggregates can be mixed in a conventional mixer equipped with a heater, which raises the temperature of the mix to 140° C in a matter of minutes. Preheating the aggregates to about 180° C and addition of silica flour produces a more homogeneous flowable mixture and more uniform products. The colour can be varied with different aggregates. Sulphur concrete can be cut with a saw and drilled.

• *Sulphur coating* on weak, flexible and porous materials makes them strong, rigid and waterproof. By dipping, spraying or painting, almost any material can be impregnated with sulphur.

• *Sulphur bonding*, by using molten sulphur as an adhesive, or applying it externally over non-adhering joints, can produce extremely strong bonds between two components.

• *Sulphur foams*, produced by introducing small amounts of foaming agents, are light (weighing about 170 kg/m³), rigid, and have excellent thermal resistance, low shrinkage and water absorption.

- *Sulphurized asphalts*, in which either the aggregate or the asphalt (as used in road and pavement construction) is partially replaced by sulphur, thus raising the viscosity at high temperatures or lowering it at lower temperatures.
- *Sulphur-infiltrated concrete*, produced by introducing molten sulphur into moist-cured lean concrete, in order to increase its strength and water resistance.

Demonstration of the use of sulphur in Dubai, United Arab Emirates: casting sulphur-concrete hollow interlocking blocks. (Photo: A. Ortega, Montreal)

Applications

- Blocks, bricks and tiles of any desired shape made from sulphur concrete for load-bearing floor and wall constructions. Blocks are most appropriately made hollow and interlocking, facilitating accurate and quick constructions, and the cavities to be filled with reinforced concrete (eg in earthquake regions) or with insulating material (eg in colder climates).

• Impregnation of weak and porous materials (such as thatch roofs; panels of reeds, woven mats, cloth or paper stretched on wooden frames; timber components; and even low-strength concrete) to provide strength and water resistance. For example, a large piece of cloth, stretched on a frame and impregnated with sulphur, forms a bowl shape, which hardens and - when turned upside down - becomes a strong, waterproof dome-shaped panel.

• Rigid walls made by laying bricks or concrete blocks dry and then applying a sulphur coating onto the internal and external surfaces. Strong lintels have also been made by laying hollow concrete blocks in a row and bonding them by applying molten sulphur across the joints on the two vertical outer surfaces.

• Thermal insulation of buildings with sulphur foams, or production of lightweight, non-loadbearing wall and ceiling panels.

• Paving of courtyards and other outdoor surfaces, walkways, etc. with sulphurized asphalts.

• Pipes, cisterns and a variety of precast elements made of sulphur-infiltrated concrete for better chemical resistance, higher mechanical strength and impermeability, despite lower proportion of cement.

Advantages

• Pure elemental sulphur is abundantly available in many regions; can be stored indefinitely and reused any number of times; requires relatively little energy and only simple equipment to melt; adheres to a wide range of materials; has no taste or smell (except when heated or cut with an electric saw) and does not act on the skin; and is a poor heat and electricity conductor.

• Sulphur concrete gains 90 % of its ultimate strength in 6 to 8 hours (normal portland cement requires 30 to 60 days to gain the same strength); it is not attacked by salts (hence unwashed aggregates and even sea sand can be used); it does not require water (of special significance in desert regions, which incidentally also produce large amounts of by-product sulphur from oil refining); it can be cast to produce building components with precise dimensions and sharp edges (especially suitable for the manufacture of interlocking blocks, which can be assembled without the use of mortar or special skills); it has a chemically resistant, non-absorbing, smooth, hard and appealing surface (which is easy to keep clean by merely washing), eliminating the need for plastering or painting; and it retains most of the characteristics of pure elemental sulphur.

• Sulphur coating can considerably increase the strength and prolong the service life of many materials.

• Sulphur surface bonding reduces construction time, saves cement and produces strong, waterproof bonds.

- Sulphur foams have similar thermal insulation characteristics, but higher compressive strengths than conventional rigid foams, such as expanded polyurethane.
- Sulphurized asphalts can be stronger and cheaper than standard paving materials.
- Sulphur-infiltrated concrete requires less cement than concretes of the same strength and impermeability.

Problems

- Sulphur has a low melting point (about 119° C) and ignites at about 245° C. Sulphur combustion is self-sustaining and thus, once ignited, will continue to burn until extinguished. Burning sulphur produces sulphur dioxide, a toxic gas.
- Pure sulphur becomes brittle and powdery (orthorhombic crystalline form) on cooling, making it unsuitable for a variety of applications.
- Sulphur has a much higher coefficient of thermal expansion than portland cement concrete, and sulphur concrete tends to contract on cooling.
- Under humid or wet conditions, reinforcing steel tends to corrode in the presence of sulphur, making sulphur concrete unfit for structural uses.

Remedies

- Sulphur should not be used as a building material where temperatures are likely to exceed 80° C.
- A sulphur fire in an enclosed structure can be smothered by closing all entrances and denying it air; it can also be extinguished with water or sand.
- Apart from avoiding all potential sources of fire (eg cookers, heaters) close to sulphur-based components, a precautionary measure is to add a fire resistant material to the molten sulphur. A suitable material is dicyclopentadiene.
- The tendency of sulphur to become brittle and powdery is overcome by adding a plasticizer which retards the crystallization of sulphur. Dicyclopentadiene was also found to be effective for this purpose, as well as to increase the thermal stability of sulphur concrete.
- Shrinkage of sulphur concrete in precast components (eg hollow blocks) is best overcome by overfilling the mould, and after cooling, sawing off the extra concrete.
- Thermal expansion of sulphur concrete should be taken into account by providing sufficiently wide joints.
- The brittleness and thermal movement of sulphur-based materials can be reduced by fibre reinforcement, but further research is needed on this aspect.

General

Although the term "Wastes" is in common use, it may be misleading. Not all wastes are useless rubbish and freely available. It is also mainly a matter of definition: from one point of view a material can be of no use, while it is a valuable resource from another.

In this context, wastes can be defined as by-products (of agricultural, forestry, industrial or even household processes), which do not essentially have anything to do with building, but which, with special processing and treatment, or in conjunction with other materials, can economically substitute (or even improve the quality of) conventional building materials. Exceptions to these wastes are recycled materials from demolished buildings, which continue to serve as building materials, though perhaps in a different way.

Discarded consumer goods (such as bottles, tins, car tyres), which have been experimented with in several industrialized countries, are of less significance in developing countries, as such materials already have numerous other uses (eg household articles, musical instruments, shoes).

The materials referred to in this section are extremely diverse, but are basically of two types: organic and inorganic wastes. As a further sub-division, organic wastes are generally agricultural or forestry by-products and also household and urban wastes, while inorganic wastes are mainly obtained from industrial processes and demolition of old buildings, but there are several exceptions.

Organic Wastes

Rice husks

• The outer skin of rice grains can be used in the dry state, chemically treated, or in the form of ash.
• Full or crushed husks mixed with clay in brick production, help to burn the brick uniformly, creating voids, and thus producing lightweight bricks.
• Water glass (sodium silicate), a useful binder, can be manufactured from rice husks. This can be used in the bonding of full or crushed husks to produce particle boards. Other binders can also be used.
• Rice husk ash (RHA) is a useful pozzolana, which can be mixed with lime to produce a cementitious binder. (Details are given in the section on *Pozzolanas*).
• RHA mixed with soil, nodulized and sintered in a kiln, makes lightweight aggregates for concrete.

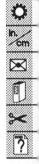

Coconut wastes

• These include fresh husks, coconut shells and waste from the coir industry.
• The husks consist of 15 - 35 cm long fibres (about 60 % of husk), with high tensile strength, which is affected by moisture. The fibres, and more so the pith (soft cork-like material), are chemically reactive, as long as they are kept dry. During the retting process (softening by soaking in water) they become inert. The difference in reactivity between retted and fresh husks necessitates different methods of conversion into building materials.
• Unretted husks, hot-pressed (at 150° C, 1 MPa pressure for 15 to 25 minutes) without any additives, produce strong particle boards.
• Unretted pith, obtained by defibrating mature husks, hot-pressed without additives, produce strong, moisture resistant boards. Lighter, resilient boards are made in the same way, but with addition of retted pith (low density, highly elastic granular material).
• Retted pith mixed with cashew nut shell liquid resin (rubbery substance) produces an expansion joint filler, which is resistant to temperature and moisture fluctuations and to insect and fungal attack.
• Retted pith granules as an aggregate in concrete are useful for thermal insulation.
• Unretted fibres, mixed with paraffin wax and hot-pressed, make strong and flexible hardboards (fibre boards).
• Coir shearing waste, containing fibre, pith and dust, bonded with an adhesive, produces particle boards with an attractive mottled appearance.
• Coir waste, mixed with portland cement and moulded under compression, produces large corrugated roofing sheets (see section on *Fibre concrete*).
• Coconut shell chips and conventional adhesives make good quality particle boards.
• Coconut shell tar, obtained during the destructive distillation of the shells, is a slightly viscous liquid with anti-microbial properties.

Wood residues

• Sawdust, woodchips, wood shavings and other wood residues from sawmills can be used in the conventional ways to produce particle, fibre and woodwool boards.
• With sawdust as aggregate in concrete, preferably with magnesium oxychloride cement, precast lightweight concrete components (eg door and window frames) can be made.
• Wood waste, mixed with inorganic materials (cement, trass, lime, pozzolana) in a mixer/ pulper machine, produce pulp cement boards for various non-loadbearing uses.
• Tannin is extracted from the bark of various timber species (obtained in timber processing) to produce tannin-based adhesives for the manufacture of particle board.

Reeds and straw

• Straw from wheat, barley, rice and other plants are hot-pressed, without any binders, to produce rigid boards, faced with paper on both sides (Stramit process).
• Flexible boards are also made by placing reeds (or stiff varieties of straw) side by side and then stitching them across with ordinary galvanized wire.
• Straw and other dried fibrous material, chopped to lengths of 10 to 20 cm, softened in water, and mixed with wet clayey soil, can be compacted in formwork to make stiff, thermal insulating walls (straw clay construction).

Bagasse

• This is the fibrous residue from sugar cane processing. It is not suitable for reinforcement of cement based products, as the residual sugar retards the setting of cement.
• With a suitable organic adhesive, particle boards and fibre boards can be made from bagasse.

Banana stalks and leaves

• Banana fibres have been successfully used in fibre concrete.
• Stalks and leaves, chopped up and boiled in water, form a thick liquid, which is applied on soil walls and roofs for waterproofing and higher resistance to abrasion and cracking.

Cashew nut shell liquid

• A by-product from cashew nut processing is a viscous liquid extracted from the mesocarp. The CNSL severely blisters the skin of any person coming into contact with it, but is a useful anti-microbial and waterproofing agent. It is therefore used to protect materials which are susceptible to biological decay (eg thatch roofing), and is applied with a brush. It can also be sprayed if mixed with kerosene to reduce viscosity.

Water hyacinth

• This beautiful plant, originally found only in Brazil, has become a serious problem, clogging tropical waterways worldwide and invading paddy fields in Southeast Asia. It is now widely used to produce biogas, mulch for soil improvement and silage as animal feed.

Water hyacinth products at the Housing & Building Research Institute, Dhaka, Bangladesh (Photo: K. Mukerji)

Asphalted corrugated sheets manufactured in India
(Photo: National Buildings Organization, New Delhi)

Bricks made from sewage sludge compared with normal burnt clay bricks, at Nanyang Technological Institute, Singapore.
(Photo: K. Mukerji)

• Research in India and Bangladesh has shown that tough, flexible hardboard can be made from a fibrous pulp of chopped water hyacinth stems.

Miscellaneous vegetable wastes

• A large variety of other agricultural wastes (eg jute and corn stalks, peanut shells) can be used in similar ways to those mentioned above. The most common uses are in the manufacture of particle board or fibre board.
• If used with cement as a binder, this is only possible if the waste material contains no cement "poison" (which retards setting), if the material has no cavities (which entrap and thus waste cement), and if the particles or fibres are long enough to provide strength by interlocking.
• Some non-edible grains are suitable for carbonization (conversion into carbon by slow burning) to produce particles of a fine cellular structure containing entrapped air. They are similar to, and used in the same way as, conventional lightweight aggregate (eg polystyrene beads), are biologically inert, fire resistant (up to 2000° C) and highly resistant to water and chemicals.

Waste paper and textiles

• While these are collected for other uses (such as recycled paper, packaging material, shoddy, bags, rag dusters, mats, etc.), shredded waste paper and cloth strips can serve as thermal insulations, for instance, in wall cavities and sandwich panels. Fire resistance can be achieved by soaking in a solution of borax, and drying.
• Asphalted corrugated sheets are produced by making a pulp out of washed and beaten paper and textile wastes, forming the pulp into sheets, drying in the sun or drying chamber, trimming, passing through an oven with corrugating rolls and finally dipping in a bath of hot asphalt.

Sewage sludge

• Sludge from wastewater treatment plants is normally dewatered and used for land-filling. This causing a serious disposal problem in the small island-state of Singapore led to research on utilization of the sludge as building materials (at Nanyang Technological Institute).
• Burnt bricks made of clay mixed with 40 % dried sludge or 50 % sludge ash showed better results with the ash, though higher percentages are not advisable.

• By adding pulverized sludge ash, to replace up to 20 % of the cement in concrete, its workability improves, the setting time remains unaffected, but the compressive strength decreases with increasing proportions of sludge ash.
• The sludge ash can be partially crushed and used as graded aggregate in lightweight concrete, or as coarse aggregate in no-fines concrete, with satisfactory results.

Coal wastes

• Coal is an organic material, but the wastes referred to here are largely inorganic, and can thus be ascribed to either group.
• Gangue is a by-product of coal production and is chiefly composed of silicon and aluminium with 75 % oxide. In China large amounts are used as building material: mainly as masonry blocks, aggregate in lightweight concrete, and as a cement replacement material.
• The burning of coal in thermal power plants produces basically two types of residues: cinder (or clinker), formed by burning lump coal, or pulverized coal which fuses to lumps and falls to the bottom of the furnace (also called "bottom ash"); fly ash (or pulverized-fuel ash) formed by burning pulverized coal, producing a fine dust, which is carried upwards by the combustion gases. Coal ashes can contain unburnt carbon in varying proportions.
• Cinder and sintered fly ash are used as lightweight aggregate in concrete construction and blockmaking.
• Fly ash and/or crushed cinder can be used in making burnt clay brick, masonry mortars and aerated concrete. (For further details about fly ash see section on *Pozzolanas*.)

Inorganic Wastes

Blast furnace slag

• This is the molten material which settles above the pig iron at the bottom of the furnace. (Details are given in the section on *Pozzolanas*.)

Bauxite waste

• The washings of bauxite ore in the production of alumina are collected in ponds, which dry out leaving a residue called red mud.
• The red mud can be mixed with clay to make fired bricks and tiles, or pelletized and fired to produce lightweight aggregate for concrete. The fired pellets can also be finely ground to produce a high quality pozzolana.

Lime sludge

• The sludge, in the form of finely precipitated calcium carbonate (with varying amounts of free lime), is obtained from fertilizer plants, sugar and paper factories, tanneries, soda-ash and calcium carbide industries.
• Lime sludges are used for the manufacture of portland cement and to produce sand-lime bricks.
• The lime sludge can also be moulded into bricks and fired in kilns to produce quicklime (calcium oxide).
• Dried lime sludge mixed with rice husks and fired in an open clamp produce a hydraulic binder (see section on *Pozzolanas*).

Phosphogypsum

• Phosphogypsum (calcium sulphate, contaminated with phosphates) is produced as a slurry in the manufacture of fertilizers and phosphoric acid. It contains several impurities, which have to be removed by expensive washing, thermal or chemical treatments. It is also to some extent radioactive and thus not recommended for building.
• If the amount of impurities and radioactivity is sufficiently low, the purified gypsum can be used as a set-retarder in portland cement, or to produce gypsum plaster, fibrous gypsum plaster boards or gypsum blocks.
• Cements from phosphogypsum have delayed setting and slow rate of strength development at early ages, but strengths at later ages (28 days) are comparable with those of ordinary cements.

Demolition waste

• Demolished buildings can provide a vast number of materials that can be recycled in new constructions. Careful dismantling and separation of various individual components (metal parts, timber boards and beams, windows, doors, tiles, pipes, etc.) help to conserve limited resources and save the immense costs and energy required to produce new components.
• Brick waste can be finely ground and used as a pozzolanic binder (see "Burnt clay" in section on *Pozzolanas*). It can also be crushed to a maximum size of 20 mm and used as coarse aggregate in concrete construction (especially important in countries, like Bangladesh, in which natural aggregates are scarce). Brick aggregate absorbs water, so that more water is required in preparing the concrete mix.
• Broken concrete serves well as aggregate in new concrete.

Metal scrap

• The collection and reuse of metal scrap is one of the world's largest industries with regard to the number of companies, people employed, weight of material handled and value of equipment used. Metal scrap can be collected at construction sites (eg off-cuts of reinforcing steel and mesh, wire and nails), demolition sites, engineering workshops (off-cuts from lathes, drills, etc.), garages and factories (scrap cars, oil drums, disused machinery, etc.), households (tin cans, domestic appliances, broken tools, furniture, etc.) and refuse dumps.
• The collected and sorted metal scrap can be melted in small decentralized foundries to produce new metal components; reshaped on a forge; cut into suitable pieces; welded together to form new products; or reused without special processing.
• Discarded beverage cans, of which large quantities accumulate in industrialized countries, are less common in the Third World. In places where they are abundantly available, they have been successfully used as bricks to construct light, thermally insulating masonry walls.
ᵒ Swarf (metal off-cuts from lathes, drills, etc.), if it is not contaminated with oil, can be used as aggregate in concrete, especially where increased resistance to cracking, impact and abrasion is needed (eg road and pavement construction).
• Flattened cans, drums, car body material, serve as cheap jointing plates in timber constructions (eg for roof trusses).

Waste glass

• In most developing countries, clean, used bottles have a high resale value and will hardly be considered as material to build with. In more affluent countries, where the bottles have no value, they have been used for wall construction as bricks, permitting light to pass through and presenting an attractive appearance.
• Broken glass (cullet) can be recycled in glass manufacture, but also has some uses as building material.
• Waste glass, crushed to a fine powder and mixed with clay (7 parts powder : 3 parts clay), acts as a flux and reduces the temperature needed to fire the bricks by more than 50° C (saving nearly 50 % of the fuel). The bricks are tough and resistant to wind and rain. Very strong and resistant bricks are also made from 31 % crushed glass, 6 % clay, 7 % water and 56 % crushed old bricks.
• Crushed glass, with a continuous grading of about 3 mm to 2 µm can be used as aggregate in concrete, but certain types of glass (eg soda and pyrex glass) have been found to expand in the alkali environment of portland cement, causing cracks and ultimate disintegration of the concrete.

Sulphur

• Large amounts of sulphur are produced in the desulphurization of petroleum and natural gas. On account of its many applications as a building material, it has been dealt with in a separate section on *Sulphur*.

Applications

• Components, mainly boards, made with organic or inorganic binders, from rice husks, coconut wastes, wood residues, bagasse, banana fibres and other vegetable waste.
• Boards made by hot-pressing without binders from straw, coconut husks, wood fibres, water hyacinth.
• Thermal insulation material and lightweight aggregate in concrete from rice husk ash nodules, coconut pith, sawdust, straw, carbonized grains, paper and cloth strips, sewage sludge ash, cinder and sintered fly ash, blast furnace slag, sintered red mud pellets, foamed sulphur.
• Replacement of aggregate in concrete by brick waste and broken concrete (demolition waste), crushed glass.
• Materials for cement production and replacement (pozzolanas) from rice husks, fly ash, blast furnace slag, bauxite, lime sludge, phophogypsum, pulverized burnt clay.
• Additives in clay brick production from rice husks, wood residues, sewage sludge, cinder, bauxite waste, crushed glass.
• Corrugated roofing sheets using coir waste, woodwool, vegetable fibres, paper and textile waste.
• Adhesives and surface protection coating made from tannin, banana stalks and leaves, cashew nut shell liquid, lime sludge, sulphur.

Advantages

• Conservation of scarce and expensive resources, and utilization of locally available materials, reducing costs and transportation.
• Reduction of pollution by the use of materials that are difficult to dispose of, and avoidance of excessive production of new materials in polluting industrial processes.
• Considerable saving of the energy required to produce new materials.
• Improvement of the quality of some materials (eg by using certain artificial pozzolanas in concrete).

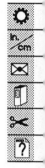

Problems

• Handling of wastes can be dangerous, eg inhaling of fine particles; blisters, burns and illness from toxic substances; severe cuts from broken glass and metal scrap.
• Although the total amount of available waste is large, it may be produced in numerous decentralized units, making collection extremely difficult.
• Once a by-product becomes a useful building material, higher prices are charged, so that the benefit of using cheap materials is quickly lost.
• Not all building materials based on wastes provide the same strength and durability as the materials they were designed to substitute (but if the price is low, this drawback can be accepted).
• The concept of using wastes and the fear of future problems that may arise due to inferior qualities of materials makes builders reluctant to use them.

Remedies

• Careful supervision and strict observance of safety precautions (eg use of gloves, goggles, protective clothing) in handling waste is of vital importance to reduce injuries and health problems.
• Producers of useful by-products need to be well instructed on appropriate methods of handling and storage of the material in order to facilitate collection.
• Especially in the case of lesser known but promising waste utilization, considerable efforts are needed to demonstrate the technology and its benefits. Prototype structures (preferably important public buildings) that are constantly used can convince most doubters.
• The use of wastes for building offers a wide field of research and should be given priority - even in the more affluent countries - as there is a great need to save resources, energy and costs, and at the same time provide more shelter for the homeless.

FUNDAMENTAL INFORMATION
ON
BUILDING ELEMENTS

134

FOUNDATIONS

General

The stability of a building depends primarily on the foundation it is built on. The construction of the foundation is in turn dependent on the type of building and, above all, on the load-bearing capacity of the ground. Soft soils, or those that become soft when wet, require more sophisticated and expensive foundations than hard soils. Natural hazards, such as earthquakes, hurricanes, floods, etc., also have an influence on foundation construction.

On account of the numerous requirements and constraints, there is a large variety of foundations. With regards to low-cost constructions, five main types are briefly dealt with here.

Types of Foundations

Linear or strip foundation

This is the most common type of foundation, consisting of a continuous strip, which supports a load-bearing wall along its full length. It is also used to bridge or cantilever over soft portions of the ground, in which case, it must be reinforced.

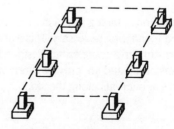

Spot or pad foundation

This is the common foundation for columns or poles (skeleton constructions), and mainly comprises a square (sometimes rectangular) footing, which is thicker than the width or diameter of the column or pole, the length and breadth each being at least three times the thickness.

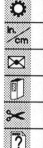

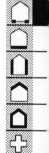

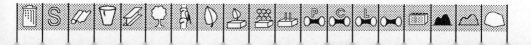

Slab or raft foundation

This type of foundation is often used for small buildings or structures with uniformly distributed loads (eg water tanks). Slabs on homogeneous ground can do without reinforcement, but over large areas, reinforcement is advisable, as non-uniform ground conditions lead to differential stresses.

Pile foundation

Building on poor soils or under water calls for this type of foundation. Holes are dug down through the weak soil up to the load-bearing layer, and filled with stable foundation material (either placed in situ or precast). The piles carry a reinforced concrete slab or are connected at the top by beams, which act like strip foundations. Lateral stability is achieved by placing some of the piles at a slant.

Stepped foundation

Building on sloping ground makes a stepped foundation necessary. It is a special form of strip foundation, designed to save material, and to provide horizontal surfaces at intervals along the slope.

Most other types of foundation are variations of the ones presented above, or are of special types, which are less relevant in low-cost constructions.

Design Considerations

Basic parts of a foundation

A linear or strip foundation is built up as follows:

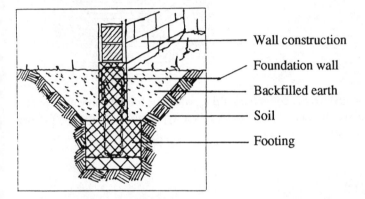

- Wall construction
- Foundation wall
- Backfilled earth
- Soil
- Footing

- The *footing* serves three main purposes: 1. to provide a solid, level base for the foundation walls; 2. to transmit the weight of the house evenly to the soil; 3. to resist the lifting forces of hurricanes.
- The *foundation wall* also serves three main purposes: 1. to provide a level base for the wall; 2. to provide the necessary bending and torsion strength for the construction of the house; 3. to prevent underground moisture from moving up into the walls.

Dimensions

- The footing must be deep enough to reach good solid earth free from plants, roots, filled-up materials, etc. Average depths are generally 50 to 100 cm, but should be considerably deeper, if washing out or shifting due to rain or flooding is expected.
- The "easy method" of determining the depth of footing is by asking neighbours, whose houses have shown good stability (without cracks or other damage). In case of doubt, deeper footings are advisable.
- Sizes of footing depend on the strength of the soil and weight of the house. The height should preferably exceed the wall or column thickness and the base should be wide enough to permit a 60° angle of load distribution. Average footing widths lie between 30 and 60 cm.
- Foundation walls should preferably be thicker than the walls they support, and high enough above ground to protect the wall from rain splash. Heights of 20 to 50 cm above the ground are common, but depend on rainfall intensity and roof overhang.

Excavation

• Foundation trenches should be carefully dug to provide a hard, level bottom surface and side walls at right angles to it. Rounded edges must be avoided.

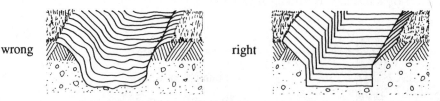

wrong   right

• The excavated soil should be retained for backfilling, when the foundation wall is ready. The backfilling should have the same characteristics (soil type, moisture, density) as the surrounding, undisturbed soil.

Materials

• Foundations can be made of several materials with differing qualities. A good reinforced concrete foundation is the strongest and best foundation for any type of residential building. Where cement is too expensive or scarce, other materials can provide satisfactory results.

Material	Quality of foundation
Reinforced concrete	Very good. Earthquake-resistant construction
Cement blocks	Poor to good
Stones and mortar	Medium to good
Burnt bricks	Medium
Stabilized mud bricks	Poor to good
Stabilized rammed earth	For arid or semi-arid regions only

Protection of foundations

• Penetration of rainwater and ground moisture is largely prevented by good waterproof concrete, natural stone, waterproof burnt bricks, but also with a waterproof coating or membrane, and protective roof overhang. Drainage tubes laid in a gravel bed alongside the footing are also effective.
• For protection against termites, see section on *Biological Agents*.

The foundation can be attacked by:

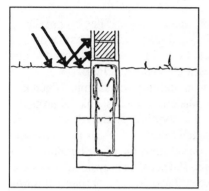

1. Rain and wind

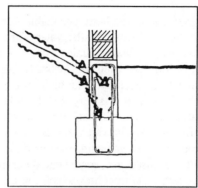

2. Hillside surface water

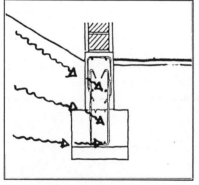

3. Hillside underground water

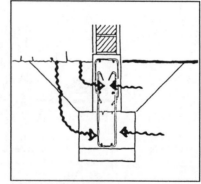

4. Seepage water

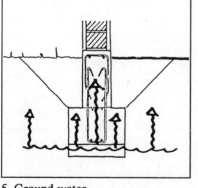

5. Ground water

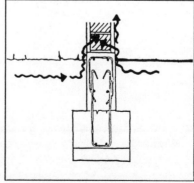

6. Termites

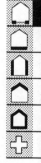

Miscellaneous Aspects

• Soft clayey soils, which are unsuitable to build on, can be consolidated by providing vertical drains which draw out the water. These can be rigid sand drains or flexible drains. Cheap and effective flexible drains using coir and jute fabric have been developed at the University of Singapore and the Central Building Research Institute in India.

• The water from fresh concrete or from the mortar in masonry foundations is quickly absorbed by the soil, if it is very dry. Therefore, foundation trenches should be properly watered before placing the foundation material, so that absorption is reduced.

• In highland regions, in which temperatures can also fall below 0° C, the water in the soil can freeze and expand, damaging the foundation and consequently the whole building. This problem, called frost heave, occurs mainly in silty soils. The problem is avoided by placing the footing below the frost line, which can lie between 50 and 100 cm, or much lower in colder climates.

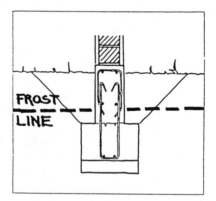

FLOORS AND CEILINGS

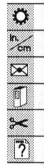

General

In many traditional societies in developing countries it is customary for all daily activities, such as working, preparing food, cooking, eating and sleeping, to take place on the floor. Hence, the floor construction and, more so, the type of surface is of great importance, especially in terms of comfort and cleanliness.

But even if activities do not take place primarily on the floor, careful thought should be given to its design and the choice of materials, particularly with respect to the local climatic and environmental conditions, as well as to traditional lifestyles and natural hazards.

Although composite climates are more common, design considerations for floor and ceiling construction in the two major climatic regions (warm humid and hot dry climates) show the two extremes, between which a variety of intermediary solutions are possible.

Design Considerations

• It is always advantageous to construct floors well above the ground surface: protection against splashing rain and flood water in predominantly humid climates, exclusion of wind-blown sand in predominantly dry regions.
• In warm humid climates, floors raised off the ground, with an air space below, are preferred mainly to facilitate air movement (needed to reduce heat and moisture) and for protection against vermin.
• In hot dry climates, floors should preferably be in contact with the ground to facilitate heat conduction from building to earth.
• In regions which may experience brief but marked seasonal cooling, the normally welcome coolness of paved flooring may be temporarily mitigated by area rugs, carpets or mats.
• The choice of colour on floors exposed to sunshine is determined by a compromise between avoiding glare and discouraging heat absorption. Smooth surfaces are best in all areas subject to dust, but non-slip surfaces must be remembered for steps in wet areas.
• Non-uniform ground conditions can cause the foundations and/or floors to subside partially, causing serious damage. Hence, in some cases, it is advisable to construct movement joints between the floor and wall (or foundation).
• A dampproof course is required where ground moisture is a problem.
• The design of ceilings must take into account the problem of sound transmission from the higher to the lower floor: resilient materials and improper ceiling-to-wall connections can cause acoustical problems.

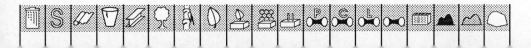

Common Materials for Floors and Ceilings

Material	Characteristics
Stone slabs or tiles	Medium costs to expensive; provides cool, clean surface; impermeable, if joints are waterproof.
Earth	Cheap; suitable for hot dry climates; in warm humid climates raised well above ground; stabilizer and/or water proofing treatment and frequent renewal required (in some regions, cow dung is traditionally used and very effective).
Burnt clay bricks and tiles	Medium costs; provides cool surface; requires careful placement to avoid unevenness; suitable for all climates; structural clay filler blocks on precast concrete joists reduce time of construction and provide good alternatives to concrete ceilings.
Concrete slabs	Expensive; strong; suitable for all climates; with reinforcement good resistance to differential settling of soil; used mainly as substructure; in situ or precast construction.
Screed and concrete tiles	Expensive; strong; screed used as jointless floor surface or as bed for floor tiles; concrete tiles available in large variety of shapes and sizes.
Bamboo	Low to medium costs; used in warm humid regions for floors without ground contact; suitable for substructure and covering, preferably with bamboo boards (split and flattened culms); very good workmanship and protection against biological agents and fire necessary.
Timber	Medium costs; similar considerations as for bamboo.
Plastics	Medium costs; mainly PVC (polyvinyl chloride) tiles and sheets as floor covering laid on rough timber or screed base.
Sulphur concrete	Medium costs; provides cool, clean and impermeable surface; protection against excessive heat necessary.
Wastes	Low to medium costs; large variety of applications as pozzolana and aggregate in concrete, thermal insulation material, adhesives, boards and tiles.

General

The main functions of walls are:
- exclusion of heat or cold, rain, wind, dust, noise, and other undesirable climatic and environmental elements;
- regulation of indoor climate (temperature, moisture, air movement);
- privacy;
- security against human and animal intrusion;
- support of ceiling and roof structure (though not the case in frame constructions with infill walls).

There are principally two ways of building a wall:
- massive or loadbearing wall construction;
- skeleton or frame construction with non-loadbearing walls.

Massive wall constructions usually comprise materials of high compressive strength (eg stone, earth, brick, concrete), by virtue of which they support their own weight and that of the ceiling or roof.

A *skeleton structure* consists of vertical, horizontal and angular members (eg timber, bamboo, reinforced concrete), which are joined together to form the loadbearing framework of the building. The space between them may remain open or can be filled in with in-situ wall construction materials (eg masonry wall, straw-clay) or prefabricated panels (eg timber and composite boards, concrete, ferrocement and brick panels). These help to strengthen the frame to prevent distortion. Well-braced frames can also carry a lightweight cladding (eg plywood and bamboo boards, fibre concrete, slate).

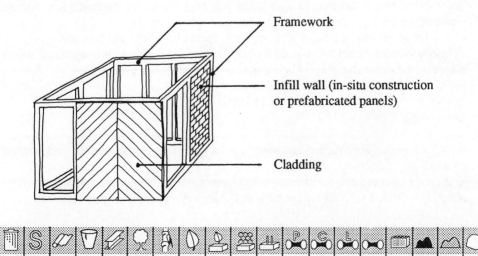

Framework

Infill wall (in-situ construction or prefabricated panels)

Cladding

Design Considerations

Climatic aspects

• In warm humid regions, diurnal and annual temperatures remain fairly constant, so that walls of low thermal capacity are required, together with large openings for cross-ventilation.
• In hot arid zones, in which diurnal and annual temperature variations are large, it is desirable for walls to absorb heat during the 9 - 12 hours of solar radiation and then to emit the heat to the interior until the cold pre-dawn hours, thus maintaining thermal comfort inside the building at all times (time-lag design theory). Small openings, located at higher levels should permit hot air to escape, and exclude solar radiation and glare.
• In all warm climates, the long axes of buildings should be orientated in east-west direction, with openings in the walls facing east and west being avoided or kept small, as it is difficult to shade them from the low morning and evening sun. Openings in walls facing south and north are easy to shade from the high noon sun by means of wide roof overhangs.
• While the east-west orientation of buildings is important, in warm humid regions priority must be given to orientation for air movement; in hot arid zones, importance must be given to exclusion of hot air, sand and dust.
• The absorption of solar heat can be greatly reduced by reflective wall surfaces. The ground adjacent to the building should be shaded or have some vegetation to avoid reflection onto walls, but heat emission at night should not be hindered.

Solid walls

• Solid walls with high thermal capacities are common in hot arid climates, as they transfer the absorbed heat to the interior with a time lag, thus restraining the heat when external temperatures are high, and releasing it when temperatures are low.
• Typical solid walls are made of stone, earth, burnt clay bricks and concrete.
• Insulation on the outside of a solid wall gives a four times greater time lag than if it were placed on the inside, but it also hinders heat dissipation during the night.

Cavity walls

• Double walled construction has many advantages, both in warm humid and hot arid regions:
• the outer layer protects the inner layer from direct solar radiation, which first heats up the outer layer. With a reflective outer surface, this heat absorption is greatly reduced;

• only a part of the heat that passes through the outer layers reaches the inner layer by radiation or convection, and if provided with a reflective surface, it will not absorb all the heat;

• if the cavity is not ventilated (as in hollow or perforated bricks), it will act as an insulator, which can be advantageous, but can also hinder the passage of heat from the inside to the outer skin;

• openings at the top and bottom of the cavities allow the hot air, which will have accumulated within, to escape at the top, while fresh air is drawn in at the lower side (however, this ventilation of the air space does not affect the radiation from the outer to the inner layer); during the day, when the fresh air is also hot, air circulation will have no cooling effect, so that it would be ideal (but not practical) to be able to close the openings during the day and open them at night;

• sound transmission is reduced by the air space.

• In warm humid climates, double walled constructions have the additional advantage of protecting the inner layer from rain and moisture penetration. Any moisture that passes through the outer layer is removed be ventilation, and condensation water can trickle down and out through the opening below.

• The materials used for cavity walls can be of various types, depending on several factors, such as temperature range, intensity and duration of solar radiation, humidity, rainfall, building usage, nature of immediate surroundings.

• In warm humid conditions, the inner skin should not be impermeable, as moisture movement is required, while the outer skin (usually thin panels or tiles on lathing) can be either impermeable or not, but care must be taken to avoid moisture bridging from the outer to the inner skin.

Solid wall and cavity wall constructions in two projects of ADAUA in Mauritania (Photos: D. Deriaz)

• In hot arid environments, materials of lower thermal capacity can be used in cavity walls, for instance, if the outer skin has good reflectivity and thermal insulation. However, the inner layer is generally a soil, brick or concrete construction, but of less thickness than for solid walls, as the heat accumulation over a 9 to 12 hour time-lag period is greatly reduced. The outer skin is typically of thin brickwork, concrete elements or a cladding of flat or corrugated sheets or tiles (eg metal, clay tiles, slate, fibre concrete).

• A disadvantage of cavity walls is that insects and vermin may nest in them. To avoid this problem, the interior surfaces of the cavity should be smooth and hard, and occasional washing will remove any accumulated dirt or insects.

Lightweight walls

• These are usually thin panels, matting, sheets or tiles of low thermal capacity, fixed to a framework. In some rare cases they can be thermally insulating.

• Such walls are only of use in warm humid regions, where heat storage is not needed. The main functions of lightweight walls are to provide shade and privacy, as well as protection from wind, rain and intruders.

• Sufficient openings facing the main wind direction are required to facilitate cross-ventilation for the improvement of indoor comfort.

• Lightweight walls are advantageous in earthquake zones, because their failure cannot cause as much devastation as heavy walls. However, in hurricane zones, lightweight walls can be susceptible to serious damage under strong wind pressure, hence strong connections, and avoidance of small elements and projecting parts are essential requirements.

Lightweight bamboo mat wall in Dhaka, Bangladesh (Photo: K. Mathéy)

Surface treatment

• Depending on the type of material and construction system, wall surfaces can be left untreated or be treated to increase their durability by protecting them against rain, abrasion and vermin, to improve the thermal and moisture performance of the wall, or to improve its appearance by covering unsightly surfaces, or applying decorative effects and colours.
• Cement or lime mortars and a variety of stabilized mud plasters are the most common types of surface treatment on concrete, brick and earth structures, whereby special knowledge and experience is required in using the correct rendering for each type of wall material.
• Other types of surface treatment are lime and cement washes, varnishes (on timber) and several types of paints (principally oil-based or emulsion paints). Wall paper is less common in tropical regions, but decorative woven fabric and mats are fairly widespread.

Wall finishes on mud constructions in Ghana: In many regions this is the work of women. (Photo: H. Schreckenbach, Bibl. 00.49)

Application of mud plaster by hand

Polishing the dried plaster with a flat granite or basalt stone

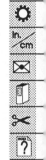

Common Wall Construction Materials

Material	Characteristics
Stone	Low to medium costs; high thermal capacity, suitable for climates with large temperature fluctuations; low earthquake resistance; surfaces often harsh, requiring rendering in building interiors.
Earth	Cheap; good material for most climates, except consistently humid areas; durability achieved by good compaction, stabilization and surface treatment (regularly renewed); low earthquake resistance.
Burnt clay bricks and concrete blocks	Medium costs; suitable for all climates; used for loadbearing masonry, infill walls and precast panels; with good workmanship, unlimited durability and good resistance to all natural hazards and fire; surface treatment not always necessary.
Concrete	Expensive; suitable for all climates, mainly for skeleton structures and loadbearing constructions; good durability and resistance to all natural hazards and fire; with good workmanship and formwork, no surface treatment needed.
Ferrocement	Medium costs; mainly used for light infill wall panels or cladding elements; otherwise same characteristics as concrete.
Fibre concrete	Low to medium costs; mainly sheets and tiles for cladding; lighter and weaker than ferrocement.
Natural fibres, grasses, leaves	Cheap; only used in warm humid climates for lightweight, infill wall panels and cladding; low durability and resistance to natural hazards, except earthquakes (lightweight and flexible).
Bamboo	Cheap; used in warm humid areas; ideal for skeleton structure, infill walls and cladding; otherwise similar to fibres, grasses, and leaves.
Timber	Medium costs; good for most climates; ideal material for skeleton structures; also lightweight infill panels and cladding; sufficiently thick sections resist fire, but otherwise low resistance to biological hazards; good earthquake and hurricane resistance.
Sulphur concrete	Medium costs; good for loadbearing walls in all conditions except extreme heat; surfaces attractive without rendering, easy to clean.

General

The roof is the most essential part of a house (a house without a roof is not considered a house). It is the part that costs the most, by area and orientation it is the part most exposed to the elements, and it is the part primarily responsible both for indoor comfort and for damage suffered during earthquakes and hurricanes. A well-designed durable roof can compensate for a great number of problems that may arise in other parts of the building.

However, technical aspects are not the only determinants of roof design. Many traditional cultures give more importance to various other criteria, such as religious belief, local lifestyles and social status, and these must be respected in designing housing schemes, especially in order to avoid the depressing monotony of present day housing colonies, which look the same in about all parts of the world.

While traditional, non-technical aspects of roof design are important, these cannot be dealt with in a technology orientated book of this kind. The basically different types of roofs and the main design criteria for roofs in the two major climatic regions, that is, those that are predominantly warm-humid and those predominantly hot-arid, are summarized below.

Common Roof Types

Flat roofs

- These can be monolithic slabs, sheets or space frame structures, or simple systems using beams, girders and decking elements of low span capability.
- By definition, roofs with inclinations less than 10° to the horizontal are classified as flat roofs. For rainwater run-off at least 2° slope is needed.
- Strong winds tend to pull off the roof by suction, hence flat roofs are less suitable for hurricane prone areas.
- Flat roofs are most common in predominantly hot arid regions, with low annual precipitation. The roofs provide additional living space (for household activities and sleeping at night) and facilitate vertical extensions of the building.
- Sheet decking must be laid in falls with large overlaps. An ingenious alternative to corrugated sheets are canaletas (trough-shaped asbestos cement roofing elements) which can span entire dwellings without supporting structures, thus saving material, costs and time of installation. A good material, in terms of strength and durability, is asbestos cement, which most likely will not be used in developing countries in the course of time (because of the health hazards). Nevertheless, galvanized iron canaletas (eg produced in Mexico) are a

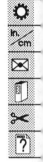

good alternative, and continued fibre concrete research will hopefully bring forth an equally good alternative to asbestos cement.
• Space frame roofs, consisting of three-dimensionally triangulated supporting members, are especially suited for large span roofs. They have great lateral rigidity and require only light roof decking.

Placing a Canaleta roof in Tegucigalpa, Honduras, 1967: rapid installation by unskilled labour (Photo: Alvaro Ortega, who developed this roofing system).

Sloped roofs

• These can be single pitched, gabled and hipped roofs, either of monolithic slabs or sheets or with a system of rafters, purlins, trusses or space frames.
• Sloped roofs are more common in predominantly warm humid regions with significant rainfall.
• Low pitches are cheaper, requiring less wall construction material and less roofing material (smaller roof surface), but suction forces are strongest at 10° pitch. In hurricane areas, minimum roof slopes should be 30° (about 1 : 1.7 or 58 %) and wide overhangs (needed for shading and rain protection) should be avoided.

- Gabled roofs leave end walls exposed; hipped roofs protect all walls, save on wall area and costs, are less susceptible to wind damage, but are more difficult to construct.
- Roofs of courtyard houses should slope inwards for better indoor climate and to facilitate rainwater collection.
- Although roof slopes are often given in degrees, angles are difficult to measure out on the site. Therefore, roof slopes should be expressed in simple relations between height and span (eg 1 : 1; 1 : 2.5; 1 : 10), preferably in round numbers.
- As the main function of roof slopes is to drain off rainwater, the lower the permeability of the roofing material, the less slope is required. Each material therefore has its own appropriate pitch, as shown in the following table.

Roof covering material	Minimum slope required	
	Ratio	Angle
Grass thatching	1 : 1	45°
Timber shingles:		
- untreated timber	1 : 1	45°
- pressure impregnated timber	1 : 1.5	33°
Burnt clay and fibre concrete roof tiles:		
- plain tiles and Spanish type	1 : 1.5	33°
- Roman type (without waterproofing membrane)	1 : 2	26°
- Roman type (with waterproofing membrane)	1 : 3	18°
Corrugated galvanized iron sheets:		
- with end laps (ie more than one sheet in direction of fall)	1 : 3	18°
- with no end laps (ie one sheet between ridge and eaves)	1 : 5	11°
Canaletas (troughed elements, with no end laps)	1 : 10	05°

Curved roofs

- These include vaults, domes, bow-string or shell structures, lightweight tensile roofs and a variety of more sophisticated types.
- Vaults and dome-shaped roofs are common in hot dry climates: the curved surface area being considerably larger than the base, receives less solar heat per unit area, thus lowering surface temperatures and facilitating reradiation after sunset. However, the acoustics inside domes can be very unsatisfactory.
- Masonry vaults and domes are likely to fail in earthquakes, while bow-string and concrete shell structures can easily withstand such hazards.
- Tensile roofs, using a system of tough membranes on cables or ropes, can cover wide spans, are relatively economical, but aerodynamically unstable with light deck, and are therefore generally used for temporary structures.

Roofs for Warm Humid Climates

• Sloped roofs with wide overhanging eaves are ideal to facilitate rapid rainwater run-off and to protect and shade outer walls and openings. Horizontal valley and internal gutters should be avoided, as these accumulate dirt and water.
• Flat roofs with good drainage are common in composite and upland climates with warm dry seasons, which permit activities and sleeping on roofs.
• Primary requirements for roofing materials (supporting structure and cladding): low thermal capacity (to avoid heat build-up, which cannot be dissipated at night, since there is no temperature drop); resistance to rain penetration, yet permeable enough to absorb moisture (eg water vapour, condensation) and release it when the air is drier; resistance to fungus, insects, rodents and solar radiation; good reflectivity (to reduce heat load and thermal movements); resistance to impact (hailstones, dropping coconuts, vandalism, etc.); resistance to temperature and moisture fluctuations; freedom from toxic materials (especially if rainwater is collected from roofs).
• Ventilated (double-layered) roofs are most effective in providing good indoor living conditions: the outer layer shades the inner building enclosure (reducing heat accumulation); any heat that builds up between the two layers is carried away by cross-ventilation; the difference between temperatures in the building interior and the ventilated air space is not so large as to cause condensation problems; any rain or moisture that penetrates through or develops beneath the outer skin evaporates or drips along the inner surface to the eaves, so that the inner roof layer remains unaffected.
• Waterproofing with an impermeable membrane can be unsuitable, since water vapour cannot escape and causes condensation.
• Insulating materials prevent release of heat during nights.
• Openings at the ridge (sloped roofs), or just below the suspended ceiling or flat roof, help to discharge accumulated heat.
• Measures for sound absorption should be considered, as tropical downpours can cause unbearable noise.

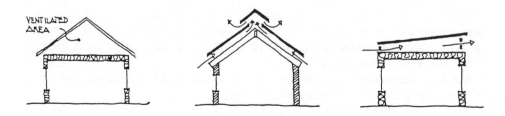

Examples of ventilated roofs (from Bibl. 00.51)

HOT-DRY CLIMATE

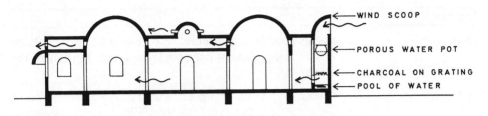

← WIND SCOOP

← POROUS WATER POT

← CHARCOAL ON GRATING
← POOL OF WATER

Roofs for Hot Dry Climates

• As rainwater run-off is no major requirement, flat roofs are most common, providing space for outdoor activities and sleeping.
• Vaults and dome shaped roofs are also common, providing good thermal comfort.
• Primary requirements for roofing materials (supporting structure and cladding): high thermal capacity (to absorb solar heat during the day and release it during the night, when the temperature drops considerably); good reflectivity (to reduce heat load and thermal movements); resistance to embrittlement (caused by repeated cycles of heating and cooling) and abrasion (caused by wind-blown sand); smooth surfaces to prevent collection of sand and dust.
• Double layered roofs (with sufficient air space to dissipate hot air and with the upper surfaces of each layer designed to reflect heat) can be of lightweight, low thermal capacity materials, whereby the outer layer can be of insulating material.
• Wind catchers (towers with openings facing the main direction of wind) are advantageous to redirect higher level breezes into the building.

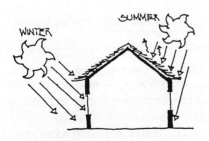

In some regions it is desirable to exclude the sun during the summer and to use the solar radiation for room heating through windows during winter. This effect can be obtained with an appropriate roof overhang. Its dimension depends on the angle of the solar radiation.

Summary of Common Roofing Materials

Material	Characteristics
Earth	Cheap; good thermal qualities; heavy construction; suitable for houses in dry climates only; not recommended in earthquake areas.
Stabilized soil tiles	Cheap; easy handling; light construction; local production of tiles; resistance to rain only effective with "over"-stabilization, thus forfeiting its economic advantage; medium resistance to hurricanes.
Burnt clay tiles	Medium costs; easy handling; light construction; good resistance to rain and hurricanes; however, tile production consumes a great deal of energy.
Reinforced concrete	Expensive; strong, heavy construction; suitable for most climates; resistant to most natural hazards; but limited availability and high cost of cement makes it less recommended for single-storey low-cost housing.
Fibre concrete roofing sheets and pantiles	Low to medium costs; promising material for village production; good thermal qualities and resistance to rain and hurricanes.
Corrugated iron sheets	Medium costs; easy handling and transport; good rain resistance; bad thermal and acoustical qualities; good for earthquake areas; good resistance to termites and fungus.
Bamboo	Low to medium costs; easy handling; good rain resistance; good for earthquake areas; low resistance to hurricanes; easily attacked by biological agents and fire.
Thatch	Cheap; easy handling; rapid decay; harbours insects; presents fire hazard.

Grass roofs (soil roofs with growing grass cover), which are becoming popular in some industrialized countries, have several advantages: use of natural, local material; maintenance of moderate outdoor and indoor micro-climate (balance of moisture and temperature); generation of oxygen and humidity; high stability through root reinforcement; good sound absorption. In hot climates, problems may arise in the dry season, requiring watering of roofs to maintain growth, and the roofs are likely to attract insects and small animals, which can be harmful to people. Research is needed to find acceptable solutions.

BUILDING SYSTEMS

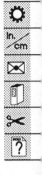

General

Building systems are generally understood as industrialized building methods, which involve a high degree of prefabrication, in order to reduce site work to a minimum. Further advantages are:
- reduced number of materials and components,
- reduced volume of materials and less wastage,
- simplified construction details and assembly procedures,
- greater accuracy and speed of construction.

In industrialized countries, in which these systems were developed and have reached a high degree of perfection, there is the additional advantage of reduced manpower, incurring lower labour costs and consequently lower costs of construction. This is rarely an advantage in developing countries, where labour costs are lower and the aim is to create more employment. Furthermore, the high capital input, quite often requiring imported machinery and equipment, makes industrialized production methods more expensive than conventional constructions (Bibl. 00.34).

There are, however, circumstances in developing countries in which industrialized systems are justified, for instance, in emergency housing and building in remote places. But, on the whole, complete systems of prefabrication will continue to be the exception rather than the rule in low-cost construction, while there is great potential in the development of partial prefabrication, dimensional coordination and simplification of procedures for the provision of higher standard constructions at greater speed and lower costs.

Complete rejection of industrialized systems is as short-sighted as the total disregard of traditional construction methods. Promising innovative solutions for developing countries always lie somewhere in between, as for example, fibre concrete roofing and the use of cement replacement materials produced from industrial and agricultural wastes.

Examples of Building Systems

In this book, the term "Building Systems" is dealt with in a broader sense. The section on *Examples of Building Systems* includes construction methods, in which the degree of prefabrication differs greatly, as well as traditional, conventional and innovative methods, in which the inherent qualities of a single material are well demonstrated.

Hence, the examples show systems with different objectives:
- systems that utilize only one material for the whole building,
- systems that improve accuracy and speed of construction,
- systems that combine the advantages of industrially produced components and those of traditional materials,
- systems that provide special protection against natural hazards,
- systems that utilize waste materials as alternatives to conventional ones.

A great number of other interesting examples could also be included, but the choice was governed mainly by the availability of information and the attempt to cover a wide range of materials and building techniques.

FUNDAMENTAL INFORMATION
ON
PROTECTIVE MEASURES

BIOLOGICAL AGENTS

General

Biological agents that can cause problems in buildings are:
• insects (termites, borer beetles, triatomine bugs, cockroaches, mosquitos, flies, etc.), which either attack and destroy building materials (such as timber, bamboo, some plastics, etc.), represent a health hazard or are simply a nuisance to the occupants;
• animals (rats, bats, birds, snakes, etc.), which can nest in uncontrolled cavities, and can not only create health problems and disturb occupants, but also restrict important functions of the building, for example, by building nests which block ventilation openings or clog drains;
• fungi (moulds, stains, rots, etc.), which develop in moist dark conditions on timber and other vegetable building materials, some fungi being non-destructive (blue stain), while others (dry rot, wet rot) lead to decay and destruction.

Many methods of protecting buildings and occupants against these agents exist, but some protective measures can create new problems, if implemented without sufficient care and consideration of the consequences. Good building design and use of materials should always be considered before resorting to using chemicals, which can destroy fungi, insects, rats, pets, children ....

Protective Measures

Insects

• Maintenance of clean conditions on the building site is vital, as dense vegetation, debris, dirt and moisture provide ideal environments for biological agents to thrive in. If termite colonies are found in the vicinity, the use of vegetable building materials should be avoided as far as possible, or used only for non-structural components.
• Good drainage of the site is essential, to avoid moist conditions (which attract insects) and standing water (in which mosquitos breed).
• Soil poisoning below and around buildings is advocated in most publications, but it should be remembered that the poison will sooner or later be washed into the ground water, losing its protective effect against termites, but contaminating drinking water supplies.
• A continuous reinforced concrete floor slab under the entire building can effectively keep out subterranean termites. If joints are necessary, these should be rough and sloping or tongue and groove joints.
• Termite shields fixed continuously around the base of the building, V-shaped grooves (45° angle) and metal caps projecting 5 - 8 cm around pipes and columns, provide sharp

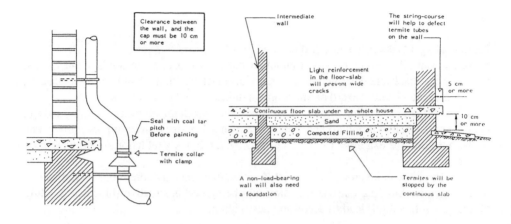

Protective measures against termites (T. Søe, Bibl. 25.12)

corners, around which termite tunnels cannot be built. These are also visible barriers that help to detect the development of tunnels, which can then be destroyed.

• Buildings raised 80 - 100 cm off the ground on poles or columns (not continuous footing wall) permit visual inspections underneath the floor (to keep away termites and other insects, and maintain clean conditions), and also facilitate ventilation (keeping the floor dry). Exposed foundations and columns should be painted in a light colour to help detect termite galleries easily from a distance.

• Foundations and floor slabs must be constructed with great care to avoid the development of cracks through differential settling. Cracks can also develop due to drying shrinkage, thermal and mechanical stresses, or bad quality materials and workmanship, and these should be carefully sealed, especially in walls, to avoid nesting of insects, such as triatomine bugs, which are responsible for the Chagas disease (an illness from which more than 20 million people in the rural areas of Latin America are suffering).

• Certain timber and bamboo species have a natural resistance to insect attack, and should be used wherever possible. However, these species are usually rare and expensive, so that less resistant species are mostly in use. Hence proper seasoning and some form of chemical treatment is necessary to avoid early deterioration. (Please refer to the sections on *Bamboo* and *Timber*.) Under no circumstance should bamboo or timber components be embedded in the ground.

• Mosquitos, flies, flying termites, and numerous other insects can be kept out of buildings by covering all openings with fine wire mesh, but this also causes a reduction of cross ventilation.

• New methods of termite control by natural means are being investigated in the Federal Republic of Germany (Bibl. 25.12): by special cross-breeding and elimination of the reproductive capacity of termites; by producing sexual hormones to disorient the termites or alarming pheromones and repellents to start a reaction of escape; by subjecting termites to certain toxic fungi (effective only in the first 3 weeks of the fungus' life). However, these biotechnical and microbiological methods still present problems that warrant extensive research.

Animals

• Rats and mice are eliminated by depriving them of nesting places and every possible source of food. Rubbish heaps, piles of stone or wood, tall grass, etc. should be removed.
• Food stores can be made rat-proof if the entrance is high enough above the ground and thus inaccessible to rats. Metal sheet strips about 30 cm wide, running parallel to and 60 cm above the ground, prevent rats from climbing up walls. Metal termite caps, projecting farther outwards (about 20 cm), prevent them from climbing up columns and pipes.

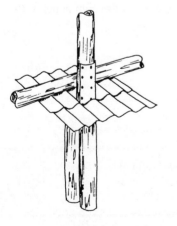

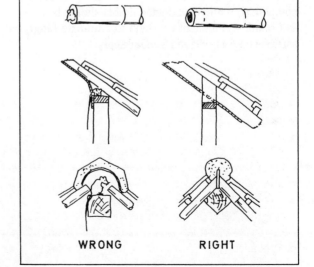

WRONG   RIGHT

A simple ratguard (Bibl. 25.08)   Prevention of rat nesting (Bibl. 13.13)

- Concrete floor slabs prevent animals from gaining access to the building from below.
- Birds and bats, which nest under roofs or in cavities, and snakes and other animals that can enter through ventilation slots and pipes, are kept out by covering all openings with a wire mesh.
- In general, smooth, hard surfaces, clean conditions and regular inspections are very effective in keeping a place free from pests.

Fungi

- Fungi are simple plants which cannot produce their own food from air, water and sunlight, but live on dead organic matter (timber, bamboo, etc.) located in damp, dark, warm and poorly ventilated places. Therefore, the best protection against fungi is to maintain clean, dry, light and well ventilated conditions. Moisture contents of timber should be less than 20 % (achieved by proper seasoning).
- Temperatures below 0° C (unrealistic in the tropics) and above 40° C also prevent fungal growth, as well as complete submersion in water.
- Designs with timber and other vegetable material should ensure quick drainage of water and avoidance of direct contact with concrete or masonry (achieved by placing a damp-proof membrane to separate the materials).
- Timber, affected by dry rot, should preferably be replaced by a fresh, unaffected component, while the affected timber should be burnt.
- Chemical treatment can help to eliminate fungi, but here again the comments in the sections on *Bamboo* and *Timber* apply.

FIRE

General

Fire is a chemical reaction which takes place when a combustible material is heated in the presence of oxygen. The liquid or solid fuel gives off vapour when heated and burns as flame.

The surface area of a material relative to its volume and density is a major criterium of its ability to burn. Thick, solid material is relatively difficult to ignite and burns only at or near the surface. Thin sheets burn rapidly, while finely divided or pulverized material can become explosive when suspended in air.

Fires can break out in buildings by accident (eg when cooking on open fires, as is common in many developing countries), by self-ignition (eg by the discharge of sparks due to friction between materials in very dry conditions, or by concentration of the sun's rays by the lens effect of some glasses), or by natural hazards (eg lightning, or earthquakes).

The damaging effects of fires in buildings depends on the materials used and the design and construction of the building. Some materials merely shrink and crack, while others may expand, melt or disintegrate causing total destruction. Lives are endangered by burns, collapsing walls and roofs, inhalation of toxic gases and smoke, panic and loss of sensibility and vision.

In hot arid zones, houses are normally built with thick, heavy materials, which do not readily ignite. In warm humid zones, combustible materials are commonly used, but humidity and rainfall can have the same effect. Nevertheless, there is always a fire risk in all climatic zones, and must be taken into consideration in all building designs.

Protective Measures

• With regard to planning in warm humid zones, where buildings are generally placed well apart for good cross-ventilation, care must also be taken to maintain a good distance between buildings in the direction of the prevailing winds, to avoid spreading of fire from one house to another.
• Climatically appropriate design in hot dry zones calls for close spacing of buildings, but sufficiently wide escape lanes and access roads for fire-fighting vehicles are essential.
• Combustible building elements should not be used closer than 1 metre to potential sources of fire (stoves, chimneys, etc.); similarly combustible materials stored in and around the house must be shielded from such sources by means of non-combustible materials (eg gypsum, glass, bricks, concrete, metals, stones, mineral wool).

- The design of cavities should take into consideration that they can act as flues, spreading fires rapidly.
- Chemical treatment of timbers and other vegetable products is possible (mainly impregnation with borax compounds), but expensive, and complete resistance is never achieved.
- A fire retardant thatch roof construction has been developed by CBRI, Roorkee in India: a non-erodable bitumen stabilized mud plaster is applied on the upper surface and the drying shrinkage cracks sealed with a slurry of soil and cow dung mixed with a small proportion of bitumen cutback. In this way the dense covering layer stops the passage of air and retards ignition for at least one hour. As an additional advantage, the roof is waterproof.
- As a general precautionary measure, it is advisable to have a water reservoir, hose pipe and pump, and/or hand fire-extinguishers close by.

Combustible and non-combustible materials (from Bibl. 00.14)

Combustible	Non-combustible
- Timber (even if impregnated with flame retardant)	- Asbestos-cement products
- Fibre building boards (even if impregnated with flame retardant)	- Fibre concrete products
- Cork	- Gypsum plaster
- Wood-wool slabs	- Glass
- Compressed straw slabs	- Glass wool (containing not more than 4 - 5 % bonding agent)
- Gypsum plaster board (rendered combustible by the paper liner)	- Bricks
- Bitumen felts (including asbestos fibre-based felt)	- Stones
- Glass wool or mineral wool with combustible bonding agent or covering	- Concretes
- Bitumen protected metal sheet	- Metals
- All plastics and rubbers	- Vermiculite
	- Mineral wool

WIND AND RAIN

General

The hazards dealt with in this section are principally of three types:
- Sand and dust
- Tropical downpours
- Cyclonic storms

Sand and dust

- These are common hazards in hot dry regions, capable of causing problems of durability of building components and great discomfort for the dwellers.
- Continuous attack by wind-blown sand causes abrasion of materials and dulling of surfaces; sand and dust can enter buildings through cracks and gaps between materials; accumulation of sand in parts of buildings can be a nuisance, but also a hazard, if loads increase on weak components; rainfall mixed with sand and dust can produce a messy sludge.
- Under normal conditions sand particles roll or bounce on hard surfaces to heights between 1 and 1.5 metres, while dust can be carried to any altitude in the earth's atmosphere.

Tropical downpours

- These can occur suddenly and with great intensity, producing floods in a very short time.
- Heavy rains in the tropics can loosen and dislocate building components; cause breakage and penetration of water; wash off coatings, insecticides and fungicides; create unbearable noise on some types of roofs.
- Inundation of buildings causes people to seek refuge on the roofs, which can collapse under the extra load.
- The softening of soils and exposure of foundations can cause severe building damages.
- Rain penetration in buildings can encourage fungal growth and corrosion of metals.

Cyclonic storms

- These storms, commonly called hurricanes (in Atlantic and Caribbean regions), typhoons (in the Pacific region) or tornados (in all inland regions), can reach wind speeds exceeding 300 km per hour. Hurricanes and typhoons are generally accompanied by torrential rains and, since they occur mainly in coastal and island regions, create storm surges, which send seawater several kilometres inland, causing floods and destruction.

• The high wind pressures affect all parts of the building, so that light structures are the most vulnerable. Roofs with slopes less than 30° can be torn off by the high negative pressure (suction) on the leeward side.
• Flying debris also cause considerable destruction; due to the lashing rain, water penetrates unprotected parts of buildings; components get dislodged and are washed away; trees, power transmission poles, chimneys, etc., fall on houses and people; and a number of other effects of tropical cyclones can account for thousands of deaths and total devastation.

Protective Measures

Sand and dust

• Wind-blown sand is effectively excluded by surrounding houses with sand barriers (eg masonry walls) of at least 1.60 m height. Better still are houses with completely enclosed courtyards, whereby the outer walls have no openings, or just small ones located at a high level.
• Vegetation around houses can greatly reduce the amount of flying sand and dust. Narrow, zig-zag streets with high walls on either side have a similar effect.
• Projecting components and cavities should be avoided on outer walls to prevent accumulation of sand and dust. Surfaces should be smooth and resistant to abrasion.

Tropical downpours

• The siting of buildings should facilitate quick drainage of water. Houses raised well above the ground surface and drainage channels surrounding them are important.
• Wide overhanging sloped roofs are required to protect outer walls and openings, and discharge the rainwater at a sufficient distance from the wall base, avoiding dirt and erosion by splashing water.
• Tight, waterproof joints and water-resistant materials or surface treatments are essential to avoid rainwater penetration. Facilities for cross-ventilation to remove indoor moisture are equally important.
• Insecticides and fungicides applied externally can be washed out, losing their function, but contaminating the surroundings; hence they should be used with great care or avoided, if possible.
• Metal connectors and components that can corrode should be protected from rainwater and well ventilated to prevent moisture retention.

• To prevent noise problems on sheet metal roofs, shorter spans between supports, bitumen coating on the underside of sheets, rubber washers at the suspension points, and an insulating layer or suspended ceiling, all contribute towards noise reduction, and are effective in combination with each other. Quite often layers of straw are placed on the roof, but must be tied down, as winds can blow them off.

• In flood prone areas, roofs must be especially strong to carry the load of dwellers seeking refuge. Provision of storage space just under the roof and openings for trapped air to escape are further useful measures. House constructions that permit the house to float on flood water can avoid a lot of damage, providing it is anchored at the same spot.

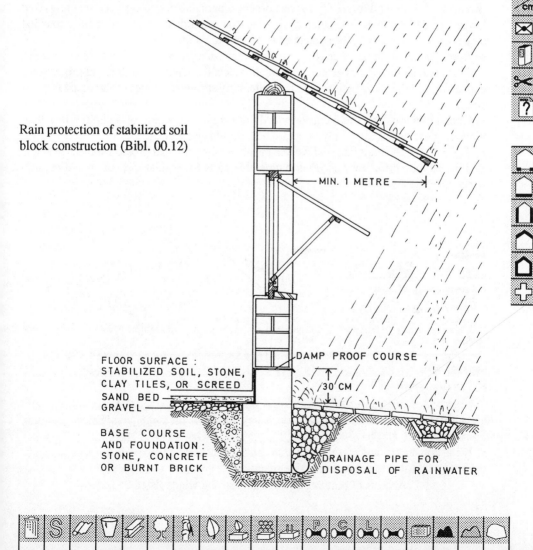

Rain protection of stabilized soil block construction (Bibl. 00.12)

MIN. 1 METRE

DAMP PROOF COURSE

FLOOR SURFACE :
STABILIZED SOIL, STONE,
CLAY TILES, OR SCREED
SAND BED
GRAVEL

30 CM

BASE COURSE
AND FOUNDATION :
STONE, CONCRETE
OR BURNT BRICK

DRAINAGE PIPE FOR
DISPOSAL OF RAINWATER

Cyclonic storms

• Building sites should preferably be at higher levels, sufficiently distant from the sea shore, and topographies or the surrounding buildings should not cause a funnel effect or increase wind velocities. Clusters of trees act as natural wind-breaks.

• Foundations should be generously dimensioned and wide at the base to resist uplifting forces or tilting due to pressure from the side. Connections between foundations and walls or columns need to be exceptionally strong.

• Stability is increased by division of floor plans into smaller rooms, the walls being strong enough to resist lateral forces (eg strong corners, diagonal bracing, etc.) and securely fixed to the foundations and roof; outer walls should be smooth and streamlined (eg rounded corners, no projections) to provide least resistance to winds.

• Roofs should be sloped at least 30°, to reduce the danger of lift-off; for the same reason, wide overhangs must be avoided (which contradicts the requirement for rain protection); connections to the substructure must be particularly strong and rigid, as forces act from all sides.

• Openings should be small and provided with shutters (folding or sliding, rather than hinged); glass panes, especially thin varieties, should be avoided.

• In general, good materials and workmanship are the principal protective measures, and designs should permit easy access to vulnerable parts for regular inspection and maintenance.

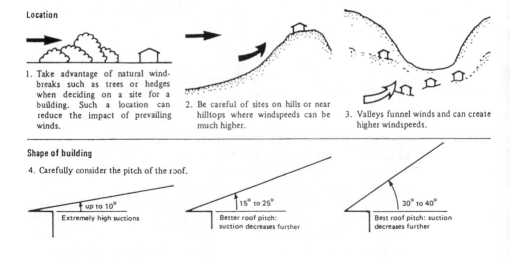

Location

1. Take advantage of natural wind-breaks such as trees or hedges when deciding on a site for a building. Such a location can reduce the impact of prevailing winds.

2. Be careful of sites on hills or near hilltops where windspeeds can be much higher.

3. Valleys funnel winds and can create higher windspeeds.

Shape of building

4. Carefully consider the pitch of the roof.

up to 10°
Extremely high suctions

15° to 25°
Better roof pitch: suction decreases further

30° to 40°
Best roof pitch: suction decreases further

Aspects of building to withstand strong winds (Bibl. 25.06)

EARTHQUAKES

General

Of all natural disasters, earthquakes cause the greatest amount of death and destruction. They generally occur without any warning and, depending on their intensity, can within a few seconds turn a prosperous town into a pile of rubble.

There are several causes for seismic tremors, the main cause being the movement of large continental plates (a few millimetres per year), which collide, move apart or rub against each other, building up immense tension within the rock formations, which at a certain point readjust themselves with a sudden violent motion, sending out seismic waves in all directions. Another cause is the leaking out of molten magma through faults in the earth's crust, which can happen deep beneath the sea or in the form of volcanic eruption. Quakes beneath the sea give rise to tsunamis (Japanese name for seismic sea waves), which can cause total devastation in coastal areas. Volcanic eruptions affect a comparatively small area and damage is mainly caused by molten lava and ash descending on houses and fields.

Artificial causes of earthquakes have recently resulted from the construction of dams, where the large water reservoirs exert great pressure on the earth's crust and lubricate faults, which release the pressure in seismic waves. The exploitation of oil and gas deposits disrupts the balance of pressures and thus can also lead to seismic tremors.

These causes make certain regions more prone to earthquakes than other areas, but exact forecasts of time and intensity are not possible so far. Special measures to minimize damage to lives and property are recommended in these regions, but complete safety cannot be achieved.

Seismic waves comprise horizontal, vertical and torsional (twisting) movements acting simultaneously. Weak, non-elastic components break apart or disintegrate; elastic materials vibrate and absorb the tremors; while tough and rigid materials can remain unaffected. Destruction of buildings mainly begins with walls falling apart; the ceilings and roofs, lacking support, follow suit, burying the dwellers and property beneath them. However, far greater damage results from secondary effects of earthquakes, such as fire, landslides, damburst, epidemics, etc. A series of smaller tremors follow major earthquakes and can lead to further collapse of buildings, greatly complicating rescue work.

The greatest casualties occur where the population is poorest and houses are built with cheap, sub-standard materials and methods, on dangerous sites, such as slopes, sea shores, valleys below dams, etc. Earthquakes of comparable intensities cause far less destruction and deaths in industrialized countries and rich areas of Third World cities, than in the poor rural areas and slums of developing countries. Hence, earthquakes are often called "classquakes".

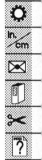

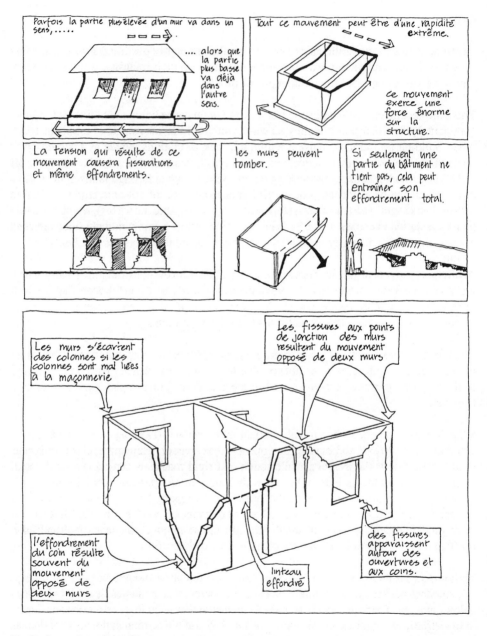

Typical earthquake effects and damage (drawings by John Norton, Bibl. 25.10)

Protective Measures

• Building sites should not be on or close to hillsides (danger of landslides, avalanches), or near the sea (risk of tsunamis); sufficient distance from neighbouring structures (danger of collapse), especially in prevailing wind direction (fire risk), and downstream from reservoirs (danger of dam-burst) should be maintained. Filled ditches and watercourses should be avoided.

• Building forms must be simple and symmetrical (both horizontally and vertically); complicated forms are possible, if subdivided into independent, simple components.

• Foundations should be of reinforced concrete, constructed on solid ground (preferably rock), maintaining uniform depths (no stepping on sloping ground) and having continuous reinforcement. On poor soils, strong slab foundations have the advantage of "floating" on seismic waves, thus avoiding damage.

• Walls should be relatively light (to lower the centre of gravity of the building and reduce the damaging effects of collapsing walls), capable of absorbing vibrations, but with rigid connections to foundations, adjoining walls and roof. Frame structures (timber, bamboo, reinforced concrete, metal) with light infill walls are most resistant to earthquakes; conventional masonry structures require a strong, continuous ring beam on top of the walls, to prevent them from falling apart.

• Openings should be small, not less than 50 cm from corners or other openings; glass panes should be avoided.

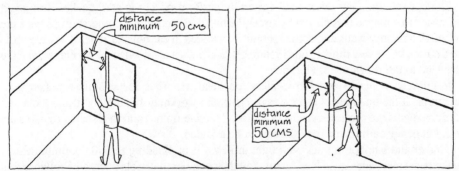

• Roofs should be as light as possible, either monolithic (with high tensile strength, eg reinforced concrete), or of strong, flexible members, firmly tied to the supporting structure; compact symmetrical shapes with spans as small as possible. Roofs must be securely fixed to the ring beam or building frame. Alternatively, roofs can be fixed to independent supports, structurally separated from the walls, which, in the event of failure, would not cause the roof also to collapse.

• Appendages (eg parapets, chimneys, water tanks), if they cannot be omitted, should be very securely fixed, to avoid their being shaken off.

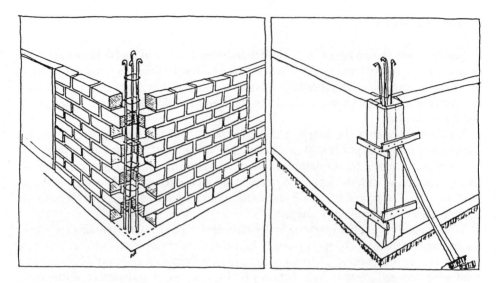

Strengthening of masonry walls with reinforced concrete (Bibl. 25.10)

• Stone, earth and clay brick walls generally perform poorly in earthquakes. Improved resistance to collapse is achieved by strengthening and reinforcing corners; ring beams are essential. Masonry walls and domes should be avoided in earthquake zones. Clay tile roofs need strong and heavy timber substructures, which are a hazard when they collapse, and the tiles tend to fall down under vibration.

• Reinforced concrete and ferrocement are ideal materials for seismic resistant constructions, if the qualities of cement, aggregate and workmanship are good, and the metal reinforcements are protected from corrosion. Concrete frames and thin shell structures are best, but heavy ceiling and roof slabs must be avoided.

• Timber and bamboo frames with light infill walls or cladding provide optimum earthquake resistance, and cause less destruction than heavier materials in case of collapse, but represent a fire hazard, which is of significance during earthquakes (due to breakage of chimneys, power and gas supply lines, etc.). Protection against biological hazards is essential to avoid weakening of the construction.

• Metal frames permit light, flexible constructions, but design and dimensioning should take into account the risk of buckling; fire protection and good resistance to corrosion are essential. Metal sheet roofs generally perform well in earthquakes.

• General precautionary measures are in all cases good workmanship and regular inspections of critical parts for maintenance and repairs; also all protective measures against fire.

EXAMPLES
OF
FOUNDATION MATERIALS

NATURAL STONE FOUNDATIONS

KEYWORDS:

Special properties	Suitable where concrete is expensive
Economical aspects	Low cost
Stability	Good
Skills required	Skilled labour
Equipment required	Masonry equipment
Resistance to earthquake	Medium to good; depends on overall design
Resistance to hurricane	Good
Resistance to rain	Good
Resistance to insects	Very good
Climatic suitability	All climates
Stage of experience	Widely used

SHORT DESCRIPTION:

• Stone foundations are made of rubble (undressed stone) or squared stone; similar construction is possible with broken brick and concrete from demolished buildings.
• The quality of mortar is of importance to achieve good strength. An example of a good mix is:
- 4 parts cement
- 1 part lime
- 12 parts clean sand
- sufficient water to make a workable mix.
• Construction should start on firm, uniform strong subsoil. It should not be started on grass, black fertile soil, filled up materials or mud.
• Under the foundation there should be a layer of lean concrete (min. 5 cm) or tamped sand; minimum depth 40 cm.
• In earthquake areas, reinforcement with wire mesh or steel rods is required, but professional advice should be sought.
Further information: Bibl. 01.01, 01.05, 01.06, 20.05.

Stone in Earth Mortar (from Vorhauer, Bibl. 20.05)

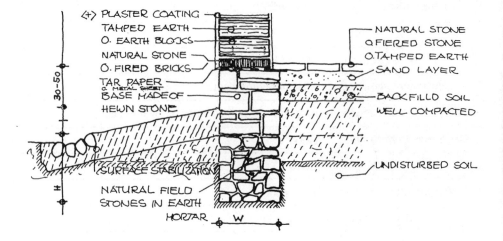

(+) PLASTER COATING
TAMPED EARTH
O. EARTH BLOCKS
NATURAL STONE
O. FIRED BRICKS
TAR PAPER
O. METAL SHEET
BASE MADE OF
HEWN STONE

NATURAL STONE
O FIERED STONE
O.TAMPED EARTH
SAND LAYER
BACKFILLD SOIL
WELL COMPACTED

30-50

SURFACE STABILIZATION
NATURAL FIELD
STONES IN EARTH
MORTAR

UNDISTURBED SOIL

W

Stone in Cement Mortar (Bibl. 20.05)

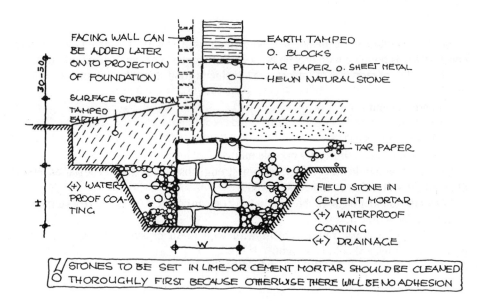

FACING WALL CAN
BE ADDED LATER
ONTO PROJECTION
OF FOUNDATION

SURFACE STABILIZATION
TAMPED
EARTH

30-50

EARTH TAMPED
O. BLOCKS
TAR PAPER O. SHEET METAL
HEWN NATURAL STONE

TAR PAPER

(+) WATER
PROOF COA-
TING

FIELD STONE IN
CEMENT MORTAR
(+) WATERPROOF
COATING
(+) DRAINAGE

W

STONES TO BE SET IN LIME-OR CEMENT MORTAR SHOULD BE CLEANED
THOROUGHLY FIRST BECAUSE OTHERWISE THERE WILL BE NO ADHESION

KEYWORDS:

Special properties	Only used for earth constructions on dry sites
Economical aspects	Low cost
Stability	Poor to medium
Skills required	Semi-skilled labour
Equipment required	Excavation and tamping equipment
Resistance to earthquake	Low
Resistance to hurricane	Low
Resistance to rain	Low
Resistance to insects	Low
Climatic suitability	Only very dry climates
Stage of experience	Traditional method

SHORT DESCRIPTION:

• Rammed earth foundations are made of well graded soil, preferably with a stabilizer for water resistance and higher strength.

• The site must be well drained and great care is needed to protect the foundation from ground moisture, especially with a plastic foil or bitumen felt. Bitumen paint, or a facing of rubble stone or burnt bricks are alternatives.

• When in doubt about suitability of rammed earth foundations, they should not be used. Stabilized soil blocks can be used instead, but similar protective measures are necessary.

• Wherever possible, the earth foundation should be placed on a concrete footing.

• The foundation is made in formwork, in the same way as the walls: layers of 10 cm soil are tamped down to 6 - 7 cm, before the next layer is filled up.

Further information: Bibl. 02.06, 02.08, 02.19, 02.32, 20.05.

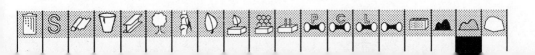

Procedure of Constructing a Rammed Earth Foundation (Bibl. 20.05)

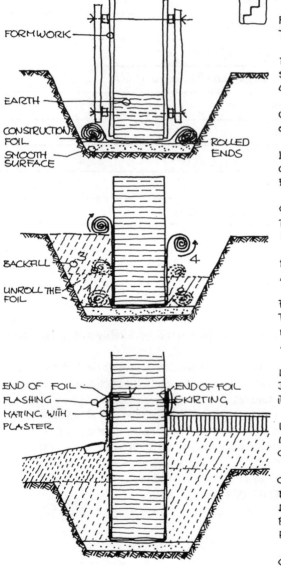

FORMWORK

EARTH

CONSTRUCTION FOIL

SMOOTH SURFACE

ROLLED ENDS

BACKFILL

UNROLL THE FOIL

END OF FOIL

FLASHING

MATTING WITH PLASTER

END OF FOIL

SKIRTING

REMOVE THE TOPSOIL TO BEARING GROUND

PLACE A THIN LAYER OF SAND OR EARTH ON THE GROUND TO SMOOTH IT

CUT THE CORNER PIECES OF THE FOIL

LAY THE FOIL ON THE GROUND FOLLOWING THE FOUNDATION LINE

OVERLAPP THE SINGLE PIECES TO GET IT WATERPPOOF > 20 CM

PROTECT THE ROLLED ENDS AGAINST DAMAGE

PLACE THE FORMWORK ON THE FOIL. PLACE THE EARTH IN LAYERS IN THE FORMWORK AND TAMP IT. O. EARTH BLOCKS

LET THE EARTH FOUNDATION DRY OUT WELL — PROTECT IT AGAINST RAIN

UNROLL THE FOIL, BACKFILL IN LAYERS, PRESS THE FOIL CAREFULLY TO THE WALL

ON THE OUTSIDE, FASTEN THE END OF THE FOIL UNDER A DRIP DEFLECTION STRIP AND PROTECT IT WITH MATTING AND PLASTER.

ON THE INSIDE, NAIL THE END OF THE FOIL TO THE WALL UNDER THE SKIRTING

BURNT BRICK FOUNDATIONS

KEYWORDS:

Special properties	Good alternative to concrete foundation
Economical aspects	Medium cost
Stability	Medium to good
Skills required	Masonry skills
Equipment required	Masonry equipment
Resistance to earthquake	Medium to good
Resistance to hurricane	Medium to good
Resistance to rain	Good
Resistance to insects	Good
Climatic suitability	Most climates, except consistently wet areas
Stage of experience	Widely used

SHORT DESCRIPTION:

• Burnt brick foundations are principally the same as masonry wall constructions, but begun under the ground, either directly on a bed of tamped sand or lean concrete, or on a concrete footing.

• A widened base is preferable to distribute the weight of the walls.

• Care must be taken to lay the bricks in perfectly level courses, and measures for waterproofing are important.

• A good mortar for masonry foundations is:
  - 4 parts cement
  - 1 part lime
  - 12 parts clean sand
  - sufficient water to make a workable mix.

• In earthquake areas, masonry foundations should be reinforced with wire mesh or thin rods. Professional advice should be sought.

Further information: Bibl. 20.04, 20.05.

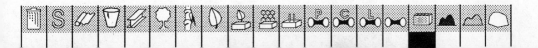

Burnt Bricks in Cement Mortar (Bibl. 20.05)

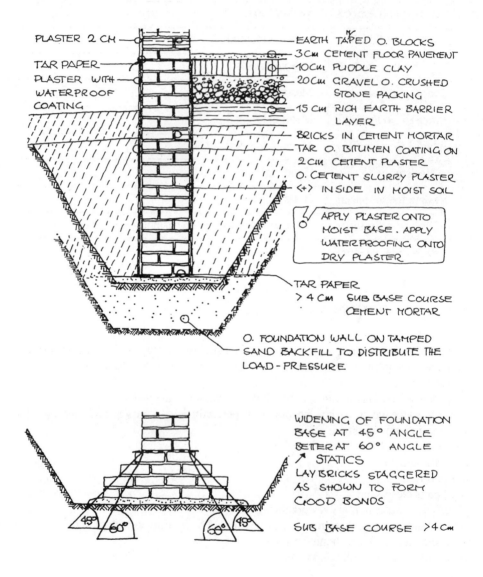

PLASTER 2 CM

TAR PAPER
PLASTER WITH
WATERPROOF
COATING

EARTH TAPED O. BLOCKS
3CM CEMENT FLOOR PAVEMENT
10CM PUDDLE CLAY
20CM GRAVEL O. CRUSHED
STONE PACKING
15 CM RICH EARTH BARRIER
LAYER
BRICKS IN CEMENT MORTAR
TAR O. BITUMEN COATING ON
2CM CEMENT PLASTER
O. CEMENT SLURRY PLASTER
(+) INSIDE IN MOIST SOIL

APPLY PLASTER ONTO
MOIST BASE. APPLY
WATERPROOFING ONTO
DRY PLASTER

TAR PAPER
> 4 CM SUB BASE COURSE
CEMENT MORTAR

O. FOUNDATION WALL ON TAMPED
SAND BACKFILL TO DISTRIBUTE THE
LOAD - PRESSURE

WIDENING OF FOUNDATION
BASE AT 45° ANGLE
BETTER AT 60° ANGLE
↗ STATICS
LAY BRICKS STAGGERED
AS SHOWN TO FORM
GOOD BONDS

SUB BASE COURSE > 4 CM

CONCRETE FOUNDATIONS

KEYWORDS:

Special properties	Strongest foundation
Economical aspects	Expensive
Stability	Very good
Skills required	Skilled labour
Equipment required	Formwork, cement mixer
Resistance to earthquake	Very good
Resistance to hurricane	Very good
Resistance to rain	Very good
Resistance to insects	Very good
Climatic suitability	All climates
Stage of experience	Commonly used worldwide

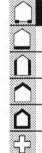

SHORT DESCRIPTION:

• Concrete foundations on hard, uniform ground can be made without steel reinforcement, if not in an earthquake or hurricane prone area.

• All non-uniform and problem soils require reinforced concrete foundations, especially in areas of medium to high rainfall and natural hazard regions.

• Depending on the strengths required, concrete mixes can vary from 1 : 3 : 4 (cement : sand : gravel) to 1 : 4 : 7, the higher proportion of cement being required for reinforced concrete.

• Water contents of fresh mixes should make them just easily workable. Excessive water leaves pores in the concrete, making it weak and water absorbant. Foundation trenches should also be properly wetted to avoid excessive absorption of the water from the mix.

• The concrete should be wet-cured for 3 to 7 days before building the walls. A damp-proof course should be laid between foundation and wall.

Further information: Bibl. 20.03, 20.04, 20.05.

Cast Concrete Foundations (Bibl. 20.05)

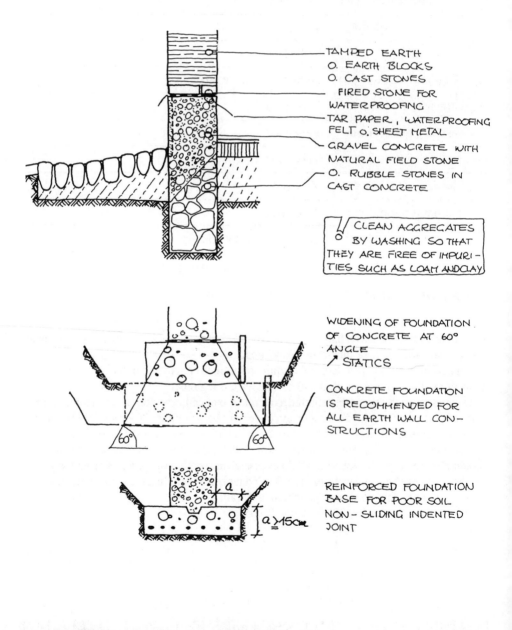

TAMPED EARTH
O. EARTH BLOCKS
O. CAST STONES
FIRED STONE FOR WATERPROOFING
TAR PAPER, WATERPROOFING FELT O. SHEET METAL
GRAVEL CONCRETE WITH NATURAL FIELD STONE
O. RUBBLE STONES IN CAST CONCRETE

CLEAN AGGREGATES BY WASHING SO THAT THEY ARE FREE OF IMPURITIES SUCH AS LOAM AND CLAY

WIDENING OF FOUNDATION OF CONCRETE AT 60° ANGLE
STATICS

CONCRETE FOUNDATION IS RECOMMENDED FOR ALL EARTH WALL CONSTRUCTIONS

60°   60°

REINFORCED FOUNDATION BASE FOR POOR SOIL NON-SLIDING INDENTED JOINT

$a \geqslant 15$cm

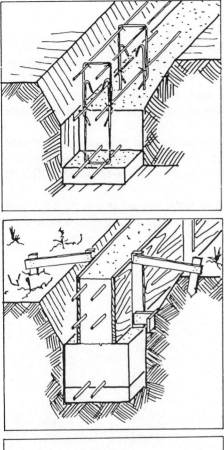

Reinforced Foundations

Placing concrete footing without shuttering: the reinforcement is laid after the lowest course of lean concrete is hardened. The richer second layer holds the reinforcement.

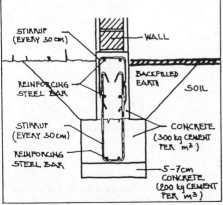

Foundation strip poured into shuttering of wood or plywood. These should be oiled before pouring concrete, to facilitate removal after hardening.

STIRRUP
(EVERY 30 cm) — WALL

REINFORCING
STEEL BAR

BACKFILLED
EARTH

SOIL

STIRRUP
(EVERY 30 cm)

REINFORCING
STEEL BAR

CONCRETE
(300 kg CEMENT
PER m³)

5-7 cm
CONCRETE
(200 kg CEMENT
PER m³)

The finished foundation, with the trench filled up with the previously excavated soil and well compacted.

Foundations on Expansive Clay (Bibl. 20.03)

•   Certain clayey soils respond to moisture movements (in rainy and dry seasons, moisture extraction by trees, etc.) with excessive swelling and shrinkage, which can severely damage foundations and consequently entire buildings.
•   Damage can be avoided by either installing foundations which penetrate through the zone of ground movement, or by constructing foundations and superstructures which are tolerant of ground movement.
•   *Pile-and-beam-foundation*: Small diameter piles are installed below the zone of clay movement; RC ground beams, which span between pile heads are constructed on compressible material (eg expanded polystyrene), which absorbs ground movement without affecting the beams and superstructure.
•   *Pad-and-beam-foundation*: Pads are installed on stable ground below the movement zone; RC columns support ground beams, which are constructed in the same way as in the pile-and-beam-foundation.

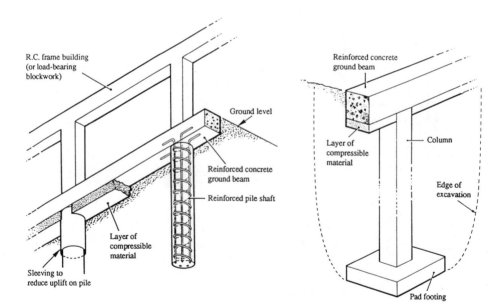

Pile-and-beam-foundation   Pad-and-beam-foundation

SPLIT–BAMBOO PILES

KEYWORDS:

Special properties	Used for subsoil stabilization
Economical aspects	Low cost
Stability	Good
Skills required	Special training
Equipment required	Drop hammer
Resistance to earthquake	Good
Resistance to hurricane	Good
Resistance to rain	Good, helps to drain water
Resistance to insects	Low
Climatic suitability	All tropical areas
Stage of experience	Experimental

SHORT DESCRIPTION:

• Split-bamboo piles have been developed to improve the bearing capacity of soft compressible soils and to reduce settlements for various types of construction works, such as buildings, roads, etc.

• The hollow bamboo culms are filled up with loosely wound coconut coir and jute thread wrapped in jute fabric; holes in the culm permit the water in the soil to trickle in, thus drying out the soil and improving its load-bearing capacity.

Further information: Dr. M.A. Aziz or Dr. S.D. Ramaswamy, Department of Civil Engineering, National University of Singapore, 10 Kent Ridge Cresent, Singapore 0511; Bibl. 20.01.

Split-Bamboo Pile

Split-bamboo piles filled up with loosely wound coconut coir strands of about 6 mm diameter each tied up with spirally wound jute thread along its length and wrapped with a layer of thickly knit jute burlap have been successfully used. Treated split-bamboo strips were holed at random points and tied up together at regular intervals with galvanized iron wire after putting the coconut coir wicks inside along its entire length (Fig. 1).

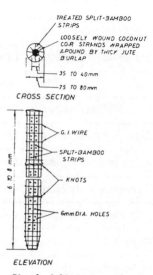

Fig. 1 Split-bamboo piles

Stabilized Area

These specially made split-bamboo piles were used in stabilizing the soft compressible subsoil of an actual construction site (Fig. 2) which consisted of a top layer of about 2 m thick soft to medium stiff sandy clayey silt underlain by a layer of about 6 m thick very soft silty clay which was again underlain by a layer of medium dense silty clayey sand. The split-bamboo piles, each about 8 m long, 80 to 90 mm diameter, were driven by a drop hammer at 2 m spacing in a square grid. After installation of the piles the entire area was covered with about 2 m surcharge of sandy materials (Bibl. 20.01).

Fig. 2 Site showing soil profile and split-bamboo piles

WOODEN POST FOUNDATION

KEYWORDS:

Special properties	Used for spot and pile foundations
Economical aspects	Low cost, if sufficient timber is available
Stability	Low to good
Skills required	Carpentry and conctruction skills
Equipment required	Carpentry and masonry equipment
Resistance to earthquake	Low to good
Resistance to hurricane	Low to good
Resistance to rain	Low to good
Resistance to insects	Low
Climatic suitability	All, except consistently wet climates
Stage of experience	Traditional methods

SHORT DESCRIPTION:

• Wooden post foundations can only be used for lightweight structures, that is buildings made of timber, bamboo and/or other vegetable material.

• The main drawback of using timber for foundations is the risk of weakening due to attack by insects (mainly termites and beetles), fungus and rodents. Hence, protective measures are necessary. (See sections on *Timber* and *PROTECTIVE MEASURES*.)

• Timber posts can be driven into the ground, if the climate is predominantly dry, the site is well drained and destructive biological agents (mainly termites) are not common in the area.

Further information: Bibl. 14.18, 14.22, 20.04, 20.05.

Simple Wooden Post Foundations (Bibl. 20.05)

Only for dry areas without termites.

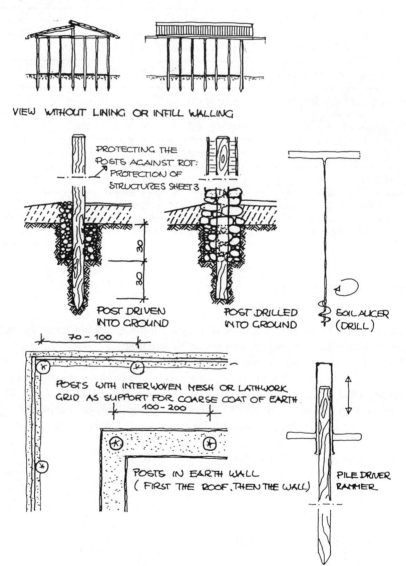

VIEW WITHOUT LINING OR INFILL WALLING

PROTECTING THE POSTS AGAINST ROT: PROTECTION OF STRUCTURES SHEET 3

30
30

POST DRIVEN INTO GROUND

POST DRILLED INTO GROUND

SOIL AUGER (DRILL)

70 - 100

POSTS WITH INTERWOVEN MESH OR LATHWORK GRID AS SUPPORT FOR COARSE COAT OF EARTH.

100 - 200

POSTS IN EARTH WALL (FIRST THE ROOF, THEN THE WALL)

PILE DRIVER RAMMER

Wooden Posts on Concrete Footings (Bibl. 20.05)

Only for dry areas without termites.

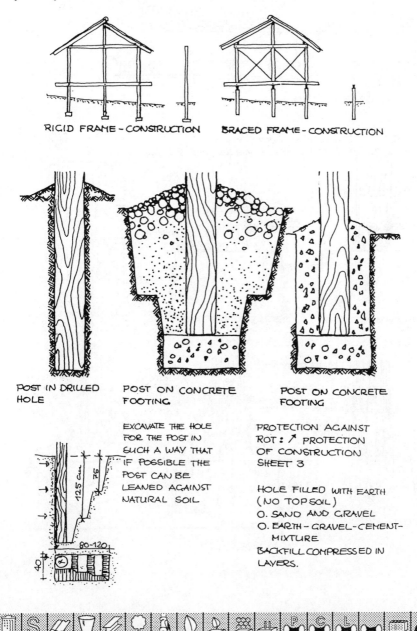

RIGID FRAME - CONSTRUCTION

BRACED FRAME - CONSTRUCTION

POST IN DRILLED HOLE

POST ON CONCRETE FOOTING

POST ON CONCRETE FOOTING

125 cm · 76

80-120

40

EXCAVATE THE HOLE FOR THE POST IN SUCH A WAY THAT IF POSSIBLE THE POST CAN BE LEANED AGAINST NATURAL SOIL

PROTECTION AGAINST ROT: ↗ PROTECTION OF CONSTRUCTION SHEET 3

HOLE FILLED WITH EARTH (NO TOP SOIL)
O. SAND AND GRAVEL
O. EARTH - GRAVEL - CEMENT - MIXTURE
BACKFILL COMPRESSED IN LAYERS.

Wooden Posts without Ground Contact (Bibl. 20.05)

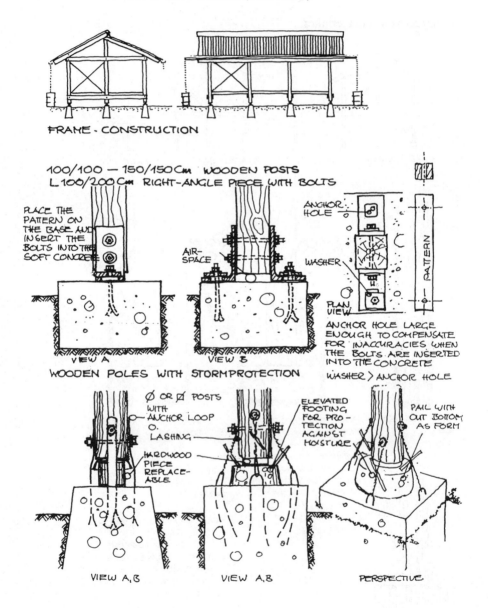

FRAME - CONSTRUCTION

100/100 — 150/150 Cm WOODEN POSTS
L 100/200 Cm RIGHT-ANGLE PIECE WITH BOLTS

PLACE THE PATTERN ON THE BASE AND INSERT THE BOLTS INTO THE SOFT CONCRETE

VIEW A

AIR-SPACE

VIEW B

ANCHOR HOLE

WASHER

PLAN VIEW

PATTERN

ANCHOR HOLE LARGE ENOUGH TO COMPENSATE FOR INACCURACIES WHEN THE BOLTS ARE INSERTED INTO THE CONCRETE

WASHER > ANCHOR HOLE

WOODEN POLES WITH STORMPROTECTION

Ø OR Ø POSTS WITH ANCHOR LOOP O. LASHING

HARDWOOD PIECE REPLACE-ABLE

ELEVATED FOOTING FOR PRO-TECTION AGAINST MOISTURE

PAIL WITH OUT BOTTOM AS FORM

VIEW A,B

VIEW A,B

PERSPECTIVE

EXAMPLES
OF
FLOOR MATERIALS

STABILIZED EARTH FLOORS

KEYWORDS:

Special properties	Natural, local material
Economical aspects	Low cost
Stability	Low to medium
Skills required	Experience in soil construction
Equipment required	Rammer or vibrating plate; soil block press
Resistance to earthquake	Low
Resistance to hurricane	Low, if water enters the house
Resistance to rain	Low, if water enters the house
Resistance to insects	Low
Climatic suitability	Dry climates
Stage of experience	Experimental

SHORT DESCRIPTION:

• Earth floors are common in all developing countries, especially rural housing: the top soil (with organic matter) is removed and filled up with inorganic soil (clay, sand, gravel) well compacted. Surface coats of a clay - cow dung mix provide some stabilization, but have to be renewed frequently, to be effective.

• At Kassel College of Technology, Federal Republic of Germany, a rammed earth floor was developed, using a finely grained soil mix, stabilized with linseed oil: the clay content of the soil should be less than 15 %; no coarse sand or gravel; for 100 litres of dry soil, 3 – 4 litres of linseed oil (depending on clay content) are diluted with 1 – 2 litres of water.

• Several layers are required (see description overleaf) and the surface can be plain rammed earth in a grid of wooden lathing or small timber blocks embedded in the soil mix. Alternatively, compressed, stabilized soil blocks (made in a soil block press) can be used instead of the timber blocks.

Further information: Bibl. 21.10.

Floor Construction

• On a well-compacted, planed surface, coarse gravel (15 cm) is laid to prevent moisture absorption by capillary action.
• This is covered by a 3 - 5 cm layer of fine gravel or coarse sand and sealed with a waterproof membrane.
• In cold regions, a 10 cm layer of insulating material (eg expanded clay nodules) can be placed before
• the first layer of stabilized soil is evenly spread out and tamped with a manual rammer or vibrating plate.
• A grid (1.80 x 1.80 m) of sawn timber (10 x 10 cm) is laid on the first layer and filled with the soil mix and tamped.
• A grid (30 x 30 cm) of wooden laths (2 x 4 cm) is placed on the second layer and the final layer is filled in and carefully tamped. The top surface is then smoothed with the edge of a trowel under considerable pressure, to get "shiny" appearance.
• After several months of hardening, the surface can be treated with a thin coat of hard wax polish, for greater durability and moisture resistance (however, the strong smell may be a problem).
• Instead of the last two layers of soil mix, wooden blocks can be laid and the joints carefully filled with the same mix.
• Alternatively, stabilized soil blocks, made with a block press (see *ANNEX*) can be used instead of timber blocks. However, the blocks must be well stabilized (eg with lime or cement) to resist abrasion and moisture penetration.

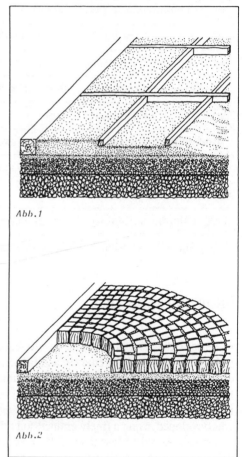

Abb.1

Abb.2

BURNT CLAY AND CONCRETE COMPONENTS

KEYWORDS:

Special properties	Simple prefabrication systems, rapid construction
Economical aspects	Medium to high costs
Stability	Very good
Skills required	Masonry skills and semi-skilled labour
Equipment required	Standard equipment for masonry and concrete work
Resistance to earthquake	Good
Resistance to hurricane	Good
Resistance to rain	Good
Resistance to insects	Good
Climatic suitability	All climates
Stage of experience	Experimental

SHORT DESCRIPTION:

• These prefabrication techniques for ceilings were designed to achieve strong and durable constructions of qualities approaching those of reinforced concrete, but with considerably less cement.

• Ceilings and roofs can be constructed without or with considerably less timber formwork, than is required for standard reinforced concrete constructions. Saving on timber not only reduces costs, but also helps to conserve the rapidly diminishing forests.

• The materials and constructions are capable of withstanding all kinds of destructive agents in the same way as reinforced concrete.

• However, the main precondition for the implementation of these techniques is the availability of good quality bricks and tiles, a requirement that may not always be fulfilled by local brick production in rural areas.

Further information: Bibl. 00.12, 00.41, 21.03, 21.07, 21.09, 23.12.

Reinforced Brick / Tile Panels

• The brick / tile panels described here were developed in India.

• In principle, the panels are made by assembling bricks or tiles on an appropriate surface, laying reinforcing rods in the longitudinal joints and bonding the components with mortar. Reinforced concrete joists of relatively small cross-section are precast in lengths corresponding to the roof span. These are placed manually on top of the walls at distances slightly greater than the length of the panels. The joists are propped and the panels arranged in parallel across them. Reinforcing rods are laid along and at right angles to the joints. A 1 : 3 (cement : sand) mortar is filled in the joints and concrete spread about 30 mm thick over the panels, thus forming a T-beam structure, with the deck concrete acting as the flange.

• The *flat panels*, developed by the Central Building Research Institute in Roorkee, are made of standard burnt bricks, forming 75 mm thick panels of 560 mm width and lengths of 1040 or 1200 mm.

• Similar panels have been developed at ASTRA, Indian Institute of Science in Bangalore. Extruded hollow tiles are used instead of solid bricks, thus reducing the dead load. The tile height of 50 mm also reduces the panel thickness while the tile dimensions of 250 x 125 mm result in panel sizes of 400 x 800 mm and 400 x 1050 mm with 9 and 12 tiles respectively.

• *Arched panels* can also be produced and used for ceilings. They are capable of carrying greater loads than the flat panels, but need more deck concrete to even out the curvature for the floor above.

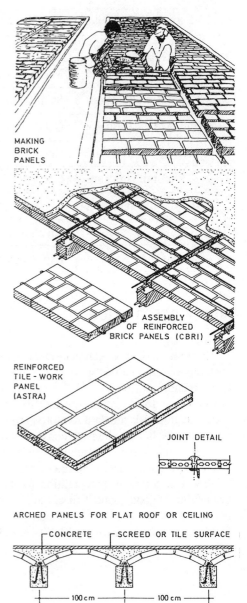

MAKING BRICK PANELS

ASSEMBLY OF REINFORCED BRICK PANELS (CBRI)

REINFORCED TILE - WORK PANEL (ASTRA)

JOINT DETAIL

ARCHED PANELS FOR FLAT ROOF OR CEILING

CONCRETE   SCREED OR TILE SURFACE

|← 100 cm →|← 100 cm →|

Structural Clay Joist and Filler Elements

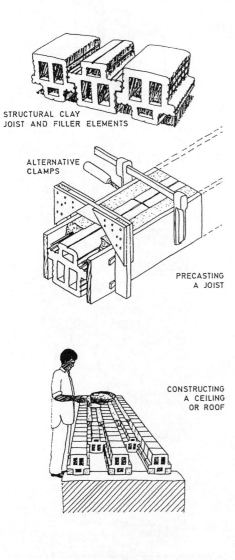

STRUCTURAL CLAY
JOIST AND FILLER ELEMENTS

ALTERNATIVE
CLAMPS

PRECASTING
A JOIST

CONSTRUCTING
A CEILING
OR ROOF

• An extruded structural clay unit, which by virtue of its shape is used both as joist and filler elements, has been developed at CBRI, Roorkee. The dimensions of the unit are 16.5 x 15.0 x 19.0 cm. It has three rectangular cavities, and the outer faces have grooves for better bonding of mortar and concrete.

• The prefabrication of a joist is done by laying the fired clay units end to end on a flat surface, in a row of desired length, with the wider base below, and joined with a 1 : 3 (cement : sand) mortar. Two wooden planks, cleaned and oiled are placed on either side and held together with clamps. The gaps between the clay units and planks are filled with concrete, in which reinforcing rods are embedded. The planks can be removed after 45 to 90 minutes, depending on the weather conditions; the joists are water-cured for 7 days and air-cured for 21 days, before use.

• When constructing the ceiling or roof, the joists, which weigh about 80 - 90 kg, are inverted and laid manually in parallel lines, at distances of 30 cm (centre to centre). For rigidity and levelling, they are placed on levelling pads of cement-sand mortar, and temporarily propped where necessary. The structural clay units, with their wider base below, are laid between the joists as filler units, ensuring that the joints in the joist member and filler units are broken (by using half length units at the ends). The joints and gaps are filled with mortar, reinforcement and concrete, as in the prefabrication of the joists, and the completed slab kept wet for 14 days, before finishing the floor surface.

Reinforced Concrete - Brick Composite Beams

• In order to reduce the need for timber formwork, which is becoming increasingly expensive and environmentally unacceptable, in view of the rapidly depleting forests, a substitute for reinforced concrete beams was developed at Chulalongkorn University in Bangkok.

• U-section clay tiles are laid in a row of required length and bonded together with cement-sand mortar, thus forming a channel. Longitudinal steel bars and stirrups are placed in the channel, which is subsequently filled with concrete. One or more layers of structural clay bricks (wetted from all sides) are laid in between the stirrups, forming the centre portion of the beam. The joints are filled with cement-sand mortar. The top compression zone can comprise another row of U-section tiles filled with concrete.

• Alternatively, this top layer (and even the centre portion) can be completed after installing the beam, which is lighter and can be placed manually. The top layer can also be integrated in a cast-in-place floor slab, producing a T-beam structure.

• In addition to the simplicity of construction, the composite beams have been found to cost 11 - 35 % less than reinforced concrete beams of the same dimensions and reinforcement.

(Source: Bibl. 21.09)

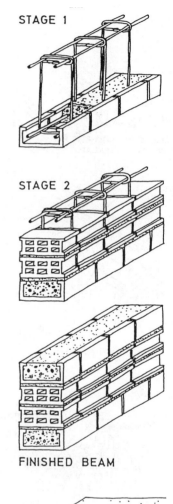

STAGE 1

STAGE 2

FINISHED BEAM

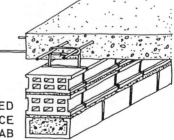

BEAM INTEGRATED IN A CAST-IN-PLACE FLOOR SLAB

PRECAST CONCRETE CEILING COMPONENTS

KEYWORDS:

Special properties	Simple prefabrication and installation
Economical aspects	Medium to high costs
Stability	Very good
Skills required	Semi-skilled labour, carpentry and masonry skills
Equipment required	Formwork (of wood and steel), vibrator
Resistance to earthquake	Good
Resistance to hurricane	Good
Resistance to rain	Good
Resistance to insects	Good
Climatic suitability	All climates
Stage of experience	Practical applications in India and China

SHORT DESCRIPTION:

• These reinforced concrete components can be precast on the building site without expensive equipment or lifting gear.

• They are designed to provide high strength with a minimum volume of concrete, thus requiring only manual operations in production and installation, and reducing cement consumption.

• The major advantages of using precast concrete components are the avoidance of shuttering for ceiling construction (apart from a few props) and the speed of installation.

• Depending on the costs and availability of cement, these construction methods can be more expensive than non-concrete ceilings, but provide greater strength and durability without special maintenance.

Further information: Bibl. 21.01, 21.04, 21.08.

Channel Units (Bibl. 21.04)

• The units, developed at the Central Building Research Institute, Roorkee, India, are 13 cm high and 30 or 60 cm wide, while the lengths can vary according to the required span, but not more than 4 m, as greater lengths reduce stiffness and load-bearing capacity.
• The moulds can be of timber or steel. The corrugations on the outer sides and the vertical grooves at the ends provide the necessary shear key action.
• The mould is oiled, the reinforcement cage placed with 12 mm spacers and concrete filled and compacted with a plate vibrator. The fresh unit is moist cured for 2 days, after which it is demoulded and cured for 12 days, keeping the trough filled with water. A further 14 days of air-curing is needed before installation in the building.
• Assembly is possible without props by placing the channel units in parallel on top of the walls, and filling the joints with concrete and a reinforcing rod.

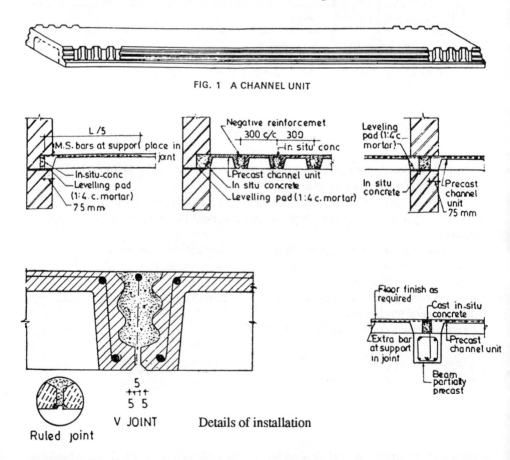

FIG. 1   A CHANNEL UNIT

V JOINT   Details of installation

Ruled joint

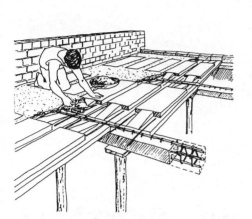

Reinforced Concrete Planks (Bibl. 21.01)

• The system, also developed in India, mainly comprises a 3 cm thick reinforced concrete plank measuring 30 x 145 cm, with a 6 cm thick haunch portion in the centre, and 10 cm wide tapering fillets to strengthen the plank during handling. Joists of 15 x 15 cm cross-section, with stirrups projecting out on the top side, are also precast in simple timber or steel moulds.

• The joists are placed at 150 cm centres and propped at mid-span. The planks are placed over the joists side by side. After fixing reinforcements across the joists, screed is cast in-situ. Once it attains its final strength, the props are removed. No structural deck concrete is required over the planks.

The mould...

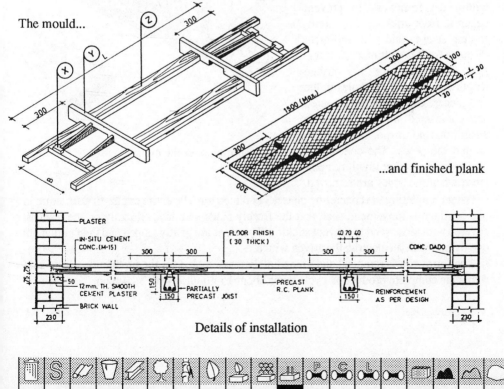

...and finished plank

Details of installation

Hollow Floor Slabs (Bibl. 21.08)

The mould

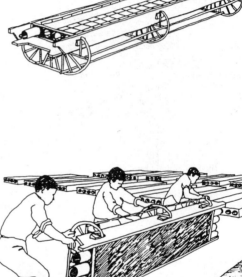

- This is a simple method for the on-site-prefabrication of reinforced concrete hollow floor slabs, a technology developed and practised in China. 20 - 25 slabs of 333 x 60 x 12 cm can be produced during a normal working day.
- The wooden framework is fixed to a cradle-like, (rocking), welded steel substructure. The steel end-pieces with 4 openings define a trapezium-shaped cross-section of the floor slab, so that when finally assembled, the V-shaped gaps between slabs can easily be filled with concrete.
- A canvas-like cloth is placed within the formwork to prevent concrete from sticking to it. Reinforcing steel is laid with sufficient distance from the ultimate slab surface. Four steel pipes are pushed lengthwise through the holes in the end-pieces, the concrete is poured and compacted simultaneously, to ensure that no air-pockets develop around the pipes. The concrete is cast very dry so that it will not collapse when the pipes are removed.

Turning over the mould

- After completing the concreting phase, 3 or 4 men turn the entire cradle-like structure in one continuous movement, such that the freshly made slab lands directly on the ground, covered with loose sand to prevent sticking. The pipes are gently tapped and then pulled out one by one with an electrically-driven winch.
- The formwork is removed and immediately reassembled for the production of the next slab. One complete production cycle takes about 15 minutes with 3 - 4 men.

BAMBOO FLOORS

KEYWORDS:

Special properties	Light, flexible, replaceable
Economical aspects	Low cost
Stability	Medium to good
Skills required	Traditional skills
Equipment required	Tools for cutting and splitting bamboo
Resistance to earthquake	Good
Resistance to hurricane	Medium to good
Resistance to rain	Medium
Resistance to insects	Low
Climatic suitability	Warm humid regions
Stage of experience	Traditional

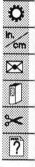

SHORT DESCRIPTION:

• Bamboo floors are common in bamboo structures and to some extent in timber framed houses.

• The simplest method is to lay bamboo culms in parallel, tied to the supporting framework. However, this gives a very uneven surface and can be uncomfortable to sit or stand on for long.

• More even surfaces are achieved by using bamboo board (split and flattened culms), or by cutting bamboo strips, which are woven into boards.

• Since bamboo components cannot be joined together without leaving gaps, the floors are well ventilated, improving the indoor climate and preventing moisture accumulation.

• Precautionary measures are required to minimize attack by biological agents and fire (see *PROTECTIVE MEASURES*).

Further information: Bibl. 13.02, 13.04, 13.05, 13.09, 13.10, 13.12, 13.13.

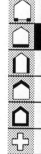

Bamboo Floors (after Dunkelberg, Bibl. 13.02)

Whole culms

Bamboo board (flattened culms)

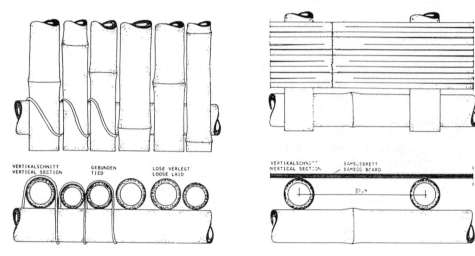

Bamboo floors made of woven bamboo strips

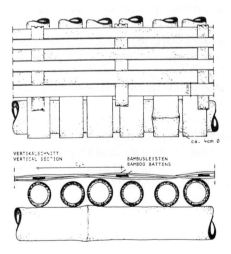

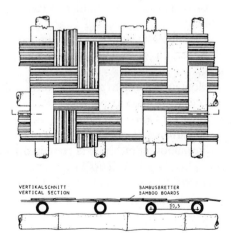

TIMBER FLOORS

KEYWORDS:

Special properties	Suitable for prefabrication, quick assembly
Economical aspects	Medium costs
Stability	Good
Skills required	Carpentry skills
Equipment required	Carpentry tools
Resistance to earthquake	Good
Resistance to hurricane	Low to medium
Resistance to rain	Low to medium
Resistance to insects	Low
Climatic suitability	Warm humid climates
Stage of experience	Standard construction

SHORT DESCRIPTION:

- Wooden floors are standard constructions in all parts of the world.
- They are principally made of wooden planks, nailed onto a sawn timber sub-structure. The smaller the distance between the members of the supporting structure, the stronger the floor or ceiling and the less the vibration and sound transmission, but also the higher the costs (as more timber is needed).
- Protective measures against biological agents and fire are essential (see section on *PROTECTIVE MEASURES*).
- The illustrations on the next three pages are taken from the excellently illustrated UNIDO Manual on Wooden House Construction, which was prepared by the Instituto de Pesquisas Tecnológicas (IPT), São Paulo, Brazil, for a self-help community building project at Coroados, Manaus, under a contract with the Housing Society for the Amazon State (SHAM).

Further information: Instituto de Pesquisas Tecnológicas (IPT) do Estado de São Paulo, S.A., P.O. Box 7141, 05508 São Paulo, Brazil; Bibl. 14.22.

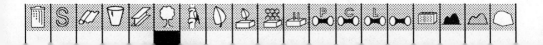

Timber Floor Construction (Bibl. 14.22)

THE NAILING OF JOISTS SPACERS IS DONE LIKE THIS . . .

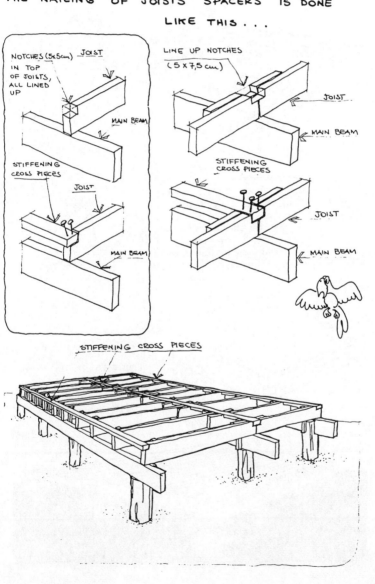

NOTCHES (5x5cm) IN TOP OF JOISTS, ALL LINED UP

JOIST

MAIN BEAM

STIFFENING CROSS PIECES

JOIST

MAIN BEAM

LINE UP NOTCHES (5 X 7,5 cm)

JOIST

MAIN BEAM

STIFFENING CROSS PIECES

JOIST

MAIN BEAM

STIFFENING CROSS PIECES

AND FINALLY YOU CAN PLACE THE FLOOR BOARDS...

THE FLOOR BOARD JOINTS MUST BE VERY TIGHT. TO NAIL THE FLOOR BOARDS USE THREE $l = 7,5$ cm NAILS IN EACH OF THE BOARDS, ON THE LINES OF THE JOISTS.

VERIFY THAT THE EDGES OF THE FLOOR PLATFORM ARE FACED AND WELL FINISHED.

SULPHUR CONCRETE FLOORS

KEYWORDS:

Special properties	Strong, durable and water-resistant
Economical aspects	Medium costs
Stability	Very good
Skills required	Experience in use of sulphur
Equipment required	Conventional mixer equipped with a heater
Resistance to earthquake	Good
Resistance to hurricane	Good
Resistance to rain	Good
Resistance to insects	Good
Climatic suitability	All climates
Stage of experience	Experimental

SHORT DESCRIPTION:

• Sulphur concrete floors comprise elemental sulphur and an inorganic aggregate, usually coarse and fine sand (see section on *Sulphur*).

• The sulphur concrete can either be poured in situ or precast as floor tiles of any appropriate shape.

• In situ constructions require skill, experience and speed, as the molten sulphur hardens rapidly on cooling.

• Sulphur concrete tiles can be laid in sand beds in the same way as fired clay, concrete and other floor tiles.

Further information: Alvaro Ortega, Research Consultant, 3460 Peel Street, Apt. 811, Montreal P.Q., Canada; Bibl. 18.01, 18.04, 18.05, 18.06, 18.07.

Learning Resources
Centre

210

Experimental Sulphur Concrete Floors

Sulphur concrete topping on bamboo-polyurethane ceiling construction, developed by Christopher Alexander for a low-cost housing scheme in Peru (PREVI – Proyecto Experimental de Vivienda, international competition sponsored by the United Nations, Peruvian Government and Housing Bank, 1969).
(Bibl. 18.01)

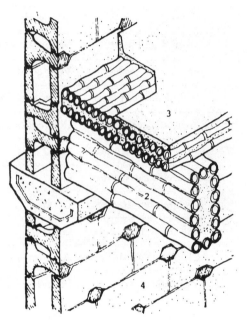

Sulphur concrete floor tiles used in the Ecol Operation (Bibl. 18.06). The 5 cm thick tiles were cast in cake tins (household utensils for baking cakes), and laid in a sand bed.

COMMON FLOOR FINISHES

KEYWORDS:

Special properties	Medium to high standard durable flooring
Economical aspects	Medium to high costs
Stability	Very good
Skills required	Special skills
Equipment required	Standard construction equipment
Resistance to earthquake	Good
Resistance to hurricane	Good
Resistance to rain	Good
Resistance to insects	Good
Climatic suitability	All climates
Stage of experience	Standard constructions

SHORT DESCRIPTION:

• The functions of floor finishes, which are the finishing layers over or covering of the structural floor, have been aptly summarized in Bibl. 21.11 as follows:
  - to have a high wearing resistance and long life span;
  - to provide a safe, non-slip and easy-to-clean surface of the floor;
  - to increase the structural floor's fire-, insect- and termite resistance;
  - to reduce sound transmission and to provide insulation;
  - to contribute to the aesthetic effect of the interior of a building;
  - to have a high enough degree of flexibility; so as not to be affected by slight shrinkage, settlement or thermal movement in the structural floor (or sub-floor).
• Some common floor finishes are illustrated on the following pages, showing a variety of good construction details.
• Since in developing countries a number of activities (eg food preparation, cooking, playing games, meeting friends) take place outdoors (on verandahs, in courtyards, on rooftops, etc.), an example of verandah floor construction is also shown.
Further information: Bibl. 00.55, 21.11.

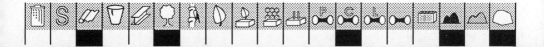

Floors and Floor Finishes (Bibl. 21.11)

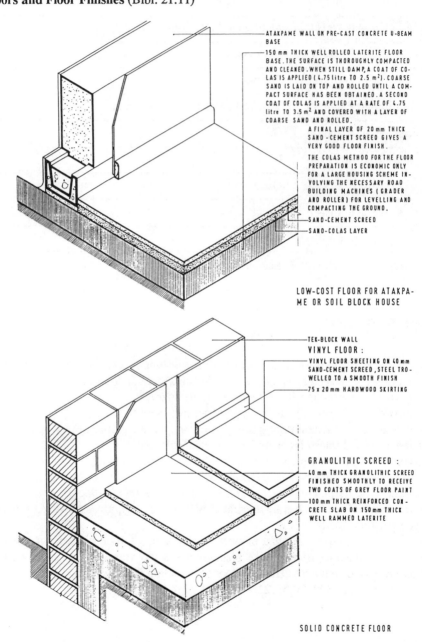

ATAKPAME WALL ON PRE-CAST CONCRETE U-BEAM
BASE

150 mm THICK WELL ROLLED LATERITE FLOOR
BASE. THE SURFACE IS THOROUGHLY COMPACTED
AND CLEANED. WHEN STILL DAMP, A COAT OF CO-
LAS IS APPLIED (4.75 litre TO 2.5 m²). COARSE
SAND IS LAID ON TOP AND ROLLED UNTIL A COM-
PACT SURFACE HAS BEEN OBTAINED. A SECOND
COAT OF COLAS IS APPLIED AT A RATE OF 4.75
litre TO 3.5 m² AND COVERED WITH A LAYER OF
COARSE SAND AND ROLLED.

A FINAL LAYER OF 20 mm THICK
SAND - CEMENT SCREED GIVES A
VERY GOOD FLOOR FINISH.

THE COLAS METHOD FOR THE FLOOR
PREPARATION IS ECONOMIC ONLY
FOR A LARGE HOUSING SCHEME IN-
VOLVING THE NECESSARY ROAD
BUILDING MACHINES (GRADER
AND ROLLER) FOR LEVELLING AND
COMPACTING THE GROUND.

SAND-CEMENT SCREED

SAND-COLAS LAYER

LOW-COST FLOOR FOR ATAKPA-
ME OR SOIL BLOCK HOUSE

TEK-BLOCK WALL

VINYL FLOOR :

VINYL FLOOR SHEETING ON 40 mm
SAND-CEMENT SCREED, STEEL TRO-
WELLED TO A SMOOTH FINISH

75 x 20 mm HARDWOOD SKIRTING

GRANOLITHIC SCREED :

40 mm THICK GRANOLITHIC SCREED
FINISHED SMOOTHLY TO RECEIVE
TWO COATS OF GREY FLOOR PAINT

100 mm THICK REINFORCED CON-
CRETE SLAB ON 150 mm THICK
WELL RAMMED LATERITE

SOLID CONCRETE FLOOR

BURNT BRICK WALL, FAIRFACED EXTERNALLY, RENDERED INTERNALLY WITH 12.5mm THICK SAND-CEMENT PLASTER

P.V.C. TILES :

P.V.C. TILES ON 50mm THICK SAND-CEMENT SCREED (WITH FINE AGGREGATE), STEEL TRO-WELLED TO A SMOOTH FINISH

90 x 20 mm HARDWOOD SKIRTING

IN-SITU TERRAZZO :

IN-SITU TERRAZZO, BLACK AND WHI-TE MOTTLED (20 mm TERRAZZO TOPPING ON 30 mm THICK SAND-CE-MENT SCREED), WITH BLACK PLA-STIC DIVIDING STRIPS TO FORM PANELS , WITH A BLACK PRE-CAST TERRAZZO SKIRTING

DAMP-PROOF MEMBRANE

125 mm THICK REINFORCED CON-CRETE SLAB ON 150 mm BASE COUR-SE FILL

TERMITE SHIELD , ACTING AT THE SAME TIME AS DAMP-PROOF COURSE

THIS FLOOR DETAIL IS SUITABLE FOR AREAS WITH MOIST CONDI-TIONS AND SUBTERRANEAN TER-MITES.

SUSPENDED REINFORCED CON-CRETE FLOOR

FIG. 277 :
GALVANIZED PRESSED STEEL FLOOR CLIPS SET 600 mm APART INTO THE SCREED . (FROM :"FLOORS " BY G.HALE, MACMILLAN PRESS LTD. LONDON)

BURNT BRICK WALL

90 x 20 mm HARDWOOD SKIRTING

20 mm THICK HARDWOOD STRIP FLODRING , TONGUED AND GROO-VED , SECRET NAILED TO 50 x 35 FLOOR BATTENS (PRESERVATIVE TREATED), WHICH ARE FIXED TO GALVANIZED FLOOR CLIPS

40 mm THICK SAND-CEMENT SCREED

D.P.M.

125 mm THICK REINFORCED CON-CRETE SLAB ON 150 mm FILL

TERMITE SHIELD

HARDWOOD STRIP FLOORING ON SUSPENDED CONCRETE FLOOR

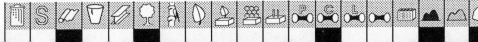

Verandah Floors (Bibl. 00.55)

- The construction of a verandah floor differs from that of an indoor floor in three ways:
- Verandah floors are built with a small slope (about 1 %) towards the outside, so that rainwater can run off quickly (a).
- A projecting outside edge (b) is provided (2 or 3 cm are sufficient) to prevent the development of cracks, which would otherwise soon appear along the edge.
- Expansion gaps, filled with wet sand (c), are constructed to accommodate thermal movement caused by direct exposure to the sun.

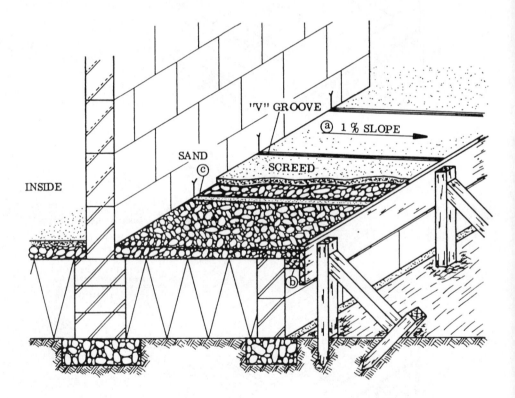

EXAMPLES
OF
WALL MATERIALS

STONE MASONRY BLOCK WALLS

KEYWORDS:

Special properties	Improvement of random rubble masonry
Economical aspects	Medium to high costs
Stability	Very good
Skills required	Masonry skills
Equipment required	Steel formwork, plate vibrator, masonry tools
Resistance to earthquake	Medium to good
Resistance to hurricane	Very good
Resistance to rain	Very good
Resistance to insects	Very good
Climatic suitability	All climates
Stage of experience	Increasing use on the Indian Sub-continent

SHORT DESCRIPTION:

• The drawbacks of random rubble masonry, common in many hilly areas, are the excessive use of stones, mortar and labour, also its non-uniformity and the risk of water penetration. By precasting the stones into uniform concrete blocks these drawbacks are eliminated.

• The technique, developed in India, basically involves steel moulds, a plate vibrator and trowels. A concrete casting platform and the inner surfaces of 4 or 5 battery moulds are oiled. The moulds are arranged side by side on the platform. Into each mould 2 or 3 stones are placed, with the flattest side of each stone resting on the casting platform. Gaps between stones or between stones and mould should be at least 15 mm.

• A concrete mix of 1 : 5 : 8 (1 cement : 5 sand : 8 graded course aggregate of 10 mm and less) is filled into the moulds, compacted with the plate vibrator, and finished with a trowel. The blocks are demoulded 5 to 10 minutes later (depending on the climatic conditions), water cured for two weeks and kept dry for another two weeks.

• The bottom face with the exposed stone texture forms the external face during construction. The blocks, typically 29 x 19 x 14 cm (l x b x h), are used in conventional masonry construction, permitting single brick thick walls (20 cm) for 3-storeyed buildings. Special blocks with recesses for reinforcement can be used, thus also achieving earthquake resistance *Further information:* Bibl. 22.01.

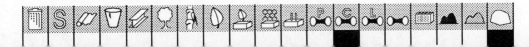

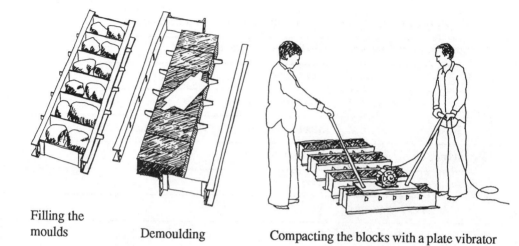

Filling the
moulds   Demoulding   Compacting the blocks with a plate vibrator

The precast stone elements consume slightly more cement in the production and laying of
the blocks, than random rubble masonry, but waterproofing is achieved without or with far
less plastering. Thinner load-bearing walls are possible and the construction time is greatly
reduced. Even earthquake resistance can be achieved, which must be rated higher than the
costs of construction. Below is an example of a stone masonry construction (in Kathmandu,
Nepal) with the wall partially rendered. (Photo: K. Mukerji)

RAMMED EARTH WALLS

KEYWORDS:

Special properties	Good impact resistance and durability
Economical aspects	Low cost
Stability	Good
Skills required	Experience in earth construction
Equipment required	Formwork, rammer
Resistance to earthquake	Low to medium
Resistance to hurricane	Good
Resistance to rain	Medium
Resistance to insects	Medium
Climatic suitability	Hot dry climates, upland climates
Stage of experience	Traditional

SHORT DESCRIPTION:

• This method of construction has been used for centuries in various parts of the world and is commonly known by its French name "Pisé".

• Earth is filled into formwork in layers of up to 10 cm and thoroughly compacted to a thickness of 6 - 7 cm with a ramming tool. When the formwork is full, it is dismantled and moved (usually horizontally) to the next position, fixing it firmly over a previously completed row. In this way the building goes up gradually, layer by layer, row by row.

• Other than patching up cracks, holes and damaged edges immediately after removing the formwork, no surface treatment is normally required.

• To a large extent, the choice of formwork and ramming device influences the speed, cost and quality of construction, so that experience and/or several trials with alternative equipment is necessary. As far as possible, the use of stabilizing agents (eg cement, lime, etc.) should be avoided, as they complicate the whole procedure. However, this is only possible with optimum soil qualities and good building design.

• Rammed earth is a natural material, constructed with only a small fraction of the energy input required for other materials to produce structures of similar strength and durability. It also causes no wastage or pollution, and when demolished, soils that contain no stabilizer can be reused over again. *Further information:* Bibl. 02.06, 02.19, 02.28, 02.32.

220

Soil

• The most appropriate soil for rammed earth construction contains: 50 to 75 % fine gravel and sand; 15 to 30 % silt (pulverized sand) and 10 to 20 % clay (cohesive particles).

Formwork

• The formwork must be more rigid than standard concrete shuttering, because of the high outward pressure of compacted earth;
• it must be light and easy to dismantle and assemble, so that the work does not become too tiring and time-consuming;
• it should be the largest size that can be reasonably handled, in order to reduce the number of moves;
• and it should permit the wall thickness to be varied.
• Different types of formwork are illustrated. The formwork is normally moved horizontally after each section is completed. In order to avoid the horizontal cracks that tend to develop between successive rows of rammed earth (since each row dries out separately), a climbing formwork was developed at the Kassel College of Technology, Federal Republic of Germany (Bibl. 02.28, Vol. 2).
• The length of formwork can range between 150 and 300 cm, the height between 50 and 100 cm. As the ratio of wall thickness to wall height should be between 1 : 8 and 1 : 12 (the latter requiring good quality control), rammed earth walls can be as thin as 30 cm. However, for a man to stand between the two sides of the form to compact the soil, a minimum of 40 cm is recommended.

Test to determine optimum sand and clay content

Making a soil cigar

Optimum soil mix

between 8 & 12 cm

Too much sand, add clay

less than 8 cm

Too much clay, add sand

more than 12 cm

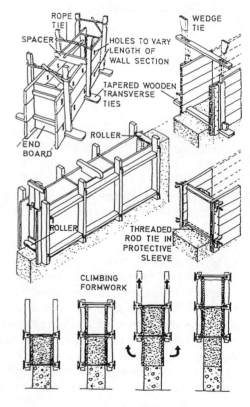

ROPE TIE
WEDGE TIE
SPACER
HOLES TO VARY LENGTH OF WALL SECTION
TAPERED WOODEN TRANSVERSE TIES
ROLLER
END BOARD
ROLLER
THREADED ROD TIE IN PROTECTIVE SLEEVE
CLIMBING FORMWORK

Rammers

• Manual rammers consist of a wooden or steel rod with a heavy wooden or metal striking head. The heavier it is, the better the compaction, but the more tiring for the user.
• Pneumatic rammers imitate the manual rammers, but achieve much higher impact frequencies, thus reducing construction time. The main drawback is their high cost.
• An alternative is a small vibrating plate, developed at the Kassel College of Technology. An electric motor with an eccentric rotating mass transmits vibrations to the plate, thus causing the machine to move. An automatic switch makes it move back and forth in the formwork, without manual guidance.

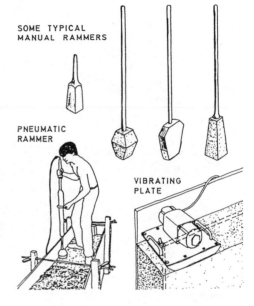

SOME TYPICAL MANUAL RAMMERS

PNEUMATIC RAMMER

VIBRATING PLATE

Construction

• A stone, burnt brick or concrete foundation and base course (at least 30 cm above ground level and exactly as wide as the earth wall) are required to start with. The top surface must be horizontal (requiring steps on sloping sites) and should never project beyond the external face of the earth wall. A damp proof course between the footing and wall is recommended in moist environments.
• The sides of the formwork should overlap the wall section below by at least 10 cm to stand firmly. The work should always begin at a corner.
• The soil is filled in the formwork in layers of not more than 10 cm. The person who rams the soil stands on it or on the top edges of the formwork, and strikes the soil systematically, first along the sides and then in the centre. The operation is completed, when the sound of each stroke of the rammer changes from a dull to a solid clear sound. Once the formwork is moved to the next section, the previous section should be covered with an appropriate material (grass, leaves, cloth, plastic sheets) for protection against rain, wind or direct sunshine.
• Care must be taken to stagger the joints between each row (just as in masonry work) and wall junctions should be made to interlock connecting walls. Wall anchors and reinforcements (eg at corners) made of metal strips or rods, strong twigs, split bamboo or rope, can be placed in these junctions and building corners during compaction.

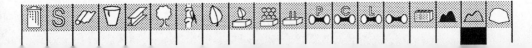

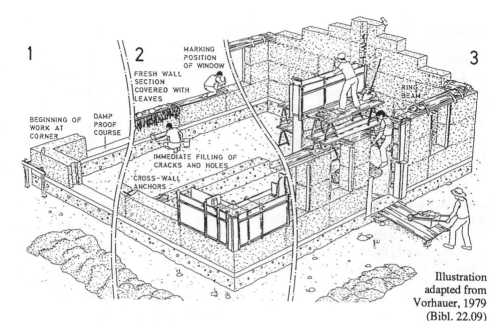

1   2   3

MARKING
POSITION
OF WINDOW

FRESH WALL
SECTION
COVERED WITH
LEAVES

RING
BEAM

BEGINNING OF
WORK AT
CORNER

DAMP
PROOF
COURSE

IMMEDIATE FILLING OF
CRACKS AND HOLES

CROSS-WALL
ANCHORS

Illustration
adapted from
Vorhauer, 1979
(Bibl. 22.09)

Openings

- These should be well planned so that their sides correspond to the ends of formwork sections, their height is in line with the top of the last layer, and the ring beam substitutes the lintel. It is also possible to insert the window and door frames within the form-work and attach anchors, so that the frames are rigidly fixed to the wall. Small openings can also be easily cut into the finished wall by means of a pisé saw (a length of barbed wire with handles at each end) used by two men.

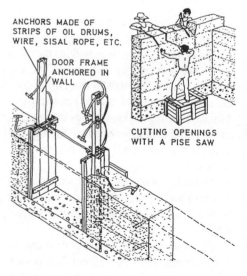

ANCHORS MADE OF
STRIPS OF OIL DRUMS,
WIRE, SISAL ROPE, ETC.

DOOR FRAME
ANCHORED IN
WALL

CUTTING OPENINGS
WITH A PISE SAW

Surface Treatment

It is important for the durability of the wall that broken edges, cracks and holes are filled and compacted, *immediately* after removing the formwork, as the patching material does not bond with partially dried up walls.

COMPRESSED SOIL BLOCK WALLS

KEYWORDS:

Special properties	Comparable to burnt clay brick walls
Economical aspects	Low cost
Stability	Good
Skills required	Semi-skilled workers
Equipment required	Manual block press
Resistance to earthquake	Good
Resistance to hurricane	Good
Resistance to rain	Medium, depends on stabilization
Resistance to insects	Medium
Climatic suitability	All except very wet climates
Stage of experience	Widely used in many countries

SHORT DESCRIPTION:

• A suitable soil, with a good grain size distribution and a clay content of 10 to 25 %, can be compacted in a slightly moistened state to produce strong, dimensionally stable blocks.

• In order to increase their durability, a binder and/or waterproofing agent is added to the soil. Common binders are cement, lime and bitumen, and their proportions vary according to the quality of soil (see *Earth, Soil, Laterite* and *Soil Stabilizers*).

• The advantages of building with stabilized soil blocks compared with most other soil construction techniques are:

• higher compressive strength and greater water resistance;

• ability to carry away by hand immediately after production;

• small drying and storage space requirement, as the block can be stacked immediately or on the day after production;

• easy transportation of dried blocks with low breakage rate;

• possibility of building walls with a higher height to thickness ratio;

• savings in cost, material and energy, as no external rendering is needed on well stabilized compressed blocks;

• lower cost of production and energy input than for equivalent volume of burnt clay bricks or concrete blocks, which are alternatives to stabilized compressed soil blocks.

Soil Selection

• The most appropriate soils for stabilized block production have sand contents of about 75 %, and minimum clay content of 10 %. The shaded area in the chart gives the impression that very few soil types fall within this group, but in reality their availability is almost universal. It is excavated after removing 10 - 15 cm of the topsoil in order to exclude organic matter.

• To achieve satisfactory results, however, a series of field tests are essential. Wherever laboratory facilities are available, they should be made use of, as field tests are not sufficiently accurate.

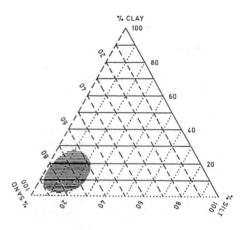

Soil Preparation

• Soils are rarely found in the state required for block production. In most cases, they need to be ground and screened through a 5 mm wire mesh.

• Mixing should take place close to the block mould and all additives thoroughly blended in the dry state. Unlike mixing concrete, the predetermined quantity of water must be sprinkled for even distribution.

• Each mix must be checked by squeezing a lump in one hand and allowing it to drop on a hard surface from about 1 metre height. If the lump remains together, it is too moist; if it disintegrates completely, it is too dry. The correct moisture content will not moisten the hand, but will make a firm lump which breaks apart into several smaller pieces when dropped. When using cement as the binder, only so much material should be prepared, as can be used up in about 20 minutes.

CORRECTION OF
GRAIN SIZE DISTRIBUTION

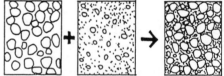

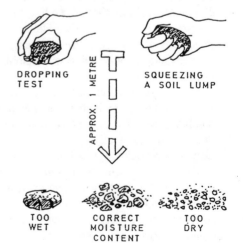

DROPPING TEST   APPROX. 1 METRE   SQUEEZING A SOIL LUMP

TOO WET   CORRECT MOISTURE CONTENT   TOO DRY

Making the Blocks

• Compaction of the soil mix in a mould can be done dynamically (ie sudden impact by tamping) or statically (ie gradual compression). Static pressure is obtained by blockmaking machines, which has become the most common method.

• The simplest, but slowest and most tiring method of block production is by tamping the soil in a mould (usually with hinged or detachable parts).

• More efficiently, a block press is used, in which the soil mix is compressed to 60 %, or even 50 %, of its original volume. The machines are either manually operated or motorized, but the procedure always involves filling the mould(s), compacting the soil (sometimes after pre-compaction), demoulding the block and removal to the drying area (see *ANNEX: Machines and Equipment*). On average, a team of 3 people is generally needed to operate the machine and remove the blocks. They must be assisted by a team of 4 - 6 workers, who excavate and prepare the soil at the same pace as the blocks are produced.

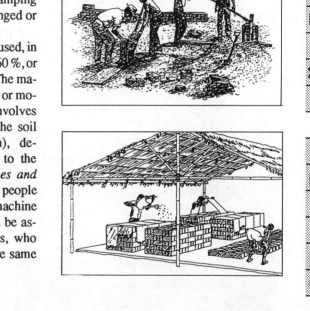

Drying and Curing

• Unlike traditional unstabilized, hand-moulded mud blocks, which have to be left to dry where they are made, compressed soil blocks are carried to a shaded curing area. Weakly compacted blocks are laid in rows on the ground and stacked a day later, while denser blocks can be stacked up to 5 layers immediately.

• If bitumen stabilizer is used, drying can be completed within 5 days, whereas cement requires about 15 days and lime 25 days. With both cement and lime, the blocks must be kept moist for the first 5 days by daily sprinkling.

LOK BRIK System (Bibl. 22.04)

• This system, developed by Dr. A. Bruce Etherington of AIT, Bangkok, is a variation of standard compressed soil block constructions, by which the walls can be built with great accuracy and speed, even with unskilled labour.

• The interlocking soil-cement bricks are made in a modified CINVA-Ram brickmaking machine (see *ANNEX*), which has two parallel upward thrust pistons (to ensure more accurate dimensions of the finished block) and a system of positive and negative frogs (to form recesses or protruding parts).

• No mortar is needed for laying the bricks, but vertical holes are provided, into which grout (thin fluid mortar) is poured. Vertical steel reinforcement can also be inserted wherever necessary, making the construction earthquake resistant.

• Apart from costs saved in material and labour, the uniformity and accuracy of construction gives it an appealing finish, so that no rendering is needed and further costs are saved.

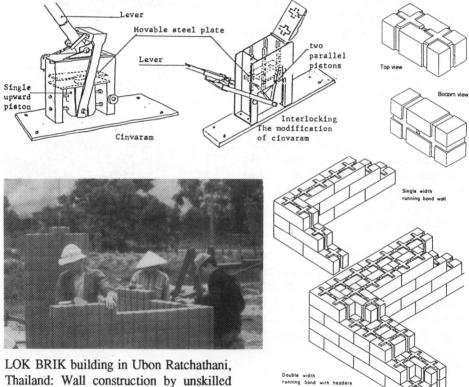

LOK BRIK building in Ubon Ratchathani, Thailand: Wall construction by unskilled workers. (Photo: W. Wilkens, DESWOS)

BAMBOO REINFORCED EARTH WALLS

KEYWORDS:

Special properties	High earthquake resistance
Economical aspects	Low cost
Stability	Good
Skills required	Traditional earth construction skills
Equipment required	Bamboo cutting tools, formwork, tamper
Resistance to earthquake	Good
Resistance to hurricane	Good
Resistance to rain	Low
Resistance to insects	Low
Climatic suitability	All except very humid climates
Stage of experience	Experimental and traditional techniques

SHORT DESCRIPTION:

• Rammed earth walls generally have low earthquake resistance, but with bamboo reinforcements this problem can be overcome.

• The examples on the following pages (taken from Bibl. 22.09) show traditional methods, generally known as wattle and daub (or "bajareque" in Latinamerica), and an innovative construction developed by Prof. Gernot Minke of Kassel College of Technology (Federal Republic of Germany) and implemented in a village in Guatemala (in cooperation with the University Francisco Marroquin and CEMAT, Guatemala).

• The traditional examples can also be built with low quality timbers, but bamboo provides straight components (for uniform constructions) and higher tensile strengths.

• The example from Guatemala combines the advantages of rammed earth construction (high density walls) and tensile strength of bamboo. The walls comprise a number of independent vertical sections, which are held together at the top by a bamboo ring beam. During an earthquake each section can respond to seismic forces individually, thus avoiding differential stresses within the whole wall, which can subsequently collapse. The roof rests on timber supports which are structurally separated from the walls, so that any wall movements will not cause to roof to collapse.

• Treatment of the bamboo is essential to avoid biological destruction.

WALL CONSTRUCTION
BAJAREQUE · PROCEDURE

ALTERNATIVES:

TWIN BAMBOO POSTS
VERTICAL COVERING

INSIDE POSTS
OUTSIDE COVER.

POSTS WITH
WICKER WORK

FOUNDATION: 50 cm ABOVE GROUND LEVEL. DAMPPROOF COURSE ON TOP OF THE FOUNDATION WALL.
CONSTRUCTION: BAMBOO > 7 cm ⌀ FRAME WORK WITH A HARD WOOD BASE RING BEAM. THE POSTS ARE ABOUT 50 cm APART. (ALT.: WITH RESTRAINED HARD WOOD POSTS.) DIAGONAL STRUTS IN THE CORNERS (+) CORNER POSTS OF HARD WOOD.
INFILLING: BOTH SIDES ARE COVERED WITH A PLANKING OF SPLIT BAMBOO. (ALT.: THE INSIDE IS COVERED WITH BAMBOO BOARDS.)

SOIL IS PACKED BETWEEN THE INNER AND EXTERIOR LINING AND LIGHTLY TAMPTED.
PLASTERING: AFTER THE INFILLING HAS DRIED A WEEK IT IS PLASTERED WITH MUD PLASTER AND PAINTED WITH LIME.
ADVANTAGE: EARTHQUAKE RESISTANT. NO SHUTTERING REQUIRED. THIN WALLS, NOT MUCH SOIL IS REQUIRED.
DISADVANTAGE: WOOD AND BAMBOO PARTS ARE INDANGERED BY TERMITES AND FUNGUS.

WALL CONSTRUCTION
LADDER BAJAREQUE · PROCEDURE

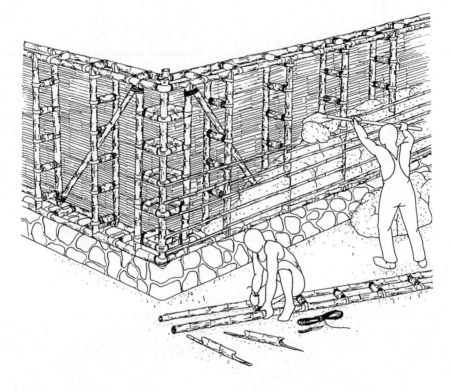

FOUNDATION: 50 cm ABOVE GROUND LEVEL. DAMPPROOF COURSE ON TOP OF THE FOUNDATION WALL.
CONSTRUCTION: THE LADDERS ARE PREFABRICATED OUT OF GREEN BAMBOO $\emptyset \geqslant 4$ cm.
THE OUTSIDE BAMBOO SPLIT COVERING IS NAILED OR FASTENED TO THE LADDERS IN SUCCESSIVE LAYERS AS THE SOIL IS FILLED.
THE CORNERS ARE BRACED DIAGONALLY.

IN EARTH-QUAKE AREAS IT IS RECOMMANDED THAT THE BASE FRAME LYING ON THE FOUNDATION WALL BE SECURED BY A COURSE OF LIME SOIL MORTAR.
ADVANTAGES: THE WALL IS THICKER THAN NORMAL BAJAREQUE (CLIMATE) EARTH-QUAKE RESISTANT. THIN $\emptyset$.
DISADVANTAGE: ONE NEEDS MORE BAMBOO AND SOIL.

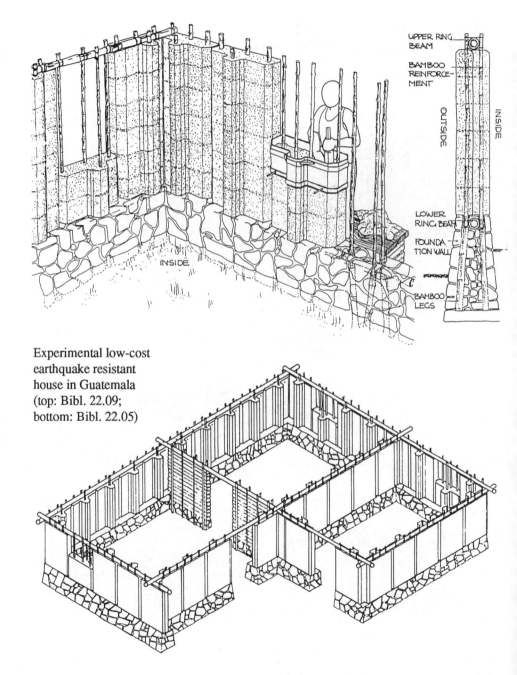

Experimental low-cost
earthquake resistant
house in Guatemala
(top: Bibl. 22.09;
bottom: Bibl. 22.05)

BURNT CLAY BRICK WALLS

KEYWORDS:

Special properties	Improved method of bricklaying
Economical aspects	Medium costs
Stability	Very good
Skills required	Masonry skills
Equipment required	Simple frames and string holders
Resistance to earthquake	Good
Resistance to hurricane	Very good
Resistance to rain	Very good
Resistance to insects	Very good
Climatic suitability	All climates
Stage of experience	Increasing applications in India

SHORT DESCRIPTION:

• This example, developed at the CBRI, Roorkee, India, shows how simple devices and a well organized work place can not only increase the speed of construction (field trials resulted in a 30 percent increase), but also greatly improve the accuracy and quality of brickwork. All that is needed is a set of end-frames for different wall thicknesses and heights, string holders that can be used with any straight, vertical member, of rectangular cross-section (eg concrete columns), boards to hold the mortar, a few accessories, and a well worked out plan of action.

• The mortar used for laying the bricks and for plastering must satisfy a number of requirements: it must be easy to spread, remain plastic as long as it is being applied, but then harden rapidly to resist deformation.

• Mortars basically consist of sand and a suitable binder, in most cases ordinary portland cement, in proportions varying from 1 : 3 to 1 : 12 (cement : sand), depending on the strengths required. However, the use of OPC alone makes a harsh mortar, which achieves undesirably high strengths. Hence it is advisable to add lime, which makes a more workable mortar, prevents cracking and achieves strengths that correspond to those of the bricks.

• The high costs of OPC can be reduced by replacing 30 % of it by a suitable pozzolana (see section on *Pozzolanas*). *Further information:* Bibl. 22.03.

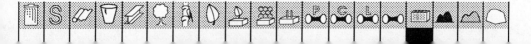

Bricklaying With Higher Efficiency

• With a few end-frames (as illustrated) the usual, time- consuming process of plumbing and stringing the wall is avoided. Each end-frame consists of two wooden planks held at right angles by a welded steel frame. The widths of the boards correspond to the wall thickness, ie half, one, or one and a half brick length.

• Simple L-shaped wooden string holders, which are held in place by the tension of the string, are slid along the edge of the frame as required. Accurate marks on the frame, corresponding to the height of the brick plus mortar joint, eliminiate the need for measurements at each layer.

• Higher efficiency is also achieved by improving the layout of the work place. The principal idea is to place stacks of bricks and mortar boards in alternate succession parallel to the wall under construction, at a distance of 50 - 60 cm for the mason to move along. The bricks are placed on edge for the bricklayer to grip easily. The mortar is placed on the boards, substituting the traditional metal pans, which the masons normally hold in one hand. Bricks and mortar are continuously supplied from the other side by helpers.

• The mortar is picked up on a trowel and unloaded on the wall while moving along it for a distance of about 1 m. Then 8 - 10 bricks are placed in line with the string, each time filling the vertical joints with mortar. The procedure is then repeated for the next metre and so on. For each new layer the string holders are just pushed up to the next mark.

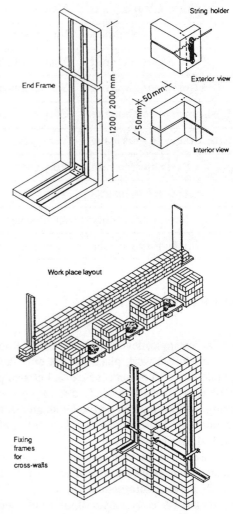

String holder

End Frame

1200 / 2000 mm

50mm × 50mm

Exterior view

Interior view

Work place layout

Fixing frames for cross-walls

• The string holders can also be used independently for filler brick walls in framed buildings by fixing them directly on the reinforced columns. The method is equally applicable for work on scaffolding.

CONCRETE HOLLOW BLOCK WALLS

KEYWORDS:

Special properties	Strong, light walls; rapid construction
Economical aspects	Medium to high costs
Stability	Very good
Skills required	Masonry skills
Equipment required	Blockmaking equipment, masonry tools
Resistance to earthquake	Very good
Resistance to hurricane	Very good
Resistance to rain	Very good
Resistance to insects	Very good
Climatic suitability	All climates
Stage of experience	Widely used method

SHORT DESCRIPTION:

- The use of concrete hollow blocks has several advantages:
- they can be made much larger than solid bricks, and if lightweight aggregate is used, can be very light, without forfeiting much of their load-bearing capacity;
- they can be made to any shape and size, and remain dimensionally stable;
- they require far less mortar than solid bricks (because of the cavities and less proportion of joints, due to the large size), and construction of walls is easier and quicker;
- the cavities can be filled with reinforcement and concrete, achieving high earthquake resistance;
- the air-space provides good thermal insulation, which is of advantage in highland and cooler regions (alternatively, the cavities can be filled with thermal insulation material);
- the cavities can also be used as ducts for electrical installation and plumbing.
- The concrete hollow blocks can be made in simple hand moulds and vibrator (for production on the building site) or in expensive, stationary or "egg-laying" machines (for mass production).

Further information: Bibl. 22.07, 22.08.

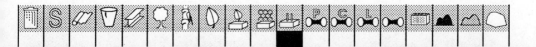

Standard Hollow Blocks

• Concrete hollow blocks generally have
two cavities and the length is twice the
width plus 1 cm (thickness of joint).
• In order to be able to divide the block into
two identical halves, a narrow cavity in the
centre is needed. Division of blocks is done
with a few knocks along the centre line with
the edge of a hammer.

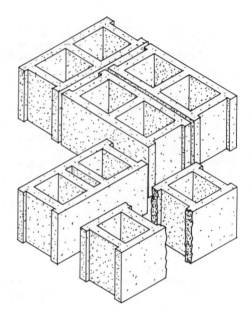

The Zipbloc System (Bibl. 22.08)

• This system is based on a special type of
hollow block (53 x 25 x 14 cm), which can
be used for different types of walls, as well
as for ceiling and roof construction.
• For wall constructions, the blocks are
assembled vertically with a little mortar.
The gaps between these vertical units
are filled with concrete 1 : 3 : 6 (1 cement :
3 sand : 6 aggregate). Reinforcing steel is
placed in the vertical cavities and also filled
with concrete. In most cases, it is sufficient
to fill only one cavity. Door and window
frames are eliminated, as the shape of the
block provides the necessary jamb for fixing shutters.
• For ceilings and roofs, inverted T-beams
of required length are precast and placed on
the walls at 60 cm centres and propped at
mid-span. The concrete hollow blocks are
placed to span two beams (as illustrated).
On top of this a welded steel mat is provided
(for temperature stresses) and screed is cast
in-situ.

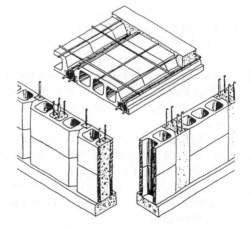

BAMBOO WALLS

KEYWORDS:

Special properties	Light, flexible; great variety of constructions
Economical aspects	Low cost
Stability	Low to medium
Skills required	Traditional bamboo construction skills
Equipment required	Tools for cutting and splitting bamboo
Resistance to earthquake	Good
Resistance to hurricane	Low
Resistance to rain	Low
Resistance to insects	Low
Climatic suitability	Warm humid climates
Stage of experience	Traditional

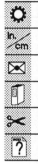

SHORT DESCRIPTION:

• In bamboo-growing regions the climate is generally warm and humid, requiring construction materials of low thermal storage capacity and designs which permit good cross-ventilation. Bamboo constructions ideally satisfy these requirements, which is why they have long been used for housing in warm humid climates.

• Plain bamboo walls cannot be made air-tight or waterproof, so that cross-ventilation is a natural feature, providing indoor comfort and removing moisture.

• The flexibility and high tensile strength makes bamboo walls highly earthquake resistant, and in case of collapse, their low weight causes less damage to people and property; reconstruction is relatively quick and easy.

• Special skills are required to handle bamboo, but these are traditionally available in most bamboo-growing regions.

• The main drawbacks are the relatively low durability (due to biological hazards), the low resistance to hurricanes and fire, therefore protective measures are essential (see section on *PROTECTIVE MEASURES*).

Further information: Bibl. 13.02, 13.04, 13.05, 13.09, 13.10, 13.12.

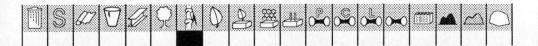

Examples of Traditional Bamboo Wall Construction (Bibl. 13.02)

Halved bamboo culms arranged vertically like Spanish roof tiles

Bamboo battens (made from culms split into eight segments) nailed to a light frame

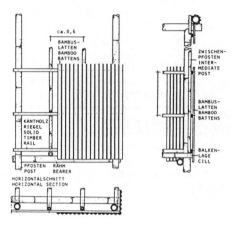

Bamboo boards (split and flattened culms) interwoven with the frame

Panels of woven bamboo strips nailed and/or tied to the bamboo frame

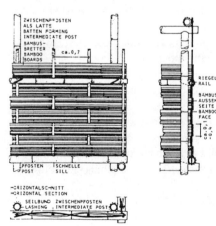

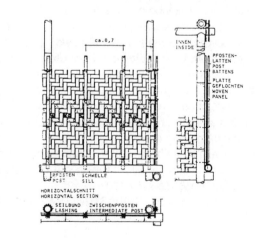

TIMBER PANEL WALLS

237

KEYWORDS:

Special properties	Suitable for prefabrication, quick assembly
Economical aspects	Medium costs
Stability	Good
Skills required	Carpentry skills
Equipment required	Carpentry tools
Resistance to earthquake	Good
Resistance to hurricane	Low to medium
Resistance to rain	Low to medium
Resistance to insects	Low
Climatic suitability	Warm humid climates
Stage of experience	Standard construction

SHORT DESCRIPTION:

• With a well coordinated, modular design, only a few types of wall panels need to be prefabricated, and the less the number of different components, the quicker and cheaper is the process of prefabrication.

• Well seasoned timber should be used in order to prevent moisture movements and distortions which could make assembly difficult and cause dangerous stresses in the course of time.

• Protective measures against biological agents, hurricanes and fire are essential (see section on *PROTECTIVE MEASURES*).

• The illustrations on the next three pages are taken from the excellently illustrated UNIDO Manual on Wooden House Construction, which was prepared by the Instituto de Pesquisas Tecnológicas (IPT), São Paulo, Brazil, for a self-help community building project at Coroados, Manaus, under a contract with the Housing Society for the Amazon State (SHAM).

Further information: Instituto de Pesquisas Tecnológicas (IPT) do Estado de São Paulo, S.A., P.O. Box 7141, 05508 São Paulo, Brazil; Bibl. 14.22.

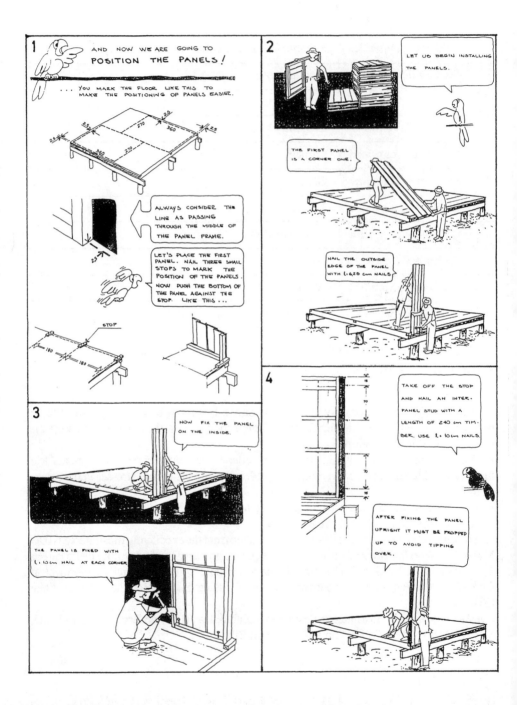

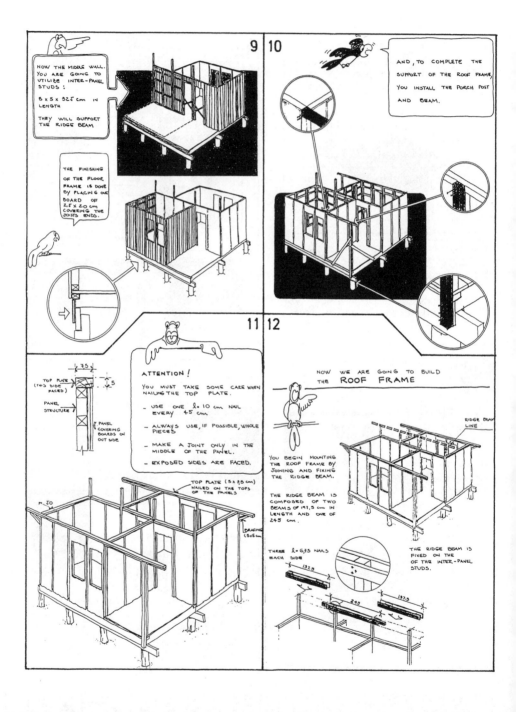

SULPHUR CONCRETE WALLS

KEYWORDS:

Special properties	Cheaper alternative to cement concrete walls
Economical aspects	Low to medium costs
Stability	Very good
Skills required	Experience in use of sulphur
Equipment required	Concrete mixer with heater
Resistance to earthquake	Very good
Resistance to hurricane	Very good
Resistance to rain	Very good
Resistance to insects	Very good
Climatic suitability	All climates
Stage of experience	Experimental

SHORT DESCRIPTION:

• The ingredients of sulphur concrete are elemental sulphur, sand and a plasticizer. Sulphur concrete remains unaffected by impurities, such as salts, which are harmful to reinforced cement concrete.

• The most appropriate use of sulphur concrete for walls is to make hollow blocks, especially interlocking blocks, which can be assembled with great speed and accuracy.

• Block production requires some skill and experience in the use of sulphur, as the molten sulphur hardens quickly. Because of the short curing time, only few moulds are required. Any broken blocks can be remelted and recycled.

• The illustrations overleaf show a practical example of interlocking sulphur concrete block walls in Dubai, United Arab Emirates. The blocks were based on the LOK BLOK system, developed by Professor Bruce Etherington (see *LOK BILD System*) and adapted to sulphur concrete by Bernard Lefebvre.

Further information: Alvaro Ortega, Research Consultant, 3460 Peel Street, Apt. 811, Montreal P.Q., Canada; Bibl. 18.06, 18.07.

Sulphur Concrete Block Walls in Dubai, United Arab Emirates (Photos: A. Ortega)

- The interlocking blocks are quickly assembled without mortar.
- The smooth, non-absorbing marble-like surfaces eliminate the need for plastering or painting, and can easily be cleaned by washing with plain water.
- Depending on the aggregates, different coloured blocks can be made, producing attractive wall surfaces.

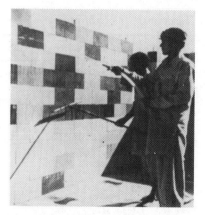

WALLS FROM AGRO-WASTE

KEYWORDS:

Special properties	Promising use of local waste materials
Economical aspects	Low cost
Stability	Good
Skills required	Average construction skills
Equipment required	Wooden hand mould, masonry equipment
Resistance to earthquake	Good
Resistance to hurricane	Good
Resistance to rain	Depends on stabilization
Resistance to insects	Medium
Climatic suitability	All except very wet climates
Stage of experience	Experimental

SHORT DESCRIPTION:

• The system described here, developed at the Forest Products Research and Development Institute, Philippines, uses hollow soil-cement blocks, which contain a certain amount of beach sand and agricultural wastes, such as rice husks, sawdust, wood chips and coconut-trunk particles.

• The blocks (10 x 20 x 40 cm with 3 rectangular holes) are made in wooden hand moulds. The raw mixture, with a moisture content similar to that for common soil cement blocks, is filled into the mould, tamped and levelled, after which the blocks can be demoulded and placed on their narrow sides for moist curing (about 10 days).

• Wall construction is the same as for concrete hollow blocks, and extremely rigid constructions are achieved by filling the cavities with steel reinforcement and concrete.

Further information: Forest Products Research and Development Institute, Los Baños, Laguna, Philippines; Bibl. 19.11.

The hand mould and finished hollow block

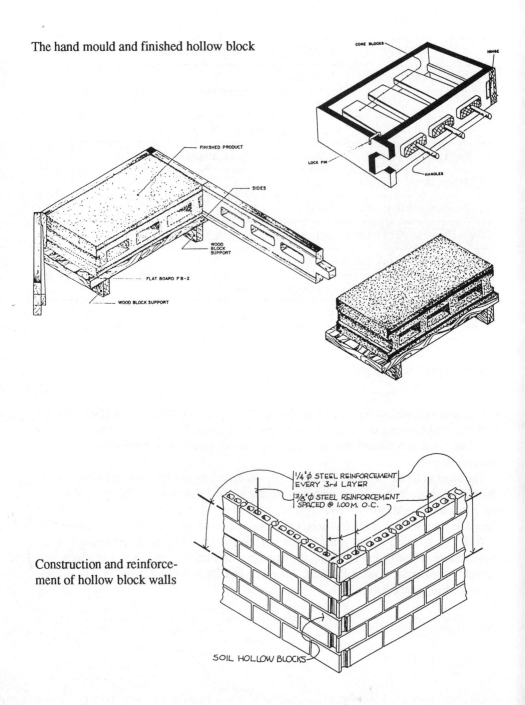

Construction and reinforcement of hollow block walls

EXAMPLES
OF
ROOF MATERIALS

EARTH REEL ROOFS

KEYWORDS:

Special properties	Heavy, high thermal capacity roof
Economical aspects	Low cost
Stability	Good
Skills required	Experience in earth construction
Equipment required	Standard construction equipment
Resistance to earthquake	Low
Resistance to hurricane	Good
Resistance to rain	Depends on finishing coat
Resistance to insects	Low
Climatic suitability	Hot dry or highland climates
Stage of experience	Traditional

SHORT DESCRIPTION:

- This roof construction system is suitable for sloping and flat roofs.
- Its density and heat retaining capacity make it well suited for hot dry or highland regions, where days are hot and nights are cool.
- The main component is a reel, made by rolling long vegetable fibrous material (generally straw) and a wet clayey soil around a wooden spindle (3 - 5 cm Ø, 80 - 100 cm long).
- The reels are laid between the timber purlins when still moist and pressed against each other, the space between them being filled with a fibre-soil mix.
- After drying, the cracks are filled with a mud slurry, on top of which a 2 cm layer of soil, stabilized with finely chopped fibres and lime is applied.
- Finally, the roof is covered with a bitumen roofing felt and a layer of sand or fine gravel.
- On account of the large proportion of vegetable fibres and timber, the risk of termite attack is great.

Further information: Bibl. 02.19, 23.24.

Preparation of Earth Reels
and Construction of Roof
(Drawings: Vorhauer, Bibl. 23.24)

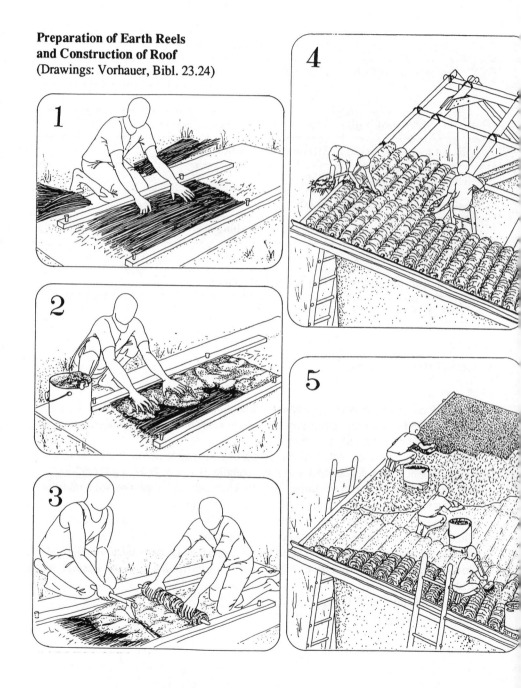

SOIL BRICK ROOF

KEYWORDS:

Special properties	Simple self-help prefabrication system
Economical aspects	Low to medium costs
Stability	Good
Skills required	Average construction skills
Equipment required	CINVA-Ram block press, formwork for beams
Resistance to earthquake	Low
Resistance to hurricane	Good
Resistance to rain	Depends on finishing coat
Resistance to insects	Good
Climatic suitability	Hot dry climates, highland climates
Stage of experience	Experimental, numerous houses built in Tunisia

SHORT DESCRIPTION:

• This roof construction method was developed by the Swedish Association for Development of Low-Cost Housing, Lund University, Sweden, for a pilot project in Rohia, Tunisia, based on "organized do-it-yourself building".

• Apart from the self-help aspect, the aim was to design a strong roof (that could be walked on), using local materials other than timber, which is in short supply and expensive.

• The principal material chosen was the local soil, called Torba, a finely grained soil, containing 60 % CaO (lime). This was used to make soil-cement blocks with a CINVA-Ram block press.

• The slightly sloped roofs were constructed with precast concrete beams placed very accurately in parallel, at a distance just sufficient to place two soil-cement blocks such that they lean against each other (for which the blocks were made with one short end slanting). The block pairs were bonded with a lime-cement mortar. The completed roof received a coat of cement slurry and later a roughly 5 cm thick layer of compacted soil-cement, which was finally whitewashed.

Further information: SADEL, Arkitektur 1, P.O. Box 118, 221 00 Lund, Sweden; Bibl. 00.01.

Construction of the Cement Stabilized Torba Roof
(Photos: Bibl. 00.01)

Left row: Precasting of soil-
cement and concrete components

Right row: Construction of the roof

CLAY TILE ROOFS

KEYWORDS:

Special properties	Durable, waterproof cladding for sloped roofs
Economical aspects	Low to medium costs
Stability	Good
Skills required	Skilled labour
Equipment required	Clay tile production unit, roof construction equipment
Resistance to earthquake	Low
Resistance to hurricane	Medium to good
Resistance to rain	Very good
Resistance to insects	Very good
Climatic suitability	All climates, but most common in humid areas
Stage of experience	Traditional

SHORT DESCRIPTION:

- Burnt clay tile roofs are only used for sloping roofs between about 20° and 50° inclination of rafter, and the tile shapes differ for each range of slope. It should be remembered that the rafter pitch is always steeper than the tile pitch (see illustration overleaf).
- Clay tile production is a traditional village craft in many regions, but uniform shapes and qualities are difficult to achieve. Mechanized plants produce good quality tiles, but at higher costs. An appropriate intermediate solution is provided by mobile presses with interchangeable moulds for different tile shapes (see *ANNEX: Machines and Equipment*).
- Depending on the clay type and production method, a major problem of clay tiles is the immense loss (in India about 35 %) due to cracking and breakage. A good remedy has been found in the use of ammonium chloride as an admixture varying between 0.1 and 1.0 %, depending on the type of soil (Bibl. 00.41).
- Clay tiles are heavy, requiring a strong substructure and closely spaced battens. Therefore, tile designs (eg Mangalore tiles), which require wider spacing of battens, are lighter and more economical. But generally, the weight of the roof and loose connection of tiles, make them susceptible to destruction in earthquakes.
- Good quality tiles with good overlaps are perfectly waterproof. The red colour, however, tends to absorb solar radiation, so that a suspended ceiling may be needed for indoor comfort.

Relation of Rafter Pitch and Tile Pitch

Some Typical Clay Roofing Tiles and their Minimum Rafter Pitch
(reduced by 5°, if the tiles are placed over a waterproof membrane)

Other Clay Roofing Elements

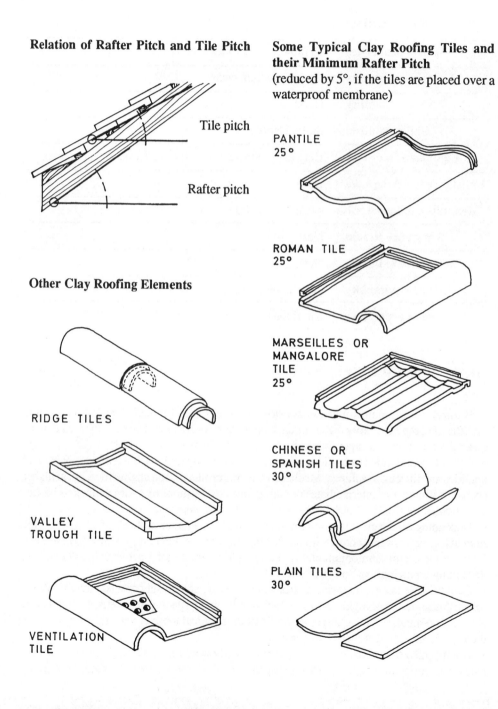

Tile pitch

Rafter pitch

PANTILE
25°

ROMAN TILE
25°

MARSEILLES OR
MANGALORE
TILE
25°

CHINESE OR
SPANISH TILES
30°

PLAIN TILES
30°

RIDGE TILES

VALLEY
TROUGH TILE

VENTILATION
TILE

GYPSUM–SISAL CONOID

KEYWORDS:

Special properties	Innovative material and design
Economical aspects	Low to medium costs
Stability	Good
Skills required	Special training
Equipment required	Simple wooden framework
Resistance to earthquake	Good
Resistance to hurricane	Good, if protected from rain
Resistance to rain	Low
Resistance to insects	Good
Climatic suitability	Dry climates
Stage of experience	Experimental

SHORT DESCRIPTION:

• This is an experimental unit, developed by Prof. Roberto Mattone and Gloria Pasero at the Turin Polytechnic, Italy.
• The conoid unit has a shape which makes it suitable for use as roofing as well as wall components.
• The aim was to produce a strong, versatile component from gypsum and sisal (which are abundantly available in some regions), using simple formwork and equipment.
• Laboratory tests showed a good strength to weight performance, since the fibres have high tensile strength and bond well with the gypsum. Furthermore, resistance to fire and biological attack is good.
• The main drawback is the solubility of gypsum in water, which calls for a completely waterproof surface protection.
Further information: Prof. Roberto Mattone, Facoltà di Architettura, Politecnico di Torino, Viale Mattioli 39, Torino 10125, Italy; Bibl. 23.15.

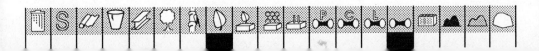

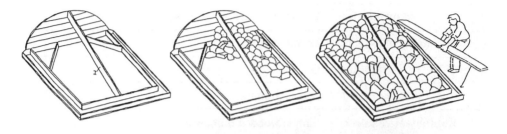

Preparing the formwork: the timber frame is filled with broken bricks and stone, first large pieces, then small pieces and finally a fine sand, which is smoothed to the desired shape, and covered with a polythene sheet. On this the gypsum-sisal mortar is spread to form the conoid.

Practical strength test of finished conoid

Potential assembly of the modules

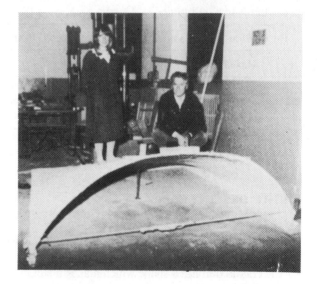

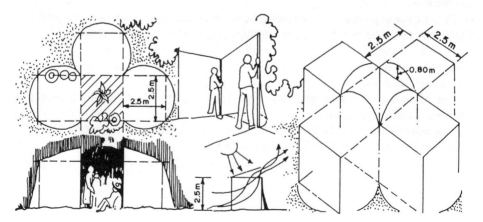

PRECAST CONCRETE CHANNEL ROOF

KEYWORDS:

Special properties	High production rate, minimum formwork and space
Economical aspects	Medium to high costs
Stability	Very good
Skills required	Average construction skills
Equipment required	Special steel moulds
Resistance to earthquake	Good
Resistance to hurricane	Good
Resistance to rain	Good
Resistance to insects	Very good
Climatic suitability	All climates
Stage of experience	Experimental

SHORT DESCRIPTION:

• This roofing system, developed at the National Building Research Institute, Pretoria, South Africa, is based on a precast concrete trough-shaped element, which is cast with great speed and ease, requiring very little working space.

• The cross-sectional dimensions are shown in the diagram overleaf and the length used in the project was 4.27 m, resulting in a total weight of about 107 kg (or 25 kg/m). Seven 4 mm steel bars provide reinforcement along its length, and stirrups of 3.3 mm steel are placed every 30 cm. The elements are self-supporting, and can span 3.50 m with a cantilever on either side of the walls.

• The assembly of the roof is done manually. After placing the troughs side by side, the gaps between them and the top of the walls are closed by inserting precast filler blocks and sealed around the edges. A polythene sheet is laid over the troughs, which are covered with a 20 mm layer of loose gravel, for improved thermal performance and to protect the sheet. The gravel is kept in place by precast, shaped, no-fines concrete blocks placed dry at the ends of the troughs. Rainwater that collects in the troughs percolates through the no-fines concrete and can be collected. Hence, a 5 % slope is suitable.

Further information: Jorge L. Arrigone, Senior Chief Research Officer, National Building Research Institute, P.O. Box 395, Pretoria 0001, South Africa; Bibl. 23.02.

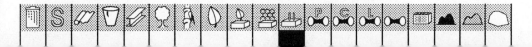

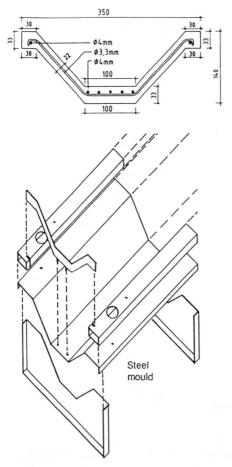

Steel
mould

Precasting the Trough–Shaped Units

The steel mould consists of a trough-shaped base with supporting ribs, fixed to the concrete floor, as well as moveable parts, ie side risers and end closer plates. The inner surface of the mould is covered with a polythene sheet and pushed in place with a steel trough-shaped form. The side and end risers are bolted into position, and a fairly dry mortar mix 1 : 3 (cement : coarse sand) poured and distributed evenly, 33 mm thick on the horizontal parts and 22 mm thick on the sloping sides. The reinforcing grid of 4 mm steel bars is placed on the mortar, pushed down, and the surface evened out by tapping the sides of the mould.

About an hour later, a new polythene sheet is placed over the element, pushed in place with the steel form, the side and end risers bolted down and the procedure repeated as before. Up to 10 units are cast one on top of the other, each one taking about 20 minutes to complete. On average, six roofing units are made per mould per 8-hour working day. The units are cured wet for two weeks and dry for another two weeks.

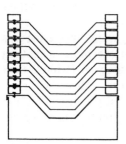

Stack-casting
of roofing units

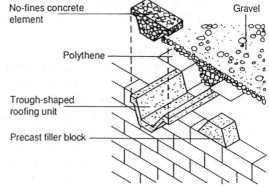

No-fines concrete element

Gravel

Polythene

Trough-shaped roofing unit

Precast filler block

FERROCEMENT ROOFS

KEYWORDS:

Special properties	Higher strength : weight ratio than reinforced concrete
Economical aspects	High costs
Stability	Very good
Skills required	Special training
Equipment required	Formwork, masonry tools
Resistance to earthquake	Very good
Resistance to hurricane	Very good
Resistance to rain	Very good
Resistance to insects	Very good
Climatic suitability	All climates
Stage of experience	Experimental

SHORT DESCRIPTION:

• Ferrocement components are extremely thin (15 to 25 mm), but have a higher percentage of reinforcement than reinforced concrete, thus achieving a higher tensile-strength-to-weight ratio. Further strength and rigidity is achieved by curvature or folds.

• Ferrocement roofs can be made in situ or with precast components, the former being useful for free forms, the latter being appropriate for modular and repetitive constructions.

• Depending on the design, ferrocement roofs can be made to span large areas without supporting structures, thus saving costs and providing unobstructed covered areas. If the ferrocement surface is properly executed (complete cover of wire mesh, dense and smooth finish, cracks sealed) no surface protection is needed, thus saving further costs. However, it is advantageous to apply a reflective coat on the outer surface to reduce solar heat absorption.

Further information: Bibl. 10.02, 10.03, 10.04, 23.01, 23.13, 23.22.

Framed Ferrocement Roof (Bibl. 23.01)

• Once the walls are erected, no reinforced concrete ring beam is required, as the roof is designed to clamp the walls together.
• Around the top, outer edge of the walls, a timber frame (6 x 6 cm) is fixed, as well as two tripod frames above the floor area. The surfaces described by these frames are hyperbolic paraboloids (hypars), which are made up of straight lines. This simplifies the fixing of the wire mesh.
• The mesh (2 or 3 layers) is stretched over the frame and nailed or stapled onto it. The frame is only needed to hold the mesh during construction, as the structure will be self-supporting once plastered.
• Reinforcing bars are fixed around the wall and along the folds of the roof.
• The roof is plastered by a team on top forcing the mortar through the mesh, while another team below recovers the falling mortar to plaster the inside.
• This curved roof system, developed by P. Ambacher, France, permits the wind to blow around smoothly, making it very suitable for hurricane prone areas.

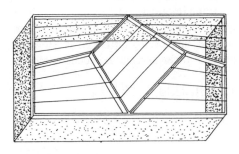

Timber frame placed on walls

The completed roof

Precast Trough Element (Bibl. 23.22)

• These elements function on the principle that folded plates have much higher strength than plates of the same thickness but without folds.
• The roofing element shown here, developed at the Structural Engineering Research Centre, Roorkee, is made either on a stationary brick-and-concrete mould or on a portable wooden mould, and can be in the form of a trough or inverted.
• A reinforcement cage is prepared on the mould.
• Before placing the mortar, a thin coat of rich cement slurry is applied to the reinforcement cage with a brush. The mortar is then applied and pressed into the reinforcement. This is done in 2 or 3 layers. A specially designed vibrator, operated by two men, compacts the mortar.
• The finished element is moist cured for one week, before it is removed from the mould. The lower side is finished with a coat of cement slurry and cured for at least another week, before handling and installation.

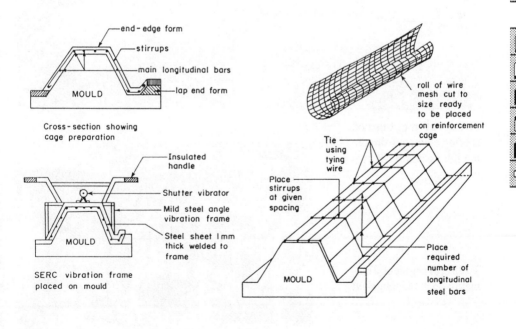

Cross-section showing cage preparation

end-edge form
stirrups
main longitudinal bars
lap end form
MOULD

roll of wire mesh cut to size ready to be placed on reinforcement cage

Insulated handle
Shutter vibrator
Mild steel angle vibration frame
Steel sheet 1mm thick welded to frame
MOULD

SERC vibration frame placed on mould

Tie using tying wire
Place stirrups at given spacing
MOULD
Place required number of longitudinal steel bars

Precast Segmental Element (Bibl. 23.13)

• The alternative to trough elements, shown on the previous page, is a segmental element, made principally in the same way.

• The segmental element shown here was developed at the Regional Research Laboratory, Jorhat, India.

• The element is 60 cm wide, 250 cm long and 2 cm thick. The reinforcement in each element consists of 5 bars of 6 mm Ø in the longitudinal direction and 10 bars of the same diameter in the transverse direction, with two layers of hexagonal chicken wire mesh. The mortar comprised 1 part cement : 2 parts sand by weight.

• Long-term performance tests have shown very satisfactory results.

Lifting of the finished roofing element from the mould; assembly of two elements

Testing of segmental elements on a bicycle shed

CORRUGATED FIBRE CONCRETE ROOFING SHEETS 261

KEYWORDS:

Special properties	Local, low-cost method
Economical aspects	Inexpensive durable roofing material
Stability	Good, if properly manufactured and installed
Skills required	Thorough training and constant quality control
Equipment required	Simple, locally made, transportable moulds
Resistance to earthquake	Uncertain
Resistance to hurricane	Good, if well installed and secured
Resistance to rain	Good
Resistance to insects	Good
Climatic suitability	All climates
Stage of experience	Fairly mature technology

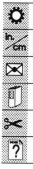

SHORT DESCRIPTION:

Corrugated FC sheets
• were the first FC roofing elements to be developed, as the aim was to substitute gci and ac sheets;
• require fairly simple, locally made equipment and a very well coordinated working team of at least two workers;
• consume about the same amount of cement as asbestos cements sheets (15 kg per m²), on account of their greater thickness and production method by manual tamping, but require no electricity;
• are difficult to handle when fresh and to cure in water tanks, because of their large size;
• are difficult to transport and install without breakage, and do not tolerate inaccurately constructed and flexing supporting structures;
• withstand strong wind forces because they are heavy and have few overlaps.
In most cases FC/MC tiles are easier to produce and install than FC sheets and therefore represent the more appropriate solution.
Further information: RAS c/o SKAT, Vadianstrasse 42, CH-9000 St. Gall, Switzerland; Bibl. 11.03, 11.05, 11.07, 11.08, 11.12, 11.15.

262

Production of Corrugated FC Sheets

Materials and equipment
• *Cement:* ordinary portland cement (5 kg per 10 mm thick corrugated sheet of 60 x 60 cm) corresponding to cement : sand ratio of 1 : 1; a pozzolana (eg rice husk ash) can be added to improve fibre durability and reduce cement content, but causes slow setting, which necessitates a larger number of moulds and larger workspace.
• *Sand:* (5 kg per sheet) preferably with angular particles and good grain size distribution between 0.06 and 2 mm, free from silt and clay.
• *Fibre:* (0.1 kg per sheet) mainly natural, such as sisal, jute, coir, or banana fibre, but also synthetic fibres, eg polypropelene or glass fibre, can be used. Long fibres can be used, but require a different (more difficult) manufacturing process and result in weaker products. Short fibres, chopped to lengths of 12 to 25 mm, are easy to process, provide cohesiveness to the wet mortar, permitting reshaping without cracking, and also help to prevent cracking due to drying shrinkage.
• *Water:* preferably drinkable water, just enough to make the mortar mix workable (water: cement ratio 0.5-0.65 by weight).
• *Admixtures:* such as waterproofers may be used, if the sand is not well graded, and colorants, if the grey cement colour is not desired.
• *Screeding board:* a flat horizontal board with outer frame, to define the FC sheet size and clamp down the polythene interface sheet.
• *Corrugated setting moulds:* gci or ac sheets, enough for two days production. All sheets should be obtained from a single batch made from a single master mould, as sheets from different batches or different producers are likely to have dissimilar corrugations. Accuracy in the corrugations is vital for proper installation and trouble-free performance.
• *Other equipment:* standard workshop tools.

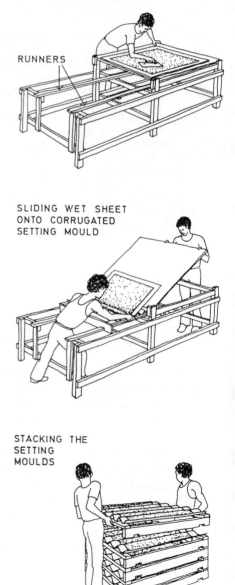

SPREADING FC MIX
ON SCREEDING BOARD

RUNNERS

SLIDING WET SHEET
ONTO CORRUGATED
SETTING MOULD

STACKING THE
SETTING
MOULDS

Moulding and curing
• The correctly proportioned and well-mixed mortar is trowelled evenly onto the polythene sheet, which is fixed on the screeding board; the mortar is tamped, levelled to a uniform thickness of 10 mm and smoothed off with the trowel.
• The frame is removed, the edges of the mortar layer trimmed and the screeding board tilted, such that the polythene sheet with the wet fibre concrete is allowed to gradually slide onto the corrugated mould held below.
• The fresh FC sheet and mould is placed on a stack for primary curing for 24 hours, after which they are hard enough to be demoulded and placed upright for further curing (by regular watering), or completely immersed in water tanks for about 2 weeks.
• Demoulding should not be done later than 48 hours after moulding, as the sheets tend to shrink on drying, and will crack if resisted by the setting mould.

Production of FC Ridge Tiles

• *Materials and equipment:* same as for sheets, but different shape of frame, and screeding board made with hinges, so that it can be bent and used as the setting mould, held in a template.
• *Moulding and curing:* same as for sheets.

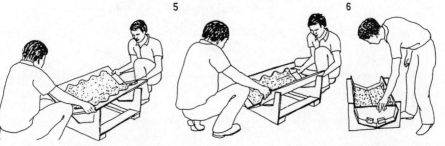

Installation of FC Roofing with Corrugated Sheets

The *corrugated FC sheets* are laid on timber roof structures in much the same way as gci and ac sheets. However, FC sheets are less flexible and can be damaged if the loads are not evenly distributed. Therefore, care must be taken in constructing the substructure, to ensure that the top edges of all members are properly aligned. If nails or bolts are used, holes (of slightly larger diameter) should be drilled beforehand. Alternatively, nibs with wire loops can be cast-in during moulding, avoiding the need for drilling. Mitred corners are essential for a weathertight fit.

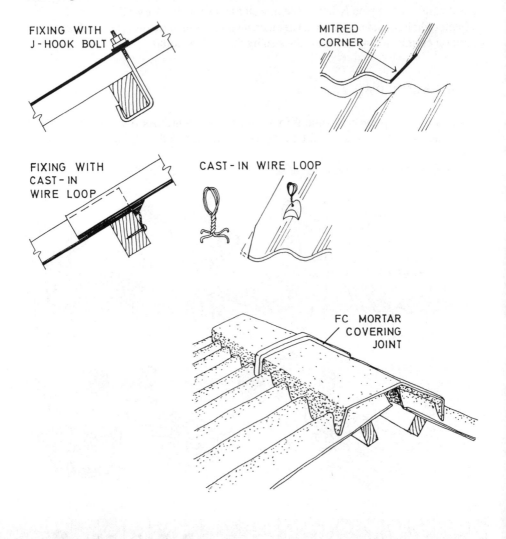

FIXING WITH
J-HOOK BOLT

MITRED
CORNER

FIXING WITH
CAST-IN
WIRE LOOP

CAST-IN WIRE LOOP

FC MORTAR
COVERING
JOINT

FIBRE AND MICRO CONCRETE TILES

KEYWORDS:

Special properties	Promising, local, low-cost method
Economical aspects	Inexpensive locally produced durable roofing material
Stability	Good, if properly manufactured and installed
Skills required	Thorough training and constant quality control
Equipment required	Imported, transportable production kit
Resistance to earthquake	Good
Resistance to hurricane	Satisfactory, if well installed and secured
Resistance to rain	Good
Resistance to insects	Good
Climatic suitability	All climates
Stage of experience	Mature technology

SHORT DESCRIPTION:

FC/MC tiles
• were developed to overcome most of the problems encountered in producing and installing corrugated FC sheets (previous example);
• are made most efficiently on a small vibrating table (hand powered or run by electricity, eg. a car battery), which can be operated by a single trained worker;
• can be made thinner (6 mm) than FC sheets (10 mm), and their cement : sand ratio (between 1 : 2 and 1 : 3) is less than for FC sheets (1 : 1), so that the cement used for making tiles is only between 5 and 7 kg per m² of roofing;
• are easy to handle when fresh and to cure in water tanks;
• do not tend to break as easily as sheets during transport and installation, and minor inaccuracies in the supporting structure have no negative effects;
• are easily torn off by strong wind forces, if they are not well fixed to the substructure.
Further information: RAS c/o SKAT, Vadianstrasse 42, CH-9000 St. Gall, Switzerland; Bibl. 11.03, 11.05, 11.07, 11.08, 11.15.

Production of FC/MC tiles

Materials and equipment
- *Cement:* same as for FC sheets, but about 0.4 kg per 6 mm thick pantile of 50 x 25 cm, corresponding to cement : sand ratio of 1 : 3.
- *Sand:* same as for sheets, but 1.2 kg per tile.
- *Fibre:* same as for sheets, but 0.02 kg per tile, used in FC tiles only.
- *Aggregate:* for MC tiles aggregate is used instead of fibre. The ratio sand to aggregate is between 2:1 and 1:1.
- *Water* and *admixtures:* same as for sheets.
- *Screeding machine:* comprising a vibrating screeding surface and interchangeable, hinged frame (for products of different shapes and thicknesses), whereby the vibrating mechanism is either powered by a 12 volt car battery or hand-powered. (A variety of models, depending on different user requirements and desired output rates are available from the Intermediate Technology Workshops, United Kingdom).
- *Setting moulds:* these are part of the pantile production kit, and are generally made of impact-resistant pvc, with rib markings (for accurate positioning of the tile edge) and supporting frame for stacking.
- *Other equipment:* same as for sheets.

1
PLACING
POLYTHENE
INTERFACE
SHEET

2
FIXING
FRAME
HOLDING
CATCHES

3
PLACING
FC MIX
UNDER
VIBRATION

4
SMOOTHING
UNDER
VIBRATION

Moulding and curing

• The wet mix is trowelled onto the polythene interface sheet on the screeding machine and, under vibration, smoothed with a trowel to the same level as the surrounding steel frame. At a predetermined spot at the top end of the tile, a matchbox-size nib is formed and a wire loop pushed into it (required for fixing to the roof).

• The steel frame is lifted off the screeding surface and the polythene sheet slowly pulled over the pvc setting mould, ensuring correct positioning of the tile edge to achieve uniform curvature.

• The mould with the fresh tile is then placed on a stack of moulds for initial setting and curing (24 hours), after which the tiles can be demoulded and cured for 2 weeks in water tanks or in an airtight container with vapour saturated air (vapour curing).

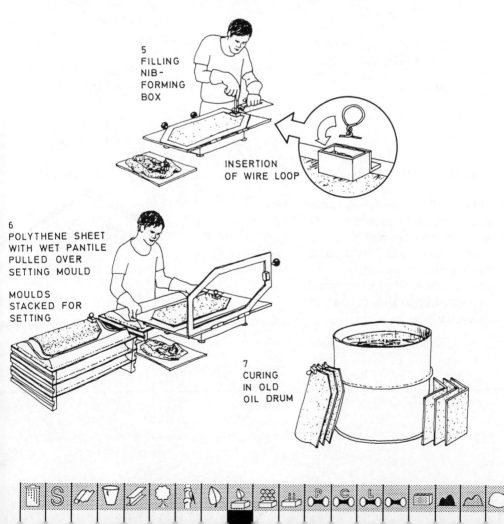

5
FILLING
NIB-
FORMING
BOX

INSERTION
OF WIRE LOOP

6
POLYTHENE SHEET
WITH WET PANTILE
PULLED OVER
SETTING MOULD

MOULDS
STACKED FOR
SETTING

7
CURING
IN OLD
OIL DRUM

Pantiles and Roman tiles

Two types of tiles are common:
* *The pantile:* is of a sinuscourve like shape and can easily be placed on a slightly uneven roof.

* *The Roman tile:* gives a neater roof surface but requires an even roof structure.

Production of FC/MC Ridge Tiles

* *Materials and equipment:* same as for tiles, but with a different steel frame and setting moulds.

* *Moulding and curing:* same as for tiles, but with nibs and wire loops fitted after the tile is placed on the setting mould.

Installation of FC/MC Roofing

The *FC/MC tiles* are laid on timber laths (spaced at 40 cm centres) in the same way as clay roof materials. Slight inaccuracies do not cause major problems especially in the case of pantile. The tiles are fixed with wire loops, nailed or tied onto the timber laths.

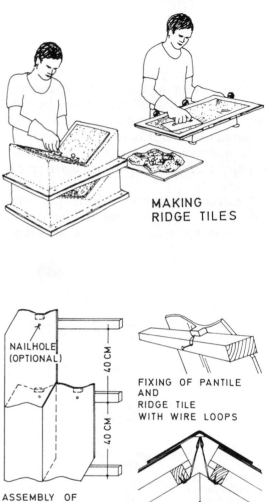

MAKING
RIDGE TILES

NAILHOLE
(OPTIONAL)

40 CM

40 CM

ASSEMBLY OF
PANTILES

FIXING OF PANTILE
AND
RIDGE TILE
WITH WIRE LOOPS

DURABLE THATCH WITH STIFF–STEM GRASSES

KEYWORDS:

Special properties	Excellent thermal and sound insulation
Economical aspects	Low cost
Stability	Good, depends on material and workmanship
Skills required	Special training and experience
Equipment required	Locally made thatching tools
Resistance to earthquake	Very good
Resistance to hurricane	Depends on fixing and roof structure detailing
Resistance to rain	Medium to good
Resistance to insects	Low
Climatic suitability	All zones where material is available
Stage of experience	Traditional

SHORT DESCRIPTION:

• Thatch is the most commonly used roof covering in the world, although it is barely recognized by construction experts. In India, for example, some 40 million houses are thatched. Almost any vegetable material, from the bark of trees to finely-tapering water reeds, can be used, though grasses, reeds and palms are most common.

• Traditional types of thatch have short durability and performance, but in certain regions (N.W. Europe, Southern Africa, Japan) skilled workmanship produces good quality functional roofing, with life expectancies between 25 and 70 years.

• Thatch uses renewable, local materials requiring minimal or zero artificial energy input in production, and costing less than most other types of roofing. Their application is labour-intensive – an important advantage in terms of employment generation. At the end of their useful life, thatching materials can be composted or compacted for use as fuel.

• The main drawback is its combustibility, but this is significantly reduced through good quality workmanship and common-sense precautions. Thatch is also susceptible to biological decay and weathering.

• The best thatching materials are stiff-stem grasses and reeds of 1 to 2 metres length and up to 10 mm diameter at the cut end. They should be straight (no bends at nodes), tapering and preferably hollow stemmed, as solid culms tend to dry out slowly and thus rot quickly.

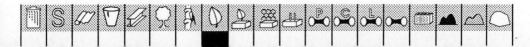

Materials: Harvesting and Processing

• Thatch may come from three different sources: first from naturally occurring indigenous vegetation, secondly as a by-product of food or cash-crop agriculture, and thirdly through the cultivation of a plant grown specifically for thatching.

• Water reed is most durable, but cereal straw (mainly wheat, but also rye, barley and rice) is more widely available. The less artificial fertilizer is used, the less susceptible they are to fungal attack.

• Harvesting is best done by hand, as modern combine harvesters break the straw. The mature (fully grown, dried) stem is cut about 5 cm above the ground.

• To facilitate tight and even thatching, the straw should be combed (with a hand-held rake) to remove dead leaves and other debris, then bundled and stored in a dry place. (The labour involved in combing the straw will be amply repaid, as it lasts more than twice as long as uncombed straw.)

• The bundles should measure 55 cm in circumference at the binding, which is tied about 30 cm from the cut end. Once bundled the straw is ready for thatching.

Grass is laid at 35°

Exposed grass is only 1 cm

Roof pitch is 45°

battens

rafter

tilting board

A leggatt

Roof Structure

• Almost any shape of roof with a minimum pitch of 45° can be thatched. Thatch will mould itself to any curve except a convex-shaped roof.

• Pole timbers and split battens may be used, and simple configurations work best, that is, valleys and other changes of roof pitch are not recommended.

• The structure should be capable of supporting up to 40 kg/m², which is the weight of the heaviest material - reed.

• A tilting board, 35 mm thicker than subsequent battens, fixed along all the eaves and barges at eave level, is essential to force the first course into tension, making the rest of the thatch more tightly compacted.

Thatching Method

• Roof-work tools: pen-knife for opening bundles and cutting ties; leggatt (thatcher's mallet) for beating the thatch upwards to tighten the thatch coat; trimming knives for tidying completed work.

• Grass is sorted: short grass for eaves, gable edges and top course; long grass for rest of roof.

• Thatching begins at a right-hand verge (unless the thatcher is left-handed) and can be worked in vertical lanes (more common) or horizontal sections.

• The first course of thatch performs the same function as the foundations of a wall, and as it has the greatest vulnerability to wind damage, it needs to be very secure.

• Thatch is placed in horizontal layers, approx. 20 cm thick, secured by stitching, layer by layer, at approx. half-way between cut end and ear. Layers overlap as tiling, so fixings are covered and protected. Total thatch thickness is 30 cm. After fixing, the grass is wedged tightly into the ties with a leggatt. The compacted surface forms a pitch, identical to that of the rafters, and exposes only 2 - 3 cm of each stem. A slight lip should be left at the top of each course and will be driven back with the next course to form a neat and invisible junction.

• The ridge is the most vulnerable part of the roof and can be made of a variety of very durable materials, eg half-round burnt clay tiles, sheet metal, ferrocement, but they are expensive and detract from the appearance of the roof. More appealing and cheaper is a flexible grass wrapped over the apex, covering the upper course fixings and held with horizontal stitching.

• Material requirements are approx. 10 bundles grass per m² of roof area; tough local string or steel wire for fixing ties. Experienced workers should fix 10 to 20 m² per day.

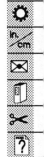

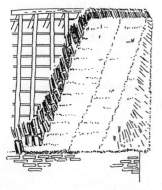

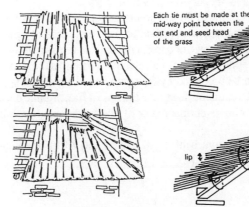

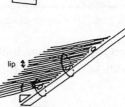

Each tie must be made at the mid-way point between the cut end and seed head of the grass

All the fixing ties must be at the same depth on every course

lip

Rainwater Collection

• Thatch roofs are generally not suitable for rainwater collection, unless a wide gutter - 30 cm minimum - is provided. A method called "tile substitution", developed and tested by Nicolas Hall, makes collection at eaves more efficient.
• Burnt clay tiles are substituted for thatch on the first course, producing a hard, straight eave.
• By doing so, the eaves are significantly strengthened (increasing the life of the roof); only a 10 cm gutter is needed (cheap, easily available, easily fixed); and the fire risk is considerably reduced.
• The main drawback of collecting rainwater from thatch roofs is that debris will first be washed off, contaminating the water. Hence, methods should be employed to discard the first flush of debris laden water.

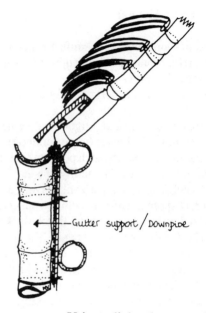

Using split bamboo guttering with palm thatch

Durability

• A competently-laid grass thatch might last up to 40 years or more, though a grass ridge will need renewal every 8 - 10 years.
• Thatch is combustible and common-sense is the best protection against fire: avoidance of high building densities (urban areas); avoidance of open fires near thatched buildings; avoidance of chimneys, or careful design and construction only at the ridge, well insulated, regularly swept; protection of all electrical fitting in the roof space. In addition, the underside of thatch can be protected by fixing an incombustible board ceiling to the rafters.
• Chemical treatments to reduce the risk of fire, organic decay and weathering are possible, but none are cheap, permanent or of good value, and prohibit rainwater collection.

Further information: Bibl. 12.02, 12.03 and 23.11 or contact Nicolas Hall, 48a Hormead Road, London W9, U.K.

BAMBOO ROOF STRUCTURES

KEYWORDS:

Special properties	High strength, flexibility, great variety of forms
Economical aspects	Low cost
Stability	Good
Skills required	Traditional bamboo craftsmanship
Equipment required	Tools for cutting, splitting, tying bamboo
Resistance to earthquake	Very good
Resistance to hurricane	Good
Resistance to rain	Depends on protective measures
Resistance to insects	Low
Climatic suitability	Warm humid climates
Stage of experience	Experimental

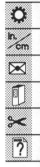

SHORT DESCRIPTION:

The main advantages of using bamboo for roof constructions are:
• It is a traditional technology, which is well understood by local artisans. No special tools are required.
• The large-scale utilization of bamboo has no disastrous environmental consequences (as in the case of timber), on account of its quick replacement within 4 or 5 years.
• The physical properties of bamboo make it an ideal construction material for seismic areas.
• Compared with most other building materials, bamboo is cheap to buy, process and maintain.

There are, however, drawbacks that need to be overcome, for example:
• limited durability, mainly on account of excessive wetting and drying, insect and fungal attack, physical impact, and wear and tear;
• limited social acceptability, as a result of the limited durability of bamboo.
Further information: Bibl. 13.05, 13.06, 13.07.

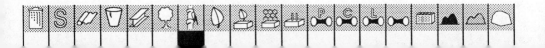

Barrel Vault (Bibl. 13.05)

- This construction system was developed at the Research Laboratory for Experimental Construction, Kassel College of Technology, Federal Republic of Germany, headed by Prof. Gernot Minke.
- It demonstrates an unusual use of bamboo, in which the construction obtains its stability by compressive forces, acting perpendicularly to the bamboo's axis.
- On the principle of masonry barrel vaults, full-section bamboo culms are laid horizontally, one on top of the other following a curve, defined by an inverted catenary. (This is a curve formed by hanging a uniform chain freely between two points. The tensile forces induced by gravitation run along the line connecting the points of contact of each chain link. Since the curve remains stable when reversing the direction of forces, an inverted catenary is the ideal shape of a barrel vault.)
- Split bamboo strips of equal length are hung such that their ends are exactly the same distance apart as the ultimate roof span. The full-section bamboo culms are laid horizontally forming an inverted vault. Split bamboo strips are then laid on the inside, exactly opposite the outer ones. Holes are drilled through the split and whole bamboo and fixed by bolts or rivets.
- The whole structure is then turned over and fixed on the top of the walls, which preferably should have a timber or concrete ring beam, onto which the roof is connected.
- The roof should be covered with a waterproof membrane for rain protection. This can be covered by a suitable local thatching material, or more appropriately by a 10 cm layer of soil on which grass can grow. For initial reinforcement (to prevent slipping) the soil should be held down by a strong net (as used for fishing). The dense structure of the grass roofs will give the soil cover its ultimate stability.

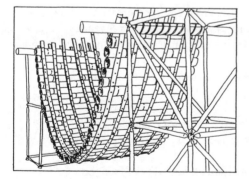 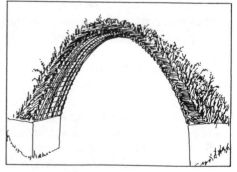

Small Geodesic Dome (Bibl. 13.05)

- This construction system was also developed and tested by Prof. Minke and his team.
- The supporting structure of the dome is made up of approx. 1.5 m long pieces of full-section bamboo culms, connected in a series of triangles, making it rigid. The lengths of the bamboo members are determined by a geometrical design, which requires fairly accurate cutting to achieve a uniform shape. However, the simple connection system allows for adjustments during assembly. For a tighter fit at the connecting points, at which in alternate succession six and five members meet, the bamboo ends are bevelled (slanted).
- In the example described, the span of the dome was 5 m, a size that is easy to prefabricate and transport manually with 5 people.
- Sand filled tin cans served as footings, providing simple adjustment to differing loads. These were placed in foundations made of old steels drums, which were filled with building rubble and lean concrete.
- A strong waterproof membrane is needed to cover the dome, on which several roofing materials may be used, eg palm leaf or soft stem grass thatch, or wooden shingles on lathing. The structure erected at the Kassel College of Technology had a grass roof.

Connection detail

Grid Shell on a Square Base (Bibl. 13.05)

• The aim of this project, carried out by the Aachen Technical College, Federal Republic of Germany, was to develop a low-cost, earthquake resistant roof structure for developing countries, using only local materials and tools. The result was a bamboo grid shell, which is prefabricated on a flat surface and later lifted in the centre to give it its ultimate shape.

• The bamboo cane used had an average diameter of 30 mm and length of approximately 4 m. For the required length 7.2 m, each grid bar required the joining of two canes. Tests showed that the strongest joints were obtained by inserting thinner bamboo pieces in the cavities at the connecting ends and fixing them by means of short dowels.

• With these lengthened bars, a grid is laid out on the ground forming grid sectors of 50 x 50 cm. Each cross point had a dowel connection which was tied with string to prevent slipping, but to allow a scissor-like movement. After lifting the centre of the grid to the required height, 1 m cane pieces are placed approximately diagonally to the rhombic grid sections, in the direction of slope, and firmly tied to the grid, giving it stability.

• The edges of the grid form a square of 6 x 6 m, corresponding to the wall dimensions. A vertical bamboo piece is embedded in each corner of the walls and a kind of bamboo ring tie beam is fixed to them. This in turn holds the grid shell roof in place. The roof is covered by a waterproof membrane and a suitable local thatching material, other than stiff-stem grass. A possible alternative to thatch is a ferrocement cover, which would remain in place even if the bamboo grid shell should cease to support it.

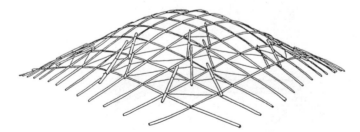

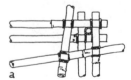

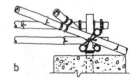

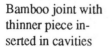

Bamboo joint with thinner piece inserted in cavities

Corner detail with ring tie beam (a. top view, b. section)

Irregularly Shaped Grid Shells (Bibl. 13.05)

- In order to construct spatially curved load-bearing structures using relatively thin bars, the same principle of inverting catenary lines, as described under "Barrel Vault", is applied. The shape of such grid shells is, therefore, not designed, but determined by using suspended models (eg with chain nets). Several such structures using split bamboo have been developed and erected on a joint project of the Institute of Lightweight Structures, Stuttgart, Federal Republic of Germany, and the School of Architecture, Ahmedabad, India.
- Corresponding to the chain net, the grid is assembled on the ground and tied at each cross point. For irregular base plans, each bar will have a different length, which is measured off the suspended model. Since the split bamboo gets more twisted, the steeper the slope of the grid shell, dowel joints cannot be used, while rope tie joints maintain a harmonious curvature of the structure.

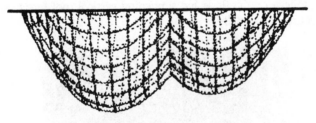

Suspended chain net model

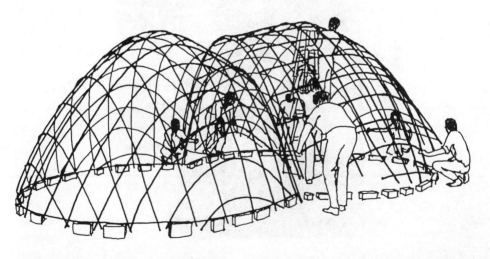

Bamboo Trusses (Bibl. 13.06, 13.07)

• In many regions, bamboo is traditionally used for truss constructions, but often use more bamboo than necessary and are not always structurally sound.
• A research project, conducted by Dr. Jules Janssen of the Eindhoven University of Technology, Netherlands, developed and tested four types of bamboo joints and an improved truss design.
• Joint 1: plywood on both sides of the bamboo and held by steel bolts.
• Joint 2: the diagonal member rests against pins inserted through the upper member, whereby the pins support both the purlin and the diagonal member. An intermediate layer (a kind of washer) considerably improves the strength.
• Joint 3: two "horns" at the end of the diagonal fit into two holes in the upper member. (Disadvantage: requires craftsmanship, time and excludes prefabrication).
• Joint 4: bamboo pin passing through three bamboo members, the outer two being parallel.
• The improved bamboo truss, built with joint 2 and a free span of 8 m, was tested in the laboratory by placing it on the floor and simulating vertical roof loads, by a system of hydraulic jacks acting horizontally.

POLE TIMBER ROOF STRUCTURES

KEYWORDS:

Special properties	Cheaper and stronger than sawn timber
Economical aspects	Low to medium costs
Stability	Good
Skills required	Carpentry skills
Equipment required	Carpentry tools
Resistance to earthquake	Very good
Resistance to hurricane	Good
Resistance to rain	Depends on protective measures
Resistance to insects	Low
Climatic suitability	All climates
Stage of experience	Partly traditional, partly experimental

SHORT DESCRIPTION:

• Unprocessed roundwood is cheaper and more easily available than sawn timber, and is mainly used for frame structures, ie skeleton wall and roof structures, trusses and the like.

• The advantages of using pole timber from young trees (5 - 7 years old) as compared to those of using sawn timber are numerous. The main ones are:

• The cost and wastage of sawing are eliminated.

• 100 % of the harvested timber's strength is utilized, while the immense original strength of large tree trunks is forfeited by sub-division or lost in the sawing wastes.

• A timber pole is stronger than sawn timber of equal cross-sectional area, because the fibres flow smoothly around natural defects and do not end as sloping grain at cut surfaces.

• Poles have large tension growth stresses around their perimeters and this assists in increasing the strength of the compression face of a pole in bending.

• Sawn timber is a product of trees that have grown for several decades. Since their replacement takes so long, excessive felling can cause serious environmental problems.

• Hence, from the points of view of economy, strength characteristics and environmental acceptability, the use of pole timber (eg from mangrove swamps, thinnings from eucalyptus or softwood plantations, etc.) can be far more appropriate for a range of building constructions than the use of sawn timber.

Scrap Metal Plate Connections
(Bibl. 00.39)

• This simple and cheap technique, developed at the Intermediate Technology Workshop in Cradley Heath, U.K., uses thin sheet metal, cut to the required size and shape, which is wrapped around the joints and firmly nailed onto the timber.

• The most suitable application of this method is in the prefabrication of pole timber trusses. To ensure uniform dimensions, the trusses are made with the help of a template laid on the ground and held in place by wooden or steel pegs. The poles are placed as accurately as possible on the template, then cut to size and joined together as described above.

Joint detail

Steel Flitch Plate Connections (Bibl. 14.10)

• The nailed flitch plate connection, developed at the Building Research Establishment, Garston, U.K., consists of mild steel sheets inserted into longitudinal saw cuts in the timber poles and connected to them by nails driven through the timber and the steel at right angles to the plate.

• Mild steel sheets up to 1 mm thickness can be easily penetrated by normal round wire steel nails without pre-drilling. Thicker sheets require drilling or the use of hard steel nails. Tests have shown that for most applications and timber species two 1 mm plates provide sufficient strength of the connections. (Considerations of cost suggest that it is better to increase the number of 1 mm plates rather than their thickness.) Stronger timbers may require flitch plates of larger areas to achieve appropriate design stresses.

• The ability of the nailed flitch plate connection to sustain loads after initial failure is a characteristic which could prove valuable in areas where buildings may be subjected to earthquakes and high winds.

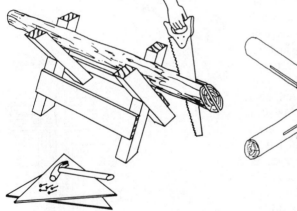

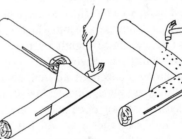

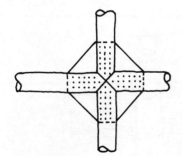

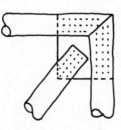

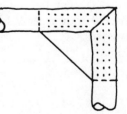

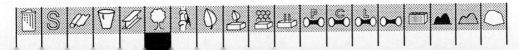

Timber Jointing with Dowels
(Bibl. 14.02)

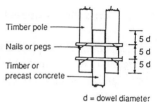

Timber pole
Nails or pegs
Timber or
precast concrete

5 d
5 d
5 d

d = dowel diameter

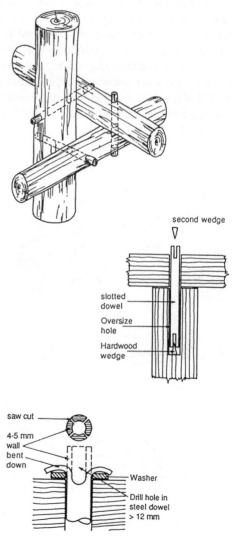

second wedge

slotted
dowel

Oversize
hole

Hardwood
wedge

saw cut
4-5 mm
wall
bent
down

Washer

Drill hole in
steel dowel
> 12 mm

• Nails and toothed plate connectors are quite often impossible to use on harder timber species. When used on softwoods, they tend to loosen when the timber shrinks.
• A more appropriate alternative, developed at the University of Nairobi, Kenya, is the use of dowels, which are fitted into predrilled holes. Where structural considerations permit, these are preferably wooden dowels, as they are cheaper and do not corrode. They should, however, be prevented from slipping out by means of nails or pegs, inserted at different angles.
• Alternatively, holes can be drilled into the ends of the wooden dowels, into which hardwood wedges can be fitted to keep the dowel in place. Thus the hole into which the dowel is inserted can be slightly oversized to facilitate and speed up work.
• Where strong connections are vital, steel bolts and nuts are most suitable, but also very expensive, costing three to four times that of the mild steel rods from which they are made. Using the rods straight away as dowels is cheaper and equally effective. To prevent them from slipping out of the timber, 10 - 12 mm deep holes should be drilled into the ends of the dowels, as described above in the case of wooden dowels. With a cross saw cut, the end pieces can be bent back like flower petals, holding down a steel washer.

Space Frame Connections (Bibl. 23.10)

• A method of using short length, local pole timber to construct space frames for large covered areas (such as meeting halls, workshops, markets, etc.) was developed in Sweden by Habitropic. The system is based on special space frame connectors, comprising a cross-component of welded steel, and tail end connectors with screws, washers and nuts.

• The poles are all cut to the same length, say 1.5 m, and cut lengthwise at both ends with a saw. Holes for bolts are drilled at each end, the steel tail-end connectors inserted in the saw cut and fixed with bolt, washer and nut. After prefabricating all the required poles, they are assembled on the ground, directly below their final position and lifted into place by a pulley system.

• With pole thicknesses of 5 - 6 cm the weight per m² is 20 kg, and the consumption of material per m² is approximately 3.5 poles and 1.1 space frame connectors.

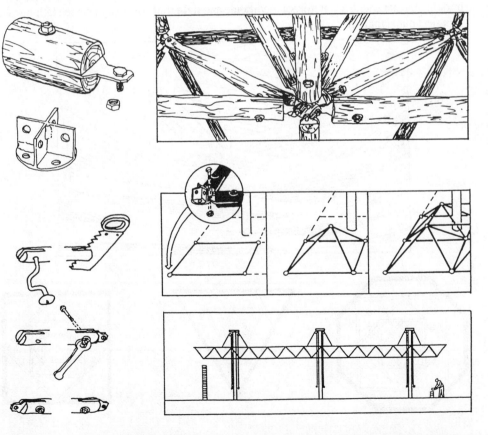

Hogan Roof Construction (Bibl. 23.16)

• The North American Navajo Indians traditionally build their homes (hogans) with this simple method. A hogan is usually an octagonal house covered by several layers of timber poles, which are laid across the corners of the layer below, thus reducing the void with each new layer. The same system can be used to cover triangular, square or other polygonal structures, without the need for supports other than at the periphery of the roof.

• A well designed roof with accurately cut and assembled poles should in theory be stable with only a few bolt or dowel connections at certain strategic points. However, it is advisable to fix each pole firmly to the one below to avoid excessive lateral movement, especially in earthquake or hurricane prone regions.

• Traditionally, the hogan roof is covered with earth to provide a high thermal capacity, which is advantageous in climates with large diurnal temperature fluctuations. Lighter roofs with low thermal capacity are also possible by merely constructing a framework and bridging the gaps with a waterproof membrane and light roof cover (eg wooden lathing and shingles, mats, thatch).

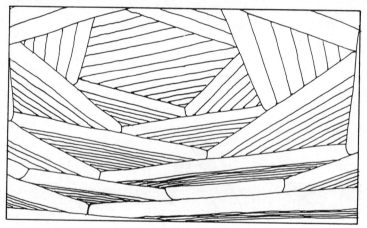

BAMBOO AND WOOD SHINGLES

KEYWORDS:

Special properties	Attractive, durable roof cover with replaceable elements
Economical aspects	Low to medium costs
Stability	Good
Skills required	Traditional craftsmanship
Equipment required	Bamboo cutting tools, shingle knife, hammer
Resistance to earthquake	Good
Resistance to hurricane	Depends on fixing
Resistance to rain	Good
Resistance to insects	Low
Climatic suitability	Warm humid and highland zones
Stage of experience	Widely used

SHORT DESCRIPTION:

• Shingles are used to cover pitched roofs (and quite often walls) on a supporting grid of bamboo or wooden laths. The appearance is typically a fish-scale structure, but some types of bamboo shingles rather resemble Spanish tiles.

• Appropriate lengths of bamboo culms or timber logs are cut and the shingles are split off these vertically, whereby bamboo culms are split into quarter or half sections, and wood shingles are flat tiles cut with a special knife and hammer.

• For fixing bamboo shingles, pre-drilled holes are needed for nailing or tying with a tough string. Quarter-cut bamboo shingles can also be made with splints which are hooked onto the lathing.

• Timber shingles are nailed onto the battens, whereby the curvature of the shingles after drying must be taken into consideration.

• The minimum roof pitch for shingles is 45°. Pressure impregnated timber and bamboo can have lower pitches, but are not recommended: higher costs; chemicals are gradually washed out and become ineffective; rainwater cannot be collected from the roof.

Further information: "The Shingle Roofing Manual" (available from the Forest Products Research Centre, Box 1358, Boroko, Papua New Guinea); Bibl. 00.19, 23.24.

Bamboo Shingles with Splint or String Fixing (Bibl. 23.24)

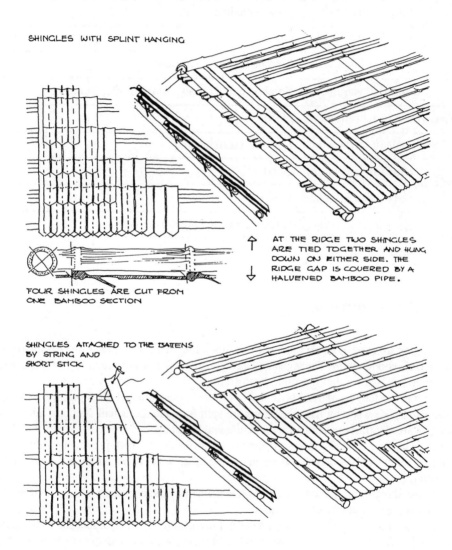

SHINGLES WITH SPLINT HANGING

FOUR SHINGLES ARE CUT FROM
ONE BAMBOO SECTION

AT THE RIDGE TWO SHINGLES
ARE TIED TOGETHER AND HUNG
DOWN ON EITHER SIDE. THE
RIDGE GAP IS COVERED BY A
HALVENED BAMBOO PIPE.

SHINGLES ATTACHED TO THE BATTENS
BY STRING AND
SHORT STICK

Bamboo Shingles as Spanish Tiles (Bibl. 23.24)

BAMBOO SHINGLES LIKE SPANISH TILES
MADE OF SHORT PIECES

THE SHINGLES ARE
BOUND TO PAIRS OF
BATTENS.
AT THE EAVES A BATTEN
WITH A BIGGER DIAMETER
EQUALIZES THE PITCH.

BAMBOO SHINGLES LIKE
SPANISH TILES MADE OF
PITCH LONG PIECES

THE PIPES ARE NAILED
TOGETHER AT THE RIDGE
AND THE CAP IS CLOSED
BY AN OTHER HALF PIPE.

THE BAMBOO PIPES
ARE SPLIT IN TWO.
THE NODGES ARE
CUT OUT.

IN ORDER NOT TO BE
LIFTED A 'SECOND EAVES
PURLIN' RUNS ACROSS
THE COVERING.

Wood Shingles (Bibl. 23.24)

NAILS ARE MADE OF DRY BAMBOO 4/4 mm AND 4 CM LONG.

THE SHINGLES ARE CUT OF CROSS SECTIONS (70 CM LONG) OF A STRAIGHT GRAIN TIMBER LOG. THE BARK AND THE CORE ARE THROWN AWAY. THE SHINGLES ARE ABOUT 2 CM THICK AND 70CM LONG. THE WIDTH WILL VARY.

THE SHINGLES ARE LAID FROM THE EAVES TO THE RIDGE. EACH SHINGLE IS FIXED WITH A SINGLE NAIL TO THE BATTENS. LAY THE SHINGLES CLOSE TO THE NEXT ONE AND TAKE CARE THAT THE JOINTS STAGGER. THE NAILS ARE COVERED WITH THE NEXT LAYER. WHEN THE UPPER SURFACE GETS ROTTEN TAKE ALL SHINGLES OFF AND NAIL THEM AGAIN UPSIDE DOWN. NO NAIL

NO NAIL MAY GO TROUGH TWO SHINGLES

JUST NAILED ON   AFTER DRYING

CORE SIDE DOWNWARD

CORE SIDE DOWNWARD SPACED LAYING

CORE SIDE UP AND DOWNWARD ALTERNATING

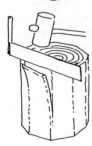

CORRUGATED METAL SHEET ROOFING

KEYWORDS:

Special properties	Light roofs, quick assembly
Economical aspects	Medium costs
Stability	Low to medium
Skills required	Average construction skills
Equipment required	Carpentry tools
Resistance to earthquake	Very good
Resistance to hurricane	Low
Resistance to rain	Good, but extremely loud
Resistance to insects	Very good
Climatic suitability	Warm humid climates
Stage of experience	Widely used in almost all countries

SHORT DESCRIPTION:

• The metal sheets are either galvanized iron or aluminium, whereby gi is susceptible to rapid corrosion if the zinc coating is not sufficiently thick (a common problem with cheaper varieties). Aluminium is lighter, more durable and reflects heat more efficiently, but is more expensive and produced with an extremely high energy input.

• The corrugations make the thin sheets stiff enough to span between two purlins without sagging. Thus large areas can be roofed with a minimum of supporting construction, making the roof light (good in earthquake zones) and cheaper (less timber or steel framework).

• Thin gauge sheets are often too weak to walk on, can be dented, punctured or torn off by strong winds.

• Major problems of metal sheet roofing are the immense heat transmission to the interior (less severe with aluminium) during sunshine, and water condensation on the underside when the roof cools down at night; unbearable noise caused by heavy rains; havoc caused by whirling sheets that are ripped off in tropical windstorms; poor fire resistance.

• Many of these problems can be alleviated with good design, material qualities and workmanship.

Further information: Bibl. 00.55, 23.17, 25.06.

Construction of Corrugated Metal Sheet Roofing

• Such roofing should be avoided in areas of intense solar radiation and rapid temperature changes, to avoid hot indoor climate and condensation problems.
• In most cases it is advisable to construct a suspended ceiling (of a light reflective material), providing a ventilated air space which removes the accumulated heat before it can reach the interior.
• The air space also reduces the noise problem during rains. In addition, shorter distances between purlins, as well as felt or rubber washers at the suspension points, rigid bolt connections and thicker gauged sheets help to reduce sound transmission.
• Similarly, thicker sheets, rigidly fixed hook bolts with large metal washers (underlaid with felt or rubber to avoid bimetallic corrosion) and avoidance of overhangs, are measures to prevent damage by strong winds.
• A fire-resistant suspended ceiling and other common-sense fire precautions can eliminate the fire risk completely.

Overlaps of roofing sheets must take into consideration the main direction of wind.

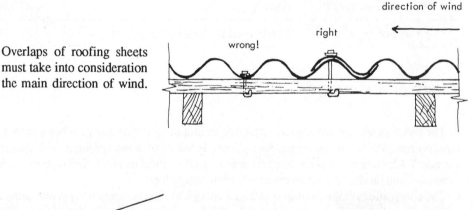

direction of wind

right

wrong!

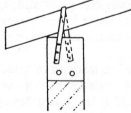

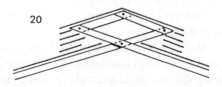

20

Rafters should be firmly held by a fastening strap or reinforcing bar, which is embedded in the concrete or masonry.
(Bibl. 25.06)

A ridge ventilator can help to improve indoor climate and also reduce internal pressure and thus decrease the total roof uplift.
(Bibl. 25.06)

291

EXAMPLES
OF
BUILDING SYSTEMS

MUD BRICK VAULTS AND DOMES

KEYWORDS:

Special properties	Building system without centering or shuttering
Economical aspects	Low cost
Stability	Good
Skills required	Special training
Equipment required	Masonry equipment
Resistance to earthquake	Low
Resistance to hurricane	Very good
Resistance to rain	Depends on external finish
Resistance to insects	Medium to good
Climatic suitability	Hot dry climates
Stage of experience	Traditional in countries like Egypt and Iran

SHORT DESCRIPTION:

• While vaults and domes are self-supporting structural forms when completed, they normally need support and centering while under construction. This usually involves first building an identical vault in wood over which the masonry vault rests, until complete and dried.

• In countries where timber is scarce, this type of vaulting is hardly advantageous. A system of building vaults and domes, without this framework, or shuttering, evolved in countries like Egypt and Iran.

• The drawings overleaf show the sequence of construction of a small house, which the founder members of Development Workshop and some friends built in New Gourna, Upper Egypt, in 1973. They worked as apprentices alongside two Nubian master masons, skilled in the techniques being used.

• The house was built with mud bricks and served, amongst other objectives, as a practical opportunity to master and evaluate the Nubian techniques of building without the use of shuttering, and to obtain a clear guide regarding the relationship of roof span to wall thickness and height for mud brick walls.

• The house stands amongst the buildings designed by Hassan Fathy, who revived this building technique in the 1940s (Bibl. 02.14).

Building Sequence of Experimental House in New Gourna, Upper Egypt
(Illustrations by Development Workshop, Bibl. 24.03)

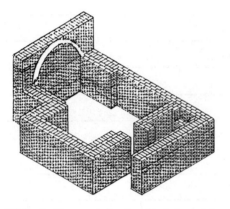

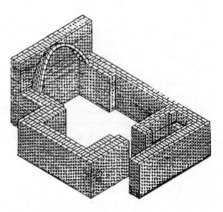

Walls built up to the level of the spring points of the vaults. End wall built up for vault to lean on. Inverted catenary form traced on end wall.

Vault building with courses leaning towards end wall so that no formwork or shuttering is required.

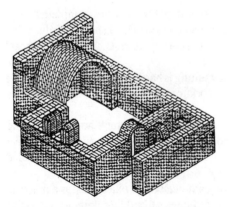

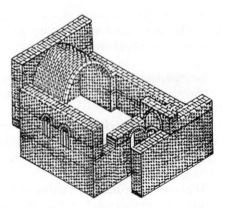

Vault is completed; each course of bricks is less inclined, until vault is flush with side walls. Window openings built up with dry bricks - no mortar.

Walls built up. Arches built over dry brick in windows.

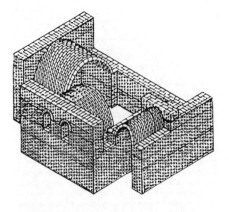

Small vault built in same way as large ones. Loose bricks removed from window openings.

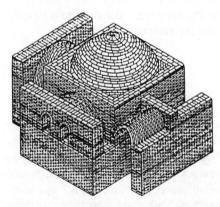

Circular arches built over vaults to form a base for the dome.

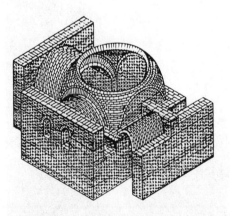

Pendentives completed, forming continuous course from which dome can be completed.

Brick courses of dome incline increasingly until dome is finished.

- *Further information*: Development Workshop (coordinating office in Canada), Box 133, 238 Davenport Road, Toronto, Ontario M5R IJ6, Canada, or (Europe office in France) B.P. 10 Montayral, 47500 Fumel, France.

New Developments

Arches constructed with old car tyres
(Bibl. 24.12)

Simple arches can be constructed over
openings by using old car tyres as formwork. This was tried out on a project in India
(1986) and found extremely easy to carry
out. The sides of the opening, which has the
width of the tyre, are erected up to the level
at which the arch begins. The tyre is placed
on a dry stack of bricks, such that the axis is
in line with the top brick layer. The bricks
should be laid alternately on each side of the
tyre, since excessive load on one side can
deform the tyre and distort the shape of the
arch. Care must be taken that the lower
edges of the bricks touch each other without
leaving any gaps. Since the tyre is flexible,
it can be removed with ease.

Catenary shaped dome

A catenary shaped template, which rotates
around a vertical axis at the centre of the
dome, is used to place the bricks with great
accuracy to form a curvature which permits
only compressive forces to act within the
structure. This gives a more stable dome
construction than hemispherically shaped
domes.

This innovative construction method was
developed and tested in 1987 at the Research Laboratory for Experimental Construction, Kassel College of Technology,
Federal Republic of Germany, headed by
Prof. Gernot Minke.

EARTHQUAKE RESISTANT MUD/BAMBOO STRUCTURES

KEYWORDS:

Special properties	Self-help construction with local materials
Economical aspects	Low cost
Stability	Very good
Skills required	Semi-skilled labour
Equipment required	Traditional local building equipment
Resistance to earthquake	Very good
Resistance to hurricane	Low to medium
Resistance to rain	Low to medium
Resistance to insects	Low
Climatic suitability	All except extremely wet climates
Stage of experience	Experimental

SHORT DESCRIPTION:

• This building system was developed and implemented by John Norton, Development Workshop, France, in a USAID technical assistance project in the Koumbia region of North West Guinea, following the December 1983 earthquake.

• Traditional houses were generally made of wattle and daub walls, and thatch roofs. Similar materials, techniques and house forms had to be used in reconstruction, in order to be sure of acceptance by the people. But the new houses had to be earthquake resistant.

• The solution arrived at was to construct the walls with sun-dried mud bricks and to strengthen them by tying bamboo frames on either side. This external reinforcement can be easily checked for termite or other damage and replaced if necessary, thus avoiding the problem faced by traditional houses, in which the concealed bamboo lattice was usually destroyed and consequently failed during the earthquake.

• With this construction, it was possible to retain the traditional house form and thatch roofing, so that no problems of social acceptance arose.

Further information: John Norton, Development Workshop, B.P. 10 Montayral, 47500 Fumel, France; Bibl. 24.13, 24.14, 25.10.

Plan and Section through Traditional Round House, Koumbia Area

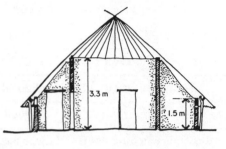

Scale
0 1 2 3 4 m.

Earthquake Resistant Mud Brick Wall with Bamboo Framework "Sandwiching" (Bibl. 24.13, 24.14)

Load bearing brick wall

Framing helps restrain wall when shaken

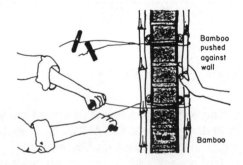

Bamboo tightened by pulling on short sticks attached to wire ends

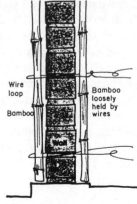

Tightening the bamboo framework with looped wires passed through the brick wall during construction

Detail of exposed bamboo reinforcement: immediate detection of termite or other damage; easy replacement of affected members

Construction of bamboo roof framework on the
completed bamboo reinforced mud brick walls

Completed "case" (traditional round house)

ADOBE BRICK HOUSE

KEYWORDS:

Special properties	Improved traditional building system
Economical aspects	Low to medium costs
Stability	Good
Skills required	Traditional construction skills
Equipment required	Formwork for bricks and concrete, building equipment
Resistance to earthquake	Good
Resistance to hurricane	Good
Resistance to rain	Depends on soil stabilization
Resistance to insects	Medium to good
Climatic suitability	All except extremely hot dry climates
Stage of experience	Increasing applications

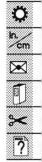

SHORT DESCRIPTION:

• This building system was implemented in a housing development project in El Salvador, Central America, initiated by GATE and conducted by the Institute for Tropical Building, Starnberg, Federal Republic of Germany, headed by Dr.Ing. Georg Lippsmeier.

• The aim was to improve the earthquake resistance of traditional adobe brick houses, by self-help methods and with little additional costs.

• The improvements were: strengthening of the site-produced mud bricks by adding lime; providing reinforced concrete foundations and ring beams; rigid connection between roof and supporting walls.

Further information: GATE, Postfach 51 80, 6236 Eschborn, Federal Republic of Germany; Bibl. 00.18, 24.01.

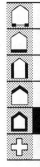

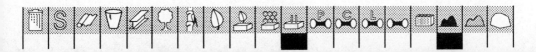

Construction Details of
Wall, Ring Beam and Roof
(Bibl. 24.01)

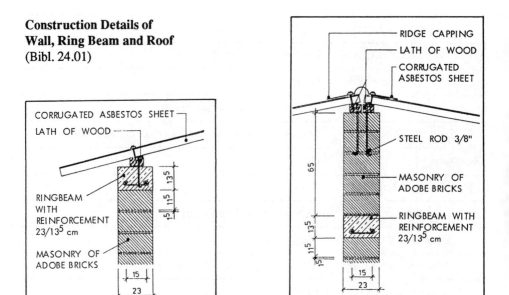

CORRUGATED ASBESTOS SHEET
LATH OF WOOD

RINGBEAM
WITH
REINFORCEMENT
23/13⁵ cm

MASONRY OF
ADOBE BRICKS

15
23

13⁵
11⁵
5

RIDGE CAPPING
LATH OF WOOD
CORRUGATED
ASBESTOS SHEET

STEEL ROD 3/8"

MASONRY OF
ADOBE BRICKS

RINGBEAM WITH
REINFORCEMENT
23/13⁵ cm

65
13⁵
11⁵
5

15
23

MODULAR FRAMED EARTH BLOCK CONSTRUCTION

KEYWORDS:

Special properties	Earthquake resistant, light frame, easy assembly
Economical aspects	Low cost
Stability	Good
Skills required	Average construction skills
Equipment required	Soil block press, simple construction equipment
Resistance to earthquake	Good
Resistance to hurricane	Good
Resistance to rain	Depends on soil stabilization
Resistance to insects	Medium to good
Climatic suitability	All except extremely hot dry climates
Stage of experience	Applications in relief projects in Africa

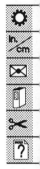

SHORT DESCRIPTION:

- The key elements of this building system are hollow steel connectors and specially formed earth blocks made in a manual block press (with a system of inserts).
- The steel connectors have either square or circular cross-sections and are used to connect straight pipes of square or circular section, or even sawn timber or bamboo components, to form the basic framework, which carries a light, corrugated aluminium sheet roof.
- The earth blocks, produced on the MARO Block Press (see *ANNEX*), are made to interlock with the framework to form durable walls. This system is ideally suited for disaster relief housing projects. A single truck-load of connectors, roofing sheets and a few block presses can be sufficient to build a group of houses with local soil and bamboo.
- The framework should rest on concrete strip foundations, though for temporary structures no foundation is needed.
- The walls can initially be plastic sheets (for immediate shelter), which are gradually replaced by earth blocks or even locally available burnt clay bricks, such that the quickly erected refugee tent camps are efficiently converted into permanent housing by self-help and low-cost methods. Extensions are possible in all directions.

Further information: Mark Klein, MARO Enterprise, 95 bis Route de Suisse, CH-1290 Versoix (Geneva), Switzerland.

MARO Construction System

Steel connectors with square
and circular sections

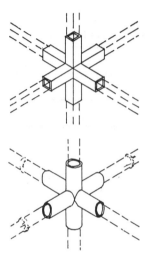

Earth block wall construction
interlocking with framework

Block press with inserts
Special earth blocks
Completed framework

LOK BILD SYSTEM

KEYWORDS:

Special properties	Interlocking blocks, high strength, easy assembly
Economical aspects	Medium to high costs
Stability	Very good
Skills required	Average construction skills
Equipment required	Special framework, standard building equipment
Resistance to earthquake	Very good
Resistance to hurricane	Very good
Resistance to rain	Very good
Resistance to insects	Very good
Climatic suitability	All climates
Stage of experience	Increasing applications; widely tested system

SHORT DESCRIPTION:

• The LOK BILD System was developed by Dr. A. Bruce Etherington of AIT Bangkok and University of Hawaii, and has been tested in Malaysia, Thailand and the Philippines using cement concrete, and in the United Arab Emirates using sulphur concrete.

• The hollow blocks are designed to be assembled without mortar, producing perfectly aligned walls without special masonry skills. The system also includes precast concrete joists, which interlock with the concrete block walls to support in situ floors and roofs, and channel blocks, which are placed on top of the walls to make reinforced concrete ring beams.

• The interlocking blocks have narrow vertical recesses and a central cavity, which when assembled form continuous, vertically aligned holes over the full height of the wall. When cement grout is poured into them, the blocks become permanently locked together. Wherever necessary, eg at corners, cross-walls, or around openings, the large hollow cores can be filled with reinforcement and concrete, providing earthquake resistance.

Further information: Dr. A. Bruce Etherington, Human Settlements Division, Asian Institute of Technology, P.O. Box 2754, Bangkok 10501, Thailand; Bibl. 24.05.

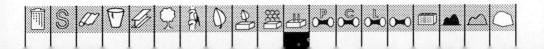

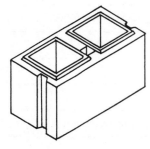

Ordinary block

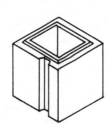

Half block

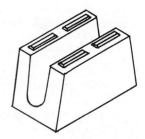

Channel block

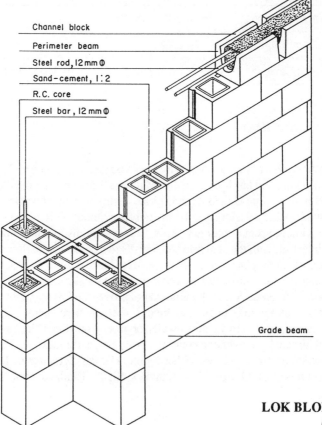

Channel block
Perimeter beam
Steel rod, 12 mm ⌀
Sand-cement, 1 : 2
R.C. core
Steel bar, 12 mm ⌀

Grade beam

LOK BLOK Assembly
(Bibl. 24.05)

Floor Assembly

REINFORCED STEEL ROD Ø 12 mm.

1˝ square WIRE MESH 3˝ OVERLAP

CONCRETE FLOOR

STEEL FORM 1 mm. THICK

1˝ square WOODEN SUPPORT

JOIST (A)

CHANNEL BLOCK

CONCRETE

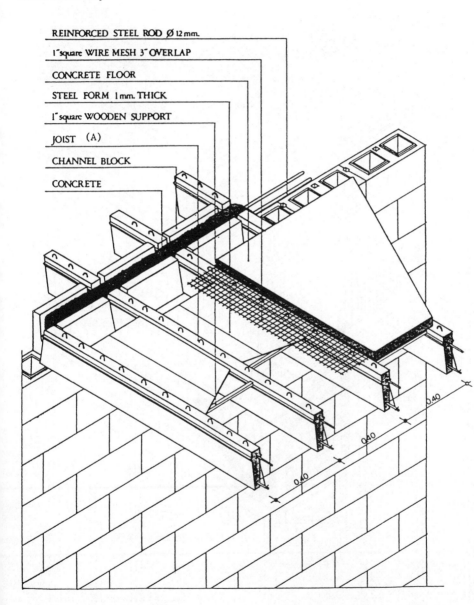

House Isometric

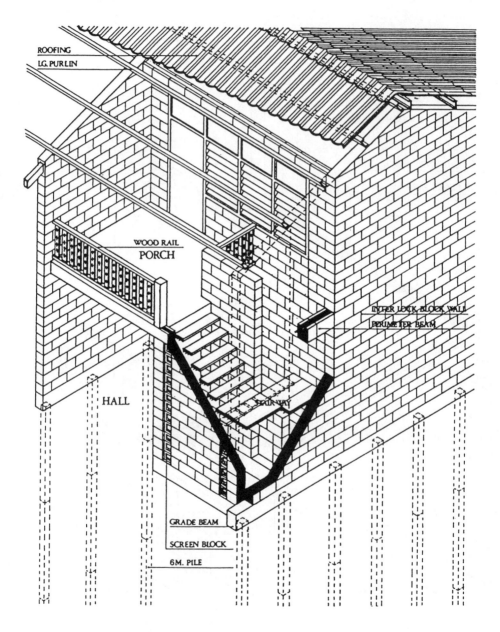

ROOFING
I.G. PURLIN
WOOD RAIL
PORCH
INTER LOCK BLOCK WALL
PERIMETER BEAM
HALL
STAIRWAY
GRADE BEAM
SCREEN BLOCK
6M. PILE

CONCRETE PANEL HOUSE

KEYWORDS:

Special properties	Prefabrication system, quick assembly
Economical aspects	Medium to high costs
Stability	Very good
Skills required	Average construction skills
Equipment required	Formwork for concrete, standard building equipment
Resistance to earthquake	Very good
Resistance to hurricane	Very good
Resistance to rain	Very good
Resistance to insects	Very good
Climatic suitability	All except very hot dry climates
Stage of experience	Experimental

SHORT DESCRIPTION:

• This building system was implemented in housing development projects in Nicaragua and Colombia, initiated by GATE and conducted by ARCO Grasser and Partner, Munich, Federal Republic of Germany.

• The prime requirements were earthquake resistance, simple prefabrication and rapid construction, which resulted in a system of reinforced concrete panels held by vertically fixed U-profiled steel frames, and a timber roof structure with corrugated galvanized iron sheets.

• The precast panels are connected by V-shaped tongue and groove joints, sealed with cement grout after assembly. The ring beam at the top can be of sawn timber or in situ concrete. Wooden door and window frames are made to the same width as the panels and inserted likewise between the steel frames.

• The panels can alternatively be made of wooden or bamboo boards, pumice concrete, ferrocement, or other locally available material.

Further information: GATE, Postfach 51 80, 6236 Eschborn, Federal Republic of Germany; Bibl. 24.02.

Construction Details of Wall, Ring Beam and Roof
(Bibl. 24.02)

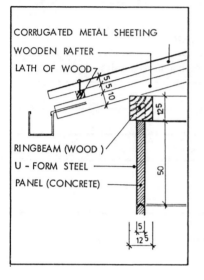

CORRUGATED METAL SHEETING

WOODEN RAFTER

LATH OF WOOD

RINGBEAM (WOOD)

U – FORM STEEL

PANEL (CONCRETE)

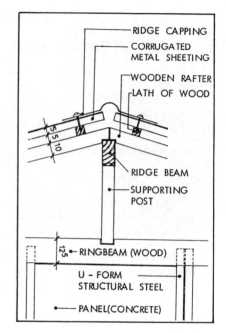

RIDGE CAPPING

CORRUGATED METAL SHEETING

WOODEN RAFTER

LATH OF WOOD

RIDGE BEAM

SUPPORTING POST

RINGBEAM (WOOD)

U – FORM STRUCTURAL STEEL

PANEL(CONCRETE)

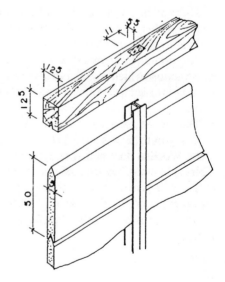

FERROCEMENT HOUSING UNITS

KEYWORDS:

Special properties	Thin but very rigid wall construction
Economical aspects	Low to medium
Stability	Good
Skills required	Average construction skills
Equipment required	Simple construction tools
Resistance to earthquake	Good
Resistance to hurricane	Good
Resistance to rain	Good
Resistance to insects	Good
Climatic suitability	Warm humid climates
Stage of experience	Experimental

SHORT DESCRIPTION:

• A simple ferrocement house was constructed in 1977 on the Caribbean island of Dominica by Richard Holloway.

• Readily available round-wood poles were used for the load-bearing framework. Chicken-wire was stretched between the poles and plastered with cement mortar, first a rough layer, then a smooth finish. The timber frame remained exposed.

• Care was taken to protect the timber from rainwater and termite attack, by mounting the vertical members on galvanized pipe supports, embedded in exposed concrete footings.

• The roof was made of galvanized iron sheets with a gap left at the top of the wall plate for ventilation. The floors, doors and windows were made of reject quality wood and old boxes, which after painting showed no great difference from new wood.

Further information: Bibl. 24.09.

Construction Details
(Bibl. 24.09)

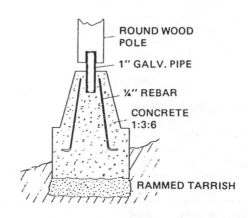

Details of footing

ROUND WOOD POLE

1" GALV. PIPE

¼" REBAR

CONCRETE 1:3:6

RAMMED TARRISH

Method of joining large poles

Chicken wire reinforcement

Completed timber framework

Completed ferrocement house

FIBRACRETO BUILDING SYSTEM

KEYWORDS:

Special properties	Comfortable housing
Economical aspects	Medium to high costs
Stability	Good
Skills required	Masonry skills
Equipment required	Masonry equipment
Resistance to earthquake	Good
Resistance to hurricane	Good
Resistance to rain	Good
Resistance to insects	Good
Climatic suitability	All climates
Stage of experience	Widely used

SHORT DESCRIPTION:

• This building system, patented in Peru under the name FIBRACRETO, basically consists of wood-wool cement panels structured with reinforced concrete columns and beams (Bibl. 24.15).

• It is used for one and two storey houses and is said to reduce construction costs by 35 to 40 % compared to conventional constructions.

• The foundations are 10 cm thick platforms, strengthened below and above the platforms along the axes of the walls.

• The 7.5 cm thick wood-wool cement boards (50 x 200 cm) are assembled with horizontal mortar joints and held together by wooden formwork. When the walls are assembled, the formwork is filled with concrete to produce strong columns, spaced 200 cm apart.

• The roof is made of the same (or thicker) wood-wool cement boards supported by cast-in-situ reinforced concrete beams, and can be flat or sloping.

• The walls and roof are plastered with cement mortar.

Further information: L.R. & T. Arquitectura y Construcción S.A., Arq. Manuel I. de Rivero D'Angelo, Shell # 319 - 702 Miraflores, Lima, Peru.

314

FIBRACRETO Building System

BAMBOOCRETE CONSTRUCTION

KEYWORDS:

Special properties	Cheaper than other equally strong structures
Economical aspects	Low to medium costs
Stability	Good
Skills required	Bamboo and masonry construction skills
Equipment required	Carpentry and masonry tools
Resistance to earthquake	Good
Resistance to hurricane	Good
Resistance to rain	Good
Resistance to insects	Low
Climatic suitability	All except very hot dry climates
Stage of experience	Experimental

SHORT DESCRIPTION:

• The bamboocrete house shown overleaf was implemented in 1976 by Dr. U.C. Kalita, et al (Bibl. 24.11), Regional Research Laboratory, Jorhat (Assam), India.

• On a concrete foundation with burnt brick base course and flooring, a framework of secondary species timber provides the structural support for infill panels and curved roofing elements made of split bamboo lattice-work, plastered with cement mortar.

• The use of bamboo to substitute steel reinforcement in concrete is of considerable economic interest, as steel is expensive and often imported. However, bamboo shrinks on drying - over 4 times more than the concrete - so that there is no bond between the bamboo and concrete. Furthermore, the alkalinity of concrete gradually destroys the bamboo fibre, which finally loses all its strength.

• Recent research (Bibl. 24.10) has shown some possible remedies: 1. Coating the bamboo with hot bitumen and improving bonding by covering it with coarse sand, driving in 25 mm nails or tying coconut fibre ropes around the bamboo (developed by D. Krishnamurthy); 2. Using only the outer section of bamboo (because of its higher tensile strength and elasticity) and twisting bundles of three split-bamboo strips around each other(developed by O. Hidalgo López).

• Further research is necessary, especially with a view to fibre deterioration.

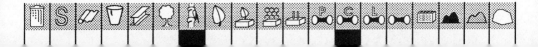

Bamboocrete House (Bibl. 24.11)

Preparation of the split bamboo lattice-work; completed house

BAMBOO HOUSES

KEYWORDS:

Special properties	High strength, flexibility, numerous designs possible
Economical aspects	Low to medium costs
Stability	Good
Skills required	Traditional bamboo craftsmanship
Equipment required	Tools for cutting, splitting, tying bamboo
Resistance to earthquake	Very good
Resistance to hurricane	Good
Resistance to rain	Depends on protective measures
Resistance to insects	Low
Climatic suitability	Warm humid climates
Stage of experience	Traditional

SHORT DESCRIPTION:

• The examples of bamboo houses shown on the following pages are taken from the excellently illustrated bamboo construction manual by Oscar Hidalgo López (Bibl. 24.07).
• All the structural components and most of the non-structural parts (floors and wall cladding) are made of bamboo. Only very little timber is used and the roof covering can be of any suitable, locally available material (eg thatch, fibre concrete, ferrocement, metal sheeting, cement mortar, or even stabilized, water-resistant soil mortar).
• The bamboo components are joined either by means of lashing materials, dowels, bolts or nails. A great number of possible bamboo connections is shown in the construction manual.
• On account of its low resistance to biological attack and fire, protective measures are necessary (see section on *Bamboo*).
Further information: Oscar Hidalgo López, Universidad Nacional de Colombia, Apartado Aéreo 54118, Bogotá, Colombia.

Construction of a Coffee Plant (also suitable for dwelling)
(Bibl. 24.07)

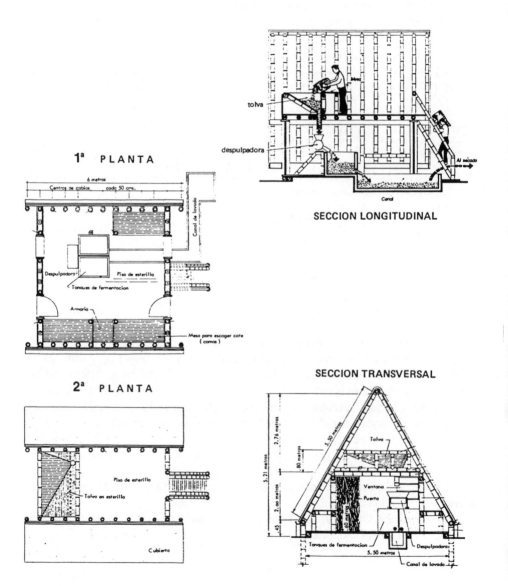

1ᵃ PLANTA

2ᵃ PLANTA

SECCION LONGITUDINAL

SECCION TRANSVERSAL

● MANUAL DE CONSTRUCCION CON BAMBU ● OSCAR HIDALGO LOPEZ ● CIBAM ● UNIVERSIDAD NACIONAL DE COLOMBIA ● FACULTAD DE ARTES ●

Positioning of the supports and erecting the structural framework

LOCALIZACION DE LOS SOPORTES - TRAZADO

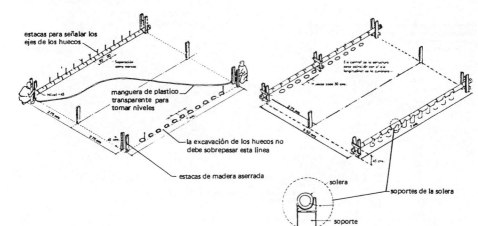

estacas para señalar los ejes de los huecos

manguera de plastico transparente para tomar niveles

la excavación de los huecos no debe sobrepasar esta linea

estacas de madera aserrada

solera

soportes de la solera

soporte

ERECCION DE LA ESTRUCTURA

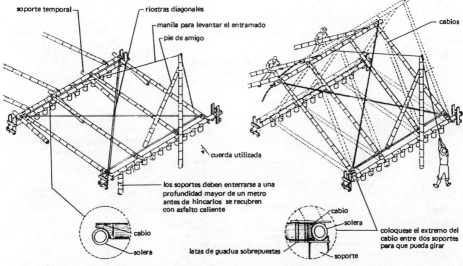

soporte temporal

riostras diagonales

manila para levantar el entramado

pie de amigo

cabios

cuerda utilizada

los soportes deben enterrarse a una profundidad mayor de un metro antes de hincarlos se recubren con asfalto caliente

cabio

solera

cabio

solera

latas de guadua sobrepuestas

soporte

coloquese el extremo del cabio entre dos soportes para que pueda girar

● MANUAL DE CONSTRUCCION CON BAMBU ● OSCAR HIDALGO LOPEZ ● CIBAM ● UNIVERSIDAD NACIONAL DE COLOMBIA ● FACULTAD DE ARTES ●

Fixing the rafters and construction of upper and lower floors (upper floor and wall cladding with split-bamboo or wooden laths, lower floor covered with stabilized rammed earth).

COLOCACION DE LOS CABIOS

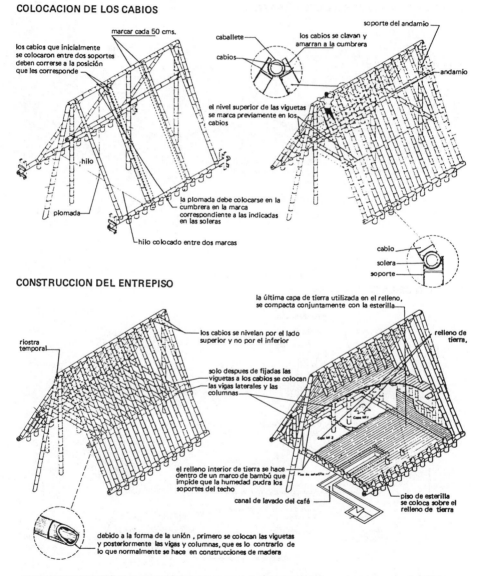

marcar cada 50 cms.

los cabios que inicialmente se colocaron entre dos soportes deben correrse a la posición que les corresponde

caballete

cabios

los cabios se clavan y amarran a la cumbrera

soporte del andamio

andamio

el nivel superior de las viguetas se marca previamente en los cabios

hilo

la plomada debe colocarse en la cumbrera en la marca correspondiente a las indicadas en las soleras

plomada

hilo colocado entre dos marcas

cabio
solera
soporte

CONSTRUCCION DEL ENTREPISO

la última capa de tierra utilizada en el relleno, se compacta conjuntamente con la esterilla

riostra temporal

los cabios se nivelan por el lado superior y no por el inferior

relleno de tierra,

solo despues de fijadas las viguetas a los cabios se colocan las vigas laterales y las columnas

el relleno interior de tierra se hace dentro de un marco de bambú que impide que la humedad pudra los soportes del techo

canal de lavado del café

piso de esterilla se coloca sobre el relleno de tierra

debido a la forma de la unión , primero se colocan las viguetas y posteriormente las vigas y columnas, que es lo contrario de lo que normalmente se hace en construcciones de madera

Bracing of roof structure and completion of roof covering (first with split-bamboo or wooden laths, fixed with nails and wire, then covered with cement mortar, stabilized waterproof mud mortar or thatch).

ARRIOSTRAMIENTO DE LA ESTRUCTURA

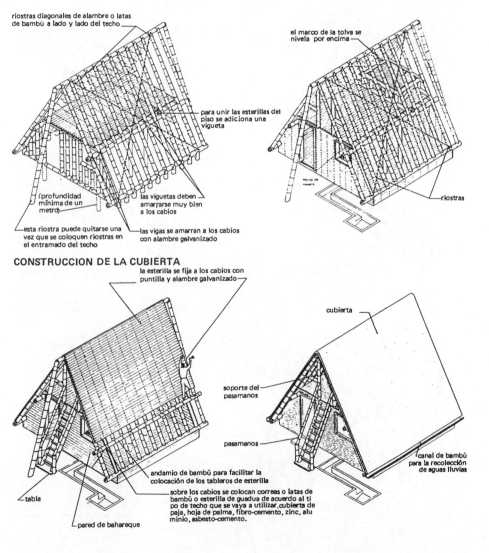

riostras diagonales de alambre o latas de bambú a lado y lado del techo

el marco de la tolva se nivela por encima

para unir las esterillas del piso se adiciona una vigueta

(profundidad mínima de un metro)

las viguetas deben amarrarse muy bien a los cabios

riostras

esta riostra puede quitarse una vez que se coloquen riostras en el entramado del techo

las vigas se amarran a los cabios con alambre galvanizado

CONSTRUCCION DE LA CUBIERTA

la esterilla se fija a los cabios con puntilla y alambre galvanizado

cubierta

soporte del pasamanos

pasamanos

andamio de bambú para facilitar la colocación de los tableros de esterilla

canal de bambú para la recolección de aguas lluvias

tabla

sobre los cabios se colocan correas o latas de bambú o esterilla de guadua de acuerdo al tipo de techo que se vaya a utilizar,cubierta de paja, hoja de palma, fibro-cemento, zinc, aluminio, asbesto-cemento.

pared de bahareque

● MANUAL DE CONSTRUCCION CON BAMBU ● OSCAR HIDALGO LOPEZ ● CIBAM ● UNIVERSIDAD NACIONAL DE COLOMBIA ● FACULTAD DE ARTES ●

Bamboo Structure with Prefabricated Space Frame Roof
(Wooden boards serve as template and temporary bracing during prefabrication; the walls of the house are not necessarily made of bamboo).

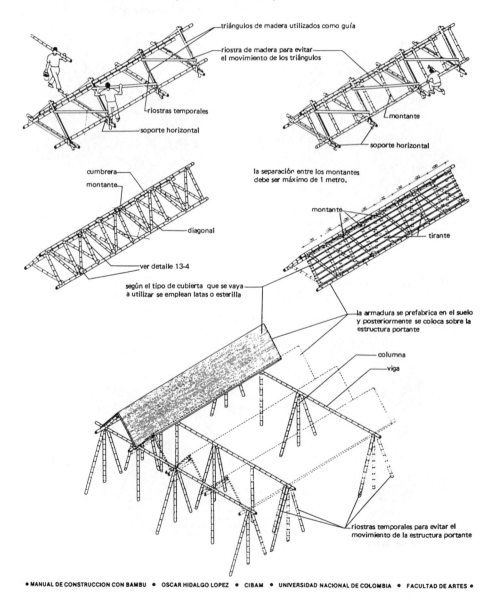

triángulos de madera utilizados como guía

riostra de madera para evitar el movimiento de los triángulos

riostras temporales

soporte horizontal

montante

soporte horizontal

cumbrera

montante

diagonal

ver detalle 13-4

según el tipo de cubierta que se vaya a utilizar se emplean latas o esterilla

la separación entre los montantes debe ser máximo de 1 metro.

montante

tirante

la armadura se prefabrica en el suelo y posteriormente se coloca sobre la estructura portante

columna

viga

riostras temporales para evitar el movimiento de la estructura portante

Bamboo House on Stilts

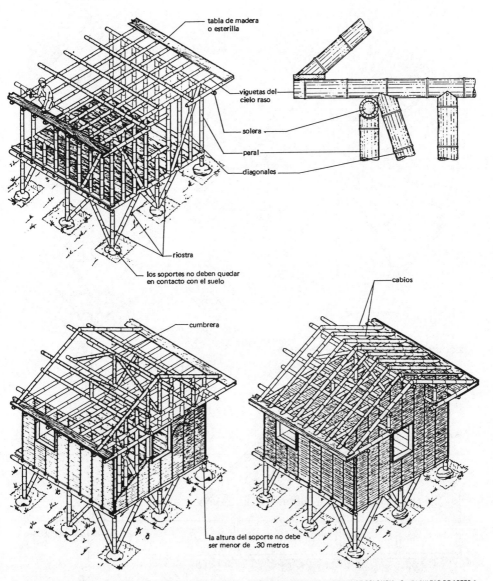

tabla de madera
o esterilla

viguetas del
cielo raso

solera

paral

diagonales

riostra

los soportes no deben quedar
en contacto con el suelo

cabios

cumbrera

la altura del soporte no debe
ser menor de .30 metros

● MANUAL DE CONSTRUCCION CON BAMBU ● OSCAR HIDALGO LOPEZ ● CIBAM ● UNIVERSIDAD NACIONAL DE COLOMBIA ● FACULTAD DE ARTES ●

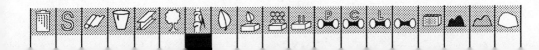

Round House with Thatched Conical Roof
(Structural stability is obtained by a bamboo tension ring along the top of the bamboo columns).

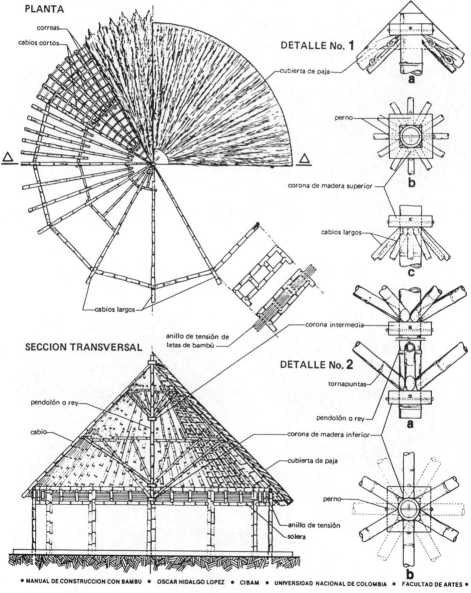

PLANTA

correas

cabios cortos

DETALLE No. 1

cubierta de paja

a

perno

corona de madera superior

b

cabios largos

c

cabios largos

corona intermedia

anillo de tensión de latas de bambú

SECCION TRANSVERSAL

DETALLE No. 2

tornapuntas

pendolón o rey

pendolón o rey

cabio

corona de madera inferior

cubierta de paja

a

anillo de tensión

solera

perno

b

• MANUAL DE CONSTRUCCION CON BAMBU • OSCAR HIDALGO LOPEZ • CIBAM • UNIVERSIDAD NACIONAL DE COLOMBIA • FACULTAD DE ARTES •

PREFABRICATED TIMBER HUT

KEYWORDS:

Special properties	Folding structure, quick assembly, easy transports
Economical aspects	Medium to high costs (depends on timber)
Stability	Good
Skills required	Carpentry skills
Equipment required	Carpentry tools
Resistance to earthquake	Very good
Resistance to hurricane	Good
Resistance to rain	Depends on cladding
Resistance to insects	Low
Climatic suitability	All climates
Stage of experience	Proven design, numerous applications

SHORT DESCRIPTION:

• Based on a German emergency housing design (Prof. Kleinlogel, 1952), a prefabricated timber hut was developed at the Central Building Research Institute, Roorkee, India.
• The aim was to construct a prefabricated house, which can be easily dismantled, transported and re-erected at different sites, particularly for disaster housing.
• The hut is designed to withstand wind velocities up to 130 km/h and a snow load of 100 kg/m².
• The main structural component is a collapsible timber frame, which defines the cross-section of the house. The length of the building is determined by the number of frames, which are erected 2.44 m apart.
• The standard hut has gci sheets for cladding and roof covering, and plywood boards for interior lining and suspended ceiling. However, any other locally available materials can be used. In cold climates, the cavity between the external cladding and interior lining can be filled with insulating material.
• All that is required is a level piece of ground. The frames can be spiked into the ground or erected on a prepared concrete foundation, if a more permanent structure is required.
Further information: CBRI, Roorkee 247 667, India; Bibl. 24.04.

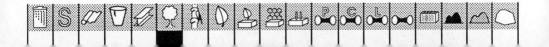

Prefabricated Timber Hut (Bibl. 24.04)

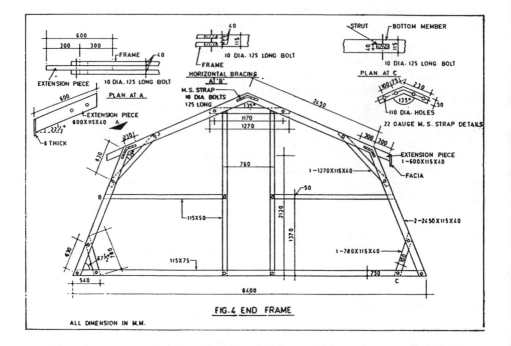

FIG. 4 END FRAME

ALL DIMENSION IN M.M.

Structural timber frame

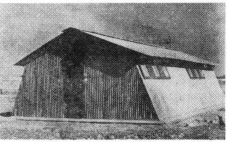

Completed hut

PREFABRICATED WOODEN HOUSE

KEYWORDS:

Special properties	Suitable for self-help projects
Economical aspects	Medium costs
Stability	Good
Skills required	Carpentry skills
Equipment required	Carpentry tools
Resistance to earthquake	Good
Resistance to hurricane	Low to medium
Resistance to rain	Low to medium
Resistance to insects	Low
Climatic suitability	Warm humid climates
Stage of experience	Standard construction

SHORT DESCRIPTION:

• The step-by-step construction of this house is shown in an excellently illustrated instruction manual published by UNIDO, which was prepared by the Instituto de Pesquisas Tecnológicas (IPT), São Paulo, Brazil, for a self-help community building project at Coroados, Manaus, under a contract with the Housing Society for the Amazon State (SHAM).

• Impressions of the contents of this manual are given in *Examples of Floors* and *Walls*. The instructions are straightforward and easy to follow.

• An experimental group of 40 houses was built in 1981 - 82, demonstrating the feasibility of the design.

• The fact that the entire house (with the exception of the roof covering) is made of wood calls for very careful consideration of protective measures against biological agents and fire (see section on *PROTECTIVE MEASURES*).

Further information: Instituto de Pesquisas Tecnológicas (IPT) do Estado de São Paulo, S.A., P.O. Box 7141, 05508 São Paulo, Brazil; Bibl. 14.22.

Prefabricated Wooden House
(Bibl. 14.22)

THE HOUSE IS MADE OF WOOD OF SUITABLE SPECIES (AND DEPENDING ON THE USE EITHER NATURALLY DURABLE OR PRESERVATIVE TREATED - SEE TABLES AT END OF MANUAL). CONSTRUCTION IS SIMPLE AND YOU CAN EASILY DO IT YOURSELF.

YOU CAN MAKE YOUR HOUSE BIGGER OR SMALLER THAN OUR MODEL, AS WELL AS IDENTICAL TO IT.
IF YOU ARE NOT ABLE TO BUILD A BIG HOUSE AT THE MOMENT, START WITH A SMALLER ONE AND MAKE IT BIGGER LATER.

TIMBER HOUSES FOR FLOOD AREAS

KEYWORDS:

Special properties	Elevated houses and floating structures
Economical aspects	Low to medium costs
Stability	Good
Skills required	Carpentry skills
Equipment required	Carpentry tools
Resistance to earthquake	Good
Resistance to hurricane	Depends on timber connections
Resistance to rain	Good
Resistance to insects	Low
Climatic suitability	Warm humid regions
Stage of experience	Experimental

SHORT DESCRIPTION:

• The great floods of 1982 and 1983, which affected the entire Parana - La Plata region of Paraguay, led to the development of prototype houses, designed to provide safe shelter, even if the floods submerged single storey houses, as they did in 1983.
• The design was jointly developed in 1983 by students of the Catholic University, Asunción, and flood victims, under the guidance of Prof. Thomas Gieth, Centre for Appropriate Technology, Asunción, and Dr. Wolfgang Willkomm, University of Hanover, Federal Republic of Germany (Bibl. 24.06, 24.17).
• The design criteria were: protection and escape from floods, low building costs, use of local materials and techniques, suitability for self-help construction.
• The solution was a two-storeyed house with an external stairway and platform around the upper floor. During floods the dwellers can take refuge on top, and planks can be laid between neighbouring houses to serve as bridges, where boats are not available. Local caranday palm logs were used for the framework, wall cladding, windows, doors, and even roof (made by alternately laying hollowed out halved logs, like Spanish tiles).
• To overcome the foundation problems associated with this design, an alternative solution was worked out in 1984 by Behrend Hillrichs, architectural student at the University of Hanover (Bibl. 24.08), suggesting houses that can float on the flood waters.

Construction System of Houses for Flood Areas
CTA, Paraguay

Grouped houses
with escape platforms

pasarelas

nivel de aqua

nivel del terreno natural

Roof detail: halved palm logs,
hollowed and laid like Spanish tiles

Details of
structural frame

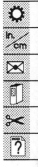

Completed house ...

... during minor floods

Principles of Floating Houses for Flood Areas (Bibl. 24.08)

Normal position of houses on dry ground

Position of houses during flood: the poles keep them in a stable position.

View of houses from above: short bridges connect the platforms.

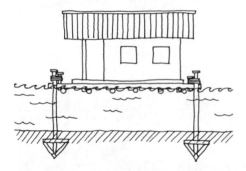

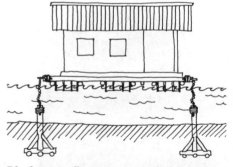

Normal raft-type platform
Advantages: simple construction; stable position during floods.
Problems: gradual wetting of floor; sinking of raft with increasing load of people and belongings and with gradual water absorption; risk of pole buckling under lateral water pressure.

Platform on floats (eg empty oil barrels)
Advantages: platform raised above water level; high load-bearing capacity; no gradual sinking.
Problems: more complicated construction; maintenance of good condition of floats (no holes!); instability during floods (tendency to "dance" on the waves).

RHA–LIME PROTOTYPE HOUSE

KEYWORDS:

Special properties	Substantial replacement of cement
Economical aspects	Medium costs
Stability	Very good
Skills required	Standard construction skills
Equipment required	Conventional building equipment
Resistance to earthquake	Very good
Resistance to hurricane	Very good
Resistance to rain	Very good
Resistance to insects	Very good
Climatic suitability	All climates
Stage of experience	Experimental

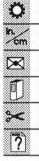

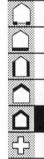

SHORT DESCRIPTION:

• The first house to be built, using to a large extent rice husk ash (RHA) and lime as substitute for cement, stands on the premises of the National Building Research Institute, Karachi, Pakistan (also see *Pozzolanas*).

• Portland cement was used to stabilize the soil for the foundation (3 % cement); for compressed soil blocks (5 % cement) used to construct the plinth; for the floor; and for concrete door and window frames.

• Structural components such as the roof, beams, lintels, projection slabs (sunshade), overhead water tank, were also made with portland cement, but with 30 % of the required amount replaced by RHA and lime.

• The hollow blocks and mortar used for the load-bearing walls were made only with RHA and lime as binder, just as the external plaster.

• The appearance, structural performance and durability of the house is no different from conventional constructions, using portland cement as the only binder, but it saved 37 % of the costs and showed a way to solve a waste disposal problem.

Further information: National Building Research Institute, F-40, S.I.T.E., Hub River Road, Karachi, Pakistan; Bibl. 24.16.

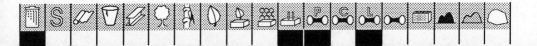

RHA–Lime Prototype House at NBRI, Karachi (Bibl. 24.16)

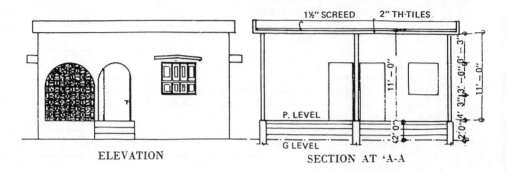

ELEVATION

SECTION AT 'A-A

HOLLOW BLOCK

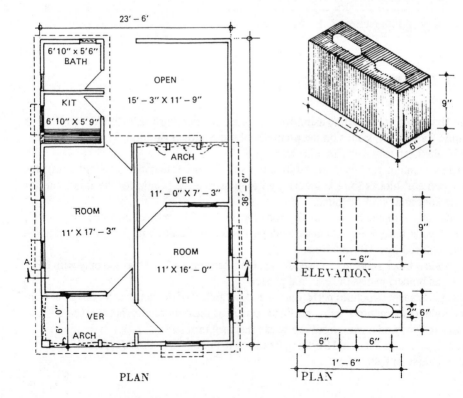

PLAN

PLAN

ANNEXES

General

Construction efficiency depends not only on the builders' skills, but to a large extent on the machines and equipment used. These are required for a variety of purposes, for instance:
• to improve the quality of raw material,
• to improve the strength and durability of a product, without increasing the quantity of expensive constituents (eg cement),
• to obtain more uniform products and better quality finishes,
• to achieve higher production rates,
• to simplify or eliminate tiring operations.

The machines and equipment presented on the following pages are of necessity only a small selection. Their inclusion does not represent a valuation or recommendation, but mainly depended on the availability of up-to-date information. In each case, the manufacturer and/or source is given, such that further details can be obtained directly.

The machines and equipment covered in this annex are:
• *Soil crushers* (required to pulverize dry lumps of clay, in order to get uniform grain sizes and better quality mixes for the production of burnt clay bricks and tiles, or air-dried soil blocks);
• *Clay brick and tile moulding equipment* (with which more uniform products can be made, with less effort and greater speed, than by traditional methods);
• *Soil block presses* (which produce compacted, stabilized or unstabilized soil blocks, which can be used without firing);
• *Block clamps* (which require only one hand to lift large, heavy blocks and place them accurately in masonry walls, providing uniform vertical joints between the blocks);
• *Concrete hollow block moulds* (which are designed for compaction by manual tamping or mechanical vibration);
• *Portable compaction devices* (for rammed earth construction or production of concrete components);
• *Fibre concrete roof tile plants* (for small and large scale production of pantiles and ridge tiles, using hand powered or electric screeding machines, and a set of moulds);
• *Wire lacing tool* (used to make strong bamboo and timber connections with 2 to 5 mm thick galvanized steel wire).

SOIL CRUSHERS

ITW/Parry
Pendulum Clay Crusher

Intermediate Technology
Workshops
Overend Road, Cradley Heath,
West Midlands B64 7DD
United Kingdom

The ITW Pendulum clay crusher is designed to meet the needs of small scale product manufactureres such as brickmakers. Dry clay lumps are fed into the hopper. The reciprocating crusher head grinds against a static plate reducing the clay to small particles which pass over an oscillating screen. This yields an output of fine powder which can then be easily turned into a smooth malleable clay by the addition of water. The resulting clay will be free of lumps and ready for moulding into high quality bricks or other clay products.
Source: ITW information leaflet

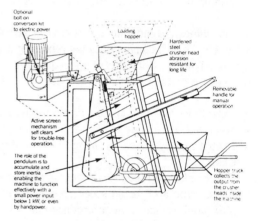

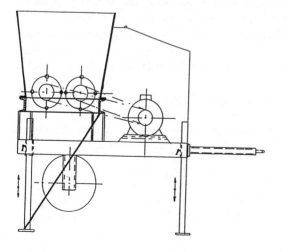

Appro-Techno Soil Pulverizer

APPRO–TECHNO
24 Rue de la Rieze
B–6404 Couvin - Cul-de-Sarts
Belgium

Two counterrotating cylinders with solid steel rods pulverize the clay by a hammering action; powered by electric motor or diesel engine.
Source: CRATerre, France

CERADES H2 Clay Disintegrator

CERATEC
Rue du Touquet, 228
B–7793 Ploegsteert
Belgium

This is an impact rotor crusher consisting of two counterrotating hollow drums (squirrel box type). Output: up to 9 m³/hour. Available with electric motor or diesel engine, with or without soil evacuation belt conveyor
Source: CERATEC information leaflet

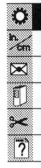

Uni-400, Universal shredder for nurseries and landscape gardening

CONSOLID AG, CH–9467 Frümsen, Switzerland (machine manufactured in France)

Shreddering and treatment of cuttings of trees and hedges (up to a diametre of 7 cm) all kinds of organic refuses, compost, soil (also stony soil), feuillage, splittery materials as for example bones or wooden cases, paper, cardboard, as well as all other organic refuses.
Source: CONSOLID leaflet

CLAY BRICK AND TILE MOULDING EQUIPMENT

ITW/Parry Type E Brick Press

Intermediate Technology Workshops
Overend Road, Cradley Heath,
West Midlands B64 7DD
United Kingdom

The rated output of the Type "E" press is 800 bricks per
day. Some of our customers achieve in excess of 1'000
bricks in an 8 hour shift.
Standard Mould Size
After drying and firing this produces a brick of internatio
nal standard (S1) in work dimension 225 x 112.5 x
75mm. Non standard sizes are possible for an additional
tooling change.
Source: ITW information leaflet

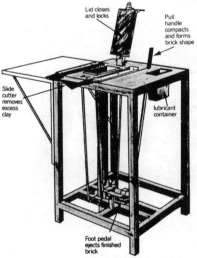

CBRI Clay Brick Table Mould

Central Building Research Institute, Roorkee 247 667, India

On this table the bricks are moulded without mechanical compression other than the compaction
achieved by throwing the clot of clay forcibly into the mould cavity. A slightly modified table mould
is also available for making roofing tiles, for which a lid is provided and pressure is applied manually.
Source: CBRI Building Research Note No. 6

CRDI Lever Press for Roof Tiles

Ceramic Research and Development Institute, Jalan Jenderal Ahmad Yani 392, Bandung, Indonesia

The machine, operated by 3 people, requires a force of 30 kg on the lever arm to apply a force of 800 kg on the fresh tile. Two moulds are provided so that one mould can be demoulded and loaded while the other one is being compressed. Output: 70 - 85 tiles per hour.
Source: CRDI information leaflet

Some soil block presses, presented on the following pages, have been designed with interchangeable moulds, in order to be able to make smaller bricks, floor and roof tiles for firing. Especially with regard to roof tiles, mention must be made of the CERAMAN and TERSTARAM machines, which can produce 3 or 4 different varieties of roofing tiles.

SOIL BLOCK PRESSES

CINVA-Ram

METALIBEC S.A.
Apartado 11798
Carrera 68B no. 18-30
Bogotá 6
Colombia

First portable manual block press developed in
Colombia in 1956. Steel mould box with a piston
at the bottom and a lid which is opened for filling.
A long metal handle is manually operated,
moves the compression piston via a toggle link-
age. All connections welded. Block size 29 x 14
x 9 cm. Production of one block per cycle, 40 - 60
blocks per hour.
Source: METALIBEC (correspondence)

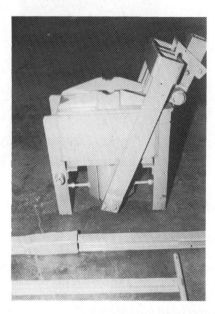

CTA Triple-Block Press

Centro de Tecnología Apropiada
Universidad Católica "Nuestra
Señora de la Asunción"
Casilla de correos 1718
Asunción
Paraguay

Modified CINVA-Ram, producing 3 blocks per
cycle, about 150 blocks per hour. Block size 24
x 11.5 x 11.3 cm.
Source: CTA (correspondence)

CETA-Ram

Centro de Experimentación
en Tecnología Apropiada
Apartado 66-F
Guatemala, C.A.

Modified CINVA-Ram to produce hollow
blocks (for placement of reinforcing rods in
aseismic wall construction). CETA-Ram II
produces both hollow and solid blocks, size
32.3 x 15.7 x 11.5 cm, with 6 cm Ø holes. Output
same as CINVA-Ram.
Source: CETA information brochures

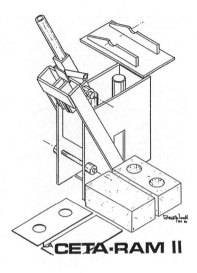

LA **CETA·RAM II**

CRATerre AMERICA LATINA Block Press

CRATerre AMERICA LATINA, Apartado Postal 5603, Correo Central, Lima - 1, Peru

Manual press on wheels, designed to make specially shaped blocks (single 28 x 28 x 8 cm or double
28 x 12.8 x 8 cm) for earthquake resistant construction. Precompaction by forceful closing of lid and
by vertical stroke piston. Side tables for soil mix and finished blocks facilitate handling.
Source: CRATerre, France

344

UNATA Manual Presses 1003 and 1004

UNATA C.V., G.V.D. Heuvelstraat 131, B-3140 Ramsel-Herselt, Belgium

UNATA 1003: slightly modified CINVA-Ram, with a lever that has to be passed from the pressing mechanism to the ejector and vice versa. Output: 70 blocks per hour. UNATA 1004: further modification by reducing the number of manual operations per cycle, cover attached to lever arm, raised mould for easier handling. Output: 100 blocks per hour. Block sizes 29 x 14 x 9 cm.
Source: UNATA (correspondence)

DSM Manual Press

La Mécanique Régionale
23, rue de la Gare
F-51140 Muizon
France

Modified CINVA-Ram with cover sliding sideways; lever action for compression and ejection of block only on one side of the machine. Block size 29 x 14.5 x 10.5 cm, output 50 to 90 blocks per hour.
Source: CRATerre, France, and Bibl. 02.07

MARO DC Press

M. Klein - MARO Enterprise, 95 bis Route de Suisse, CH-1290 Versoix, Switzerland

Modified CINVA-Ram with sliding cover and one-sided lever operation; assembled only with screws and bolts (easy to dismantle for transports); all moving parts with sealed, greased for life ball bearing; available with double compaction; can also be supplied with a tray for easy filling of mould. Block size 30 x 15 x 10.5 cm, output 60 to 80 blocks per hour.
Source: MARO Enterprise (correspondence)

GEO 50

ALTECH
Société Alpine de
Technologies Nouvelles
Rue des Cordeliers
F-05200 Embrun
France

Manual press developed by ARCHECO (Centre de Terre, 31590 Verfeil, France). Lever action only on one side, double compaction. Block size 29 x 14 x 9 cm, output 60 to 80 blocks per hour.
Source: CRATerre, France, and Bibl. 02.07

ELLSON Blockmaster

Kathiawar Metal & Tin Works Private Limited, 9 Lati Plot, Sadgurunagar, Post Box 202, Rajkot 360 003 (Gujarat State), India

Originally produced in South Africa, this is one of the oldest soil block presses still being produced. It has a lever-linkage toggle mechanism and high compaction is achieved by the forceful closing of the lid and "jumping pull" of the lever. Interchangeable moulds allow for different block, brick and tile sizes. Largest block 30.5 x 22.8 x 10 cm, smallest tile 29 x 14 x 5 cm.
Source: Kathiawar Metal & Tin Works (correspondence)

ASTRAM Soil Block Machine

Aeroweld Industries
B9, HAL Industrial Estate
Bangalore 560 037
India

Manual block press, developed at ASTRA, Bangalore, based on the principle of the ELLSON Blockmaster, but lighter construction. Block size 30 x 14.5 x 10 cm or 23 x 19 x 10cm, output 40 - 50 blocks per hour.
Source: ASTRA (correspondence)

T.A.R.A. BALRAM Mud Block Press

Development Alternatives
B-32, Institutional Area
TARA Crescent
New Mehrauli Road
New Dehli-110 016
India

Manual press to make compressed earth blocks.
The standard mould produces two conventional
sized blocks of 23 x 10.8 x 7.5 cm per cycle. A
team of 5 persons can make an average of i,200
blocks per day. Optional mould of 23 x 23 x 7.5
cm is available. Robust construction with
machined and arc-welded steel body. Easily
dismantled and maintained.
Development Alternatives provides training at
Delhi, Bangalore and field sites to supervisory
staff and machine operators. Cost of machine
and accessories is US $ 600 [exfactory].
Source: Development Alternatives (correspondence)

TEK Block Press

Mechanical Engineering Dept.
Faculty of Engineering
University of Science
and Technology (U.S.T.)
Kumasi
Ghana

Sturdier version of the CINVA-Ram,
with simplified handling (cover connected to lever), wooden lever (easy replacement) and larger block size (29 x
21.6 x 14 cm). Output 50 blocks per
hour.
Source: U.S.T. (correspondence)

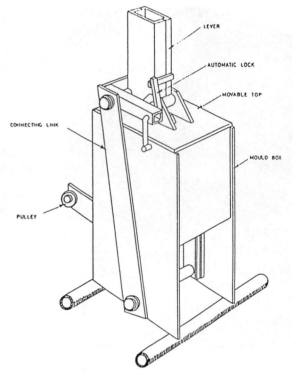

VS CINVA-Ram

Sohanpal Metal Works Ltd.
P.O. Box 904
Tanga
Tanzania

Modified CINVA-Ram, designed with
the assistance of GATE. Design allows
for variable compression ratios. Very
robust, overloading impossible, easy
transportation, improved safety measures.
Source: GATE (correspondence)

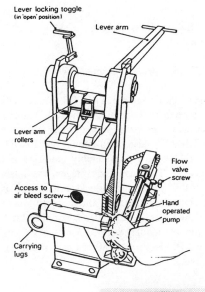

Lever locking toggle
(in 'open' position)

Lever arm

Lever arm rollers

Access to air bleed screw

Carrying lugs

Flow valve screw

Hand operated pump

BREPAK Machine

Concrete Machinery Systems Ltd.
CMS
Satellite Business Park
Blackswarth Road
Bristol BS5 8AX
England

Designed at the Building Research Establishment, the machine is based on the CINVA-Ram, but has a compaction pressure 5 times that of the CINVA-Ram, achieved by means of a hand operated hydraulic pump, acting through a piston beneath the base plate of the mould. Block size 29 x 14 x 10 cm, output 30 - 40 blocks per hour.
Source: BREPAK Operators Manual

CLU 3000 Mobile Soil Brick Plant

INTREX GmbH, P.O. Box 1328, D-42477 Radevormwald, Federal Republic of Germany

Designed by CONSOLID AG, CH-9467 Frümsen SG, Switzerland, the mobile plant is an automatic, integrated unit, equipped with a mixer, hopper and 4 station rotating table with hydraulic press for one brick each time. Brick size 25 x 12 x 7.5 cm (slight variations possible), output 350 bricks per hour. Powered by electric motor or diesel engine.
Source: CONSOLID information brochure

Both machines on this page are manufactured by:
APPRO-TECHNO, 24 Rue de la Rieze, B-6404 Couvin - Cul-des-Sarts, Belgium
Source: APPRO-TECHNO pamphlets and CRATerre, France

TERSTARAM Hand Operated Press

Based on the design of LA SUPER MADELON (developed at the beginning of the 20th century), which was later manufactured under the name STABIBLOC, also well-known as LAND-CRETE, but now considerably modified and improved.. The main advantages are interchangeability of moulds (blocks, bricks, various roof tiles), easy operation and mobility. Maximum block size 40 x 20 x 10 cm, common brick size (double mould) each 22.5 x 10.5 x 6 cm, outputs 70 blocks and 180 bricks per hour respectively.

SEMI-TERSTAMATIQUE Motor Operated Press

Greatly improved version of the successful Belgian machine LA MAJO, with semi-automatic compression and ejection of blocks. The moulds are interchangeable for different block shapes and sizes, similar to TERSTARAM, but excluding roof tiles. Outputs range between 200 and 400 blocks per hour. Powered by electric motor or diesel engine.

Both machines on this page are manufactured by:
CERATEC, Rue du Touquet 228, B-7793 Ploegsteert, Belgium
Source: CERATEC pamphlets (and correspondence)

CERAMAN Manual Press

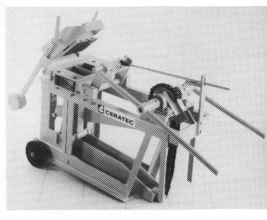

Principally the same as TERSTARAM, but with automatic ejection of blocks. The soil is piled onto the open mould, the cover pushed down with force for pre-compaction. Compression of bricks is effected by turning and pressing down two lever arms by two men (one on either side). When releasing the pressure, the clamp opens, and the bricks are automatically ejected. Maximum block size 40 x 20 x 10 cm, outputs between 100 and 300 blocks per hour.

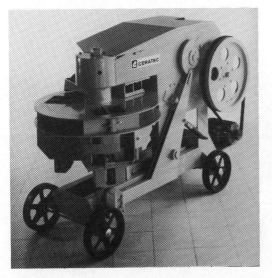

CERAMATIC Automatic Brick Press

Greatly improved version of the successful Belgian machine LA MAJO-MATIQUE, with 3 station rotating table: automatic precompaction (with cone-shaped roller), compression and ejection. Only two men operate the machine (one for filling soil, one for removal of bricks). Single moulds with blocks of 29.5 x 14 x 7 cm, and double moulds with 22 x 10.7 x 7 cm are available, outputs at least 700 and 1400 blocks per hour respectively. Powered by electric motor or diesel engine.

DSH Hydraulic Press

La Mécanique Régionale
23, rue de la Gare
F-51140 Muizon
France

Semi-automatic machine designed for transportation with a fork lift. Three station rotating
mould system set in motion manually. Standard
block size 30 x 15 x 12 cm, output 150 - 180
blocks per hour. Powered by electric motor or
diesel engine.
Source: CRATerre, France, and Bibl. 02.07

PACT 500 Mechanical Press

ALTECH
Société Alpine de
Technologies Nouvelles
Rue des Cordeliers
F-05200 Embrun
France

Motorized press (electric motor), equipped with
wheels for mobility. Four station rotating table
manually set in motion, mechanical compression transmitted by a cam. Largest block size 30
x 20 x 10 cm, output 250 blocks per hour.
Source: CRATerre, France, and Bibl. 02.07

GEOBETON ONE PRESS BLOC 80 TM

GEOBETON ONE, 169 Boulevard Denis Papin, F-53000 Laval, France

Mobile production unit on 4 wheels, incorporating a vibrating sieve, a horizontal shaft mixer, a hopper and a press, all powered by a single diesel engine. Feeding the sieve with soil, water and stabilizer is done manually, the remaining operations function automatically (computer controlled). Block size 29 x 14 x 9 cm, output 320 blocks per hour. *Source*: CRATerre, France, and Bibl. 02.07

RAFFIN DYNATERRE 01-4M

Ets RAFFIN, 700 route de Grenoble, B.P. 9 Domène, F-38420 Le Versoud, France

Integrated production unit on two wheels, equipped with a conveyor belt, mixer, water tank, motor pump and spraying device, hopper and press. The outstanding feature is that the soil is vibrated during compression (dynamic compression), producing superior quality blocks and tiles of various shapes and sizes. Output 250 blocks per hour. The unit has an electric motor, a diesel generator can be supplied. *Source*: CRATerre, France, and Bibl. 02.07

MPACT 500

Southwest Alternatives LTD, P.O. Box 1363, Corrales, New Mexico 87048

Compact mobile production unit on two wheels, fed and operated manually. The blocks of 30 x 14 x 9 cm are compressed hydraulically. Output about 960 blocks per day. Also manufactured is the Impact 501 which is capable of producing 1440 blocks per day.
Source: Impact information leaflet

BLOCK CLAMPS

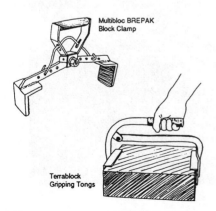

Multibloc BREPAK Block Clamp

Terrablock Gripping Tongs

The problem of handling heavy blocks and placing them accurately in walls is overcome with simple block clamps that enable a person to lift a block with one hand and place it in line with the adjoining block. The thickness of the steel angle and rubber pad that hold the block, provides a uniform vertical joint between the blocks, so that little skill is required to achieve accuracy. Two examples are shown here:
• The Multibloc Brepak Block Clamp, developed at the Building Research Establishment, Garston, U.K.
• Terrablock Gripping Tongs, developed by Terrablock, Earth Technology Corporation, 175 Drennen Road, Orlando, Florida 32806, U.S.A.

MACHINES FOR CONCRETE HOLLOW BLOCKS

SENA Máquina para Hacer Bloques

División de Desarrollo Tecnológico
Servicio Nacional de Aprendizaje
Apartado Aéreo 9801
Bogotá
Colombia

Simple block mould, equipped with a tray for preparing the cement-sand mix. The filled mould is tamped manually and the top surface smoothed with a trowel. The lever is used to lower the cavity inserts and the hollow block is tilted out on a wooden pallet, ready for curing.
Source: SENA instruction manual

BLOKORAMA

Estructuras Desarmables, S.A.
Apartado Postal 1669
México, D.F.

Automatic "egg-laying" machine: the raw mix is filled in on one side, the hollow blocks are moulded (under vibration) on the ground and left standing as the machine moves to the next moulding position.
Source: BLOKORAMA information brochure

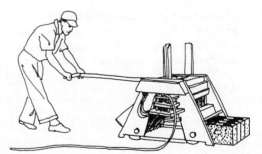

The concrete block machines on this page are manufactured by:
Kathiawar Metal & Tin Works Private Limited, 9 Lati Plot, Sadgurunagar, Post Box 202,
Rajkot 360 003 (Gujarat State), India
Source: SKAT Working Paper 05/84

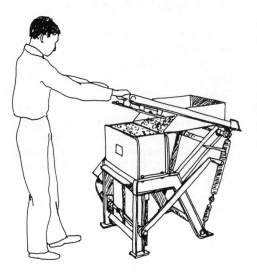

*Combination Plain and Hollow Concrete Block
Machine*

A large tray facilitates filling of concrete mix
into the mould. The surplus concrete is scraped
off and the tamper lid-plate brought down with a
few sharp blows to compact the block. The lever
is used to eject the block, which is removed on
the wooden base plate for curing.

ELLSON-VIBRO

The machine has a mechanical vibrator driven by
an electric motor or diesel engine and flat faced
drive-pulley (both not supplied with machine).
All operations are manual and simple to carry
out. The moulds are interchangeable, producing
dense blocks of various shapes and sizes.

ITW 80 B Vibro-Compaction Block Mould

Intermediate Technology Workshops
Overend Road, Cradley Heath,
West Midlands B64 7DD
United Kingdom

Portable block mould equipped with vibrator, which works off a car battery (not supplied). Use of mechanical vibration in place of manual tamping saves up to 1 kg of cement for every block. Block size 45 x 23 x 23 cm with 40 % hollow.
Source: ITW information leaflet

MULTIBLOC Super Minor

CMS Ltd, Satellite Business Park, Blackswarth Road, Bristol BS5 8AX, England

The machine comprises three main parts: the frame, mould box and tamping head with vibrator. The machine is operated by one man: filling mould box, vibrating and tamping, ejecting blocks, and moving machine to repeat the cycle. Various hollow and solid blocks can be produced.
Source: Multibloc information leaflet

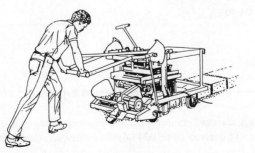

PORTABLE COMPACTION DEVICES

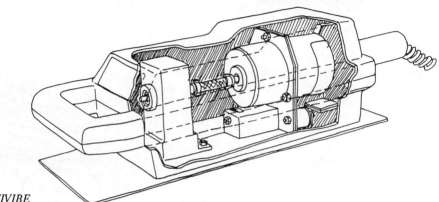

MULTIVIBE

Intermediate Technology Workshops, Overend Road, Cradley Heath, West Midlands B64 7DD, United Kingdom

Detachable vibrator, which works from a 12 volt DC supply (car battery or ordinary battery charger). It can be used to make concrete blocks, tiles, window elements, and any other concrete products, as well as fibre concrete roofing tiles and water pipes.
Source: ITW information leaflet

RAM 30   RAM 15A   RAM 11G   RAM 06

Pneumatic Earth Rammers

Atlas Copco Tools, P.O. Box 100 234, D-4300 Essen, Federal Republic of Germany

Hand-held rammers for high standard rammed earth construction. The rammers require a separate compressor, which supplies 3 litres/sec. (for RAM 06) to 14 litres/sec. (for RAM 30).
Source: Bibl. 02.28

FIBRE CONCRETE ROOF TILE PRODUCTION KITS

ITW/Parry Roof Tile Plants

Intermediate Technology Workshops
Overend Road, Cradley Heath
West Midlands B64 7DD
United Kingdom

Hand powered vibration screeding machine

A variety of roof tile plants is available, depending on the required output: mini plants for outputs of 250 to 500 tiles/week, small-scale industrial plants for 1000 to 2000 tiles/week. The smaller plants are either hand or electric powered, while the larger plants can be semi-mechanized (with handling trucks and solar curing bins). The production procedure is shown in *EXAMPLES OF ROOF MATERIALS*.
Source: ITW information leaflets

Production unit for 1000 roof tiles per week

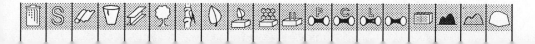

WIRE LACING TOOL

Delft Wire Lacing Tool

Materials Science Section, Civil Engineering Department, Delft University of Technology, 4 Stevinweg, NL-2628 CN Delft, The Netherlands

Hand operated device used for tying 2 to 5 mm thick galvanized steel wire around any object, but mainly around bamboo pipes and timber connections. The tool stretches the wire, twists the two ends and cuts off the surplus wire, leaving a 3 cm twisted piece which is bent over or covered with a piece of plastic tubing.

Stretching
the wire

Twisting
the wire ends

Cutting and
removing tool;
securing sharp
twisted end

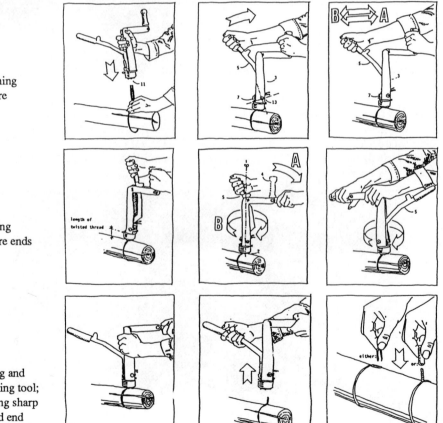

CONVERSION FACTORS FOR SI–UNITS

General

One of the main aims of this book is to provide practical information for builders in all parts of the world. But its practical value is reduced in places where the systems of measurement differ from those in the book – and this is true for any technical book.

The two main systems of measurement are the English (Imperial) and the metric systems, and their use in each country was mainly determined by its historical development. The metric system is now the official system in most of the countries that were accustomed to the Imperial system, but the change of systems has always proved to be a difficult and slow process, as the people have to readjust themselves to a new way of thinking. A further problem is that the Imperial system is still officially used in North America.

The basic units of the Imperial system are foot, pound and second, while the basic units of the metric system are metre, kilogram and second (MKS), which later also included ampere (MKSA). The inclusion of kelvin (thermodynamic temperature), mole (amount of substance) and candela (light intensity) led to a new internationally standardized system of measurement, called *SI-Units* (Système International d'Unités).

The units of measurement given in this book are mainly SI-units, as they are the most widespread. In order to make the book equally useful to those readers, who are less acquainted with the metric units, some of the most important conversion factors are given on the following pages.

IMPERIAL UNITS	CONVERSION FACTORS	METRIC / SI–UNITS

Length

Units: inch (in)	1 in = 25.4 mm	*Units:* millimetre (mm)
foot (ft)	0.39 in = 1 cm	centrimetre (cm)
yard (yd)	1 ft = 30.48 cm	metre (m)
mile (mile)	39.37 in = 1 m	kilometre (km)
	1 yd = 91.44 cm	
12 in = 1 ft	0.6214 mile = 1 km	10 mm = 1 cm
3 ft = 1 yd	1 mile = 1.6093 km	100 cm = 1 m
1760 yd = 1 mile		1000 m = 1 km

Area

Units: square in (sq in; in²)	1 in² = 6.4516 cm²	*Units:* square mm (mm²)
square ft (sq ft; ft²)	10.76 ft² = 1 m²	square cm (cm²)
square yd (sq yd; yd²)	1 ft² = 0.0929 m²	square m (m²)
square mile (sq mile)	1.196 yd² = 1 m²	hectare (ha)
	1 yd² = 0.8361 m²	square km (km²)
	1 acre = 4046.86 m²	
144 in² = 1 ft²	2.471 acre = 1 ha	100 mm² = 1 cm²
9 ft² = 1 yd²	0.3861 mile² = 1 km²	10000 cm² = 1 m²
4840 yd² = 1 acre	1 mile² = 2.59 km²	10000 m² = 1 ha
640 acre = 1 sq mile		100 ha = 1 km²

Volume

Units: cubic in (cu in; in³)	1 in³ = 16.3871 cm³	*Units:* cubic cm (cm³)
cubic ft (cu ft; ft³)	1 ft³ = 28.3 dm³	cubic deci-
cubic yd (cu yd; yd³)	35.31 ft³ = 1 m³	metre (dm³)
	1.308 yd³ = 1 m³	cubic m (m³)
1728 in³ = 1 ft³	1 yd³ = 0.7646 m³	
27 ft³ = 1 yd³		1000 cm³ = 1 dm³
100 ft³ = 1 register ton		1000 dm³ = 1 m³

IMPERIAL UNITS	CONVERSION FACTORS	METRIC / SI–UNITS

Capacity / Volume of Liquids and Gases

Units: fluid ounce (fl oz)	1 fl oz (UK) = 28.4 ml	*Units:* millilitre (ml)
gill (UK gill, US gill)	0.035 fl oz = 1 ml	cubic centimetre
pint (UK pt, US pt)	1 gill (UK) = 142 ml	(cm³, ccm, cc)
quart (UK qt, US qt)	1 gill (US) = 118.3 ml	litre (l)
gallon (UK gal, US gal)	1 pt (UK) = 568 ml	cubic dm (dm³)
	1 pt (US) = 454 ml	kilo litre (kl)
5 fl oz = 1 UK gill	1 qt (UK) = 1136 ml	cubic metre (m³)
4 fl oz = 1 US gill	1 qt (US) = 909 ml	
4 gills = 1 pt (UK, US)	1 gal (UK) = 4.546 l	1 ml = 1 cm³
2 pt = 1 qt (UK, US)	1 gal (US) = 3.785 l	1000 ml = 1 l
4 qt = 1 gal (UK, US)	0.22 gal (UK) = 1 l	1 l = 1 dm³
1 UK gal = 1.2 US gal	0.26 gal (US) = 1 l	1000 l = 1 kl = 1 m³

Mass

Units: ounce (oz)	1 oz = 28.3 g	*Units:* milligram (mg)
pound (lb)	0.035 oz = 1 g	gram (g)
stone (stone)	1 lb = 0.454 kg	kilogram (kg)
hundredweight (cwt)	2.205 lb = 1 kg	tonne (t)
ton (ton)	1 stone = 6.35 kg	
	1 UK cwt = 50.8 kg	1000 mg = 1 g
16 oz = 1 lb	0.98 long ton = 1 t	1000 g = 1 kg
14 lb = 1 stone	1 long ton = 1.016 t	1000 kg = 1 t
8 stone = 1 UK cwt (long)	1.1 short ton = 1 t	
112 lb = 1 UK ton (long)	1 short ton = 0.907 t	
100 lb = 1 US ton (short)		

Density

Units: lb/cu ft (lb/ft³)	1 lb/ft³ = 16.02 kg/m³	*Unit:* kg/m³
lb/UK gal	1 lb/UK gal = 100 kg/m³	
lb/US gal	1 lb/US gal = 120 kg/m³	

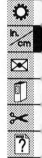

IMPERIAL UNITS	CONVERSION FACTORS	METRIC / SI–UNITS

Force
Units: lbf
tonf

1 lbf = 4.448 N
1 tonf = 9.964 kN

Units: newton (N)
kilonewton (kN)

Pressure
Units: lbf/in² (psi)
tonf/ft²

1 lbf/in² = 6895 Pa
145 lbf/in² = 1 MPa
1 UK tonf/ft² = 0.107 MPa
9.32 UK tonf/ft² = 1 MPa

Units: pascal (Pa)
megapascal (MPa)
newton/mm²
(N/mm²)
bar (bar)

1 Pa = 1 N/m²
1 MPa = 1 N/mm²
1 bar = 0.1 N/mm²

Energy, Work, Heat
Unit: British thermal
unit (Btu)

1 Btu = 1055 J
0.948 Btu = 1 kJ
1 Btu = 0.000293 kWh
3413 Btu = 1 kWh

Units: joule (J)
kilojoule (kJ)
calorie (cal)
kilowatt hour (kWh)
watt second (Ws)
newton metre (Nm)
pascal cubic metre
(Pa m³)

1 J = 1 Nm = 1 Ws = 1 Pa m³
1 J   = 0.239 cal
1 kWh = 3600 kJ

Power, Energy Flow Rate
Units: Btu/h
ft lbf/s
horsepower (hp)

1 hp = 550 ft lbf/s
1 hp = 2545 Btu/h

1 Btu/h = 0.293 W
3.412 Btu/h = 1 W
1 ft lbf/s = 1.356 W
0.74 ft lbf/s = 1 W
1 hp = 745.7 W

Units: watt (W)
joules/second (J/s)
hp metric

1 W   = 1 J/s
1 hp metric = 735.5 W

IMPERIAL UNITS	CONVERSION FACTORS	METRIC / SI–UNITS

Thermal Conductivity

Unit: Btu/ft²h deg F

1 Btu ft²h deg F = 0.144 W m deg C
6.94 Btu/ft²h deg F = 1 W/m deg C
1 Btu/ft²h deg F = 0.124 kcal/m h deg C
8.06 Btu/ft²h deg F = 1 kcal/m h deg C

Units: W/m deg C
kcal/m h deg C

1 W/m deg C =
0.861 kcal/m h deg C
1 kcal/m h deg C =
1.163 W/m deg C

Velocity

Units: ft/s
miles per hour (mph)

1 ft/s = 0.305 m/s
3.28 ft/s = 1 m/s
1 mph = 1.609 km/h
0.62 mph = 1 km/h

Units: m/s
km/h

MISCELLANEOUS CONVERSION FACTORS

Temperature

Difference of temperature
1 degree on the Centigrade or Celsius scale (deg C)
= 1.8 degrees on the Fahrenheit scale (deg F)

Temperature reading on thermometer
0°C = 32° F (water freezing point)
100°C = 212° F (water boiling point)

Calculation of temperature difference
1 deg C = 9/5 deg F
1 deg F = 5/9 deg C

Calculation of temperature level
°C = 5/9 x (°F−32)
°F = 9/5 x °C+32

100° C	212° F
90° C	194° F
80° C	176° F
70° C	158° F
60° C	140° F
50° C	122° F
40° C	104° F
30° C	80° F
20° C	68° F
10° C	50° F
0° C	32° F
- 10° C	14° F
- 20° C	- 4° F
- 30° C	- 22° F
- 40° C	- 40° F

Angles and Slopes

These are mainly required for sloping roofs, which are generally expressed in degrees, but which are difficult for the worker to measure out on the site. Therefore roof slopes are best expressed in simple relations between height and span, preferably using round numbers. Since they are difficult to visualize, the approximate relations between some common slopes (given in ratios and percentages) and angles (in degrees) are shown in the following table:

Ratio of slope	Percentage of slope	Angle
1 : 50	2 %	≈ 1°
1 : 25	4 %	≈ 2°
1 : 20	5 %	≈ 3°
1 : 10	10 %	≈ 5.5°
1 : 5	20 %	≈ 11.5°
1 : 4	25 %	≈ 14°
1 : 3	33.3 %	≈ 18.5°
1 : 2	50 %	≈ 26.5°
2 : 3	66.7 %	≈ 33.5°
3 : 4	75 %	≈ 37°
4 : 5	80 %	≈ 38.5°
1 : 1	100 %	45°
5 : 4	125 %	≈ 51.5°
4 : 3	133.3 %	≈ 53°
3 : 2	150 %	≈ 56.5°
2 : 1	200 %	≈ 63.5°
3 : 1	300 %	≈ 71.5°
4 : 1	400 %	≈ 76°
5 : 1	500 %	≈ 78.5°
10 : 1	1000 %	≈ 84.5°

USEFUL ADDRESSES

Argentina

Asociación Vivienda Económica
Centro Experimental de la
Vivienda Económica (CEVE)
Igualdad 3600 Villa Siburu
Estafeta 14
5000 Córdoba

Low-cost housing research centre; manuals and brochures on construction

Australia

National Building Technology Centre
P.O. Box 30
Chatswood, N.S.W. 2067

Research and development of construction materials and technologies (mainly cementitious materials)

Austria

UNIDO
United Nations Industrial
Development Organization
Vienna International Centre
P.O. Box 300
1400 Wien

Financing and coordination of research studies, expertise, publications, international conferences

Bangladesh

Housing & Building Research Institute
Darus-Salam, Mirpur
Dhaka - 18

Research and development of local construction materials and technologies

Belgium

ATOL
Study and Documentation Centre on Appropriate Technology in Developing Countries
Blijde Inkomststraat 9
3000 Leuven

AT centre with bookshop; coordination of research studies and publications; joint publishers of AT journal "AT Source" (formally VRAAGBAAK)

COTA
Collectif d'Echanges pour
la Technologie Appropriée
18, rue de la Sablonnière
1000 Bruxelles

Documentation, information and research centre; cooperation with NGOs mainly in French- and Portuguese-speaking countries

Katholieke Universiteit Leuven
Post Graduate Centre Human Settlements
Kasteel Arenberg
3030 Leuven (Heverlee)

Educational and study group; co-organizer of international colloquium on "Earth construction technologies appropriate to developing countries" (Dec. 1984)

UNATA (Union for Adapted
Technological Assistance)
G.V.D. Heuvelstraat 131
3140 Ramsel-Herselt

Technical assistance group, producing simple machines (eg soil block presses); publish a quarterly newsletter "UNATA-PRESS"

Université Catholique de Louvain
Centre de Recherches en Architecture CRA
Place du Levant 1
1348 Louvain-la-Neuve

Educational and study group; co-organizer of international colloquium on "Earth construction technologies appropriate to developing countries" (Dec. 1984)

Bolivia

SEMTA
Servicios Multiples de Tecnologías Apropiadas
Casilla 20410
La Paz

Appropriate technology information centre, providing consulting services; technical co-operation project implementation

Botswana

Botswana Technology Centre
Private Bag 0082
Gaborone

Provides information services (SATIS network), conducts technical cooperation projects

Rural Industries Promotions (RIP)
Private Bag 11
Kanye

Rural industries innovation centre, providing assistance in various appropriate technologies

Brazil

CEPED
Centro de Pesquisas e Desenvolvimento
Km 0 da BA-536
Caixa Postal 09
42.800 Camaçari (BA)

Governmental research institution; development of low-cost construction technologies (project THABA), mainly soil cement, ferrocement and fibre concrete

Instituto de Pesquisas Tecnológicas
do Estado de São Paulo S.A. (IPT)
P.O. Box 7141
05508 São Paulo

Governmental research and documentation centre; technical cooperation projects; produced UNIDO Manual on Timber House Construction (Bibl. 14.22)

Canada

Development Workshop (DW)
238 Davenport Road
P.O. Box 133
Toronto M5R 1J6

Technical assistance group for Human Settlements in the Third World; wide experience in low-cost building technologies

IDRC
International Development Research Centre
P.O. Box 8500
Ottawa K1G 3H9

Research centre for adaptation of science and technology to the needs of developing countries

McGill University
School of Architecture
Minimum Cost Housing Group
3480 University Street
Montréal 101, Quebec H3A 2A7

Research and development of various low-cost housing technologies; experience in sulphur concrete construction, interesting publications

Chile

CETAL
Centro de Estudios en Tecnología
Apropiada para Latinoamérica
Subida Mackenna 1246 - Vinn
Apartado Postal 197 - V
Valparaíso

Research and documentation centre, dealing with technical cooperation; several technical publications

SELAVIP
Servicio Latinoamericano y Asiático
de Vivienda Popular
German Yungue 3825
Apartado Postal 871
Santiago

International low-cost housing finance and consultancy institution, publish SELAVIP News

China

Beijing Institute of Architectural Design
62 South Lishi Road
Beijing

One of the main building design institutions, primarily concerned with new housing projects, which are generally high-rise in Beijing

Building Research Institute
No. 1 Construction Bureau
China State Construction
Engineering Corporation (CSCEC)
Nan Yuan
Beijing

Leading institution with specialized departments on all aspects of building materials and construction research, also with international cooperation, eg experimental passive solar houses in Daxing, with West German assistance

China Building Technology
Development Centre (CBTDC)
19 Che Gong Zhuang Street
Beijing

Implementing agency of MURCEP, providing technology consultancy services, also conducting international cooperation projects

Dalian Institute of Technology
Department of Civil Engineering
Dalian 116 024

Materials research and development, especially use of industrial wastes

MURCEP
Ministry of Urban-Rural Construction
and Environmental Protection
Bureau of Science and Technology
Bai Wan Zhuang, Westsuburb
Beijing

Governmental organization; administration in urban-rural development; coordination of international cooperation on research and development. (Under same address: Architectural Society of China; China National Waterproof Building Materials Corporation)

Shanghai Research Institute
of Building Sciences
75 Wan Ping Road
South Shanghai

Materials research and development, especially use of industrial wastes

Colombia

ARIT
arquitectura investigación en tierra
cra. 3A no. 30 - 33
Bogotá

Technical assistance group, dedicated to promoting soil construction technologies

ENDA AL
Medio Ambiente y Desarrollo
del Tercer Mundo
c/o Naciones Unidas
Apartado Aéreo 091369
Bogotá

Dissemination of appropriate technologies and support of self-help housing projects

FEDEVIVIENDA
Federación Nacional de
Organizaciones de Vivienda Popular
Diagonal 60 No. 23 - 63
Bogotá

Organization supporting housing construction by community self-help, also investigating socially appropriate technologies

PROCO
Fundación para la promoción de la
comunidad y el mejoramiento del habitat
Diagonal 60 No. 23 - 63
Bogotá

Technical assistance group supporting self-help housing projects

SENA
Servicio Nacional de Aprendizaje
División de Desarrollo Tecnológico
Apartado Aéreo 9801
Bogotá

Development of low-cost technologies, eg machine for making concrete hollow blocks

Universidad Nacional de Colombia
Facultad de Artes
Apartado Aéreo 54118
Bogotá

University faculty with a Centro de Investigación de Bambú y Madera (CIBAM), internationally recognized institution with considerable experience in bamboo and timber construction

Denmark

Statens Byggeforskningsinstitut (SBI)
Dr. Neergaards Vej 15
Postboks 119
2970 Hørsholm

Government research institute; low-cost construction

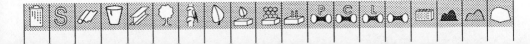

Technological Institute - Wood Technology
Gregersensvej
Postboks 141
2630 Taastrup

Research and documentation centre; technical
cooperation

Dominican Republic

CETAVIP
Centro de Tecnología Apropiada
para la Vivienda Popular
Apartado Postal 20-328
Avenida 27 de Febrero
Plaza Criolla, Local 10
Santo Domingo

Low-cost housing research, development,
training and information centre; executive
branch of CII-Viviendas (Consejo Inter-
Institucional para la Coordinación de Programas
de Viviendas, Inc.)

Ecuador

CATER
Centro Andino de Tecnología Rural
Universidad Nacional de Loja
Casilla 399
Loja

University research and documentation centre;
technical cooperation projects

CITA-EC
Centro de Ingeniería para
Tecnologías Adecuadas
Casilla 1024
Cuenca

AT centre, providing information and development assistance; technical cooperation projects

FUNHABIT
Fundacion Ecuatoriana del Habitat
Pedro de Texeira 273
Casilla 17-15-0086-C Sucursal 16
EC-Quito
Equateur

El Salvador

Fundación Salvadoreña de
Desarrollo y Vivienda Mínima
Apartado Aéreo 421
San Salvador

Research and documentation centre on low-cost
housing; technical cooperation projects

Ethiopia

Addis Ababa University
Faculty of Technology
P.O. Box 40874
Addis Ababa

Building materials research and development, eg fibre concrete roofing materials

UN Economic Commission of Africa
Africa Mall
P.O. Box 3001
Addis Ababa

United Nations body, providing development assistance in low-cost housing

France

ARCHECO
Centre de Terre
Lavalette
31590 Verfeil

Research and development centre for earth construction, developed soil block presses, eg GEO 50

BASIN-EAS
Earth Building Adviory Service
c/o CRATerre-EAG

Partner of the Building Advisory Service and Information Network (BASIN), specialised in earth construction.

CRATerre-EAG
International Center for Earth Construction
Centre Simone Signoret
B.P. 53
38090 Villefontaine

Leading earth construction research development and information centre; provides consultancy services and technical assistance. Many publications provide professional training and post graduate courses on the subject.

CSTB
Centre Scientifique et Technique du Bâtiment
24, rue Joseph Fourier
38400 St. Martin d'Heres

Government research institute on building materials and construction

Development Workshop
B.P. 13
82110 Lauzerte

Technical assistance group for Human Settlements in the Third World; wide experience in low-cost building technologies

ENTPE
National School of State Public Work
Laboratory Géo Matériaux
rue Maurice Audin
69120 Vaulx-en-Velin

Research laboratory for building materials; experience in earth construction technologies

GRET
Groupe de Recherche et
d'Echanges Technologiques
213, rue Lafayette
75010 Paris

Research and development organization, provides information and technical assistance; many interesting publications

RILEM
International Union of Testing and Research
Laboratories for Materials and Structures
12, rue Brancion
75700 Paris Cedex 15

Organizes international workshops and conferences on low-cost building materials

Germany, Federal Republic of

BASIN-WAS
Wall Building Advisory Service
c/o GATE

Partner of the Building Advisory Service and Information Network (BASIN), specialised in wall construction

BGR
Bundesanstalt für Geowissenschaften
und Rohstoffe
Stilleweg 2
30655 Hannover 51

Research and information centre on mineral resources; wide experience on laterites

BORDA
Bremer Arbeitsgemeinschaft für
Überseeforschung und Entwicklung
Bahnhofplatz 13
28195 Bremen 1

Bremen Overseas Research and Development Association; rural and urban development projects (eg Pune, India)

DESWOS
Deutsche Entwicklungshilfe für soziales
Wohnungs- und Siedlungswesen e.V.
Bismarckstrasse 7
50672 Köln 1

Small non-profit organization which provides research, development and financial assistance in cooperative housing projects, mainly Latin America and Southern Asia

GATE-GTZ
German Appropriate Technology Exchange
Dag-Hammarskjöld-Weg 1
Postfach 51 80
65726 Eschborn

Division of the German Agency for Technical Cooperation; provides extensive information service and conducts research and development projects worldwide; numerous useful publications

Gesamthochschule Kassel
Forschungslabor für Experimentelles Bauen
Menzelstrasse 13
34121 Kassel

Research laboratory for experimental building; leading German centre for soil building research and development of various other innovative constructions

Institute for Lightweight Structures (IL)
University of Stuttgart
Pfaffenwaldring 14
70569 Stuttgart 80

Research and development institute, dealing with natural and synthetic materials for light, tensile roof structures; research project in India on innovative bamboo constructions

IRB
Informationszentrum Raum und Bau
Fraunhofer-Gesellschaft München
Nobelstrasse 12
70569 Stuttgart 80

Documentation and information centre for all aspects of building and planning

KfW
Kreditanstalt für Wiederaufbau
Palmengartenstrasse 5 - 9
60325 Frankfurt 11

Finance institution, providing development assistance in many fields

Technische Universität Berlin
Planen und Bauen in Entwicklungsländern
Fachbereich 8, Institut II, Sekr. A 53
Strasse des 17. Juni 135
10623 Berlin 12

Educational and research institution on all aspects of planning and building in developing countries

Technische Hochschule Darmstadt
Fachgebiet Planen und Bauen
in Entwicklungsländern
Petersenstrasse 15
64287 Darmstadt

Educational and research institution on all aspects of planning and building in developing countries

TRIALOG
Vereinigung zur wiss. Erforschung des Planens
und Bauens in Entwicklungsländern e.V.
Ploenniesstrasse 18
64289 Darmstadt

Association of experts of all fields related to planning and building in developing countries; quarterly journal TRIALOG (mainly in German)

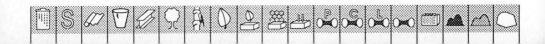

Ghana

BRRI
Building & Road Research Institute
P.O. Box 40 University
Kumasi

Well-known research institute; wide experience in laterite and soil construction; many publications

University of Science and Technology
Faculty of Architecture
Department of Housing and Planning
University Post Office
Kumasi

Educational and research institution, (developed the TEK-Block soil block press); technical assistance and advisory services provided through the Technology Consultancy Centre (TCC)

Guatemala

CEMAT
Centro de Estudios Mesoamericanos
sobre Tecnología Apropiada
4a avenida 2-28, zona 1
Apartado Postal 1160
Guatemala Ciudad

AT organization providing information services and development assistance; experience and publications on low-cost housing technologies; quarterly publication RED Newsletter

Centro de Tecnología Apropiada
"Manuel Guarán"
Apartado 1779
Guatemala Ciudad

Research and development of local construction materials and appropriate technologies

CETA
Centro de Experimentación
en Tecnología Apropiada
Apartado 66-F
Guatemala Ciudad

Research centre for appropriate technologies; developed the CETA-Ram soil block press

ICAITI
Instituto Centroamericano de
Investigaciones y Tecnología Industrial
Apartado Postal 1552
Guatemala Ciudad

Central industrial research institute of Central America, providing information and technical assistance; several publications

India

Asian and Pacific Centre
for Transfer of Technology
P.O. Box 115
Bangalore 560 052

Technology information centre of UN ESCAP;
publishes bimonthly newsletter "Asia-Pacific
Tech Monitor"

ASTRA
Indian Institute of Science
Malleswaram
Bangalore 560 012

Centre for the Application of Science & Technology to Rural Areas; research and development of low-cost building techniques; design of
ASTRAM block press

ATDA
Appropriate Technology
Development Association
P.O. Box 311
Ghandi Bhawan
Lucknow 226 001

AT organization, providing information, training, development assistance; special experience
in small-scale cement production; newsletter
"ap-tech"

Auroville Building Center (AV-BC)
Earth Architecture Department
Ind-605101 Auroshilpam
Tamil Nadu

Resource center for Appropriate Building Technologie course and production of equipment for
many constructions.

CBRI
Central Building Research Institute
Roorkee 247 667

Leading Asian research institute for building
materials and technologies, numerous useful
publications

CORT
Consortium on Rural Technology
D-320, Laxmi Nagar
New Delhi 110 092

Institution which promotes and disseminates
information on rural technologies; no research of
its own, but coordination of research between
other institutions

Council of Scientific & Industrial Research
Regional Research Laboratory, Trivandrum
Trivandrum 695 019

Research institution; improvements in low-cost
building materials, especially thatch roofing

CSV
Centre of Science for Villages
Magan Sangrahalaya
Wardha 442 001

AT organization, providing information and
technical assistance; newsletter "Science for
Villages"

Development Alternatives
B-32, Institutional Area
TARA Crescent
New Mehrauli Road
New Delhi-110 016

Non-profit organization providing multi-disciplinary expertise in low-cost building technologies (especially soil constructions); designed the BALRAM soil block press

Forest Research Institute
New Forest
Dehra Dun 248 006

Research and training on applications of forestry products for building

Habitat Technology Network
Building Centre, Sarai Kale Khan
East Nizamuddin
New Dehli 110013

Indian Institute of Technology (IIT)
Department of Civil Engineering
Building Technology Division
Madras 600 036

Educational and research institute on building technologies; designed the IIT Cam block press

National Buildings Organization
"G" Wing, Nirman Bhavan
Maulana Azad Road
New Delhi 110 011

Central coordinating organization for housing and building research and implementation; numerous useful publications; UN regional centre of ESCAP

National Council for Cement
and Building Materials
M-10 South Extension Part-II
New Delhi 110 049

Leading coordination and information centre of the Indian cement and building materials industries

Regional Research Laboratory (C.S.I.R.)
Applied Civil Engineering Division
Jorhat 785 006, Assam

Building materials and technology research institute; experience in bamboocrete, ferrocement, agro-wastes

SERC
Structural Engineering Research Centre
CSIR Campus
Taramani
Madras 600 113

Research institution with specialization in precast concrete and ferrocement construction

University of Roorkee
Department of Civil Engineering
Roorkee 247 667

Educational and research institution on various fields of building technology

Indonesia

Ceramic Research and Development Institute
Jalan Jenderal Ahmad Yani 392
Bandung

Government research institute, providing infor-mation and assistance in improving clay brick and roof tile production

Yayasan Dian Desa
P.O. Box 19
Bulaksumur
Yogyakarta

AT organization, with some experience in bamboocrete and fibre concrete; monthly bulletin "TARIK" and other publications

Institute of Human Settlements (IHS)
Agency for Research and Development
Ministry of Public Works &
UN Regional Centre for Human Settlements
84, Jalan Tamansari
Bandung

Leading building material and technology research institute, providing information and development assistance; UN regional centre of ESCAP

Italy

Facoltà di Architettura
Politecnico di Torino
Viale Mattioli 39
Torino 10125

Department of Turin Polytechnic involved in building technology research (eg gypsum-sisal conoids)

FAO
Food and Agriculture Organization
of the United Nations
Via delle Terme di Caracalla
00142 Roma

UN organization providing information on building materials from agricultural and forestry products and wastes

Jordan

Yarmouk University
Department of Civil Engineering
Irbid

Research on cementitious building materials

Kenya

HABITAT
United Nations Centre for Human Settlements
(U.N.C.H.S.)
P.O. Box 30030
Nairobi

Central coordinating body on housing, building and planning; project implementation, international conferences; numerous publications; "HABITAT News" published three times a year

HRDU
Housing Research and Development Unit
University of Nairobi
P.O. Box 30197
Nairobi

Leading research institution on all aspects of low-cost housing and building materials

Intermediate Technology Kenya
22 Chiromo Access Road
Off Riverside Drive
P.O. Box 39493
Nairobi

Project work on small-scale production of concrete products and building stone, low cost housing, marketing of building products and appropriate building standards. Dissemination of information and local networking in the areas of housing and building materials through the Shelter Forum

Malaysia

Ministry of Housing and Local Government
Jalan Cendersari
50646 Kuala Lumpur

Research and Technology Planning Division concerned with building materials and construction technologies for low-cost housing

University Technology Malaysia
Faculty of Built Environment
Karung Berkunci 791
80900 Johor Bahru

Educational and research institution dealing with low-cost housing technologies

Mexico

Centro nacional de investigaciones de
construccion con tierra y energias alternativas
M. Imaz Ferriz Alberto, Directeur Général
Saltillo N° 31, Col. Condesa
Mex-Mexico D.F.

COPEVI
Centro Operacional de Vivienda y Poblamiento
Tlaloc 40-2
Col. Tlaxpana
México DF 11370

Housing research and development institution, providing information and assistance in project implementation

Sociedad Mexicana de Ingeniería Sísmica A.C. Camino Santa Teresa 187 Apartado Postal 70-227 México DF 04510	Information and advisory centre for earthquake resistant construction

Nepal

His Majesty's Government of Nepal Department of Housing, Building & Physical Planning Babar Mahal Kathmandu	Building research institution; experience in soil-cement, stone, concrete products

Netherlands

CIB International Council for Building Research Studies and Documentation Weena 704 P.O. Box 20704 3001 JA Rotterdam	Association of building research experts and organization which coordinates research activities and information dissemination through technical working commissions, conferences and publications
Delft University of Technology CICAT (Centre for International Cooperation and Appropriate Technology) P.O. Box 5048 Stevinweg 1 2600 GA Delft	AT organization which undertakes numerous research and development projects in developing countries; several useful publications, "AT News" published 3 times a year, joint publishers of "AT Source"
SATIS Socially Appropriate Technology International Information Services Postbus 803 3500 AV Utrecht	Information and documentation centre for appropriate technologies in all fields; publishes a comprehensive catalogue of useful AT publications
Technical University Den Dolech 2 P.O. Box 513 5600 MB Eindhoven	Educational and research institution; special field of research of the Faculty of Architecture and Building: bamboo constructions

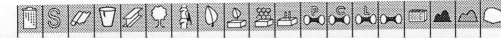

TOOL
Technische Ontwikkeling Ontwikkelingslanden
(Technical Development
with Developing Countries)
Sarphatistraat 650
1018 AV Amsterdam

AT centre with bookshop; coordination of
research studies and publications; joint
publishers of AT journal "AT Source" (formally
VRAAGBAAK)

Nigeria

National Commission for Museums and
monuments
M. Ogunsusi Valentine Adebowale
WAN-Jos PMB 2031
Nigeria

Resource and training centre on earth
architecture. National Museum Jobs

Pakistan

ATDO
Appropriate Technology
Development Organization
Ministry of Science & Technology
1 - A & B 47th Street, F - 7/1
Islamabad

AT organization with regional offices in Karachi
and Lahore; ATDO Karachi (St. No. 10-A,
Block No. 4, Gulshan-e-Iqbal, Scheme No. 24,
Karachi) specializes in building materials
(eg soil cement blocks, concrete hollow blocks)

NBRI
National Building Research Institute
F-40, S.I.T.E.
Hub River Road
Karachi

Government research institute, mainly dealing
with cementitious materials and products; built
first RHA-lime house (Bibl. 24.16)

Panama

Grupo de Tecnología Apropiada
Apartado 8046
Panamá 7

AT organization, providing information and
technical assistance

Papua New Guinea

SPATF
South Pacific Appropriate
Technology Foundation
P.O. Box 6937
Boroko

AT organization with experience in soil block construction and fibre concrete roofing; publish "Liklik Buk" and quarterly newsletters "Yumi Kirapim" and "SPATF NIUS"

Paraguay

Centro de Tecnología Aproiada
Universidad Católica
"Ntra. Sra. de la Asunción"
Facultad de Ciencias y Tecnología
Casilla de Correos 1718
Asunción

AT organization with main emphasis on building technologies: developed CTA Triple soil block press, timber flood resistant housing, comprehensive research project on rural housing improvements to prevent the Chagas disease

Peru

CRATerre AMERICA LATINA
Apartado Postal 5603
Correo Central
Lima 1

Technical assistance group, dedicated to promoting soil construction technologies; developed a soil block press for earthquake resistant soil block construction

Intermediate Technology Peru
Casilla 18-0620
Lima 18

Project work on community-based planning, housing, especially disaster resistant housing, and work on building materials production in collaboration with local ngo's

Philippines

CIAP
Construction Industry Authority
of the Philippines
6th Floor, Trade & Industry Centre
Tordesillas St., Salcedo Village
Makati, Metro Manila

Principal agency concerned with building materials and construction technologies, conducting a Construction Technology Research and Development (CTRD) program for better R & D coordination and implementation

FPRDI Forest Products Research and Development Institute Los Baños Laguna	Leading research institute on timber and vegetable building materials, and use of agro- and forestry wastes; several publications
National Housing Authority Elliptical Road Diliman Querzon City	Government institution responsible for housing development and implementation
PCATT Philippine Center for Appropriate Technology and Training 224 Diego Silang Street Batangas City 4201	AT information centre; various publications, but only few on building materials, eg bamboo, coconut palm
UNDP/UNIDO Regional Network in Asia for Low-Cost Building Materials Technology and Construction Systems (RENAS-BMTCS) Office of the Regional Secretariat 10th Floor, Allied Bank Building Ayala Avenue, Makati Metro Manila	Regional information centre designed as a facility to merge common interests and promote mutual assistance among building research institutions in Asia and the Pacific; publish quarterly newsletter NETWORK MONITOR, and several monographs on low-cost building materials

Singapore

Nanyang Technological Institute School of Civil & Structural Engineering Nanyang Avenue Singapore 2263	Research on alternative building materials, eg sewage sludge for brick production
National University of Singapore Department of Civil Engineering Kent Ridge Singapore 0511	Educational and research institute with wide experience in ferrocement and fibre concrete constructions, also in waste utilization, soil consolidation, etc.

South Africa

National Building Research Institute P.O. Box 395 Pretoria 0001	Development of various innovative low-cost building techniques, especially adobe and concrete constructions

Sri Lanka

National Building Research Organization
99/1 Jawatta Road
Colombo

Government research institute, experience in soil-cement, clay brick and concrete construction

Sudan

Building and Road Research Institute
University of Khartoum
P.O. Box 321
Khartoum

Government research institution with experience in fibre concrete construction and other low-cost housing technologies

Sweden

HABITROPIC
Birkagatan 27
113 39 Stockholm

Product development enterprise for appropriate technologies; developed a low-cost space frame construction

NFC- Natural Fibre Concrete AG
P.O. Box 1512
S-172 29 Sundbyberg

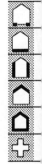

SADEL
Swedish Association for
Development of Low-Cost Housing
Arkitektur 1
P.O. Box 118
Sölvegatan 24
221 00 Lund

Technical research and development assistance group, attached to Lund University; special low-cost housing experience in Tunisia

Swedish Cement and
Concrete Research Institute
100 44 Stockholm

Amongst other research, specialization in the durability of natural fibres in fibre concrete

Switzerland

BASIN-RAS
Roofing Advisory Service
c/o SKAT

Partner of the Building Advisory Service and Information Network (BASIN), specialised in roof construction

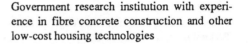

ETH Hönggerberg Institut für Hochbautechnik 8093 Zürich	Research institute, with specialization in soil technologies and ferrocement
ILO International Labour Organization 4, route des Morillons 1211 Geneva 22	UN body, providing development assistance in low-cost building technologies; many publications
SKAT Swiss Centre for Development Cooperation in Technology and Management Vadianstrasse 42 9000 St. Gallen	AT organization with bookshop; coordination of research studies and publications; technical advisory services, especially on roofing

Tanzania

Ardhi Institute Centre for Housing Studies P.O. Box 35124 Dar es Salaam	Professional training and research institute with information and documentation unit
Building Research Unit Mpakani Road P.O. Box 1964 Dar es Salaam	Government vocational training and research institute, with information and documentation unit
Small Industries Development Association (SIDO) P.O. Box 2476 Dar es Salaam	Local promotion of small industries including those of building materials production, for example in the areas of clay bricks, concrete roofing tiles and lime

Thailand

AIT Asian Institute of Technology P.O. Box 2754 Bangkok 10501	Leading research institution, with Human Settlements Division (LOK BILD system and other technologies) and International Ferrocement Information Center
Chulalongkorn University Faculty of Architecture Phya Thai Road Bangkok 10500	Educational and research institute with experience in low-cost constructions

ESCAP Economic and Social Commission for Asia and the Pacific The United Nations Building Rajadamnern Avenue Bangkok 10200	UN body, with a special ESCAP/UNIDO Division of Industry, Human Settlements and Technology, which conducts international conferences (eg on building materials, 1987), research studies and training seminars; numerous publications
National Housing Authority 905 Sukapibal 1 Bangkapi Bangkok 10240	Government institution responsible for housing development and implementation
Thailand Institute of Scientific and Technological Research (TISTR) 196 Phahonyothin Rd. Bangkhen Bangkok 10900	Leading research institution covering all fields of low-cost building materials and construction technologies

Togo

Centre de la Construction et du Logement (CCL) B.P. 1762 Lomé	Building research and information centre, specialized in low-cost building materials

United Kingdom

AHAS Associated Housing Advisory Services P.O. Box 397 London E8 1BA	Research organization with information and consultancy services on all aspects of low-income housing and self-help construction
BASIN-CAS Cements and Binders Advisory Service c/o ITDG	Partner of the Building Advisory Service and Information Network (BASIN), specialised in cements and binders
Cambridge Architectural Research Limited The Oast House Malting Lane Cambridge CB3 9HF	Consultancy specialized in various disciplines related to architecture, including appropriate climatic design and construction technology in developing countries

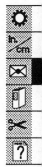

ITDG Intermediate Technology Development Group Myson House Railway Terrace Rugby CV21 3HT	Leading AT organization, whose establishment gave birth to the worldwide AT movement; provides information and consultancy services, and conducts technical cooperation projects
Intermediate Technology Publications Ltd. 103 - 105 Southhampton Row London WC1B 4HH	Publishing arm of ITDG; largest selection of AT literature in the IT Bookshop; publish quarterly journals "Appropriate Technology" and "Waterlines", among numerous important publications
Intermediate Technology Workshops Overend Road Cradley Heath Warley, West Midlands B64 7DD	Private organization involved in the development of improved techniques for building materials production; developed numerous machines and equipment
Overseas Development Administration Foreign and Commonwealth Office Eland House Stag Place London SW1E 5DH	Government agency for development assistance
TERRE 109, High Street Portsmouth P01 2HJ	Consultancy specialized in the development of non-metallic rock and mineral resources and building materials industries

United States of America

Agency for International Development (AID) Department of State Washington, D.C. 20523	United States development aid organization, providing financial and technical assistance, and information service
AT International 1331 H Street, N.W. Washington, D.C. 20005	Development assistance corporation, promoting small enterprise development by evaluation and transfer of AT
HUD U.S. Department of Housing and Urban Development Office of International Affairs Washington, D.C. 20410	Development assistance institution with extensive documentation on all aspects of housing, building and planning

International Council of Earth Builders (ICEB)
419 North Larchmont Blvd., Ste. 72
Los Angeles, California 90004

INTERTECT
International Disaster Specialists
P.O. Box 10502
Dallas, TEX 75207

Organization that deals with disaster mitigation
and post-disaster shelter and housing; "International Newsletter: Earthen buildings in seismic
areas"

TRANET
Transnational Network
for Appropriate Technology
P.O. Box 567
Rangeley, ME 04970

Non-profit organization with subscription-paying members; facilitates exchange of information and ideas among members from numerous
countries and professional fields

VITA
Volunteers in Technical Assistance
1815 North Lynn Street, Suite 200
P.O. Box 12438
Arlington, VA 22209

Organization providing technical assistance to
groups involved in the development of small-scale low-capital investment tools and techniques

Volunteers in Asia
Appropriate Technology Project
P.O. Box 4543
Stanford, CA 94305

Information and documentation unit, which
publishes the most comprehensive bibliographical reference book: "Appropriate Technology
Sourcebook" (Bibl. 00.07)

Vietnam

The Institute of Building Materials
Ministry of Construction
Thuong Dinh
Dong Da
Hanoi

R. & D. on production and use of appriopriate
building materials such as cement, lime, fired
clay bricks, board and sheet materials and fibre-reinforced concrete

Zimbabwe

Intermediate Technology Zimbabwe
Gorlon House, 2nd Floor
7 Jason Moyo Avenue
Harare

Project work on building terials production and
housing concentrating on clay brick production
and stabilised soil blocks and networking with
local organisations.

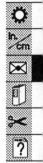

BIBLIOGRAPHY

390

Language of publication: (E) = English, (F) = French, (S) = Spanish, (G) = German

* *= available at SKAT Bookshop*

00. GENERAL

00.01 Andersson, L.A.; Arnsby, L.; Johansson, B.; Pering, C.; Åstrand, J.: **A Solution to Rural Housing Problems,** Experiences from a pilot project in Tunisia based on organized do-it-yourself building, SADEL, S-22100 Lund, Sweden, 1986 (E)

00.02 * Bery, Sunil (Ed.): **Compendium of New Construction Techniques and Materials,** National Building Organization, New Delhi, 1987 (E)

00.03 Building Research Establishment: **Building in Hot Climates,** A selection of Overseas Building Notes, BRE, Garston, 1980 (E)

00.04 * CIB/ RILEM: **Appropriate Building Materials for Low Cost Housing,** African Region (Vol. I + II), Proceedings of an international symposium in Nairobi (November 1983), E. & F.N. Spon, London, 1983 (E, F)

00.05 Dakhil, F.H.; Ural, O.; Tewfik, M.F. (Eds.): **Housing Problems in Developing Countries,** Vols. I and II, Proceedings of IAHS International Conference at the University of Petroleum and Minerals, Dharan, Saudi Arabia, John Wiley & Sons, Chichester, 1978 (E)

00.06 * Dancy, H.K.: **A Manual of Building Construction,** IT Publications, London, 1975 (E)

00.07 * Darrow, Ken; Saxenian, Mike: **Appropriate Technology Sourcebook,** A guide to practical books for village and small community technology, A Volunteers in Asia Publication, Stanford, CA 94305, USA, 1986 (E)

00.08 Denyer, Susan: **African Traditional Architecture,** Heinemann, London, 1978 (E)

00.09 Doswald, Fritz: **Planen und Bauen in heißen Zonen** (Planning and building in hot zones), Baufachverlag, Zürich, 1977 (G)

00.10 Duly, Colin: **Houses of Mankind,** Thames and Hudson Ltd., London, 1979 (E)

00.11 Ebert, Wolfgang: **Home Sweet Dome - Träume vom Wohnen,** Dieter Fricke GmbH, Frankfurt am Main, 1978 (G)

00.12 ESCAP: **Building Technology Series,** Building Materials and Construction Technologies for Low-Cost Housing in Developing ESCAP Countries (Prepared by K. Mukerji), ESCAP (IHT Div.), Bangkok, 1987 (E)

00.13   ESCAP, RILEM, CIB: **Building Materials for Low-income Housing**, Asian and Pacific Region, Proceedings of an international symposium in Bangkok (January 1987), E. & F.N. Spon, London, 1987 (E)

00.14   Everett, Alan: **Materials**, Mitchell's Building Series, Batsford Academic and Educational Ltd., London, 1984 (E)

00.15   Fathy, Hassan: **Natural Energy and Vernacular Architecture: Principles and Examples with Reference to Hot Arid Climates**, The University of Chicago Press, Chicago, 1986 (E)

00.16   Fullerton, R.L.: **Building Construction in Warm Climates**, Vols. 1, 2 & 3, Oxford Tropical Handbooks, Oxford University Press, Oxford, 1979 (E)

00.17   GATE: **Building and Construction**, Issue No. 1/85 of "gate - questions, answers, information", Eschborn, 1985, (E)

00.18   Grasser, Klaus; Mukerji, Kiran: **Minimum Cost Housing in El Salvador**, Project Report of the Institut für Tropenbau, Dr.Ing. G. Lippsmeier, Starnberg, in cooperation with FSDVM and CIG, San Salvador, Aus der Arbeit von GATE, Eschborn, 1981 (E, G, S)

00.19   Hale, P.R.; Williams, B.D.: **Liklik Buk**, A Rural Development Handbook Catalogue for Papua New Guinea, Liklik Buk Information Centre, P.O. Box 1920, Lae, PNG, 1977 (E)

00.20   Hedley, G.; Garrett, C.: **Practical Site Management**, An illustrated guide, 2nd Ed., George Godwin, Longman Group Ltd., London, 1983 (E)

00.21 *   Institution of Civil Engineers: **Appropriate Technology in Civil Engineering**, Proceedings of conference, April 1980, Thomas Telford Ltd., London, 1981 (E)

00.22   Kahn, Lloyd (Editor): **Shelter**, Shelter Publications, Bolinas, Calif., 1973 (E)

00.23   Kahn, Lloyd (Editor): **Shelter II**, Shelter Publications, Bolinas, Calif., 1978 (E)

00.24   König, Holger: **Wege zum Gesunden Bauen**, (Construction of healthy buildings), Ökobuch, Freiburg, 1985 (G)

00.25   Koenigsberger O.H.; Ingersoll T.G.; Mayhew A.; Szokolay S.V.: **Manual of Tropical Housing and Building, Part 1: Climatic Design**, Longman Group Ltd., London, 1973 (E)

00.26   Kolb, Bernhard: **Beispiel Biohaus** (Biological and Solar Houses in German-Speaking Regions), Blok Verlag, München, 1984 (G)

00.27   Krusche, P. u. M.; Althaus, D.; Gabriel, I.: **Ökologisches Bauen** (Ecological Building), Bauverlag, Wiesbaden and Berlin, 1982 (G)

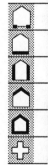

00.28 * Kur, Friedrich: **Bauen und Wohnen mit Naturbaustoffen** (Building and Living with Natural Building Materials), Compact Verlag, München, 1987 (G)

00.29 Lippsmeier, Georg: **Tropenbau - Building in the Tropics**, Callwey Verlag, München, 1980 (G, E)

00.30 Mathéy, Kosta; Mrotzek-Sampat, Rita; Mukerji, Kiran (Eds.): **TRIALOG 12: Angepaßte Technologien**, (special issue on appropriate technologies in the German journal on planning and building in the Third World), TRIALOG, Darmstadt, 1987 (G, E)

00.31 Mathéy, Kosta: **Angepaßte Baumaterialien im Wohnungsbau für untere Einkommens-gruppen in Entwicklungsländern** (Appropriate Building Materials for Low-Income Housing in Developing Countries), Article in TRIALOG 12, Darmstadt, 1987 (E)

00.32 Mathur, G.C. (Ed.): **Rural Housing and Village Planning**, Proceedings of a seminar organized by NBO, New Delhi, 1960 (E)

00.33 Minke, Gernot: **Alternatives Bauen**, Report on the work of the Research Laboratory for Experimental Building, University of Kassel, Ökobuch Verlag, Grebenstein, 1980 (G)

00.34 Mukerji, K.; Sulejman-Pasic, N.; Murison, H.S.; Hockings, J.E.: **Prefabrication for Low-Cost Housing in Tropical Areas**, I.F.T. Report 4, Institut für Tropenbau Dr.Ing. G. Lippsmeier, Starnberg, 1975 (E, G)

00.35 Oliver, Paul (Editor): **Shelter and Society**, Barrie and Jenkins Ltd., London, 1969 (E)

00.36 Oliver, Paul (Editor): **Shelter in Africa**, Barrie and Jenkins Ltd., London, 1971 (E)

00.37 * Oliver, Paul: **Dwellings - The House across the World**, Phaidon Press Ltd., Oxford, 1987 (E)

00.38 Pama, R.P.; Nimityongskul, P.; Cook, D.J. (Eds.): **Materials of Construction for Developing Countries**, Vols. I and II, Proceedings of the International Conference at AIT, Bangkok, 1978 (E)

00.39 * Parry, John; Gordon, Andrew: **Shanty Upgrading**, Technical handbook for upgrading squatter and shanty settlements, Intermediate Technology Workshops, Cradley Heath, 1987 (E)

00.40 Piltz, H.; Härig, S.; Schulz, W.: **Technologie der Baustoffe** (Technology of Building Materials), 8th Edition, Dr. Lüdecke-Verlagsgesellschaft mbh, Haslach i.K., 1985 (G)

00.41 * Rai, Mohan; Jaisingh, M.P.: **Advances in Building Materials and Construction**, Central Building Research Institute, Roorkee, 1986 (E)

00.42   Rapoport, Amos: **House Form and Culture**, Prentice-Hall Inc., Englewood Cliffs, N.J., 1969 (E)

00.43   Riedijk, W. (Editor): **Appropriate Technology for Developing Countries**, Delft University Press, Delft, 1984 (E)

00.44   Rudofsky, Bernard: **Architecture without Architects**, The Museum of Modern Art, New York, 1965 (E)

00.45   Rudofsky, Bernard: **The Prodigious Builders**, Secker + Warburg, London, 1977 (E)

00.46   Rybczynski, Witold: **Paper Heroes**, A Review of Appropriate Technology, Prism Press, Dorchester, 1980 (E)

00.47   Saini, B.S.: **Building Environment**, An Illustrated Analysis of Problems in Hot Dry Lands, Angus and Robertson Pty. Ltd., Sydney, 1973 (E)

00.48   Saini, B.S.: **Building in Hot Dry Climates**, John Wiley & Co., Brisbane, 1982 (E)

00.49   Schreckenbach, Hannah; Abankwa, Jackson G.K.: **Construction Technology for a Tropical Developing Country**, GTZ, Eschborn, 1983 (E)

00.50   Spence, R.J.S.; Cook, D.J.: **Building Materials in Developing Countries**, John Wiley & Sons Ltd., Chichester, 1983 (E)

00.51 * Stulz, Roland: **Elements of Solar Architecture**, SKAT Publication, St. Gallen, 1980 (E)

00.52   Tutt, P.; Adler, D.: **New Metric Handbook**, The Architectural Press, London, 1979 (E)

00.53   UNIDO: **Appropriate Industrial Technology for Construction and Building Materials**, Monographs on Appropriate Industrial Technology, No. 12, United Nations, New York, 1980 (E)

00.54 * van Lengen, Johan: **Manual del Arquitecto Descalzo**, (Handbook of the barefoot architect), J.v. Lengen, Av. Eugenio Sue 45, México 5, D.F. México, 1981 (S)

00.55   van Winden, John; et al: **Rural Building**, Technical Training Course in 4 books (Reference, Basic Knowledge, Construction, Drawing Book), TOOL, Amsterdam, 1986 (E)

00.56   Vorhauer, Klaus: **Low Cost/Self Help Housing**, GATE-Modul 6/6, Eschborn, 1979 (E)

00.57   Wendehorst, R.: **Baustoffkunde** (Building Materials Science), Curt R. Vincentz Verlag, Hannover, 1986 (G)

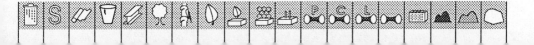

00.58   Willkomm, Wolfgang: **Selbstbau in Entwicklungsländern** (Self-help building in developing countries), Ph.D. Thesis (IB 3), University of Hanover, 1981 (G)

Addendum 1993

Andrews, V. & R.: **The Owner Builder magazine**, Bendigo, Australia (E)

Alsayyad, Nezar, ed.: **The Design and Planning of Housing**, College of Environmental Design, University of Petroleum and Minerals, Dhahran, 1984 (E)

Baker, N.V.: **Passive and Low Energy Building Design for Tropical Island Climates**, Commonwealth Secretariat Publications, London, 1987 (E)

Brown, G.Z.: **Sun, Wind and Light**, John Wiley & Sons, New York, 1985 (E)

Golany, Gideon S., ed.: **Design for Arid Regions**, van Nostrand Reinhold Company, New York, 1983 (E)

Golany, Gideon S., ed.: **Urban Planning for Arid Zones**, John Wiley & Sons, New York, 1978 (E)

Gut, Paul; Ackerknecht, Dieter: **Climate Responsive Building**, SKAT, St. Gallen, 1993 (E)

Hillmann, G.; Nagel, J.; Schreck, H.: **Klimagerechte und Energiesparende Architektur**, Verlag C.F. Müller, Karlsruhe, 1983 (G)

Konya, Allan: **Design Primer for Hot Climates**, The Architectural Press, London, 1980 (E)

Lechner, Norbert: **Heating, Cooling, Lighting**, John Wiley & Sons, New York, 1991 (E)

Mazria, Edward: **The Passive Solar Energy Book**, Rodale Press, Emmaus Penn., 1978 (E)

Niles, Philip; Haggard, Kenneth: **Passive Solar Handbook**, Califorinia Energy Commission, Sacramento, 1980 (E)

Olgyay, Victor: **Design with Climate**, Princeton University Press, Princeton, 1963 (E)

01.   STONE

01.01   Carayon, B.; Gardet, J.; Berthoumieux, G.-L.: **La Pierre** (Stone), GRET, Paris, 1984 (F)

01.02   CBRI: **Precast Stone Masonry Block Walling Scheme**, Building Research Note No. 7, CBRI, Roorkee, 1986 (E)

01.03   Everett, Alan: **Stones**, Chapter 4 in "Materials", Bibl. 00.14 (E)

01.04   Holmes, Stafford: **Stone - A Local Building Resource**, Appropriate Technology Vol. 11, No. 3, IT Publications, London, 1984 (E)

01.05   Ortega, Alvaro: **Basic Technology: Stone**, Mimar 21, Concept Media, Singapore, 1986

01.06   Rural Water Supply Nepal: **Stone Masonry Course**, Technical Training Manual No. 2, Remote Area and Local Development Department, HMG; SATA; UNICEF, Kathmandu, 1977 (E)

01.07   Spence, R.J.S.; Cook, D.J.: **Stone and Stone Masonry**, Chapter 4.5 in "Building Materials in Developing Countries", Bibl. 00.50 (E)

01.08   United Nations: **Stone in Nepal**, compiled by Asher Shadmon, UNDP and Government of Nepal, Kathmandu, 1977 (E)

Addendum 1993

Shadmon, Asher: **Stone – An Introduction**, IT Publications, London, 1989 (E)

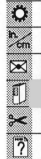

02.   *EARTH, SOIL, LATERITES*

02.01   Agarwal, Anil: **Mud, Mud,** The potential of earth-based materials for Third World housing, Earthscan/International Institute for Environment and Development, London, 1981 (E)

02.02   Andersson, Lars-Anders; Johansson, Bo; Åstrand, Johnny: **Blockmaking machines for soil-blocks**, SADEL, Lund, 1983 (E)

02.03   Architectural Society of China: **Proceedings of the International Symposium on Earth Architecture**, ASC, Beijing, 1985 (E)

02.04   Arrigone, Jorge Luis: **Appropriate Technology Adobe Construction**, A research and demonstration project on the use of Adobe for low-cost housing construction, National Building Research Institute, Council for Scientific and Industrial Research, Pretoria, 1986 (E)

02.05   Bardou, P.; Arzoumanian, V.: **Archi de Terre**, Paranthèses, Marseille, 1978 (F)

02.06 * CRATerre - Doat, P.; Hays, A.; Houben, H.; Matuk, S.; Vitoux, F.: **Construire en terre**, éditions alternatives, Paris, 1983 (F)

02.07 * CRATerre (H. Houben, P.E. Verney); ENTPE (M. Olivier, A. Mesbah, Ph. Michel): **Raw Earth Construction: The French Equipment**, CRATerre, Grenoble, 1987 (E)

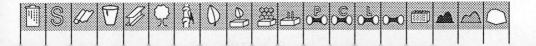

02.08   CRATerre; GAITerre: **Marrakech 83 Habitat en Terre,** (Marrakesh 83 Earth Housing), Rexcoop - Plan Construction, Paris, 1983 (F)

02.09   CRATerre (Alain Hays, et al): **Técnicas mixtas de construcción con tierra** (Various soil construction techniques), Rexcoop - Plan Construction, Paris, 1986 (S)

02.10   Department of Housing and Urban Development: **Handbook for Building Homes of Earth,** HUD, Washington, D.C., year of publication unknown (E)

02.11   Dethier, Jean: **Down to Earth: Mud Architecture - an old idea, a new future,** Thames and Hudson, London, 1982 (E)

02.12   Dye, John R.: **Assembly Manual for the Tek-Block Press,** Department of Housing & Planning Research, Faculty of Architecture, University of Science and Technology, Kumasi, Ghana, 1975 (E)

02.13   Enteiche, G.; Augusta, A.: **Soil Cement: Its Use in Building,** United Nations, New York, 1964 (E)

02.14   Fathy, Hassan: **Architecture for the Poor,** An Experiment in Rural Egypt, The University of Chicago Press, Chicago, 1973 (E)

02.15   GATE (Ed.): **Lehmarchitektur,** Rückblick - Ausblick, Proceedings of a Symposium, held in Frankfurt in March 1982, Aus der Arbeit von GATE, Eschborn, 1982 (G)

02.16   Gieth, Thomas: **Construction of Low-Cost Dwelling with Compacted Soil Blocks** (Prototype "A"), C.T.A., Catholic University, Asunción, 1984 (E)

02.17   Guérin, Laurent: **Principes directeurs pour l'emploi de la terre crue** (Principles of soil construction), ILO, Geneva, 1985 (F)

02.18   Hammond, A.A.: **Prolonging the Life of Earth Buildings in the Tropics,** Building Research and Practice (May/June 1973), Building and Road Research Institute, UST Kumasi, 1973 (E)

02.19   Houben, Hugo; Guillaud, Hubert: **Earth Construction Primer,** Project Document of AGDC/UNCHS/PGC-HS-KUL/CRA-UCL/CRATerre, Brussels, 1984 (E)

02.20   Jagadish, K.S.; Venkatarama Reddy, B.V.: **A Manual of Soil Block Construction,** Alternative Building Series - 1, Centre for Application of Science and Technology for Rural Areas (ASTRA), Indian Institute of Science, Bangalore, 1981 (E)

02.21   Lander, Helmut; Niermann, Manfred: **Lehm-Architektur in Spanien und Afrika,** Karl Robert Langewiesche Nachfolger Hans Köster, Königstein im Taunus, 1980 (G)

02.22   Lola, Carlos R.: **Research Efforts on Soil Cement Stabilization for Low-Cost Housing in Nicaragua**, University of Tennessee, Knoxville, 1981 (E)

02.23   Lola, Carlos R.: **ADAUA Earthen Construction Techniques**, AT International, Washington D.C., 1983 (E)

02.24   Lou Má, Roberto E.: **La Ceta-Ram**, Una máquina para producir bloques huecos de suelo-cemento, inspirada en el diseño de la Cinva-Ram, CETA, Guatemala, 1977 (S, E)

02.25 * Lou Má, Roberto E.: **Two Manually Operated Block Presses CETA-Ram and CETA-Ram II**, CETA, Guatemala, 1984 (E)

02.26   McHenry jr., P.G.: **Adobe and Rammed Earth Buildings**, Design and Construction, John Wiley & Sons, New York, 1984 (E)

02.27   Minke, Gernot: **Lehmbauforschung**, Development and Testing of partially mechanized rammed earth and wet soil techniques, Schriftenreihe Heft 8, Fachbereich Architektur, Gesamthochschule Kassel, 1984 (G)

02.28 * Minke, Gernot (Ed.): **Bauen mit Lehm**, Journal on Building with Soil, Reports on new developments, research studies and building projects, Ökobuch-Verlag, Grebenstein/Freiburg, 1984/1987 (G)

02.29   Mukerji, K.; Bahlmann, H.: **Laterite for Building**, I.F.T. Report 5, Institut für Tropenbau Dr.Ing. Georg Lippsmeier, Starnberg, 1978 (E, G)

02.30   Mukerji, Kiran: **Soil Block Presses**, Report on a Global Survey, GATE, Eschborn, 1986

02.31   Niemeyer, Richard: **Der Lehmbau** und seine praktische Anwendung, Nachdruck des Originalwerks aus dem Jahre 1946, Ökobuch Verlag, Grebenstein, 1982 (G)

02.32 * Norton, John: **Building with Earth**, A Handbook, IT Publications Ltd., London, 1986 (E)

02.33   Odul, Pascal: **Case Studies on Earth Construction: Synthesis**, PGC-HS, Katholieke Universiteit Leuven, 1984 (E)

02.34   Odul, Pascal; et al: **Exhibition on Earth Construction Technologies Appropriate to Developing Countries - The Technical Issue**, AGDC/UNCHSPGC-HD-KUL/CRA-UCL/CRATerre, available from ATOL, Leuven, 1984 (E)

02.35   Popposwamy (alias Reinhold Pingel): **Village Houses in Rammed Earth - an Indian Experiment**, Reihe dü scriptum, Dienste in Übersee, Stuttgart, 1980 (G, E, F)

02.36   Schneider, Jürgen: **Am Anfang die Erde - Sanfter Baustoff Lehm**, Das Buch zur ZDF-Sendung im Februar 1985, Edition Fricke, Verlagsgesellschaft Rudolf Müller, Köln, 1985 (G)

02.37 * SKAT: **Soil Block Making Equipment**, Compilation of material on some well-known systems, machines and equipment, Working Paper 05/84, SKAT, St. Gallen, 1984 (E, F, S)

02.38   Stulz, Roland: **Earth for Construction** Appropriate Technology Vol. 11, No. 3, IT Publications, London, 1984 (E)

02.39   Venkatarama Reddy, B.V.; Jagadish, K.S.; Nageswara Rao, M.: **The Design of a Soil Compaction Ram for Rural Housing**, Alternative Building Series - 4, ASTRA, Indian Institute of Sciences, Bangalore, 1981 (E)

02.40 * VITA: **Making Building Blocks with the CINVA-Ram Block Press**, Volunteers in Technical Assistance, Mt. Rainier, 1977 (E)

02.41   Volhard, Franz: **Leichtlehmbau,** alter Baustoff - neue Technik, Verlag C.F. Müller, Karlsruhe, 1983 (G)

02.42   Wolfskill, L.A.; Dunlap, W.A.; Gallaway, B.M.: **Earthen Home Construction**, A field and library compilation with an annotated bibliography, Texas Transportation Institute, College Station, 1962 (E)

Addendum 1993

AGCD, ABOS, UNCH-Habitat, **Earth construction technologies appropriate to developing countries**, Conference Proceedings, Brussels, 1984 (E)

Bourgeois, J.L.; Pelos, C.: **Spectacular vernacular. The adobe tradition.**, Aperture Foundation, New York, USA, 1989 (E)

CRATerre-EAG (Houben, H.; Guillaud, H.): **Traité de construction en terre**, Editions Parenthèses, Marseille, France, 1989 (F)

CRATerre (Guillaud, H.): **Modernité de l'architecture de terre en Afrique. Réalisations des années 80**, Grenoble, France, 1989 (F)

CRATerre-EAG, ICCROM: **5th international meeting of experts on the conservation of earthen architecture**, Grenoble, France, 1988 (E)

CARTerre-EAG: **Marrakech 87, Habitat en terre**, Grenoble, France, 1987 (F)

CRATerre-EAG, Doat, P.; Hays, A.; Houben, H.; Matuk, S.; Vitoux, F.: **Building with earth**, Rakmo Press Pvt. Ltd., New Delhi, 1991, (for sale only in South Asia) (E)

CRATerre-EAG: **Compressed Earth Block Production**, Video (25min), Eschborn, Germany, 1991 (E)

CRATerre-EAG: **Basics of Compressed Earth Blocks**, GATE, Eschborn, Germany, 1991 (E, F)

Development Workshop - pour UICN/WWF: "Conservation et Gestion des Ressources Naturelles dans l'Aïr et le Ténéré", **Les toitures sans bois**, Lauzerte, France, 1990 (F)

Houben, H.; Guillaud, H.: **Earth Construction Technology**, - 4 volumes, UNCHS (Habitat), Nairobi, 1986 (E)

Middleton, G.F.; Schneider, L.M.: **Earth-wall construction.** In Bulletin n°5. Fourth edition., National Building Technology Centre, Chatswood, Australia, 1987 (E)

Mukerji, K.; CRATerre-EAG: **Soil block presses. Product Information.** GATE, Eschborn, Germany, 1988 (E)

Mukerji, K.; Wörner, H., GATE, CRATerre-EAG: **Soil Preparation Equipment - Product Information**, Eschborn, Germany, 1991 (E)

Tibbets, J.M.: **The earthbuilder's encyclopedia**, Southwest Solaradobe School, New Mexico, USA, 1988 (E)

03. SOIL STABILIZERS

03.01 CRATerre (P. Doat, et al): **Stabilization**, Chapter VII of "Construire en Terre", Bibl. 02.06 (F)

03.02 Ferm, Richard: **Stabilized Earth Construction**, An Instructional Manual, The International Foundation for Earth Construction, Washington, D.C., 1985 (E)

03.03 Houben; Guillaud: **Soil Stabilization**, Chapter 4 in "Earth Construction Primer", Bibl. 02.19 (E)

03.04 Kafesçioglu, R.; Gürdal, E; Güner, A; Akman, M.S.: **Adobe Blocks Stabilized with Gypsum**, Proceedings of the CIB/RILEM Symposium on Appropriate Building Materials for Low Cost Housing in Nairobi, E. & F.N. Spon, London, 1983 (E)

03.05 Lunt, M.G.: **Stabilized Soil Blocks for Building**, Overseas Building Note No. 184, Building Research Establishment, Garston, 1980 (E)

03.06 Norton, J.: **Stabilization**, Cahpter 8 in "Building with Earth", Bibl. 02.32 (E)

03.07   Spence, Robin: **Making Soil-Cement Blocks**, The Technical Services Branch, Commission for Technical Education and Vocational Training, University of Zambia, Private Bag RW 16, Lusaka, (no date) (E)

03.08   Spence; Cook: **Soil and stabilized soil**, Chapter 3 of "Building Materials in Developing Countries", Bibl. 00.50 (E)

03.09   Webb, David J.T.: **Stabilized Soil Construction in Kenya**, Proceedings of the International Conference "Economical housing in developing countries: materials, construction techniques, components", RILEM, Paris, 1983 (E)

Addendum 1993

Iterbeke, M.; Jacobus, P.: **Soil-cement technology for low-cost housing in rural Thailand. An evaluation study**, Heverlee, Belgium, 1988 (E)

Ingles, O.G.: **Soil Stabilization - Principles and Practice**, Butterworths, Sydney, Australia, 1972 (E)

Smith, R.G.; Webb, D.J.T.: **Small-scale manufacture of stabilised soil blocks**, Technical Memorandum No. 12, International Labour Office, Geneva, Switzerland, 1987 (E)

Vénaut, Michel: **Le traitement des sols a la chaux et au ciment**, CERILH, Paris, France, 1980 (F)

04.   *FIRED CLAY PRODUCTS*

04.01   Bogahawatte, V.T.L.: **Non Mechanized Brickmaking in Sri Lanka**, National Building Research Organisation, Colombo, 1986

04.02   Gallegos, et al: **Construyendo con Ladrillo**, INIAVI, Lima, Peru, 1977 (S)

04.03   Hill, Neville R.: **A Clamp can be Appropriate for the Burning of Bricks**, Appropriate Technology Vol. 7, No. 1, IT Publications, London, 1980 (E)

04.04 * ILO/UNIDO: **Small-scale Brickmaking**, Technology Series, Memorandum No. 6, International Labour Office (ILO), Geneva, 1984 (E)

04.05   Keddie, James; Cleghorn, William: **Least Cost Brickmaking**, Appropriate Technology Vol. 5, No. 3, IT Publications, London, 1978 (E)

04.06   Keddie, James; Cleghorn, William: **Brick Manufacture in Developing Countries**, Scottish Academic Press Ltd., Edinburgh, 1980 (E)

04.07   Marciano, Michel: **Dossier Presses à Briques**, GRET, Paris, 1985 (F)

04.08 * Mestiviers, Bernard: Le point sur **Briques et Tuiles**, Dossier Nº 6, GRET, Paris, 1985 (F)

04.09   Parry, John: **The Brick Industry**, Energy Conservation and Scale of Operations, Appropriate Technology Vol. 2, No. 1, IT Publications, London, 1975 (E)

04.10   Parry, John: **Better Brickmaking for Developing Countries**, Appropriate Technology Vol. 5, No. 1, IT Publications, London, 1978 (E)

04.11   Parry, John: **Brickmaking in Developing Countries**, Review prepared for the Overseas Division, Building Research Establishment, Garston, 1979 (E)

04.12   Smith, Ray: **Improved Moulding Devices for Hand-made Bricks**, Appropriate Technology Vol. 7, No. 4, IT Publications, London, 1981 (E)

04.13   Spence, Robin: **Brick Manufacture using the Bull's Trench Kiln**, Appropriate Technology Vol. 2, No. 1, IT Publications, London, 1975 (E)

05.   *BINDERS*
        (see also Lime, Cement and Pozzolanas)

05.01   Apers, Jef: **Binders: Alternatives to Portland Cement**, Technisch Dossier, ATOL, Leuven, 1983 (E)

05.02   Bardin, F.: **Le Plâtre: production et utilisation dans l'habitat** (Gypsum: production and use in housing), GRET, Paris, 1982 (F)

05.03   CBRI: **Gypsum as a Building Material**, Building Research Note No. 14, CBRI, Roorkee, 1983 (E)

05.04   CBRI: **Mechanical Pan Calcination System for Gypsum Plaster and Plaster Boards**, Project Proposal No. 61, CBRI, Roorkee, 1986 (E)

05.06   Everett, Alan: **Bituminous Products**, Chapter 11 of "Materials", Bibl. 00.14 (E)

05.07   Kinniburgh, William: **Bitumen Coverings for Flat Roofs**, Overseas Building Notes No. 180, BRE, Garston, 1978 (E)

05.08   Ortega, Alvaro: **Basic Technology: Gypsum, its production and uses**, Mimar 18, Concept Media, Singapore, 1985 (E)

05.09   Smith, Ray: **Small-Scale Production of Gypsum Plaster for Building in the Cape Verde Islands**, Appropriate Technology Vol. 8, No. 4, IT Publications, London, 1982 (E)

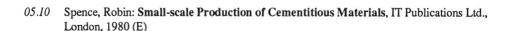

05.10   Spence, Robin: **Small-scale Production of Cementitious Materials**, IT Publications Ltd., London, 1980 (E)

05.11   Spence, R.J.S.; Cook, D.J.: **Gypsum, lime and pozzolanas**, Chapter 6 of "Building Materials in Developing Countries", Bibl. 00.50 (E)

Addendum 1993

Coburn, A.; Dudley, E.; Spence, R.: **Gypsum Plaster – Its manufacture and use**, IT Publications, London, 1989 (E)

Hill, N.; Holmes, S.; Mather, D.: **Lime and Other Alternative Cements**, IT Publications Ltd., London, 1992 (E)

06.   *LIME*
       (see also Pozzolanas)

06.01   CBRI: **Building Material from Lime Kiln Rejects**, Building Materials Note 21, CBRI, Roorkee, 1978 (E)

06.02   CBRI: **Manufacture of Lime and Lime Products**, Project Proposal No. 56, CBRI, Roorkee, 1985 (E)

06.03 * Chantry, G.: **La Chaux: production et utilisation dans l'habitat** (Lime: production and use in housing), GRET, Paris, 1981 (F)

06.04   Everett, Alan: **Limes** and Cements, Chapter 7 of "Materials", Bibl. 00.14 (E)

06.05   Ortega, Alvaro: **Basic Technology: Lime and its Production**, Mimar 17, Concept Media, Singapore, 1985 (E)

06.06   Spence, Robin: **Lime in Industrial Development**, A UNIDO guide to its uses and manufacture in developing countries, Sectoral Studies Series No. 18 (and Vol. II: Directory); UNIDO, Vienna, 1985 (E)

06.07   Spiropoulos, John: **Small Scale Production of Lime for Building**, Aus der Arbeit von GATE, Eschborn, Vieweg Verlag, Braunschweig, 1985 (E)

06.08 * Wingate, Michael: **Small-scale Lime-Burning, A Practical Introduction**, IT Publications Ltd., London, 1985 (E)

Addendum 1993

Spiropoulos, J.: **Chenkumbi Lime,** IT Publications Ltd., London, 1992 (E)

07.   CEMENT

07.01   CBRI: **Magnesium oxychloride cement based materials,** Project Proposal No. 57, CBRI, Roorkee, 1982 (E)

07.02   CBRI: **Cement Paints,** Building Research Note No. 21, CBRI, Roorkee, 1986 (E)

07.03   Everett, Alan: **Limes and Cements,** Chapter 7 of "Materials", Bibl. 00.14 (E)

07.04   Sigurdson, Jon: **Small Scale Cement Plants,** IT Publications Ltd., London, 1977 (revised 1979) (E)

07.05   Spence; Cook: **Portland and other cements,** Chapter 7 of "Building Materials in Developing Countries", Bibl. 00.50, (E)

Addendum 1993

Sinha, S.: **Mini-cement - a review of Indian experience,** IT Publications Ltd., London, 1990 (E)

8.   POZZOLANAS

08.01   Apers, J.; Pletinck, M.: **A Lime-Pozzolana Cement Industry in Rwanda,** Appropriate Technology Vol. 11, No. 4, IT Publications, London, 1985 (E)

08.02   CBRI: **Proportioning of Fly Ash Concrete Mix,** Building Digest No. 79, CBRI, Roorkee, 1970 (E)

08.03   Metha, P.K.: **Rice hull ash cement - high quality, acid resistings,** Journal of the American Concrete Institute, Vol. 72, No. 5, Detroit, 1975 (E)

08.04 *   Regional Centre for Technology Transfer - RCTT: **Rice Husk Ash Cement,** proceedings of a joint workshop organized be UNIDO, ESCAP, RCTT, PCSIR, Bangalore, 1979 (E)

08.05   Smith, Ray: **Rice Husk Ash Cement,** progress in development and application, IT Publications Ltd., London, 1984 (E)

08.06   Spence, Robin: **Lime and Surkhi Manufacture in India,** Appropriate Technology Vol. 1, No. 4, IT Publications, London, 1974 (E)

08.07 * Swamy, R.N. (Ed.): **Cement Replacement Materials,** Concrete Technology and Design, Vol. 3, Surrey University Press, Blackie & Son Ltd., London, 1986 (E)

08.08 UNIDO: **Rice-Husk Ash Cements - their development and applications,** Vienna, 1984 (E)

09. *CONCRETE*

09.01 Arrigone, Jorge Luis: **Low cost roof building technology - Three case studies using locally manufactured building components,** National Building Research Institute, Pretoria, 1983 (E)

09.02 CBRI: **Deterioration of Concrete in Sulphate and Soft Waters,** Building Digest No. 36, CBRI, Roorkee, 1965 (E)

09.03 CBRI: **Precast R.C. Plank Flooring/Roofing Scheme,** Building Research Note No. 4, CBRI, Roorkee, 1982 (E)

09.04 CBRI: **Thin R.C. Ribbed Slab for Floors and Roofs,** BRN No. 5, CBRI, Roorkee, 1987 (E)

09.05 CBRI: **Concrete Floor Hardness,** BRN No. 27, CBRI, Roorkee, 1984 (E)

09.06 CBRI: **Autoclaved Cellular Concrete,** BRN No. 48, CBRI, Roorkee, 1986 (E)

09.07 CTRD (Construction Technology Research and Development Program): **Lightweight Concrete** and **High Strength Concrete in the Philippines,** Construction Industry Authority of the Philippines, Makati, Metro Manila, (no date) (E)

09.08 Everett, Alan: **Concretes,** Chapter 8 of "Materials", Bibl. 00.14 (E)

09.09 Lu Xihong; Yan Ziliang*: **Cold-drawn low-carbon steel wire prestressed concrete technology** (*Engineers of Jiangsu Research Institute of Building Construction, China), Network Monitor, Vol. 3, No. 1, UNDP/UNIDO (RENAS-BMTCS), Manila, 1986 (E)

09.10 Maher, A.; Makhdoomi, S.A.: **Appropriate Concrete Mix Proportions for Lower Cost and Higher Quality,** S.M. Report No. 2, National Building Research Institute, Karachi, 1984 (E)

09.11 Spence, R.J.S.; Cook, D.J.: **Concrete,** Chapter 8 of "Building Materials in Developing Countries", Bibl. 00.50 (E)

09.12 * Swamy, R.N. (Ed.): **New Concrete Materials,** Concrete Technology and Design, Vol. 1, Surrey University Press, Blackie & Son Ltd., London, 1983 (E)

09.13 * Swamy, R.N. (Ed.): **New Reinforced Concretes,** Concrete Technology and Design, Vol. 2, Surrey University Press, Blackie & Son Ltd., London, 1984 (E)

Addendum 1993

Simonnet J., LBTP. **Recommendations pour la conception et l'exécution de bâtiments en géobéton,** LBTP. Abidjan, Côte-d'Ivoire, 1979 (F)

10.   FERROCEMENT

10.01 BOSTID (Board on Science and Technology for International Development): **Ferrocement: Applications in Developing Countries,** National Academy of Sciences, Washington, D.C., 1973 (E)

10.02 International Ferrocement Information Center - IFIC (Ed.): **Housing Applications of Ferrocement,** Journal of Ferrocement, Vol. 11, No. 1, IFIC, Bangkok, 1981 (E)

10.03 International Ferrocement Information Center - IFIC (Ed.): **Prefabricated Ferrocement Housing,** Journal of Ferrocement, Vol. 13, No. 1, IFIC, Bangkok, 1983 (E)

10.04 International Ferrocement Information Center - IFIC (Ed.): **Ferrocement Prefabrication & Industrial Applications,** Journal of Ferrocement, Vol. 16, No. 3, IFIC, Bangkok, 1986 (E)

10.05 Shah, S.P.; Balaguru, P.N.: **Ferrocement,** in "New Reinforced Concretes", Bibl. 09.13 (E)

10.06 Spence, R.J.S.; Cook, D.J.: **Ferrocement,** Chapter 9 of "Building Materials in Developing Countries", Bibl. 00.50 (E)

10.07 * Watt, S.B.: **Ferrocement Water Tanks** and their construction, Intermediate Technology Publications, London, 1978 (E)

10.08 * Watt, S.B.: **Septic Tanks and Aqua-privies from Ferrocement,** Intermediate Technology Publications, London, 1984 (E)

11.   FIBRE CONCRETE

11.01 Aziz, M.A.; Paramasivam, P.; Lee, S.L.: **Concrete reinforced with natural fibres,** in "New Reinforced Concretes", Bibl. 09.13 (E)

11.02 Baradyana, J.S.: **Sisal fibre concrete roofing sheets,** in "Building Materials for Low-income Housing", Bibl. 00.13 (E)

11.03 * Beck, V.; Gram, H.E.; Wehrle, K.: **Fibre Concrete Roofing: Towards a mature technology**, FCR-News, SKAT, St. Gall, 1987 (E)

11.04 Berhane, Z.: **Durability of mortar roofing sheets reinforced with natural fibres: A review of the present state-of-the-art**, in "Building Materials for Low-income Housing", Bibl. 00.13 (E)

11.05 Evans, Barrie: **Understanding Natural Fibre Concrete**, Its Application as a Building Material, IT Publications Ltd., London, 1986 (E)

11.06 Fageiri, O.M.E.: **Use of kenaf fibres for reinforcement of rich cement-sand corrugated sheets**, in "Appropriate Building Materials for Low-Cost Housing", Bibl. 00.04 (E)

11.07 Gram, H.E.; Persson, H.; Skarendahl, A.: **Natural Fibre Concrete**, SAREC Report R2: 1984, Swedish Agency for Research Cooperation with Developing Countries, S-10525 Stockholm, 1984 (E)

11.08 * Gram, H.E.; Parry, J.P.M.; Rhyner, K.; Schaffner, B.; Stulz, R.; Wehrle, K.; Wehrli, H.: **FCR - Fibre Concrete Roofing**, SKAT, St. Gall, 1986 (E)

11.09 Gram, H.E.; Nimityongskul, P.: **Durability of natural fibres in cement-based roofing sheets**, in "Building Materials for Low-income Housing", Bibl. 00.13 (E)

11.10 Guimarães, S. da S.: **Some experiments in vegetable fibre-cement composites**, in "Building Materials for Low-income Housing", Bibl. 00.13 (E)

11.11 Kerr, J.G.: **Fibre reinforced concrete**, in "New Reinforced Concretes", Bibl. 09.13 (E)

11.12 Lola, Carlos R.: **Fibre Reinforced Concrete Roofing Sheets**, Technology Appraisal Report, AT International, Washington, D.C., 1985 (E)

11.13 Mawenya, A.S.: **Developments in sisal fibre reinforced concrete**, in "Appropriate Building Materials for Low-Cost Housing", Bibl. 00.04 (E)

11.14 Mwamilla, B.L.M.: **Characteristics of natural fibrous reinforcement in cement-based matrices**, in "Building Materials for Low-income Housing", Bibl. 00.13 (E)

11.15 Parry, John: **Fibre Concrete Roofing**, Intermediate Technology Workshops, Cradley Heath, 1985 (E)

11.16 Spence, R.J.S.; Cook, D.J.: **Composites**, Chapter 10 of "Building Materials in Developing Countries", Bibl. 00.50 (E)

11.17 Swift, D.G.; Smith, R.B.L.: **Sisal-cement Composites as Low-cost Construction Materials**, Appropriate Technology Vol. 6, No. 3, IT Publications, London, 1979 (E)

Addendum 1993

Gut, Paul; Gram, Hans-Erik et al: **FCR/MCR Toolkit**, elements on the various topics regarding this technology, SKAT, St. Gallen, 1991 (E)

Macwhinnie, Ian: **An Introduction to FCR/MCR Production**, A BASIN Video, ITDG/GTZ-GATE, Eschborn, 1990 (E)

SKAT: **The Basics of Concrete Roofing Elements, Fundamental Informaiton on the Micro Concrete Roofing (MCR) and Fibre Concrete Roofing (FCR) Technology for Newcomers, Decisionmakers, Technicians, Field Workers and all those who want to know more about MCR and FCR**, SKAT, St. Gallen, 1989 (E)

12. NATURAL FIBRES, GRASSES, LEAVES

12.01 Bombard, Miriam L.: **Palms - Their Use in Building**, Department of Housing and Urban Development, Division of International Affairs, Washington, D.C. 20410, 1969 (E)

12.02 Hall, Nick: **Has Thatch a Future?**, Appropriate Technology Vol. 8, No. 3, IT Publications, London, 1981 (E)

12.03 Hall, Nick: **Durable Thatching with Grasses**, Appropriate Technology, Vol. 9, No. 1, IT Publications, London, 1982 (E)

12.04 Inter Pares (Richard Kerr): **Jute - a substitute for fibreglass in Bangladesh**, Appropriate Technology Vol. 7, No. 4, IT Publications, London, 1981 (E)

12.05 Pillai, C.K.S., et al: **A Simple Process for Extending the Life of Coconut Leaf Thatch**, Appropriate Technology Vol. 12, No. 1, IT Publications, London, 1985 (E)

13. BAMBOO

13.01 Cornelius, Lorraine: **Bamboo and Rattan**, The IDRC Reports, Vol. 13, No. 4, International Development Research Centre, Ottawa, 1985 (E)

13.02 Dunkelberg, Klaus: **Bambus als Baustoff**, (Bamboo as building material), Koldewey-Gesellschaft, Rudolf Habelt Verlag, Bonn, 1978 (D)

13.03 Farralley, David: **The Book of Bamboo**, Sierra Club Books, P.O. Box 3886, San Francisco, CA 94115, USA, 1984 (E)

13.04 Hidalgo López, Oscar: **Nuevas técnicas de construcción con bambú**, Centro de Investigación del Bambú (CIBAM), Universidad Nacional de Colombia, Bogotá, 1978 (S)

13.05 * Institute for Lightweight Structures: **IL 31 Bamboo**, Karl Krämer Verlag, Stuttgart, 1985 (G, E)

13.06 Janssen, Jules J.A.: **Bamboo: its use in the construction of Roofs and Bridges**, Appropriate Technology, Vol. 10, No. 2, IT Publications, London, 1983 (E)

13.07 * Janssen, Jules J.A. (Compiler): **Bamboo**, CICA Publication 82.03, University of Technology, Eindhoven, 1982/85 (E)

13.08 Liese, Walter: **Bamboo - Methods of Treatment and Preservation**, GATE 1/81, German Appropriate Technology Exchange, Eschborn, 1981 (E)

13.09 McClure, F.A.: **Bamboo as a Building Material**, Department of Housing and Urban Development, Office of International Affairs, Washington D.C., 1953 (reprinted 1972) (E)

13.10 * Siopongco, Joaquin O.; Munandar, Murdiati: **Technology manual on bamboo as building material**, RENAS-BMTCS, UNDP/UNIDO, Manila, 1987 (E)

13.11 Subrahmanyam, B.V.: **Bamboo reinforcement for cement matrices**, in "New Reinforced Concretes", Bibl. 09.13 (E)

13.12 Taylor, Brian Brace: **Bamboo City - A Refugee Camp**, Mimar 20, Concept Media, Singapore, 1985 (E)

13.13 United Nations: **The Use of Bamboo and Reeds in Building Construction**, United Nations, New York, 1972 (E)

14. *TIMBER*

14.01 Alcachupas, Pablito L.: **Sawmilling of Coconut Trunks into Lumber in the Philippines**, Network Monitor, Vol. 2, No. 1, UNDP/UNIDO (RENAS-BMTCS), Manila, 1985 (E)

14.02 Campbell, P.A.: **Some Developments in Tropical Timber Technology**, Appropriate Technology, Vol. 2, No. 3, 1975 (E)

14.03 CBRI: **Woodwool Board**, Building Research Note No. 38, CBRI, Roorkee, 1985 (E)

14.04 CBRI: **Particle Board and its Use in Buildings**, BRN No. 55, CBRI, Roorkee, 1986 (E)

14.05 CBRI: **Making Woodwool Boards at Small Scale Level**, Project Proposal No. 33, CBRI, Roorkee, 1985 (E)

14.06   CTRD (Construction Technology Research and Development Program): Leaflets on **Coco Timber, Glue Laminated Wood, Manufacturing Considerations in Wood Gluing, Mechanical and Related Properties of Locally-Made Fibreboards (Lawanit), Particle Board, Wood Treatment/Preservation, Woodwool Cement Boards**, Construction Industry Authority of the Philippines, Makati, Metro Manila, (no date) (E)

14.07 * Doernach, Rudolf: **Natürlich bauen** (Building naturally - with pole timber), Wolfgang Krüger Verlag, Frankfurt/Main, 1986 (G)

14.08   Everett, Alan: **Timber**, Chapter 2 of "Materials", Bibl. 00.14 (E)

14.09   Forest Products Laboratory: **Wood Handbook: Wood as an Engineering Material**, Agriculture Handbook No. 72, US Department of Agriculture, Washington, D.C., 1974 (E)

14.10   Herbert, M.R.M.: **Structural connections for indigenous pole timbers**, Proceedings of the International Conference "Economical Housing in developing countries: materials, construction techniques, components", Paris, 1983 (E)

14.11   Informationsdienst Holz: **Baulicher Holzschutz** (Constructive timber protection), Entwicklungsgemeinschaft Holzbau i.d. Deutschen Gesellschaft für Holzforschung, München, 1986 (G)

14.12   Keenan, F.J.; Tejada, Marcelo: **Tropical Timber for Building Materials in the Andean Group Countries of South America**, IDRC-TS 49e, International Development Research Centre, Ottawa, 1984 (E)

14.13   Killmann, Wulf: **Coconut wood - the potential of an agricultural by-product**, GATE 4/83, German Appropriate Technology Exchange, Eschborn, 1983 (E)

14.14   NBO: **Special Issue on Timber**, Journal of the National Buildings Organization, Vol. XXX, No. 1, New Delhi, 1985 (E)

14.15   Paskaran, N.: **Timber as an Engineering Material in Developing Countries**, Appropriate Technology, Vol. 8, No. 4, IT Publications, London, 1982 (E)

14.16   Piltz; Härig; Schulz: **Holzbaustoffe** (Timber building materials), Chapter 8 in "Technologie der Baustoffe", Bibl. 00.40 (G)

14.17   Ratra, R.S.: **Secondary Timbers**, National Buildings Organization, New Delhi, 1986 (E)

14.18   Shasmoukine, Annie et Pierre: **Construire en Bois** (Building with timber), édition Alternative et Parallèles, collection AnArchitecture, Paris, 1980 (F)

14.19   Siriban, Felino R.: **Preservation of Coconut Trunk and Lumber**, Network Monitor, Vol. 2, No. 3, UNDP/UNIDO (RENAS-BMTCS), Manila, 1985 (E)

14.20   Spence, R.J.S.; Cook, D.J.: **Timber and timber products**, Chapter 5 of "Building Materials in Developing Countries", Bibl. 00.50 (E)

14.21   Tack, C.H.: **Preservation of Timber for Tropical Building**, Overseas Building Notes, No. 183, Building Research Establishment, Garston, 1979 (E)

14.22 * UNIDO: **Popular Manual for Wooden House Construction**, United Nations, Vienna/ New York, 1985 (E)

14.23 * Weissenfeld, Peter: **Holzschutz ohne Gift?**, Holzschutz & Holzflächenbehandlung in der Praxis (Timber protection without poison? Practical timber protection and surface treatment), Ökobuch-Verlag, Grebenstein/Freiburg, 1983 (G)

14.24   Wendehorst: **Holz und Holzwerkstoffe** (Timber and timber products), Chapter 2 of "Baustoffkunde", Bibl. 00.57 (G)

14.25   Willemin, Véronique: **Le Cocotier**, production et mise en œuvre dans l'habitat (The coconut palm, production and use in housing), GRET, Groupe de Recherche et d'Echanges Technologiques, Paris, 1986 (F)

Addendum 1993

Schneider, Jörg: **Holzbau**, Eidgernössische Technische Hochschule, Zürich, 1988 (G)

Sell, Jürgen: **Eigenschaften und Kenngrössen von Holzarten**, LIGNUM, Zürich, 1989 (G)

15.   **METALS**

15.01   Everett, Alan: **Metals**, Chapter 9 of "Materials", Bibl. 00.49 (E)

15.02   NBO: **Economy of Iron and Steel in Building Construction**, Report of the Committee Constituted by the National Buildings Organization, New Delhi, 1961 (E)

15.03   Overseas Building Notes: No. 124 **Corrosion of Metals**, and No. 148 **The Durability of Metals in Building**, Building Research Establishment, Garston, 1968/1973 (E)

15.04   Piltz; Härig; Schulz: **Baumetalle** (Building Metals), Chapter 7 in "Technologie der Baustoffe", Bibl. 00.40 (G)

15.05   Qiu Zhichang; Shao Bozhou: **Research and Application of Prestressed Concrete Reinforced with Cold-Drawn Low-Carbon Steel Wire in Zhejiang Province**, Paper presented at the "Workshop on Low-Cost Building Materials Technology and Construction Systems" (21.10. - 4.11.1982, Beijing-Hangzhou), China Building Information Centre, Beijing, 1983 (E)

15.06   Wendehorst: **Eisen- und Stahlwerkstoffe** (Iron and steel materials), Chapter 10, and **Nichteisenmetalle** (Non-ferrous metals), Chapter 11 of "Baustoffkunde", Bibl. 00.57 (G)

16.   *GLASS*

16.01   Everett, Alan: **Glass**, Chapter 12 of "Materials", Bibl. 00.14 (E)

16.02   Piltz; Härig; Schulz: **Bauglas** (Building glass), Chapter 6 of "Technologie der Baustoffe", Bibl. 00.40 (G)

16.03   Wendehorst: **Glas** (Glass), Chapter 14 of "Baustoffkunde", Bibl. 00.57 (G)

17.   *PLASTICS*

17.01   CBRI: **Plastics and Their Applications in Building**, Building Digest No. 134 (Revised), CBRI, Roorkee, 1979 (E)

17.02   Everett, Alan: **Plastics and Rubbers**, Chapter 13 of "Materials", Bibl. 00.14 (E)

17.03   Overseas Building Note: No. 134 **Plastics for Building in Developing Countries**, Building Research Establishment, Garston, 1970 (E)

17.04   Piltz; Härig; Schulz: **Kunststoffe** (Plastics), Chapter 10 of "Technologie der Baustoffe", Bibl. 00.40 (G)

17.05   Rai, Jaisingh: **Polymers and Plastics**, Chapter 4 of "Advances in Building Materials and Construction", Bibl. 00.41 (E)

17.06   Wendehorst: **Kunststoffe** (Plastics), Chapter 13 of "Baustoffkunde", Bibl. 00.57 (G)

18.   *SULPHUR*

18.01   Alexander, Christopher; et al: **Houses Generated by Patterns**, Center for Environmental Structure, Berkeley, California, 1969 (E)

18.02   Dale, J.M.; Ludwig, A.C.: **Fire-retarding elemental sulphur**, SWRI Report, Southwest Research Institute, San Antonio/Texas, 1967 (E)

18.03   Fike, H.L.: **Some Potential Applications of Sulphur**, The Sulphur Institute, Washington, D.C., 1972 (E)

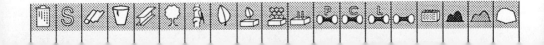

18.04 Ludwig, A.C.: **Utilization of Sulphur and Sulphur Ores as Construction Materials in Guatemala,** United Nations, New York, 1969 (E)

18.05 Malhotra, V.M.: **Sulphur concrete and sulphur-infiltrated concrete,** in "New Concrete Materials", Bibl. 09.12 (E)

18.06 Ortega, A.; Rybczynski, W.; Ayad, S.; Ali, W.; Acheson, A.: **The Ecol Operation,** Ecology + Building + Common Sense, Minimum Cost Housing Group, School of Architecture, McGill University, Montreal, 1972 (E)

18.07 Ortega, Alvaro; Lefebvre, Bernard: **The Use of Sulphur as a Building Material in Deserts,** United Nations Mission on Housing, Building and Planning to the United Arab Emirates, Dubai, 1977 (E)

Addendum 1993

ACI Committee 548: **Guide for Mixing and Placing Sulphur Concrete in Construction,** American Concrete Institue, Report No. ACI 548.2R-88, 1988 (E)

19. *WASTES*
      (see also Pozzolanas)

19.01 CBRI: **Use of Coal Ash in Building Industry,** Building Materials Note No. 1 (Revised), CBRI, Roorkee, 1979 (E)

19.02 CBRI: **Utilization of By-Product Phosphorgypsum for Building Materials,** BRN No. 9, CBRI, Roorkee, 1983 (E)

19.03 CTRD (Construction Technology Research and Development Program): **Composite Roofing and Panelling Materials from Wood Waste and Agricultural Fibrous Residues for Low-Cost Housing,** Construction Industry Authority for Low-Cost Housing, Construction Industry Authority of the Philippines, Makati, Metro Manila, (no date) (E)

19.04 * Lauricio, Feliciano M.: **Technology manual on rice husk ash cements,** RENAS-BMTCS, UNDP/UNIDO, Manila, 1987 (E)

19.05 Maher, A.: **Utilization of waste brick bats as coarse aggregate for structural concrete,** in "Building Materials for Low-Income Housing", Bibl. 00.13 (E)

19.06 NBO: **Directory of Industrial and Agricultural Wastes, Utilization in Construction Industry,** National Buildings Organization, New Delhi, 1985 (E)

19.07   Network Monitor: **Building Materials from Agro-Residues**, Vol. 1, No. 3, Newsletter of the Regional Network in Asia for Low-Cost Building Materials Technologies and Construction Systems (RENAS-BMTCS), UNDP/UNIDO, Manila, 1984 (E)

19.08   Network Monitor: **Industrial Residues**, Vol. 2, No. 2, Newsletter of RENAS-BMTCS, UNDP/UNIDO, Manila, 1985 (E)

19.09   Pawley, Martin: **Garbage Housing**, Architectural Design 12/73, London, 1973 (E)

19.10   Ramaswamy, S.D.; Murthy, C.K.; Nagaraj, T.S.: **Use of waste materials and industrial by-products in concrete construction**, in "New Concrete Materials", Bibl. 09.12 (E)

19.11   RENAS-BMTCS: **Building Materials from Agro-Residues**, Low-Cost Building Materials Technologies and Construction Systems, Monograph Series No. 1/1984, UNDP/UNIDO, Manila, 1984 (E)

19.12   Schmidt-Brümmer, Horst: **Alternative Architektur**, DuMont Buchverlag, Köln, 1983 (G)

19.13   Tay Joo Hwa: **Utilization of sludges as building material**, in "Building Materials for Low-Income Housing", Bibl. 00.13 (E)

19.14   United Nations: **Use of Agricultural and Industrial Wastes in Low-Cost Construction**, United Nations, New York, 1976 (E)

19.15 * Vogler, Jon: **Work from Waste**, Recycling Wastes to Create Employment, IT Publications, London, and Oxfam, Oxford, 1981 (E)

20.   *FOUNDATIONS*

20.01   Aziz, M.A.; Ramaswamy, S.D.: **Bamboo technology for low cost constructions**, in "Appropriate Technology in Civil Engineering", Bibl. 00.21 (E)

20.02   De, P.L.: **Foundations in poor soils including expansive clays**, Overseas Building Notes, No. 179, Building Research Establishment, Garston, 1978 (E)

20.03   Longworth, T.I.; Driscoll, R.; Katkhuda, I.E.D.: **Guidelines for Foundation Design of Low-Rise Buildings on Expansive Clay in Northern Jordan**, Overseas Building Notes, No. 191, BRE, Garston, 1984 (E)

20.04   Schreckenbach, H.; Abankwa, J.G.K.: **Foundations and Retaining Structures**, Section 5.3 in "Construction Technology for a Tropical Developing Country", Bibl. 00.49 (E)

20.05   Vorhauer, Klaus: **Foundation**, in "Low Cost/Self Help Housing", Bibl. 00.56 (E)

414

21. FLOORS AND CEILINGS

21.01 CBRI: **Precast R.C. plank flooring/roofing scheme**, Building Research Note No. 4, CBRI, Roorkee, 1986 (E)

21.02 CBRI: **Thin R.C. ribbed slab for floors and roofs**, BRN No. 5, CBRI, Roorkee, 1987 (E)

21.03 CBRI: **Reinforced brick and reinforced brick concrete slabs for floors and roofs**, BRN No. 42, CBRI, Roorkee, 1985 (E)

21.04 CBRI: **Channel unit for floor/roof**, BRN No. 52, CBRI, Roorkee, 1986 (E)

21.05 CBRI: **Clay flooring and terracing tiles from alluvial soils**, Building Materials Note No. 22, CBRI, Roorkee, 1978 (E)

21.06 CBRI: **Waffle unit floor/roof**, Building Digest No. 105, CBRI, Roorkee, 1973 (E)

21.07 CBRI: **Prefabricated floor/roof using structural clay units**, (Joist and filler scheme), Building Digest No. 105, CBRI, Roorkee, 1973 (E)

21.08 Hausmann, Ulrich: **The small-scale production of reinforced concrete floor slabs**, Appropriate Technology, Vol. 11, No. 1, IT Publications, 1984 (E)

21.09 Lukkunaprasit, P.: **Reinforced concrete-brick composite beams for low-cost construction**, in "Materials of Construction for Developing Countries", Bibl. 00.38 (E)

21.10 Minke, Gernot: **Zeitgemäße Lehmfußböden für den Selbstbau** (Contemporary earth floors for self-construction), in "Bauen mit Lehm, No. 2 (1985)", Bibl. 02.28 (G)

21.11 Schreckenbach, H.; Abankwa, J.G.K.: **Floors and Floor Finishes**, Section 5.4.2 in "Construction Technology for a Tropical Developing Country", Bibl. 00.49 (E)

22. WALLS

22.01 CBRI: **Precast stone masonry block walling scheme**, Building Research Note No. 7, CBRI, Roorkee, 1986 (E)

22.02 CBRI: **Non-erodable mud plaster for mud walls**, BRN No. 12, CBRI, Roorkee, 1986 (E)

22.03 CBRI: **Improved method of brick laying**, BRN No. 36, CBRI, Roorkee, 1985 (E)

22.04   Chatsiri, Thanmarom; Etherington, A. Bruce: **Verbreitung von Verbundsteinen für das Ländliche Wohnungs- und Siedlungswesen in Thailand** (Dissemination of Interlocking Soil Cement Brick for Rural Housing and Settlement in Thailand), Article in DESWOS-Brief (Newsletter), Vol. 13, No. 3, DESWOS, Köln, 1986 (G)

22.05   Minke, Gernot; Lau, Adolfo; Asturias, José: **A Low-Cost Housing System for Guatemala - Sistema de Vivienda de Bajo Costo para Guatemala**, Laboratory for Experimental Construction, Kassel University (Germany), Facultad de Arquitectura, Universidad Francisco Marroquin (Guatemala) and CEMAT (Guatemala), 1978 (E, S)

22.06 * Norton, John: **Introduction of earthquake resistant building techniques in the Koumbia area, N.W. Guinea**, Development Workshop, Fumel, 1985 (E)

22.07   Schreckenbach, H.; Abankwa, J.G.K.: **Walls and Wall Finishes**, Section 5.4.3 in "Construction Technology for a Tropical Developing Country", Bibl. 00.49 (E)

22.08   SERC: **Zipbloc System**, Paper prepared by the Structural Engineering Research Centre, Madras, (no date) (E)

22.09   Vorhauer, Klaus: **Wall construction**, in "Low Cost/Self Help Housing", Bibl. 00.56 (E)

23.   *ROOFS*

23.01   Ambacher, P.: **Framed Ferrocement**, in "Prefabricated Ferrocement Housing", Bibl. 10.03 (E)

23.02   Arrigone, Jorge Luis: **Low Cost Roof Building Technology - Three Case Studies Using Locally Manufactured Building Components**, National Building Research Institute, Pretoria, 1983 (E)

23.03   Baris, Danièle (Ed.): **Toitures** en zones tropicales arides (Roofs in arid tropical zones), Dossier Technologies et Développment, GRET, Paris, 1984 (F)

23.04   BOSTID (Board on Science and Technology for International Development): **Roofing in Developing Countries**, Research for New Technologies, National Academy of Sciences, Washington, D.C., 1974 (E)

23.05   CBRI: **Doubly curved tile roof**, Building Digest, No. 43, Roorkee, 1966 (E)

23.06   CBRI: **Improved method of making thatch roof**, Building Research Note No. 37, CBRI, Roorkee, 1985 (E)

23.07   CBRI: **Water-proofing of flat in situ RCC roofs**, BRN No. 54, CBRI, Roorkee, 1986 (E)

23.08   CBRI: **Corrugated roofing sheets from coir waste or wood wool and portland cement,** Project Proposal, No. 53, CBRI, Roorkee, 1985 (E)

23.09   Eygelaar, J.: **Roof structures for low-cost housing - cost comparison for various roofing materials,** Housing Research and Development Unit, Nairobi, 1975 (E)

23.10   Habitropic: **Low cost space frame roof structures,** Birkagatan 27, S-113 39 Stockholm, Sweden, 1983 (E)

23.11 * Hall, Nicolas: **Thatch - A Handbook,** IT Publications, London, 1988 (E)

23.12   Jagadish, K.S.; Yogananda, M.R.; Venkatarama Reddy, B.V.: **Reinforced-tile-work for low-cost roofs,** Alternative Building Series - 11, ASTRA, Bangalore, 1985 (E)

23.13   Kalita, U.C.; Nambiar, M.K.C.; Borthakur, B.C.; Baruah, P.: **Ferrocement roof for low-cost housing,** Indian Concrete Journal, Bombay, 1986 (E)

23.14   Mathur, G.C.: **Appropriate Roofing Materials for Low Cost Housing,** NBO, New Delhi, 1985 (E)

23.15   Mattone, Roberto: **Operational Possibilities of Sisal Fibre Reinforced Gypsum in the Production of Low-Cost Housing Building Components,** in "Building Materials for Low-Income Housing", Bibl. 00.13 (E)

23.16   Minke, Gernot: **Grass Hogan,** EX-Bau INFO 15, Forschungslabor für Experimentelles Bauen, Gesamthochschule Kassel, Federal Republic of Germany, 1981 (G)

23.17   Mukerji, K.; Whipple, J.H.; Castillo Escobar, R.: **Roof Constructions for Housing in Developing Countries,** Research Report of the Institut für Tropenbau Dr.Ing. G. Lippsmeier, Starnberg, in cooperation with ICAITI, Guatemala, Aus der Arbeit von GATE, Eschborn, 1982 (E, G)

23.18   NBO: **Report on study of methods used for water-proofing of roofs in India,** National Buildings Organization, New Delhi, 1962 (E)

23.19   Ortega, Alvaro: **Economic roofing for Central American dwellings,** Research and development of Canaletas, Internationale Asbestzement Revue, ac 22, Dr. H. Girsberger, Zürich, 1961 (E)

23.20   Pillai, C.K.S.; Venkataswamy, M.A.; Satyanarayana, K.G.; Rohatgi, P.K.: **A Simple Process for Extending the Life of Coconut Leaf Thatch,** Appropriate Technology, Vol. 12, No. 1, IT Publications, London, 1985 (E)

23.21   Rao, A.V.R.: **Roofing with Low-Cost Corrugated Asphalt Sheets,** Appropriate Technology, Vol. 1, No. 4, IT Publications, London, 1975 (E)

23.22   Sashi Kumar, K.; Sharma, P.C.; Nimityongskul, P.: **Ferrocement Roofing Element**, Do-it-yourself series booklet No. 5, International Ferrocement Information Center, Bangkok, 1985 (E)

23.23   Sperling, R.: **Roofs for Warm Climates**, BRE, Garston, 1970 (E)

23.24   Vorhauer, Klaus: **Roof Construction**, in "Low Cost/Self Help Housing", Bibl. 00.56 (E)

Addendum 1993

Schunk, Eberhard; Fink, Thomas; Jenisch, Richard; Oster, Hans Jochen: **Dach Atlas**, Institut für internationale Architektur-Dokumentation, München, 1991 (G)

Gut, Paul: **FCR/MCR Toolkit Element 24, Roof Structure Guide**, SKAT, St. Gallen, 1993 (E)

24.   BUILDING SYSTEMS

24.01   ARCO Grasser and Partner: **Building Instruction for an Adobe Brick House**, A project by GATE, Eschborn, 1982 (E) (F) (G) (S)

24.02   ARCO Grasser and Partner: **Building Instruction for a Panel House**, A project by GATE, Eschborn, 1982 (E) (F) (G) (S)

24.03   Cain, A.; Afshar, F.; Norton, J.: **Indigenous Building and the Third World**, Architectural Design 4/75, London, 1975 (E)

24.04   CBRI: **Prefabricated Timber Hut**, Building Digest No. 17 (revised), CBRI, Roorkee, 1981 (E)

24.05   Etherington, A.B.: **The LOK-BILD Construction System - An Introduction**, in "Building Materials for Low-Income Housing", Bibl. 00.13 (E)

24.06   Gieth, Thomas: **Construction of lacustrine housing with Caranday palms for zones that can be inundated (Prototype "B")**, Technical Bulletin No. 5, Centro de Tecnología Apropiada, Asunción, Paraguay, 1985 (E)

24.07   Hidalgo López, Oscar: **Manual de Construcción con Bambú**, Construcción rural 1, Estudios Técnicos Colombianos Ltda., Apartado Aéreo 50085, Bogotá, 1981 (S)

24.08   Hillrichs, Behrend: **Bauen in Überschwemmungszonen** - Entwurf eines einfachen Haustyps für die La Plata und Parana–Region Südamerikas (Building in Flood Zones - Design of a simple house type for the La Plata and Parana Region of South America), unpublished design of an architectural student at Hanover University, 1984 (G)

24.09 Holloway, Richard: **Ferrocement Housing Units in Dominica**, Appropriate Technology Vol. 5, No. 3, IT Publications, London, 1978 (E)

24.10 Janssen, Jules: **Using Bamboo as a Reinforcement**, Appropriate Technology Vol. 14, No. 2, IT Publications, London, 1987 (E)

24.11 Kalita, U.C.; Khazanchi, A.C.; Thyagarajan, G.: **Bamboocrete Wall Panels and Roofing Elements for Low Cost Housing**, in "Materials of Construction for Developing Countries", Bibl. 00.38 (E)

24.12 Mukerji, Kiran: **Regenwasser-Sammeltanks in Indien** (Rainwater Collection Tanks in India), in "TRIALOG 12: Angepaßte Technologien", Bibl. 00.30 (G)

24.13 Norton, John: **Introduction of Earthquake Resistant Building Techniques in the Koumbia Area, N.W. Guinea**, Development Workshop, Fumel, France, 1985 (E)

24.14 Norton, John: **Limitations on Improving Earthquake Resistance: the Exploitation of Local Materials**, A Case Study in Guinea - Conakry, in "TRIALOG 12: Angepaßte Technologien", Bibl. 00.30 (E)

24.15 de Rivero D'Angelo, M.I.: **Fibracreto - A Peruvian Non-Conventional Construction System**, in "Prefabricated Ferrocement Housing", Bibl. 10.03 (E)

24.16 Sulaiman, M.; Mansoor, N.; Khan, K.: **Experimental and Demonstration Low-Cost House Built with Rice Husk Ash and Lime as Cement**, National Building Research Institute, Karachi, (no date) (E)

24.17 Willkomm, Wolfgang; Wemhöner, Antje: **Angepaßte Technologien und Zusammenarbeit - einige Beispiele** (Appropriate technologies and cooperation - some examples) in "TRIALOG 12: Angepaßte Technologien", Bibl. 00.30 (G)

25. *PROTECTIVE MEASURES*

25.01 CBRI: **A cheap and effective fire retardant treatment for paddy/coconut leaves/ reeds/palmyrah thatch**, Building Research Note No. 13, CBRI, Roorkee, 1986 (E)

25.02 CBRI: **Termite control in buildings**, BRN No. 50, CBRI, Roorkee, 1986 (E)

25.03 CBRI: **Termite and rodent resistance of plastic pipes**, Building Digest No. 140, CBRI, Roorkee, 1980 (E)

25.04 CTRD: **Building to resist effect of wind**, Construction Industry Authority of the Philippines, Makati, Metro Manila, (no date) (E)

25.05   Davis, Ian: **Shelter after disaster**, Oxford Polytechnic Press, Oxford, 1978 (E)

25.06   Eaton, Keith J.: **Making Buildings to Withstand Strong Winds**, Appropriate Technology Vol. 7, No. 3, IT Publications, London, 1980 (E)

25.07   Janssen, Jules: **How to Protect Bamboo Buildings from Rat Infestation**, Appropriate Technology Vol. 8, No. 3, IT Publications, London, 1981 (E)

25.08   Moody, Tony: **Drying Maize for Storage in the Humid Tropics**, Appropriate Technology Vol. 7, No. 1, IT Publications, London, 1980 (E)

25.09   NBRI: **The Prevention of Fires in Thatched Roofs**, NBRI Information Sheet, National Building Research Institute, Pretoria, 1971 (E)

25.10   Norton, John: **Manuel de construction parasismique en Guinée** (Manual of earthquake resistant construction in Guinea), Development Workshop, Fumel, 1986 (F)

25.11 * Rauch, Egon: **Rodent and Termite Proofing of Buildings**, Working Paper WP 01/84, SKAT, St. Gall, 1984 (E)

25.12   Søe, Thorkil: **STOP Termite Attacks on Buildings**, ERLA Publishers, Svenstrup, 1982 (E)

25.13   Teodoru, G.; Beuter-Famili, K.: **Wood Durability and Termites**, in "Building Materials for Low-Income Housing", Bibl. 00.13 (E)

25.14   UNDRO: **Guidelines for disaster prevention**, A series of three volumes, Office of the United Nations Disaster Relief Co-ordinator, Geneva, 1976 (E)

25.15   UNDRO: **Disaster Prevention and Mitigation**, A series of 12 volumes, UNDRO, Geneva, 1976 - 1987 (E)

25.16 * UNDRO: **Shelter after Disaster**, Guidelines for Assistance, UNDRO, Geneva, 1982 (E)

25.17 * Wijkman, A.; Timberlake, L.: **Natural Disasters - Acts of God or acts of Man?**, Earthscan, London, 1984 (E)

ABBREVIATIONS

A

ac	asbestos cement *83, 149*
AIT	Asian Institute of Technology, Bangkok (Thailand) *77, 226, 305*
Al	aluminium *111 ff*
ASTRA	Centre for Application of Science and Technology for Rural Areas, Bangalore (India) *196*
AT	appropriate technology
ATDO	Appropriate Technology Development Organization, Islamabad (Pakistan)

B

BASIN	Building Advisory Service Information Network
BRE	Building Research Establishment, Garston (U.K.) *281, 349, 354*

C

C	concrete grade (compressive strength in N/mm²) *72 ff*
$CaCO_3$	calcium carbonate (limestone, chalk, etc.) *51 ff*
$CaMg(CO_3)_2$	dolomitic limestone *51*
CaO	calcium oxide (quicklime) *32, 51, 249*
$Ca(OH)_2$	calcium hydroxide (hydrated or slaked lime) *32, 57*
CAS	Cements and Binders Advisory Service
$CaSO_4$	calcium sulphate (anhydrite gypsum) *48*
$CaSO_4 \cdot 2H_2O$	calcium sulphate di-hydrate (gypsum) *48*
$CaSO_4 \cdot 1/2H_2O$	calcium sulphate hemi-hydrate (Plaster of Paris) *48*
CBRI	Central Building Research Institute, Roorkee (India) *38, 43, 58, 88, 104, 164, 196 ff, 200 ff, 231, 325, 340*
Cd	cadmium *111 ff*
CEB	Compressed Earth Block
CEMAT	Centro de Estudios Mesoamericanos sobre Tecnología Apropiada, Guatemala *227*
CETA	Centro de Experimentación en Tecnología Apropiada, Guatemala *343*
CFI	Commonwealth Forestry Institute, Oxford (U.K.) *104*
CH_4	methane *53*
C_3H_8	propane *53*
C_4H_{10}	butane *53*

G

GATE   German Appropriate Technology Exchange, Eschborn (Federal Republic of Germany) *84, 301, 309*

gci   galvanized corrugated iron *84, 112*

ggbfs   ground granulated blast furnace slag *65 ff*

H

HBRI   Housing & Building Research Institute, Dhaka (Bangladesh) *81, 126*

H_2O water *57*

I

IFIC   International Ferrocement Information Centre, AIT, Bangkok (Thailand) *77*

IFT   Institut für Tropenbau, Starnberg (Federal Republic of Germany) *301*

IL   Institut für leichte Flächentragwerke, Universität Stuttgart (Federal Republic of Germany) *277*

IPT   Instituto de Pesquisas Tecnológicas, São Paulo (Brazil) *205, 237, 327*

ITDG   Intermediate Technology Development Group, Rugby / London (U.K.) *84, 104*

ITW   Intermediate Technology Workshops, Cradley Heath (U.K.) *38, 266, 280, 338, 340, 357 ff*

K

KVIC   Khadi Village Industries Commission, Bombay (India) *55*

M

MgO   magnesium oxide *51*

MC   Micro concrete

MCR   Micro concrete roofing

N

NBO   National Buildings Organization, New Dehli (India) *66, 126*

NBRI   National Building Research Institute, Karachi (Pakistan) *70, 333*

NBRI   National Building Research Institute, Pretoria (South Africa) *255*

Ni   nickel *111 ff*

O

OPC   ordinary portland cement *61 ff, 67 ff, 231*

P

Pb   lead *111 ff*

PBFC   portland blast furnace cement *68*

PCP   pentachlorphenol *97*

PCSIR   Pakistan Council of Scientific and Industrial Research *69*

pfa   pulverized fuel ash (fly ash) *65 ff*

PI   plasticity index *27*

PREVI   Proyecto Experimental de Vivienda, Peru *210*

PVC   polyvinyl chloride *142*

R

RAS   Roofing Advisory Service (former FAS)

RCC   reinforced cement concrete *74 ff, 77 ff, 184*

RHA   rice husk ash *65 ff, 123, 333*

RRL   Regional Research Laboratory, Jorhat (India) *260, 315*

S

SADEL   Swedish Association for Development of Low-Cost Housing, Lund (Sweden) *249*

SENA   Servicio Nacional de Aprendizaje, Bogotá (Colombia) *355*

SERC   Structural Engineering Research Centre, Madras / Roorkee (India) *81 / 259*

SHAM   Housing Society for the Amazon State, Brazil *205, 237, 327*

SKAT   Swiss Centre for Development Cooperation in Technology and Management, St. Gall (Switzerland) *84, 90*

Sn   tin *111 ff*

U

UNIDO   United Nations Industrial Development Organization, Vienna (Austria) *205, 237, 327*

UNATA   Union for Adapted Technological Assistance, Ramsel-Herselt (Belgium) *344*

W

WAS   Wall Building Advisory Service

Z

Zn   zinc *111 ff*

INDEX

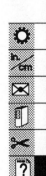

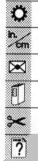

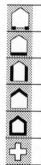

434

Learning Resources
Centre